AN INTRODUCT
DIALECTIC

CW00701667

AN INTRODUCTION TO DIALECTICS

(1958)

Theodor W. Adorno

Edited by Christoph Ziermann

Translated by Nicholas Walker

polity

First published in German as *Einführung in die Dialektik* © Suhrkamp Verlag, Berlin, 2010

This English edition © Polity Press, 2017

Polity Press
65 Bridge Street
Cambridge CB2 1UR, UK

Polity Press
350 Main Street
Malden, MA 02148, USA

ISBN-13: 978-0-7456-9311-8
ISBN-13: 978-0-7456-7944-0 (pb)

A catalogue record for this book is available from the British Library.

Library of Congress Cataloging-in-Publication Data

Names: Adorno, Theodor W., 1903–1969. author.
Title: An introduction to dialectics / Theodor W. Adorno.
Other titles: Einfuhrung in die Dialektik. English
Description: Cambridge, UK ; Malden, MA : Polity Press, [2017] | Includes
    bibliographical references and index.
Identifiers: LCCN 2016020592 (print) | LCCN 2016036294 (ebook) | ISBN
    9780745693118 (hardback) | ISBN 9780745679440 (pbk.) | ISBN
    9780745693965 (Mobi) | ISBN 9780745694894 (Epub)
Subjects: LCSH: Dialectic.
Classification: LCC B105.D48 A3613 2017 (print) | LCC B105.D48 (ebook) |
    DDC 193–dc23
LC record available at https://lccn.loc.gov/2016020592

Typeset in 10.5 on 12 pt Sabon
by Toppan Best-set Premedia Limited
Printed and bound in Great Britain by CPI Group (UK) Ltd, Croydon.

For further information on Polity, visit our website:
politybooks.com

CONTENTS

Editor's Foreword   xi

LECTURE 1   1

Prejudices against the dialectic • The double character of the
dialectic • The dialectic as method of articulating the Ideas
(Plato) • The order of concepts expresses the order of things •
The vital nerve of the dialectic • The dialectic as necessary
'exaggeration' • The positivist element of the dialectic

LECTURE 2   4

'The movement of the concept' (Hegel) • The dialectic
hypostasizes the identity of thought and being • Hegel's
dialectic as the union of identity and non-identity •
Non-identity in the process, identity in the result •
Introduction to the dialectic as a model of dialectic • The
movement of the concept is not sophistical • The movement
of the concept as the path of philosophical science • The
object of knowledge is internally dynamic • The movement
of the object is not arbitrary • The metaphysical concept of
truth • The inevitable reification of truth • Historical
movement is not the movement of being but is concrete •
The dialectic is not a philosophy of foundations • The
temporal core of dialectic

LECTURE 3   15

Critique of *prima philosophia* • Matter no first principle
either • Hegel's dialectic also a preservation of first
philosophy • All determination implies mediation • The
movement of the concept is no external contribution of
thought • A sophistical displacement of meaning in
Gehlen • The whole is the true solely as the result of all
mediations • The idea of an open dialectic • The whole is
neither a pantheistic totality of nature nor a seamless unity •
'The truth is essentially result' • Individual phenomena
intelligible only in terms of the whole • Recourse to the
whole is mediated through the self-movement of the
individual • The concept of the whole as already given

LECTURE 4   26

The traditional concept of system: derivation of the whole
from one fundamental principle • The dialectical concept of
system • Determinate negation • Contradiction in Kant •
Contradiction in Hegel • Antithesis arises from thesis • The
measure of the absolute lies in objectivity • Dialectical
criticism is necessarily immanent • Refutation of a thought
as development of the thought • The emergent absolute is
essentially temporal • The interaction of theory and
practice • The truth as result is concrete

LECTURE 5   37

The charge of universal rationalization • Dialectical thought
is not rationalistic thought • The dispute over rationalism •
Conceptual thought is indispensable • The truth moment
of irrationalism • The irrational as a moment of *ratio* •
Suffering and happiness are immanent to thought • Being in
itself, being for itself, being in and for itself • Relationship
of thesis, antithesis, synthesis • Dialectical method concerns
the contradictory life of the object • The dialectic not
immune to ideological abuse

LECTURE 6   49

Dialectical method not a formal conceptual schema • The
objectivation of truth • Every true thought becomes untrue
once it is isolated • The triadic schema irrelevant in Hegel •
The charge of universalizing contradiction • Contradiction is

not a first principle • Hegel's critique of Kant's
transcendental dialectic

LECTURE 7   60

Hegel's dialectical principle of development is a principle of
real being • Dialectic in Kant is only the negative side of the
critique of reason • The positive moment of the critique of
reason • Reflection as the principle of the speculative
self-knowledge of reason • Knowledge of knowledge also
the principle of substantive knowledge • Dialectic and
formal logic • The 'example' in Hegel • Logical form of
the judgement and the 'emphatic concept' • Dialectical
contradiction expresses the disparity of thought and world

LECTURE 8   71

Dialectic names the negative state of the world by its proper
name • Contradiction not only in thought, but is objective •
Contradiction as principle of diremption is also the principle
of unity • Dialectic as union of the a priori and experience •
The objective order of the world also conceptual in
character • Coercive character of dialectic • The systematic
claim of dialectic • Dialectical contradiction in Hegel's
political philosophy • Dialectical system not a seamless
deductive structure • The concept of experience in Hegel

LECTURE 9   82

The paradoxical task of knowledge: identifying the non-
identical • Identity of thought and being (Hegel) • Non-
identity and contradiction not resolvable in thought
(Marx) • The materialist priority of being over
consciousness is problematic • The whole and the parts
presuppose one another • The materialist critique of
literature cannot proceed from unmediated instances of
particular experience (Benjamin) • Dialectical materialism
is not vulgar materialism • The charge of metaphysically
hypostasizing the totality (Weber)

LECTURE 10   92

Knowledge of the social whole precedes individual
experience • Prior awareness of the whole not unique to
human beings • Rejection of Hegel's attempted restoration

of immediate experience • The congruence of whole and
parts as result of a process • Intuition • Theory neither
static nor complete • The danger of a dogmatic ossification
of dialectic (Lukács) • Tracing knowledge back to origins is
undialectical • Survival of obsolete philosophical notions in
the individual sciences

LECTURE 11   104

Terminological remarks on the concept of role • Neither
whole nor part enjoys priority over the other • Metaphysics
as science of the ultimate ground • Origin as mere beginning
(Hegel) • The ontological appropriation of Hegel •
'Abstract' in Hegel • The dialectic not a dynamic ontology •
'Being' in Hegel • Philosophy of immediacy as regress to
mythology • Dialectic and positivism • The 'natural'
appearance of a reified world

LECTURE 12   116

Affinity between dialectic and positivism • The constitutive
distinction of essence and appearance • Dialectic exposes the
apparent immediacy of ultimate givens • The Darmstadt
investigation • Motivational analysis in industrial sociology •
Opinion research, empirical and critical • Transition from
positivism to dialectic • Contradiction in the given as the
principle of dialectical movement

LECTURE 13   128

Scientific method in Descartes • Rationalism as the will to
control nature • The postulate of self-evidence (Descartes) •
A hermeneutic intervention • Self-evidence as a form of
ultimate metaphysical grounding • Evidence of sense-
perception already mediated • The order of knowing, the
order of the known • Experience and conceptuality •
Emphasis on analysis destroys the crucial interest of
knowing • Philosophy of nature and natural science •
Philosophy always bound to the material knowledge of the
sciences

LECTURE 14   140

Analysis alone yields no knowledge • The universal
concretized through the particular • Attitude of dialectic to
the concept of development • The family not merely a

remnant • Society not an organism but antagonistic in character • Knowledge as a continuity of steps • The unity of society constituted by discontinuity • The presumption of continuity is merely affirmative • 'Enthusiasm' a necessary moment of knowledge • The positive aspect of continuity

LECTURE 15   152

The coercive character of logic • Immanent and transcendent critique • Mobility of thought is not an evasion • Contradictions are constitutive • Against relativism • Dialectical cognition of the particular object requires explicit self-reflection • The charge of groundlessness • A sociological excursus on the mobility of thought • The substance of philosophy lies in the vital source of its concepts • Arrested movement in Heraclitus and Hegel

LECTURE 16   163

The dogmatic character of the axiom of completeness • The fulfilment of this demand in German idealism • Dialectical clarification of the objective by recourse to models • 'Ideal types' in Weber • 'Intuition of essences' in Husserl • Thinking in models • Labyrinthine communication in literary works (Kafka, Balzac, von Doderer) • Historical transformations in the concept of system

LECTURE 17   174

Consciousness as unifying principle in the modern conception of system • Critique and renewal of the concept of system in the nineteenth century • Contemporary appeal of the concept of system • The spectral afterlife of the concept of system • The need for system and the closed experience of the world • No categorical continuum among the particular sciences (Talcott Parsons) • Apologetic character of the functionalist concept of system • 'Frame of reference' • The logic of science and debased metaphysics complement one another today • Dialectic a beneficent anachronism

LECTURE 18   185

Dichotomous consciousness • Dialectical mediation not a matter of both–and • Mediation as the critical self-reflection of extremes • Role of either/or in the social sciences •

Dialectic and the negative concept of truth • Values are
neither transcendent nor merely relative • The criterion of
truth is immanent to the object • The dialectic is not a
matter of 'standpoints' • Dialectic offers no recipes •
Definition as logical form

LECTURE 19   196

The limits of *deixis* and definition with respect to the
concept • The concept is not a *tabula rasa* • Concept and
constellation • Life and fluidity of the concept as the
object of dialectic • Verbal definitions and philosophical
definitions • Philosophical definition requires prior
knowledge of the matter in question • It extends concepts
into force fields • Abbreviation as a specific feature of
philosophical definition • Operational definitions in the
particular sciences • Forfeiting the synthetic moment of
knowledge • Operational definitions and their field of
application • Dialectic as a critical mediation of realism and
nominalism • Truth moment of the phenomenological
analysis of meaning

LECTURE 20   208

Dialectical articulation of concepts as constellation and
configuration • The order of ideas in Plato as an expression
of the social division of labour • The exposition of the
matter in question not external • Exposition guarantees the
objectivity of knowledge • Contradiction in the identifying
judgement as starting point of dialectic • Truth and untruth
of the logical judgement form • Subjective synthesis and
objective reference in the judgement • An immanent critique
of logic • The phenomenological critique of inference •
Surrender of logical subordination as index of dialectical
thought • Is knowledge possible without assuming the
identity of subject and object?

Adorno's Notes for the Lectures   221
Editor's Notes   254
Index   314

EDITOR'S FOREWORD

The series of lectures which Adorno delivered at the Johann Wolfgang Goethe University in Frankfurt in the summer semester of 1958 can still be said to provide what the original announcement in the official lecture lists promised: it offers an introduction to dialectics. Presented in a free and improvised style, Adorno's theoretical reflections here are generally more accessible than comparable discussions in his writings on Hegel or in *Negative Dialectics*. The lecture course can thus certainly be regarded as a kind of propaedeutic to these texts. In reading out specific passages from Hegel and interpreting them in some detail, Adorno clarifies central motifs of dialectical thought such as the 'movement of the concept' or the meaning of determinate negation and dialectical contradiction. But he also makes it easier to approach this tradition of thought for those who already entertain sceptical or downright hostile attitudes towards it insofar as he systematically explores the difficulties it involves, addresses the resistance and the prejudices which it typically encounters, and discusses the specific challenges which dialectical thought presents. The only readers likely to be disappointed by Adorno's treatment of these questions are those who expect to be offered an instant recipe for such thinking. But, as Adorno insists, 'it belongs to the essence of dialectic that it is no recipe, but an attempt to let truth reveal itself' (Lecture 3, p. 25).

In terms of Adorno's own development, these lectures document a moment of some significance, since this is the first time that the issue of dialectics is expressly addressed. A couple of years before the plan for a work on dialectics as such assumed definite shape in

Adorno's mind, what we have here is a kind of methodological self-reflection on his previous substantive contributions, one where he explores for the first time that idea of 'an open or fractured dialectic' (Lecture 10, p. 95) which he will finally go on to develop at length in *Negative Dialectics*. This is evident, above all, from Adorno's original general plan for the lectures (pp. 221–53), which, in its almost symphonic layout, affords some insight into how his philosophy, in express relation to and with a constant eye upon the work of Hegel and Marx, attempts to situate and articulate itself. But the actual execution of the lectures, which differs significantly from the original plan in several respects, also explicates the central motifs of Adorno's own conception of dialectic: its definition as 'an attempt to do justice in thought itself to the non-identical, that is, precisely to those moments which are not exhausted in our thought' (Lecture 9, p. 82); the emphasis upon its originally critical function; its specific opposition to ontology and positivism alike; its complementary relationship to the idea of a negative metaphysics; and, finally, the question, so important to Adorno, of that individual motivation for engaging with dialectics which today – when the inner, namely dialectical, contradictions of capitalism are rousing us from a sort of post-modern somnolence – actually seems to have lost none of its relevance: namely the experience of 'diremption or alienation' (Lecture 8, p. 74) which makes us realize how 'dialectical thought itself responds to a negative condition of the world and, indeed, calls this negative condition by its proper name' (Lecture 8, p. 72), but without thereby relinquishing the hope that what strives for reconciliation is 'something itself harboured within the diremption, the negative, the suffering of the world' (Lecture 8, pp. 73–4).

Adorno delivered these one-hour lectures twice a week and presented them, as was usual with him, in a fairly free form that was based loosely on the notes and jottings he had set down beforehand. The lectures were recorded on tape as they were delivered – not specifically for subsequent publication but primarily for Adorno's own use – and were then transcribed. This transcription of the tape recordings forms the basis of the present edition and is preserved in the Theodor W. Adorno Archiv under Vo 3023–3249. On account of a one-week break after Easter, Adorno actually delivered twenty lectures rather than the twenty-two that were originally planned. No transcription has survived of the opening lecture, so that in this case the text is based on a stenograph by someone who can no longer be identified.

The presentation of the text follows the general editorial principles established for the posthumously published lectures of Adorno. This means that the primary intention here was not to produce a critical edition of the text but one that would be as immediately accessible as possible, especially since, with all the 'lectures', we are not dealing with texts which Adorno composed in written form or even autho- rized as such. In order to preserve the immediate oral character of the lectures the syntax of the original as recorded in the transcription was left unaltered as far as this was possible. The punctuation of the text here has been limited to clarifying the often rather involved sentences and periods and thus making the line of thought as clear as possible. This rule has not been observed in a small number of cases where intelligibility would otherwise be severely compromised. A number of tacit changes have also been introduced in the case of obvious verbal slips on Adorno's part or obvious mistakes in the transcription arising from typing errors or mishearing of the tape recording. All of the relevant substantive changes in relation to the transcription, which must be regarded as additions of the editor, have been identified by the use of square brackets in the text. All conjec- tural emendations where the editor felt obliged to deviate from the transcription and suggest a different reading have been specifically identified in the notes. The editor has deviated from the otherwise standard editorial practice with regard to Adorno's lectures only in two respects: firstly, the ancient Greek words and expressions which Adorno sometimes introduces into the lectures have been supple- mented with a corresponding transliteration of the Greek script in square brackets; secondly, while the German quotations from Hegel in the lectures are cited from the modern Suhrkamp edition of Hegel's writings edited by Karl Marcus Michel and Eva Moldenhauer, the editor also decided in the notes to cite the numerous quotations from Hegel's works in accordance with the editions which Adorno himself obviously used to read from in the course of his lectures. This deci- sion was motivated not by any desire to create a supposed aura in this regard but simply to clarify certain observations on Adorno's part which are intelligible only in relation to these older editions (with regard to the older orthography of *seyn* [being] for *sein* [being], for example). For ease of reference, details of the corresponding volume and pagination of the Suhrkamp edition have also been provided, along with details of the relevant English translations of Hegel's writings.

The editor's notes, insofar as they touch on substantive issues, are intended to assist the reader's understanding of the lectures and to clarify, as far as seemed possible for the editor, certain particularly obscure passages in the text. Given the length of the lecture series itself, comparable passages from Adorno's published writings have been cited in detail only rarely. The 'table of contents' which has been provided for the text, though based on Adorno's general practice, is not designed to offer an articulated account of the lectures after the event but merely intended, along with the index, to furnish a general orientation for the reader.

The editor would like to thank the publisher for permission to make available to the reader the extensive notes and sketches which Adorno produced in connection with this series of lectures. Careful attention to these materials shows that we must distinguish four levels of preparation for the lectures: 1) the general plan; 2) the detailed planning of the first two lectures of 8 and 13 May which exists as a typescript (point 1 and point 2 in the general plan); 3) the first phase of the lectures (8 May to 24 June), in which Adorno began by developing his outline for the first two lectures; because he could not keep within the allotted time he henceforth supplemented his sketches for the coming lecture with handwritten notes and jottings (either in the margin or between the lines of his existing typescript); and 4) the second phase of the lectures, in which he produced new and very detailed notes for three occasions (26 June, 3 July, and the rest of the semester from 15 July until 31 July). There is also a) a further loose sheet related to the first phase of the lectures (for 12 July); b) a sheet related to the second phase (on 'definition'); and c) a gloss which Adorno had prepared in relation to Hegel's *Phenomenology of Spirit*. The insertions subsequently added by Adorno are represented here by smaller print. Question marks in square brackets indicate words which are no longer legible. The purpose of the editor's notes provided for Adorno's own notes and sketches is limited to clarifying their specific relationship to the individual lectures where this is not evident from the dates which Adorno himself supplies.

Finally, it gives me great pleasure to thank all those who have assisted me in one way or another with the preparation of this edition: Andreas Arndt, Jelena Hahl-Fontaine, Hans-Joachim Neubauer, Wim Platvoet, Michael Schwarz and Matthias Thiel. The transcription of Adorno's notes and sketches was prepared by Henri Lonitz.

LECTURE 1

8 May 1958[1]

The concept of dialectic which we shall explore here has nothing to do with the widespread conception of a kind of thinking which is remote from the things themselves and revels merely in its own conceptual devices. Indeed, at the point in philosophy where the concept of dialectic first emerges, in the thought of Plato, it already implies the opposite, namely a disciplined form of thought which is meant to protect us from all sophistic manipulation. Plato claims that we can say something rational about things only when we understand something about the matter itself (*Gorgias* and *Phaedrus*).[2] In its origin, the dialectic is an attempt to overcome all merely conceptual devices of spurious argumentation, and precisely by articulating conceptual thinking in a truly rigorous fashion. Plato attempts to counter his opponents, the Sophists, by use of their own means.

All the same, the concept of dialectic as it has come down to us from classical thought is very different from what I mean by the term. For the ancient concept of dialectic is the concept of a philosophical method. And to a certain extent this is what it has always remained. Dialectic is both – it is a method of thought, but it is also more than this, namely a specific structure which belongs to the things themselves, and which for quite fundamental philosophical reasons must also become the measure of philosophical reflection itself.

What dialectic means for Plato is that a philosophical thought does not simply live there where it stands, as it were, but continues to live when it informs our consciousness without our realizing it. Platonic dialectic is a doctrine which enables us to order our concepts correctly, to ascend from the concrete to the level of the highest and most universal. In the first place, the 'ideas' are simply the highest general concepts to which thought can rise.[3] On the other hand, dialectic also implies that we can subdivide these concepts correctly.[4] This question regarding the correct division of our concepts brings Plato to the problem of how to articulate concepts in such a way that they are appropriate to the things which they encompass. On the one hand, what is required is the logical formation of concepts, but this must not be achieved in a coercive way in accordance with some schema; rather, the concepts must be formed in a way that is appropriate to the thing in question. This may be compared to the botanical system of Linnaeus[5] and the natural system based upon the structure of plants. The old traditional concept of dialectic was essentially a method for organizing concepts.

On the other hand, Plato was already well aware that we do not simply know, without more ado, whether the conceptual order we bestow upon things is also the order which the objects themselves possess. Plato and Aristotle emphasized the importance of framing our concepts in accordance with nature, so that these concepts might properly express what it is they grasp. But how can we know anything about the non-conceptual being that lies beyond these concepts? We realize that our particular concepts become entangled in difficulties; then, on the basis of these problems, we are obliged to develop a more adequate body of concepts. This is the fundamental experience of dialectic: the way our concepts are driven on in the encounter with what they express. We must try and compare whether what is given corresponds to the relevant concepts or not.

The dialectic is indeed a method which refers to the process of thinking, but it also differs from other methods insofar as it constantly strives not to stand still, constantly corrects itself in the presence of the things themselves. We could define dialectic as a kind of thinking which does not content itself merely with the order of concepts but, rather, undertakes to correct the conceptual order by reference to the being of the objects themselves. The vital nerve of dialectical thinking lies here, in this moment of opposition. Dialectic is the reverse of what it is generally taken to be: rather than being simply an elaborate conceptual technique, it is the attempt to overcome all merely conceptual manipulation, to sustain at every level the tension between thought and what it would comprehend. Dialectic is the method of thinking which is not merely a method, but the attempt to overcome the merely arbitrary character of method and to admit into the concept that which is not itself concept.

On the issue of 'exaggeration':[6] it is claimed that truth must always represent the simpler or primitive level, while what is more remote can only be a further arbitrary addition. This view assumes that the world is the same as the façade it presents. Philosophy should fundamentally contest this idea. The kind of thinking which shuns the effort to overcome inveterate ideas is nothing but the mere reproduction of what we say and think without more ado. Philosophy should help us to avoid becoming stupid. In a conversation with Goethe, Hegel once described dialectic as 'the organized spirit of contradiction'.[7] Every thought which breaches the façade, or the necessary illusion which is ideology, is an exaggeration. The tendency of dialectic to move to extremes serves today precisely to resist the enormous pressure which is exerted upon us from without.

The dialectic realizes that it furnishes thought, on the one hand, and that which thought strives to grasp, on the other. Dialectical thought is not merely intellectualist in character, since it is precisely thought's attempt to recognize its limitations by recourse to the matter itself. How does thought succeed within its own thought-determinations in doing justice to the matter? In the *Phenomenology*,[8] Hegel claims that immediacy returns at every level of the movement which thought undergoes. Again and again thought encounters a certain opposition, encounters what can be called nature. An introduction to the dialectic can only be pursued in constant confrontation with the problem of positivism. Such an introduction cannot proceed as if the criteria of positivism had not been developed. On the contrary, we must attempt to measure them against themselves and thereby move beyond their own concept. Positivism is not a 'worldview' but, rather, an element of dialectic.

LECTURE 2

13 May 1958

Ladies and gentlemen,[1]

Last time, I attempted to introduce you to a problem or difficulty which it is important to grasp right at the beginning if we wish to work our way towards the concept of the dialectic. And the difficulty is this: on the one hand, the dialectic is a method of thinking; on the other hand, it is an attempt to do justice to some determination, quality, or feature of the matter in question. Hegel captured this in the Preface to his *Phenomenology of Spirit*, when he spoke expressly of 'the movement of the concept',[2] where 'concept' has just this double sense: on the one hand, it is the concept which we bring to things – that is to say, the methodically practised manner in which we grasp the relevant conceptual 'moments' – yet, on the other hand, it is also the life of the matter itself; for in Hegel, as you will discover, the concept of a thing is not something which has merely been abstracted from things. Rather, it is that which constitutes the essence of the thing itself. The difficulty of approaching the concept of dialectic in the first place, the difficulty, especially for those unfamiliar with this field, of framing any idea or conception of what this is supposed to mean, lies at the very point which I have already indicated to you: in the fact that it looks as though, on the one hand, we are talking about a procedure of thought which can be learned while, on the other hand, we are also talking about something which unfolds in the thing itself.

Thus you will hear talk of the dialectical method as a procedure for explicating an object in accordance with the necessary movement of its contradictions. But then you will also hear talk of a 'real dia-lectic', to use an expression which has become rather popular, espe-cially since Hermann Wein,[3] namely a dialectic which unfolds in the thing itself, which is supposed to move in contradictions in accor-dance with its own concept. When you hear it expressed in this way, you will probably immediately think, as an inevitable logical conse-quence, that a kind of identity between thought and being must be assumed if we are to grasp this concept of dialectic in that double sense which I have attempted to point out to you. That is to say, it is only if thought (as represented by the method) and the object of thought (the thing itself which is supposedly expressed by the dialec-tic) are ultimately and properly speaking the same that we can mean-ingfully speak of dialectic in this double sense – at least if we are not simply to court confusion by using the same word to describe two quite different things. We might really be dealing with a case of simple equivocation here – that is, with the possibility that the word 'dia-lectic' is being used now to describe a particular method of thought, a particular way of presenting something (just as Marx, in what is perhaps a rather unfortunate passage, once characterized the dialectic simply as a particular 'form of presentation'),[4] and now to imagine something quite different, namely the kind of oppositions which unfold within the thing itself. I believe it is most important, if we are to develop any serious concept of dialectic, that you should be very clear from the outset that the latter cannot be regarded either merely as a method – for then it would be nothing but what we described in the preceding session as the older dialectic of ancient philosophy, simply a theory regarding the procedure of thought – or merely as a way of identifying oppositions which are empirically discovered in things themselves – for then the dialectic would fail to reveal that compulsion, that power of the whole, which is what actually enables dialectic to be a form of philosophy in the first place, and to furnish something like basic explanatory principles for the great questions of reality and of metaphysics alike. Both these aspects can certainly only be united if we concede that a dialectical philosophy must be one which posits thought and being as identical. And indeed this is quite true for the dialectic in its most fully developed philosophical form, namely for the Hegelian dialectic, which ultimately is a philosophy of identity, a philosophy which in the last instance teaches that being itself or, as Hegel puts it in the Preface to the *Phenomenology of Spirit*, that truth is subject.[5]

Now I have already introduced you to a really serious problem which lies at the heart of dialectical philosophy itself. For you will remember, if you followed the previous lecture, how I claimed that

dialectic is precisely the attempt to develop a philosophical understanding of what is not itself 'subject', that is, to ensure that the two
determinations here – the matter itself, on the one hand, the process
of thought, on the other – do not merely collapse into one another.
Yet it suddenly seems, at least as far as Hegel's conception of philosophy is concerned, that these determinations are identical with one
another after all. The supreme contradiction with which you are
confronted here – on the one hand, that dialectic is the attempt to
think non-identity – i.e., the attempt to acknowledge in thought the
opposed moments which are not simply exhausted in thought – and,
on the other hand, that dialectic is only possible as a philosophy of
identity – i.e., a philosophy which posits thought and being in a
radical sense as one – [this contradiction] already perfectly expresses
the programme which the dialectic in its idealist version, namely the
Hegelian version, specifically posed for itself. For this form of thought
expressly declared its programme to be precisely that of uniting identity with non-identity, as this is expressed in its own language.[6] Thus,
while everything is indeed to be taken up into thought, thought must
also be acknowledged as something which nonetheless differs from
its object in every instant. Here you will surely be tempted at first to
say that this is at once nothing but press freedom *and* censorship, a
manifest contradiction which makes wholly excessive demands on
thought: on the one hand, the dialectic is precisely what endeavours
to express the opposition between subject and object, the opposition
of matter and method, the opposition of cognition and the infinite
Absolute; on the other hand, the dialectic is supposed to posit all this
as one after all, and thereby expunge this opposition from the world.
How is all of this to be understood?

Now the Hegelian response here – at present I speak only of the
Hegelian and thus of the idealist version of dialectic; later on we shall
hear about the materialist version of dialectic, which is structured
quite differently – the Hegelian conception here (which furnishes you
with the very programme of a dialectical philosophy in a nutshell) is
this: it is quite true that non-identity emerges in every individual
determination that thought can articulate, and true therefore that
thought and its object do not simply coincide with one another, but
the entire range of the determinations to which thought can rise, or
the totality of all the determinations articulated by philosophy, does
produce this absolute identity within itself; or, to put this in a perhaps
more cautious and strictly Hegelian way: it produces and is this
identity precisely as the totality, as the entire range of all of the developed individual contradictions. And this is to say that, in the whole,
which philosophy for Hegel claims to be, these contradictions are

living moments which are 'sublated' [*aufgehoben*], at once superseded and preserved, in philosophy as a whole.

In short, this is the programme which the idealist dialectic specifically set for itself, and which finds expression in Hegel's claim that
the true is the whole.[7] But before we start to consider some of the
questions which arise in connection with this conception of truth, I
should like at least to read out the passage which I have already
mentioned to you, namely the one which refers specifically to the
so-called movement of the concept. For here too you will immediately
encounter a certain difficulty. And if in these lectures I am to introduce you to the dialectic rather than, say, offering you a dialectical
philosophy in its entirety, then, for the reasons indicated in our last
session, I can only begin by trying to dispel some of the difficulties
which obstruct our approach to the dialectic, and which we are
already aware of everywhere in our experience, irrespective of whether
this has been influenced or directly shaped by theoretical disciplines
of one kind or another. And since our attempt to counter these difficulties will actually serve, in each case, to express something of the
dialectical concept itself, this propadeutic can also provide a sort of
model of how you can actually think in a dialectical way.

When we speak of the concept, the idea of something like the
'movement of the concept', which I have already cited from Hegel
and perhaps introduced a little recklessly here, will once again present
quite a challenge. For in the context of your ordinary thinking, or
– and indeed even more, I would suggest – in the context of the academic or theoretical studies which you have already pursued to some
degree or other, you will all be familiar, as a matter of intellectual
discipline, with the idea of pinning down your concepts – i.e., of
defining the relevant concepts 'cleanly' by means of a certain number
of specific features; and one is expected to demonstrate this theoretical cleanliness by not confusing these concepts through the introduction of other differently defined concepts – in other words, by not
allowing our concepts to move. When I pointed out last time that the
dialectic is widely suspected as a form of sophistry, suspected of
depriving us of every stable definition or determination, you may
already recognize the source of this resistance to dialectic. For it is
believed that there is nothing to hold on to in the face of dialectic,
that our concepts are barely framed before they are immediately
snatched away from us, that we are thereby simply abandoned to the
arbitrary whims or perhaps to the suggestive rhetoric of the thinker.
Before I read you a passage from Hegel's *Phenomenology of Spirit*
which relates directly to this problem, and the first of several such
texts, I would just like to say this: the task of dialectical thinking is

not to juggle with concepts, or surreptitiously to replace certain determinations which belong to a concept with quite different determinations of the same concept. That would indeed be a road to sophistical thought rather than to the dialectical concept. Rather, what is actually required of dialectical thought in the ideal case – and I am the last to claim that this is also always realized in every dialectical operation – is to deploy the concepts themselves, to pursue the matter itself, above all to confront the concept with what it intends to the point where certain difficulties come to light between this concept and the matter which it intends. And these difficulties compel us to alter the concept in a certain way as we continue with the process of thought, but without thereby relinquishing the determinations which the concept originally possessed. Rather, this alteration comes about precisely through criticism of the original concept – that is, by showing how the original concept does not correspond to the matter it seeks to grasp, however well defined the latter may seem to be – and it thereby does justice to the original concept by insisting that the latter should correspond after all with the matter it sought to grasp. The fact that dialectical thought refuses to provide a definition is not an arbitrary decision, produced merely by toying with different possible definitions; rather, according to the idea behind dialectical thought, this refusal springs from the need to express precisely the moment of non-identity here, the fact that concept and thing are not simply equivalent. Thus the concept, in constant confrontation with the thing or matter in question, in a process we may describe as immanent critique, is convicted of its own inadequacy; and the change which the concept thereby undergoes must at the same time, at least according to Hegel's conception, be seen as a change in the thing or matter in question.

That is therefore the response which I would have to give you, in an initial and provisional way, to the question as to how the dialectic specifically relates to the concepts and their definitions with which it deals. And now I should like to read you the passage from Hegel:

> This movement of pure essences constitutes the nature of scientific method in general. Regarded as the connectedness of their content, it is the necessary expansion of that content into an *organic whole*. Through this movement, the path by which the concept of knowledge [that is, of philosophical or fully developed knowledge] is reached becomes likewise a necessary and complete process of becoming; so that this preparatory path ceases to be a casual philosophizing [that is, ceases to be an arbitrary presentation of more concepts, as I pointed out earlier] that fastens on to this or that object, relationship,

or thought that happens to pop up in the imperfect consciousness, or tries to base the truth on the pros and cons, the inferences and consequences, of rigidly defined thoughts. Instead, this pathway, through the movement of the concept, will encompass the entire sphere of worldly consciousness in its *necessary development*.[8]

This then is the programme of 'the movement of the concept'. I have started by explicating this idea of the movement of the concept or, to put it more modestly, by suggesting that it describes what happens with our concepts when we think. If you recall for a moment what I said at the beginning (that the dialectic also always shows a double character, related as it is both to how we think and to the matter itself), you may find it easier to approach this idea of 'the movement of the concept', which strikes me as central to the notion of dialectic itself, if you can form some idea of the underlying object or matter of dialectical philosophy. And this, I would emphasize, is also something which underlies dialectical philosophy in both of its principal forms, the idealist Hegelian dialectic and the materialist Marxian dialectic. To put this somewhat dogmatically to begin with, and I hope that the dogmatic and simply categorical appearance of this claim will subsequently be dispelled, this is the idea of something which is objective, something which is to be unfolded through the concept, of something which is dynamic in itself, and is thus not simply the same as itself, of something which is not identical with itself once and for all, but rather of something which is actually a process. If we are to grasp the essential point from this particular perspective, we must remember that the fundamental experience here must be approached from the side of the matter itself, from the theory of the object rather than the theory of the subject, from the thing which inspired the dialectic itself, from the experience of the fundamentally dynamic character of the matter; in other words, from the fundamentally historical character of the world itself, from the fundamental experience that there is actually nothing between heaven or on earth which simply is as it is; from the recognition that everything that is must actually be comprehended as something in movement, as something that becomes.[9] And it is already implicit in Kant's doctrine, incidentally, that time is not only a necessary form of our intuition; it also provides the ultimate condition for the capacity to connect our thoughts at all, so that nothing can be thought by us unless it can be thought as something essentially temporal.

This idea of the fundamentally historical and dynamic character of experience thus leads dialectical thought to maintain that particular 'essences' cannot in fact be grasped in rigid terms but must be conceived, in their objective interconnection and in their objective determinacy, as something which changes through history. But this approach also involves a further essential moment, one which is characteristic of Hegel and derives originally from his conception of philosophical system – i.e., from the thought of an overall and unified presentation of reality. It is the thought that this historical dynamism of the matter itself – this primacy of history over being, as we might even put it – is not merely an arbitrary process of change which befalls things which are in time, but that the necessity, the orderly development, the all-embracing process to which we are exposed is this very process of historical change. Traditional thought, pre-dialectical thought, had identified the order of necessity, or that which claims ultimate validity, with the essentially permanent and immutable, with that which once and for all just is as it is. The discovery of the historical dimension, which effectively began with Montesquieu[10] and Vico,[11] developed through Condorcet[12] in the eighteenth century, and culminated in the work of Fichte[13] and Hegel, actually represents a Copernican Turn in this respect, the significance of which can certainly be compared with the Copernican Turn which is explicitly associated with the Kantian philosophy. For it signifies that the necessity we have been talking about is not properly to be sought where things remain identical with themselves and one another. Rather, this necessity resides in the great laws of development through which the self-identical becomes something other or different from itself, and finally something which is internally self-contradictory. Thus we may consider an experience which is very close to all of us, namely that our individual fate depends fundamentally and decisively upon the major historical and dynamic tendencies in which as individual human subjects we constantly and repeatedly find ourselves caught up. And it is this experience – that the law of our existence should be understood as the historical movement of our epoch and of all epochs rather than as some so-called fundamental determinacy of Being – which is the impulse that actually springs from the matter itself, and which belongs from the start to something like the concept of dialectic itself. And if you really try and make the dialectic your own, as I strongly encourage you to do – that is, if you try to reproduce, and produce afresh, out of your own experience the motivations which ultimately give rise to dialectical thought – then it is precisely here, I believe, that you will discover what the law, what the objectivity we have been talking about, actually means, and how what actually determines our acting and thinking over and beyond our mere individuality, how what is historical is far

more than what we merely are, more than what we conceive ourselves once and for all to be.

At this point Hegel has reversed everything, as it were – and this
is a characteristic moment we find in his dialectic, and even more
perhaps in the materialist dialectic: what appeared to traditional
thought to be absolutely stable and secure, to be a fixed and ahistori-
cal self-identical truth, now itself appears as a distorted historical
image, namely as an expression of petrified relations which seek to
perpetuate themselves, the very nature of which is to perpetuate
themselves, and which have now basically lost a living relationship
to the subject, which are 'reified', to use a crucial term from this
philosophy. Thus the fixed and immutable character which strikes
ordinary or undialectical thought as the very mark of truth already
appears to this philosophy – and this holds for both forms of the
dialectic – as a phenomenon of petrifaction, so to speak, as something
which philosophy is expressly called upon to dissolve. For this is a
hypostasis, where some finite finished thing is made into an absolute
and falsely posited as the ultimate ground, as if it were the truth in
itself. The struggle against the reification of the world, against the
conventionalization of the world, where what is ossified or frozen,
where something which has arisen historically now appears as if it
were something simply given 'in itself', something binding on us once
and for all – this is what furnishes the polemical starting point for
all dialectical thinking.

It is also characteristic of dialectical thinking that it does not try
and counter this reification by appeal to some principle or other, to
another abstract or, if you like, equally reified principle, such as 'life'
for example. Rather, it seeks to overcome reification by grasping
reification itself in its necessity – that is, by deriving the phenomena
of petrifaction, of ossified institutional structures, of the alienation
encountered in what confronts us as an alien and dominating power,
from the historical concept – historical understood here in the
emphatic sense of necessity which was captured by that expression I
have tried to interpret for you, namely 'the movement of the concept',
which seeks to unite historical necessity with insight into the matter
itself. For to grasp a thing should really mean to grasp the historical
necessity of a thing in all its stages. That is what you should have in
mind when Hegel says that 'the movement of the concept' allows us
to renounce the sort of casual or arbitrary philosophizing which
simply happens to fasten on these or those particular objects, relationships, or thoughts as the case may be. Such philosophy is not
arbitrary precisely because it does not just leave the objects in question as they arbitrarily present themselves but, rather, attempts to

derive them in their necessity, or, we could say, attempts to derive even this contingent and arbitrary appearance itself in its necessity.

I think I have thus basically already indicated that the dialectic, insofar as it is a method, cannot be a way of securing one's own position in a discussion with others, although of course this is just what it is suspected of being. On the contrary, it is an attempt to bring out objective contradictions which lie in reality itself. If you recall for a moment the point about the historical character of objectivity, we can see that this historicality of objectivity means that the objects in question are not inert in themselves but rather dynamic; and where real history is concerned, this dynamic character signifies that history is broken or diremptted, that it unfolds through contradictions, and that we must explore these contradictions. But it is just on this account – and I think it is not without importance to draw your attention to the point – that the dialectic stands from the first in the sharpest possible contrast to those philosophies of being which appear to be on the rise today, philosophies which effectively adopt an undialectical approach from the start. And I would warn you not to lose sight of this sharp and emphatic contrast just because some of the contemporary defenders of ontological thought believe that they can also somehow draw Hegel into their own sphere.[14] But this generally amounts to nothing but a sort of ontologization of Hegel. In other words, they attempt to interpret that extremely radical conception of the historical character of truth itself as though we were dealing here with a specific interpretation of being. Yet dialectical philosophies, in both of the versions we have mentioned, share the conviction that they are not concerned simply with historicity, and do not rest content with the bare claim that being or truth are historical in character, but conclude from this that the task is precisely to pursue this historical character into all the concrete characteristics of objects. Thus the dialectic does not and cannot amount to some abstract assurance or 'worldview' regarding the historicity of being or the historicity of truth. If dialectic wishes to grasp the philosophical concept from which it lives, then it must concretely attempt to reveal the historical meanings of the objects which it addresses. This also implies, we note in passing, that the usual distinction between philosophy on the one side – oriented to the universal, the eternal, and the permanent – and the particular positive sciences on the other is something that dialectical thought cannot accept. For philosophy discovers its own substance in the determinations of the concrete sciences which it undertakes to interpret, while the determinations of the sciences must appear a matter of indifference to philosophy unless they are illuminated by the concept and thus begin to speak.

Here you may be able to grasp one of the most essential motivations for such dialectical thinking. In the division of labour between philosophy and the sciences which currently prevails, it really does effectively look as if, in spite of all assurances to the contrary, everything in which knowledge has its substance, everything with which it is really concerned, has been more or less abandoned to the individual sciences. The task of knowledge is thus constantly exposed to the danger of collapsing into the merely positive, of merely registering what is the case, without the question regarding the meaning of what has been registered, or indeed regarding the justification of what exists, even being raised. And then all that is left for philosophy really is the stalest and emptiest content of all, like the concept of being as such;[15] and while philosophy can produce as many manikins as it likes,[16] can struggle as much as it likes to spin something truly concrete out of this abstract concept of being, it cannot actually succeed, since all of the determinations which philosophy introduces in order to develop a higher and superior conception of this supposedly enchanted word 'being' still derive from that domain of beings, and thus of the historical, which is disdained by ontological philosophies with such pathos and misplaced arrogance. Dialectic is at once more and less modest in this regard. Dialectical thought does not claim that truth is eternal, or remains identical to itself, but endorses a concept of truth which has taken historical determinations up into itself. But, being more modest in this regard, it is in turn more immodest insofar as it fulfils itself in these material determinations and believes it can derive truly philosophical determinations precisely from such concrete objects. While the philosophies of being merely smuggle in these concrete determinations, taking them up from the whole domain of the empirical and the historical, they must at the same time deny them, proclaiming pure being instead. But dialectical philosophy, which cannot accept the opposition between pure being and merely historical existence, seeks to articulate its philosophical judgements precisely by reference to the determinations which derive from historical existence, seeks precisely to do justice to the latter.

I should emphasize that the programme which I have suggested to you here has one extremely far-reaching consequence which may well represent the most difficult of all the challenges posed by dialectical thought, challenges which I have been trying to unfold in our sessions. This is the challenge involved in the concept of truth itself. The standard conception sees truth as something essentially timeless,[17] as that which remains absolutely self-identical. On the traditional view, truth does indeed stand in time, is marked by a certain temporal index, is somehow affected by time, and it is on account of this temporal dimension that we are never really in a position to attain the full and absolute truth. But the idea of truth, from the time of Plato through to Kant, has always been identified with the idea of that which is eternally and absolutely binding. Think, for example, of the concept of the a priori in Kant, which signifies precisely that what is necessary and universal must be identified with what is utterly constant and unchangeable, which is the condition of any possible judgement whatsoever. Now the truly decisive challenge of dialectic lies not in the thought that truth must be sought within time or in opposition to time but, rather, in the idea that truth itself possesses a temporal core, or – as we might even say – that time exists in truth.[18] I have already suggested to you that this concept too has simply fallen from the heavens and, above all, is one that it is implicit in Kant himself. But you may take it as a general guide for the understanding of the problem of dialectic that dialectic must, in an eminent sense, be regarded as Kantian philosophy which has come to self-consciousness and self-understanding. I have just pointed out that Kant still upholds the traditional conception of truth in the sense of the eternally immutable a priori. But, insofar as he also makes time into a constitutive condition of knowing as such, that traditional approach is already losing its meaning in Kant's philosophy, so that time itself – one could almost say – has now become the organon of truth. Yet Kant did not recognize the full consequences of this, and it fell to his successors, and especially to Hegel, to draw out these consequences. And this then also affects the traditional conception of truth as the concordance or adequate correspondence of thought with being, an idea which must be changed and modified in the light of such philosophy.

LECTURE 3

20 May 1958

Ladies and gentlemen,

In our last session I tried to provide a foretaste of the central difficulty of dialectical thought, namely that its concept of truth itself is not a static one; that dialectical thought has broken with the notion of the 'idea' as something essentially permanent, immutable, and self-identical, a conception which has prevailed throughout the philosophical tradition since Plato, and which is defined as the ultimate truth in precisely these terms in the speech which Plato puts in the mouth of Diotima in the *Symposium*.[1] We could also express it this way – which may help to introduce the thought that must form the principal theme of this lecture, and to which we shall have to return again and again from a variety of different perspectives in order to respond to its challenge. We could say that dialectical philosophy or dialectical thought differs from traditional thought in the sense that the former does not hunt after some absolute first ground or principle. For the pursuit of such a ground ultimately involves the idea of the invariance of truth. And when philosophies of the most various kinds have constantly attempted to dig out some such first principle, the motive at work here is not simply the desire to trace things back historically as far as we can possibly go. For this quest for a first principle always invokes a certain substantive – or, if you wish, ontological – interest as well. One then imagines the first ground or principle – irrespective of whether this is understood as that which is logically prior or temporally prior – at least as something that in some way or other persists immutably and thereby essentially furnishes the key for everything that subsequently follows. The entire conception of philosophy which has prevailed in the West since Aristotle – and indeed this holds not only for idealist traditions but also for empiricist ones – is that of 'first philosophy' or πρώτη φιλοσοφία [*prōtē philosophia*] – that is, a philosophy which offers certain fundamental grounds or principles, whether of being or of thought, from which everything else is supposed to flow in a necessary fashion. Once these original grounds or principles have been secured, we then can claim to possess the decisive answers to our questions.[2] This is not to suggest, of course, that all of you have already engaged in such considerations. But I believe that, if you reflect for a moment and, above all, examine the need which would generally lead you to concern yourselves with philosophy at all, you will discover that this equation of philosophical questions with such first principles that need to be established appears self-evident.

Now the dialectical approach has directed its criticism at this very point – and I might add in parenthesis here that it is one of the signs of the degeneration of the second version of dialectical thought, namely the materialist version, that this specific impulse has not been recognized and that matter as such or the material conditions of social existence have now themselves been turned into an absolute first principle which simply needs to be secured from the start. All the talk of 'diamat'[3] thus clearly reveals itself for what it is, namely as a propagandistic device, since such talk has already negated the principle of dialectics: that the mere provision of fundamental principles is not actually enough for philosophy.

Today I should like to take some passages from Hegel's *Phenomenology of Spirit* – once again from the Preface, which is still the most appropriate text for introducing dialectic as a specific method – and to try and show you how this critique of a first ground or principle is presented in its original context – that is to say, in the first great version of a dialectical philosophy. I shall read out a couple of passages from Hegel and then interpret them from a twofold perspective, attempting in the first place to render them intelligible to you but also, in the second place, drawing your attention to some of the consequences which arise from this dialectical approach to the idea of a 'first' philosophy or philosophy of origins. Although I shall come back to this later on, I should point out right away, by way of qualification, that Hegel is an extraordinarily complex thinker in this regard, for, while he is the first one to offer a really radical critique of the concept of a 'first philosophy', there is a certain sense in which Hegel also upholds the claims of such a first philosophy, namely in the sense that he identifies the full development and articulation of the movement of the concept with such a first principle, and indeed frequently and expressly refers to Plato in this connection.[4] But we shall return to this question later. Here then is the relevant passage from the *Phenomenology*, which is also one of the most celebrated passages in all of Hegel's work, and one which can give you a certain idea of the essential character of dialectic.

> The True is the whole. But the whole is nothing other than the essence consummating itself through its development. Of the Absolute [which can here be equated with truth in the emphatic sense] it must be said that it is essentially a *result*, that only in the *end* is it what it truly is; and that precisely in this consists its nature...Though it may seem contradictory that the Absolute should be conceived essentially as result, it needs little pondering to set this show of contradiction in its true light. The beginning, the principle, or the Absolute, as at first immediately enunciated, is only the universal. Just as when I say '*all* animals', this expression cannot pass for a zoology, so it is equally plain that the words 'the Divine', 'the Absolute', 'the Eternal', etc., [and perhaps I might perhaps add 'Being' to the list here] do not express what is contained in them; and only such words, in fact, do express the intuition as something immediate. Whatever is more than such a word, even the transition to a mere proposition, contains a *becoming-other* that has to be taken back, or is a mediation.[5]

Expressed in other words, the moment you take a word like the 'Divine', the 'Absolute', the 'Eternal' – a word by which you can understand absolutely everything, and indeed only when you do so does it fulfil that claim to absoluteness with which the word itself addresses you – the moment you explicate such a word through a sentence or proposition, when you say, for example, that 'the Absolute is what remains immutably identical with itself', or 'the Absolute is the identity of thought and being', in that moment you already qualify that which precisely signified everything and to which the pathos of such a word, its claim to absolute validity, effectively clings, and in doing so you alter the concept itself. You could also express this by saying that you can determine such an exalted concept as that of the Absolute, the Eternal, or the Divine only by qualifying or altering it, and this process of alteration is what is decisive for dialectical thinking. This alteration is not something external which our own reflections impose upon such a word or such a concept; it is rather that such a word or a concept drives us, if we wish to comprehend it at all – that is, if we wish to give it any specific content, through which it first properly becomes a concept – drives us to qualify in the way that Hegel suggests. At the same time, you have here an explanation of the principle of dialectic and an exemplary case of the dialectic developed with reference to a specific concept. 'Whatever is more', as Hegel says, 'than such a word, even the transition to a mere proposition, contains a becoming-other that has to be taken back, or is a mediation.' The term 'mediation' in Hegel always signifies a change or alteration which must be expected of a concept as soon as we wish to be apprised of the concept itself. We might also say that mediation is the moment of 'becoming' that is necessarily involved in any form of 'being'. And, if dialectic is the philosophy of universal mediation, this implies that there is actually no being which could evade the process of becoming once you attempt to determine it as such.

This is the Hegelian concept of mediation, and I would ask you to bear this concept clearly in mind, for we shall naturally have to recur to it constantly in what follows. And, speaking of this mediation, Hegel continues: 'But it is just this that met with horrified rejection, as if absolute cognition were being surrendered when more is made of mediation than in simply saying that it is nothing absolute, and is completely absent in the Absolute.'[6] Now this horrified rejection which Hegel talks about is indeed that hostile attitude to dialectic which we shall still have to confront, for essential reasons, whenever we attempt to understand dialectic. For it springs from the idea that, if we fail to uphold our concepts unchanged, if we must change them in order to grasp them – if we insist, in other words, that their being is a becoming, that truth itself is actually dynamic – then this amounts to a dissolution of the concept of truth, to a kind of universal relativism that makes it impossible for us to say anything determinate about anything at all. Here I would say two things to you. In the first place, you will already have noticed one thing about the insightful Hegelian example that I have just presented to you: the movement of the concept which we have considered here – the attempt to determine a concept such as the Absolute, the Eternal, the Divine, and thereby qualify it with regard to what it actually claims, namely to be something unqualified, unconditioned, absolute – this movement of the concept is not some additional contribution of thought but is something required if you are to ascertain the significance of such a concept at all; that is to say, if you do not perform the operation which I have described – that is to say, if you do not go on to express a specific proposition concerning such a word – you cannot ascertain anything about it. It is then something meaningless. And since the word demands to be understood, if it is to possess its truth at all, this demand for change in the concept, for this other dimension which you add to it in the predicate, so that it becomes what as the subject term it is in itself, this demand does not spring from a merely sophistic form of reasoning which approaches the relevant concepts from without. It springs from the matter itself, if this matter is to be comprehended in its own right. But that means – and this compulsion is what essentially distinguishes dialectic from every form of merely external or sophistical reasoning – that the movement of the concept of which we have spoken is not some arbitrary alteration, manipulation or juggling of concepts, as many like to suppose, but something which arises of itself from the necessity of the matter. And in that sense it is the very opposite of the sophistical procedure which precisely fails to pursue the inner life of concepts, namely what they require, in and of themselves, if they are to be understood, but proceeds instead to ascribe different senses to the concepts in an arbitrary and external way.

That is the first thing which I wanted to indicate here, at the very point where Hegel himself clearly recognized, as his reference to 'horrified rejection' shows, where the real difficulty provoked by dialectic lies, and to suggest how we should respond to this rejection. For we have to see – to put this in rather drastic terms – that it is not we who bring concepts into movement. Dialectic is not the sort of thinking where we deploy concepts in very different senses in order to prove what we want to say. Arnold Gehlen tells us, for example, in his work on anthropology[7] that the human being requires 'discipline' in order to survive at all and speaks of 'raising' or 'education' in this connection, arguing that human beings must specifically be 'raised' if they are to survive the underdeveloped biological conditions of early childhood. But when he immediately goes on to insinuate[8] the other meaning of training or discipline as practised by a martinet, this second meaning of training is not the unfolding of a dialectical movement but is actually a sophism.[9] But when we say here that I must qualify a concept such as that of the Eternal, the Divine, or the Absolute in order to grasp it all, to be able to think it, and then proceed to add something else through which it first becomes what it is, so that only through this change does it become what it is, that is a case of dialectical thinking – that is to say, a movement of the concept which is drawn from the matter itself, and not something subsequently imposed upon the latter by ourselves.

The second thing which I wanted to point out to you takes us back to the very beginning of the passage from Hegel, namely to the claim that the true is the whole. These days, of course, there is so much talk of wholeness, and the expression 'wholeness' is constantly trotted out by schoolteachers, who imagine when they speak of wholeness and inveigh against mechanistic and particularistic forms of thought that they have captured something of wonderful philosophical import. And thus I can only begin by warning you emphatically about the concept of 'wholeness' which has now become so popular. Thus the task of philosophical education today, it seems to me, is to serve those who seriously desire such an education specifically by immunizing them against the countless philosophical slogans and ready-made concepts which swirl around us everywhere, and which people imagine can provide some kind of 'guide', norm, or meaningful ori-entation, while we refuse the trouble and effort involved in thinking these concepts through and subjecting them to due critical examina-tion. This kind of wholeness, this kind of organic unity, something basically unarticulated which has simply come together spontane-ously and is seen as inimical to the conceptual domain and to analyti-cal thought generally, this is not actually what Hegel means when he speaks of the whole. When Hegel makes the famous claim that the true is the whole – a claim, moreover, which I have felt compelled for crucial reasons to criticize, although I do not wish to pursue this yet at this stage in our reflections[10] – when Hegel defends this position what he basically means is this: the sum of all mediation – that is to say, the sum of all those movements which must be accomplished if our essential concepts are to receive their full meaning – this compre-hensive interrelationship of concepts, or that which ultimately emerges out of them, is the Absolute in question. And you may say, if you like, that this is the rather blunt, emphatic and even drastic response which Hegel himself would make to the charge of relativism.

But I should already say here that I do not believe that we neces-sarily have to take this step, and that we do not necessarily need to defend the claim that the whole is the true, if we wish to awaken the concept of truth in the first place, if we wish to uphold the concept of truth. You can readily see whether this is important or not, whether we accept this claim or not. For in fact you can only really defend this claim if you also maintain that the subject and the object are identical with one another. Only if subject and object ultimately coincide, as Hegel actually teaches, can you say that the comprehen-sive sum of all mediations is tantamount to the truth or the Absolute itself, just as in Hegel the Absolute is indeed defined at the highest level as subject-object.[11] But if we have serious reasons for not accept-ing this, for not conceding that subject and object are ultimately identical – and there certainly are very serious reasons for not endors-ing this extreme idealist claim – then you cannot rely upon the thought that the whole is the true because the infinite whole is not something which is ever given, at least to the finite subject; or, in other words, because not everything which is can be resolved into the pure determinations of thought. This is why the controversy which attaches to this highest principle of Hegelian philosophy, if you wish to put it that way, is of such extraordinary importance. But I believe – and this is the consolation, as it were, which I can offer you at this point – that this question regarding the Absolute as the whole does not have the absolutely decisive say regarding truth itself. For precisely in that form of mediation itself – that is, in the negation of the individual concept and in the compulsion to go beyond itself which the concept as such exerts – there lies a necessity, there lies a moment, which already vouchsafes truth even if we cannot conceive of this whole, this totality, as something ever completely given to us. Perhaps I may add here that what motivated me personally to turn to dialectics in a decisive sense is precisely this micrological motif, namely the idea that if we only abandon ourselves unreservedly to the compulsion exercised by a particular object, by a particular matter, and pursue this single and specific matter unreservedly, then the ensuing movement is itself so determined out of the matter that it possesses the character of truth even if the Absolute, as an all-embracing totality, can never be given to us. This would be the concept of an open dialectic – in contrast to the closed dialectic of idealism – and in the course of the following lectures I may perhaps be able to give you a more concrete idea of such a dialectic.

And here I should also just like to add that Hegel's concept of the whole which is meant to be the true does not refer to some kind natural totality, that this Hegelian concept of the whole is not remotely pantheistic in character and is not conceived as some kind of unfractured organic unity. For this whole is actually nothing other than what Hegel understands by 'system', namely the entire and developed range of all the relations between subject and object, and the antagonistic relations between subject and object which are unfolded on their various levels; and then, when you think all of these relations together, when you finally see how the simplest concepts with which you begin eventually return to themselves as concepts which have now been fully developed and critically clarified, only then, according to Hegel, do you have what he understands by the system or the Absolute. In other words, in Hegel, the system of philosophy is, in the highest sense, actually identical with being. But the concept of being here is not an enchanted word that stands right at the beginning and yields everything else.[12] Rather, we could almost say, that being, for Hegel, is a demand or programme, something which only becomes what it is precisely through encompassing the entire movement of the concept. You could also express this thought in the following way – which is also just how Hegel himself expresses it – and say that the

Absolute is indeed the result, or that which emerges at the end of this movement, but then you must not go on to reify this concept of result in turn, as if, for example, at the end of Hegel's great systematic works, at the end of the *Phenomenology of Spirit*, or the *Encyclopaedia of the Philosophical Sciences*, or the *Science of Logic*, this result could now simply be found resumed in a couple of summary propositions. That would still be a far too mechanical conception of dialectical thought, which indeed you can characterize as thought which resists both the merely mechanistic approach, which fails to surrender itself at every moment to the experience of the matter, and the merely organicist approach, which simply strives to grasp some irrational wholeness, where the latter turns into something blind because it is not properly thought and explored at all. Dialectic, in contrast, is precisely the kind of thinking which attempts to steer a path between the Scylla of mechanistic and the Charybdis of organicist or organological thought.

But to return to the concept of 'result': in Hegel this concept should not be envisaged as something finished that duly emerges at the end, which we can then simply carry away. When Hegel says that 'the truth is essentially result', you must take the expression 'essentially result' in its deepest and most serious sense. Perhaps from the inconspicuous example of this Hegelian phrase you can get a clear, and quite emphatic, sense of the full difference between traditional and dialectical thinking. For the phrase 'essentially result' does not mean that such a result springs forth as the conclusion of an extended method, after a long process of considered reflection. Those philosophies which appeal to some origin or first principle, in their various forms, could also say the same. Thus in a contemporary context you may learn from Husserl or from Heidegger that extensive forms of ἐποχή [*epochē*] or 'reduction', or even a kind of 'destruction', are required in order ultimately to reach something truly reliable and absolute, namely at Being or the ontological sphere of absolute origins.[13] That is not what it is decisive here. But when Hegel says that the truth is essentially result, this means that it belongs to the truth to be result. This does not concern a simple proposition or something simply valid for all time. It concerns something in which, as it is constituted now, its own genesis and origin, the process and the path which has brought it to this point, is sublated and comprehended. You could express this – and here I base myself squarely on Hegel's text – by saying that truth is at once the process and the result of the process, that truth, whatever it is, emerges only at the end of this conceptual process, but that this emergence is not simply external to this process, that the process is 'sublated' in this result, that the whole process itself belongs essentially to this truth, and is no mere propadeutic that could then simply be detached from the result which you have now finally discovered and acquired.

What 'the whole' really means for Hegel, if I may try again to make this difficult concept a little clearer to you, is quite simply that truth does not consist in defining some concept in isolation, treating it in isolation as if it were a mere sector, but rather by taking it in relation to the totality in which it stands. Those of you who are studying the sciences of society can form a really emphatic idea of this whenever you try and understand any specific social sectors – in the sociology of business, for example, any specific relations which prevail within a particular factory or within a particular branch of industry. Then you will soon encounter all of the determinations which have already emerged for you here and now, even though in reality they are not simply grounded in the particular place, the particular site, or the particular branch of industry which is the focus of investigation. For these determinations will lead back to much broader questions, such as, for example, the role of the mining industry or the conditions of mine workers in the entire process of industrial production today,[14] and ultimately to the entire structure of society in which the industrial exploitation of raw materials is involved today. It is only if you reflect upon the whole that you will also be able to understand the individual aspect properly. Thus it is necessary to grasp individual phenomena precisely in their particular character, though without simply arresting our thought at this point, and also to extrapolate from these phenomena – that is, to understand them within the totality from which they first receive their meaning and determination. This is the most essential insight which is involved in Hegel's claim that the whole is the true. And I believe that, among the most important reasons which may lead us to develop a dialectical conception of knowing in contrast to a purely positivist approach to scientific knowledge, this insight must take pride of place.

But we must add that such recourse to the whole certainly cannot be an unmediated one. I shall also try and clarify this for you. For it is indeed entirely possible that one may try and explain certain social phenomena in a quite arbitrary and, let us say, external manner, simply by proclaiming, 'Well, of course, that springs straight from the structure of capitalist society', or 'That derives from the level of productive forces or from certain things of this kind', but without showing how the necessity for this transition to the totality is actually involved in the specific character of the individual phenomenon under investigation. Yet, on the other hand – and this already holds for society, let alone for metaphysics – the totality from which the whole is to be explained is not just 'given' in the same sense in which some particular datum, or some particular phenomenon, is given to scientific study or observation. Capitalist society is not immediately given in this way as an object of study, and nor is the whole accessible to us as a mere fact, like the relations involved in some concrete and specific field of industry. Thus this transition to the whole, which the individual phenomenon requires if it is to be understood, also always involves a moment of speculative arbitrariness or, to put this in positivist terms, evinces a certain lack of scientific rigour. And here you can study the intellectual function, the practical function, of dialectic in a particularly precise fashion. For dialectic, in contrast, is not an attempt to introduce the whole, in a merely schematic or mechanical manner, from the outside in order to understand the phenomenon because the latter cannot be understood in its own terms. Rather, dialectic is the attempt to illuminate the individual phenomenon in such a way, to tarry with the phenomenon in such a way, to determine the phenomenon in such a way, that the latter intrinsically passes beyond itself through this very determination and thereby manifests precisely that whole, that system, within which alone it finds its own role and place. Expressed in concrete terms, this is the demand which dialectical thinking initially makes upon us, if I may put it this way, as naive seekers of knowledge: on the one hand, we should not be content, as rigid specialists, to concentrate exclusively upon the given individual phenomena but strive to understand these phenomena in the totality within which they function in the first place and receive their meaning; and, on the other hand, we should not hypostasize this totality, this whole, in which we stand, should not introduce this whole dogmatically from without, but always attempt to effect this transition from the individual phenomenon to the whole with constant reference to the matter itself.

But it would of course be naive[15] to believe that we could actually arrive at the whole, whatever that may be, simply on the basis of the individual phenomenon if we did not also possess some concept of this whole already. In the *Phenomenology of Spirit* this finds expression in the thought that there is always a double movement here, a movement of the object, of the objective concept, on the one hand, and a movement of the knowing subject, on the other. If I do not have some such a concept of the whole, some such a concept of the matter, or indeed ultimately an intention towards truth itself – here we could almost speak of a practical intention regarding how this truth is to be actualized – and fail to bring this to bear upon the phenomenon, then the phenomenon in turn cannot begin to speak. And I have no wish to pretend, in a kind of dialectical mysticism, that the phenomenon would somehow actually speak if I am not there to listen. But the authentically dialectical art, which you can learn from Hegel, lies precisely in this: we must allow the matter to drive us beyond the merely inert individual determinations, while we must still retain the capacity, through the experience of the specific and the individual which we have exposed, to modify that whole whose concept we must possess in order to grasp the concept of what is individual, to modify that whole in such a way that it forfeits its rigid and dogmatic character. In other words, the dialectical process is something which relates at once to both: to the parts, the individual moments, which we must pass beyond by virtue of the whole, and to the whole itself, for the whole, the concept which we already have and which should ultimately constitute the truth, must continue to change in accordance with our experience of what is individual. There is no recipe for how this is adequately to be accomplished, but then it belongs to the essence of dialectic that it is no recipe, but an attempt to let truth reveal itself.

LECTURE 4[1]

22 May 1958

Ladies and gentlemen,

I concluded the last session by interpreting the claim that the whole is the true, and also by trying to tell you something about the place of the concept of 'system' in dialectical philosophy, and specifically in the idealist and Hegelian form of dialectical philosophy. Now you may think – and this is a point of considerable importance – that the concept of system itself is precisely what cannot apply to dialectic, as I have attempted to show. For this concept suggests a philosophy of origins – that is to say, a philosophy where the totality is in a certain sense unfolded on the basis of an absolutely first principle. And, indeed, when we speak of 'system' we generally think of a seamless and wholly self-contained structure of thought, something we would describe in logical terms as a closed deductive context. And in a deductive context of this kind everything else is generally derived by inference from a single highest principle. If you proceed inductively, on the other hand, and instead of deriving everything from some such highest principle you attempt to advance from the particular to the universal, then, according to traditional logical doctrine, you can never be completely certain of the matter in question. Thus if up to this point all human beings in the past have died, and you extrapolate from this that human beings are mortal, you are not yet justified in purely logical terms in concluding that human beings in every case will actually die, since it is at least possible that one will fail to do so. But if there were something about the principle of the human being which ensured our mortality, we could be relieved of this difficulty and could confidently affirm such a claim as purely a priori. The traditional conception of system is precisely one which involves strict derivation from a single specific principle, and in that sense it represents the opposite of what I said at the start about Hegelian philosophy.

I should now like to try and show you, taking another passage from the *Phenomenology of Spirit*, that the Hegelian concept of system or, to put it in less pedantic and historical terms, that the dialectical concept of totality is actually the opposite of that approach. And here I should also like to present once again the central motif of the dialectic in a somewhat different light. I am talking about the idea that the truth can only be grasped as result, where this result is not just something that emerges at some given point but, rather, includes the process within itself as the necessary condition of its own validity, of its own meaning. The passage I wish to read to you in this context is also drawn from the Preface to the *Phenomenology*, and is particularly relevant here because it reveals the contrast with the traditional conception of system and thus also with the static conception of truth in an especially striking way. Hegel writes:

> Among the various consequences that follow from what has just been said, this one in particular can be stressed, that knowledge is only actual, and can only be expounded, as Science or as *system*; and furthermore, that a so-called basic proposition or principle of philosophy, if true, is also false, just because it is *only* a principle or basic proposition.[2]

In the specific context of the history of philosophy, this claim is explicitly aimed at Fichte's *Doctrine of Knowledge*,[3] in its first version of 1794,[4] a work which indeed in a certain sense is presupposed by Hegel's system and which does effectively attempt to derive the whole of philosophy from some such a first principle or proposition.[5] But this claim of Hegel's stands in downright contradiction to what we have just been talking about because the criterion of a deductive framework – that is, of a self-contained derivation of consequences from a highest principle – is precisely the criterion of non-contradiction. If a contradictory moment does arise, then according to the rules of traditional logic the deductive structure appears to have been violated. You can already see from this that Hegelian philosophy, for a quite specific reason, finds itself opposed not only to traditional philosophy and the traditional metaphysics of the permanent and the immutable but also even to traditional logic. This means that Hegelian philosophy does not recognize the principle of contradiction insofar as this philosophy holds that thought itself does not find its truth by proceeding in a wholly non-contradictory manner; rather, it is driven into repeated contradiction precisely through its own rigour and possesses its logical unity – its non-contradictory character – only as a fully developed totality, not in the single steps which it undertakes. This is a further challenge which dialectical thinking poses for us, a challenge which you can already appreciate right here once you properly understand this claim 'that a so-called basic principle or proposition of philosophy, if true, is also false, just because it is only a principle or basic proposition.'[6] In order to clarify this once again, we could say that, if for idealist philosophy the idea of the absoluteness of thinking stands at the very beginning, the idea that there is therefore nothing which is not thought, and that consequently, as Fichte himself expresses it, the thinking principle, the I, posits itself as something absolute, then we could say – and this step is already accomplished by Fichte – very much in Hegel's sense that this first principle is necessarily also already false, for the concept of this thinking which is posited here necessarily involves the moment to which such thinking relates. There is no thinking, there is no thought, which does not involve something thought, something to which it refers; there is thus no thought which, insofar as it thinks, is not more than merely a thought. But if we grasp the issue in this way – and Fichte most emphatically took this step which I am outlining to you here – if we ponder its full implications, then we might say that the principle with which philosophy begins – and the principle of Hegel and Fichte in this decisive point is the same – is at once true, insofar as there is indeed nothing whatsoever which is not mediated, insofar as we can know nothing which we do not know through thought. Yet at the same time it is false, for this apparently absolute origin also involves its own opposite, and the thought of an absolute and creative I or pure Idea already inevitably involves the thought of the non-I, the object to which thought relates.

Hegel continues: 'It is, therefore, easy to refute it [i.e., a first principle]. The refutation consists of pointing out its defect; and it is defective because it is only the universal or principle, is only the beginning. If the refutation is thorough, it is derived and developed from the principle itself, not accomplished by counter-assertions and random thoughts from outside.'[7] From these remarks alone you can recognize two decisive features of the dialectical method as a whole. Firstly, that 'refutation' in Hegel does not bear the usual meaning, as it does when we say that some claim or proposition is simply false. Rather, refutation here means pointing out the defect of the claim or proposition, as Hegel says. In other words, with every case of finite knowledge it is pointed out that, inasmuch as it is a merely finite knowledge – and we can express anything specific or determinate at all only as something finite – it is precisely and necessarily not yet the whole; yet, since is the whole alone which is supposed to be the true, every thought is also to that extent false, although not false in the sense of a particular arbitrary or mistaken judgement that demands correction, as a kind of intellectual defect, but rather false on account of its being a finite judgement. For every finite judgement precisely shows itself, as seems evident, not to be that whole from which alone the concept of truth according to Hegel can be derived. But this also implies that this falsehood is not an arbitrary or contingent feature for its own part, not something which is external to philosophy, to the movement of the concept, but something into which we necessarily find ourselves drawn.

In reality this thought can already be seen as a Kantian one, although in Kant it is not perhaps presented with the same consistency and clarity that it eventually acquires in Hegel. For it is the thought that there are certain types of proposition – and this is still expressed in Kant in a much more limited manner – which specifically go beyond our positive experience, that is, in which we apply our conceptual capacities beyond what can be furnished or substantiated by the material of experience. Thus we inevitably find ourselves entangled in contradictions, and Kant attempts at the same time in the second main section of the *Critique of Pure Reason*, in the Transcendental Logic, to show how we may nonetheless resolve and respond to these inevitable contradictions. This is a remarkable idea which stands right there in Kant but is not further pursued by Kant himself. On the one hand, as we are repeatedly told in the *Critique of Pure Reason*, we are necessarily caught up in these contradictions, and no epistemological reflection is capable of 'curing' us of this predicament. On the other hand, Kant does believe that he is able to offer a solution to the problem, namely by distinguishing between the different ways in which we may apply the concepts of noumena and phenomena, for which, according to him, quite different laws are supposed to hold.[8]

You can see therefore that a certain kind of contradiction is also acknowledged in Kant. But we can see that the experience of contradiction which persists in Kant – almost *malgré lui-même* we might say – is expressly raised to consciousness in Hegel, is almost turned we might say into the *organon* of philosophical thought in general. This means therefore, on the one hand, that, while reason necessarily becomes involved in contradictions, it also possesses the power to go beyond these contradictions and to correct itself. And according to

Hegel this is the very essence of the movement of the concept, the essence of philosophy itself. You have to keep both aspects in mind if you wish to understand dialectical thought properly: the unavoidability of contradictions, on the one hand, and the driving force of these contradictions, on the other, where this latter leads to the overcoming or sublation of the contradictions in a higher form of truth and also, in constant correlation with this for Hegel, in a higher form of reality. For, in Hegel, truth and reality are not conceived as entirely separate from each other, but as two interrelated dynamic moments which depend upon one another and are only constituted in relation to one another in the first place.

The second thing which I wanted to point out with regard to these few Hegelian remarks has to some extent already been anticipated in our previous reflections, and it is this: the refutation of the truth of some proposition, or the negation of some proposition, or – to introduce at last the watchword you have surely all been waiting for – the 'antithesis' to the initial 'thesis', is not something brought in from the outside but that which properly arises out of the consistent pursuit of the original thought itself. If you wish to develop a genuinely philosophical concept of dialectic, and to free yourselves from the debased and pre-philosophical conception of dialectic that can be encountered everywhere – for which dialectic just amounts to saying something like: 'Well, whatever one person may claim, one can somehow also say the opposite' – you will see [from Hegel's words] that this popular relativistic wisdom is incompatible with the thought which Hegel was actually trying to develop here. For it is the thought that the antithesis is not introduced in opposition to the initial proposition from without – something which he would certainly have repudiated as a purely sophistical dispute about contrary opinions. Rather, the opposing claim or proposition must always be derived immanently from the initial claim or proposition itself, as I have already briefly tried to suggest with regard to the relationship between the I and the non-I which indeed furnishes the fundamental theme for Hegel's *Phenomenology of Spirit*. To think dialectically, therefore, is not to confront one proposition of whatever kind with some other contrary opinion from outside. Rather, it is to drive thought to the point where it comes to recognize its own finitude, its own falsehood, and is thereby also driven on beyond itself.

I would now like to read out the rest of the paragraph from the Preface, but I should point out beforehand that, when Hegel dismisses the kind of external position which is opposed to a thought from the outside, instead of being drawn from the very thought itself, he speaks expressly of mere 'assurances' or 'random thoughts'. If you consider Hegel's philosophy as a whole, you will be able to learn a lot more from these two words than they express at this point if taken merely in isolation. For while it is true that thought itself receives this tremendous emphasis in Hegel, that it does indeed claim to develop the Absolute from out of itself, this must also always be understood to mean that thought specifically constitutes itself in and as objectivity. If we can say in an eminent sense that Hegelian dialectic is a subjective dialectic, namely if the Absolute, as Hegel puts it once, is actually Subject,[9] this means that thought, and emphatically on every individual level, finds its measure in and as objectivity. And the pathos of this dialectical philosophy in its entirety lies invariably in this: the judgement of the subject – insofar as it is a merely reflective or ratiocinatory judgement, insofar as it reaches out solely from itself to the object, without surrendering itself to the discipline, power, or density of the object with which it must engage – and the subject in question always finds itself convicted of its own arbitrary and contingent character, or, as Hegel also often likes to say, of its own vanity.[10] The contradiction or counter-claim which is not drawn from the matter itself, into which the matter itself is not immanently drawn, or which is simply introduced from the outside, all this is merely ascribed to the contingent subject in its finitude, becomes a mere 'opinion', becomes that δόξα [doxa] which you already find subjected to the severest criticism in Plato. And the path on which you will find that truth now becomes subject, becomes absolute subject, always involves the correction of all merely particular 'opinion' in and as the objectivity which thinking subjectivity encounters at every individual level.[11]

The 'refutation', as Hegel goes on to say, 'would, therefore, properly consist in the further development of the principle, and in thus remedying the defectiveness, if it did not mistakenly pay attention solely to its *negative* action, without awareness of its progress and result on their *positive* side too.'[12] This passage takes us into the innermost character of dialectical thought which I am hoping to convey to you. For the thought here involves the remarkable admission that the refutation in question is not what is normally described as a refutation in traditional logic, namely the process in which we take a certain thought and demonstrate that it is false. For refutation in Hegel's sense arises not against the original thought but rather with the thought itself, and out of its own power. Thus Hegelian dialectical thought generally, and Marxian dialectical thought too as long as it is critical thinking, is always a form of immanent critique. When we subject some structure or other to explicit critique, then this critique – and this is a popular way of expressing it – can be a case of transcendent critique – that is, it can measure the structure or reality in question against certain assumptions which seem indeed to be secure and reliable to the one who is passing judgement, but which are not grounded in the matter itself. On the other hand, it may be a case of immanent critique, that is, a process where what is criticized is measured against its own assumptions, its own principles of form. Now the path of dialectic is always that of immanent critique – that is, in the sense I have just been explaining, we cannot simply confront the matter in question with some criterion external to it or introduce any 'assurances' or 'random thoughts' of our own. Rather, the matter in question, if it is to be disclosed as it is, must be measured, in itself, against its own concept. Thus, to offer you an example from the materialist dialectic, when Marx furnishes a critique of capitalist society, he will never do so by contrasting it with a supposedly ideal society, such as a socialist society. That kind of thing is scrupulously avoided by Marx at every turn, just as Hegel never allowed himself at any point to paint utopia or the fully realized Idea as such. There is a serious taboo on this in both versions of dialectic. Therefore when Marx submits a form of society to critique he does so by measuring it against what the society in question claims of itself to be. Thus Marx will say: 'This society claims to be one of free and just exchange, so let us see if it lives up to these its own demands.' Or again: 'This claims to be a society of free subjects engaged in exchange as contracting parties; let us see how it stands with this demand.' All of these moments which actually characterize Marx's method, and which also make it so difficult to grasp Marx's method properly, instead of misinterpreting it precisely as a theory of an ideal society, something which was very far from his mind, all of these moments are already present in the Hegelian passage we have just been discussing.

But I should like at this point to go on to discuss something else. For you have already seen that dialectical negation is not a simple correction, or counter-claim, to a false thought but, rather, if you want to put it this way, the further extension, or, as Hegel rightly describes it, the development of the initial thought, and thus the remedying of its defective character. In this sense it is a genuine correction, and not something which simply eliminates the thought itself. If therefore – to take up the Marxian example again – the thought of a free and just society is subjected to critique, the idea of freedom and justice is not thereby eliminated or dissolved in the dialectical method. Rather, we are shown how this idea is not yet realized in the reality which is compared with the idea. And the concepts of freedom and justice which have prevailed hitherto are also themselves modified in the process. That is to say, they cease to be as abstract as they initially present themselves to thought, and thereby become more concrete. Now this all sounds harmless enough, and you may even breathe a sigh of relief and say: 'Well, it seems the dialectic is not so terrible after all, that all this talk of contradiction was not meant so seriously, and the whole thing does not appear to conflict that much with the rules of common sense. We do not have to be so narrow in our approach, we can expand our limited thoughts, can go beyond them and in this way eventually reach the whole.' And indeed there is something of this 'common sense' about the dialectic. Yet the matter is not nearly as simple and straightforward as this. And here once again we come to a critical point in the conception of dialectic which I would ask you to bear clearly and constantly in mind. For Hegel says that this would all be fine and good, that thought simply develops and manages to avoid refutation. But Hegel says that the critical thought – that is, the thought which measures the matter against itself, which confronts the matter with itself and drives it onwards – pays attention 'solely to its *negative* action, without awareness of its progress and result on their *positive* side'.[13] This means, in the first place, that Hegel is extraordinarily serious about refutation in his sense, that we do not simply have the whole at our disposal, that we cannot simply extend our concepts at will with the sovereign gesture of a God who assigns its proper place to everything, simply transcend the limitations of our thought and finally secure its proper place. What is demanded, rather, is that thought must really surrender itself to the dialectic without fear or favour. This springs directly from what I was trying to get over in our last session, namely that the whole is precisely not something already given, that truth is not something fixed and somehow guaranteed. On the contrary, truth itself is something which arises and emerges, is essentially result. But this also means that we cannot deploy truth by introducing it from without, that we cannot, simply by thinking dialectically, already rise above dialectic by virtue of this abstract truth. Rather, we must immerse ourselves in this dialectical process itself. We could even say that there is no other possible way for us to reach the whole except by exposure to the partial, for we do not possess the whole. Only by entrusting ourselves to this partiality, by persevering through this limitation, by recognizing the critical movement itself as the truth, is it possible for us to reach truth at all. On the other hand – and here you see how serious the concept of dialectic in Hegel really is – this means that the next step must also be taken with full seriousness. This step should not simply be relativized as such, insofar as it sees itself in turn only as a partial moment of the whole. For this implies in turn that the next step – namely that reflective negativity which manifests the defective character of the finite – is not yet itself the truth either. For this step, insofar as it inevitably misunderstands itself, turns into untruth once again and is thus driven on beyond itself. And the inevitable untruth in which it is then caught up is just what prevents it from appearing simply as an extension or correction of the false. It is what necessarily and inescapably lends it the appearance of an absolute contradiction. You can see from all this that the concept of contradiction, despite all the relevant qualifications, is indeed an extraordinarily serious matter here. To take another historical example, if the men who brought about the liberation of bourgeois society during the French Revolution had not seriously regarded this bourgeois society as the realization of a just society as something absolute, if their own limited intellectual perspective in this regard were not effectively at work as an explosive force, then the revolution as a whole would never have come to pass. But, at the same time, this defective understanding involved in turn that particular limitation which made this into a merely relative historical achievement after all.

I could perhaps express this thought in another way, which serves to bring out something I attempted to introduce at the beginning, namely the idea of the temporal core of truth itself.[14] For it is here that you probably approach the deepest point in Hegelian thought, and from which you may be able to grasp that idea. It implies that no thought can actually be thought which frees itself from time, from its own temporal core. Thus a thought, or a political thought – and the *Phenomenology of Spirit* itself is a politically conceived work in a pre-eminent sense – which tried to relate immediately to what is absolute, to a justice beyond time, instead of growing from the concrete conditions of its own time and measuring itself against them, such a thought would not actually be in a superior position to these concrete conditions of the time. It would only be more abstract, and would fall powerless precisely by virtue of this greater abstractness. It would forfeit the very power to become actual which ultimately justifies the truth of a thought from the dialectical perspective. This is, so to speak, the political or practical dimension of the idea of the temporal core of truth. This implies there is no universal truth resting statically within itself, and no such truth about society. For truth itself only ever emerges from the concrete situation, and once it absolves itself from the concrete situation, or believes that it can simply rise above the latter, it thereby finds itself condemned to powerlessness, and can only bring about the very opposite of what it believes it is able to effect.

I have introduced these reflections here as a model to show you something else which is also extraordinarily important for the general climate of dialectical thinking. I am talking about the continual interaction between an extremely theoretical thought and an orientation to praxis. Here too we find that dialectical thought is fundamentally different from traditional thought. For dialectical thought does not just present us with an elaborated theoretical system from which practical 'conclusions' are produced only after the entire theory has been duly settled. Rather, all levels of dialectical thought, we might say, effectively yield sparks which leap from the extreme pole of theoretical reflection to the extreme pole of practical intervention. And if I have indicated the logical structure of the thought here, the unavoidable limitation of the contradiction involved – or the central role of concrete political praxis in contrast to an abstract political utopia, for example – this must be recognized as a crucial issue for dialectical thought in general. We must really accustom ourselves to the idea that the unity of theory and praxis – as conceived in all dialectical thought, already in Fichte, and certainly in Hegel and Marx – is already the kind of unity which does not merely spring forth at the end but consists in just such a continual interaction as I have tried to suggest. And this itself is also a consequence of what we have called the temporal core of truth, a consequence which is fully acknowledged by Hegel. For this means that truth itself cannot be set over against time in a purely contemplative sense. Rather, in possessing a temporal configuration of its own, truth always possesses a quite emphatic relationship to possible praxis as well.

The paragraph from Hegel which we have been discussing concludes as follows:

> The genuinely *positive* exposition of the beginning is thus also, conversely, just as much a negative attitude towards it, viz. towards its initially one-sided form of being *immediate* or *purpose*. It can therefore be taken equally well as a refutation of the principle that constitutes the *basis* of the system, but it is more correct to regard it as a demonstration that the *basis* or principle of the system is, in fact, only its *beginning*.[15]

This effectively recapitulates what we already heard in the last session: that the definition of zoology, say, as the theory 'of animals' is not identical to a developed zoology, that this bare principle or proposition doesn't give you the zoology. You can only possess that when you advance concretely from this definition or its concept and explore the development of particular animals and their relationship to one another. But the passage actually says more than this. For when you hear in this way that a first principle or proposition is only a beginning, this again may sound quite harmless. Thus you might understand it in the following sense and say, 'Of course, if you have such a first principle, like Fichte's initial proposition, you have to develop it further in order to acquire richer content gradually as you proceed.' But here too I should remind you once again that conceptual expressions such as 'only a beginning' bear much more weight in Hegel, and must be taken much more seriously, than you may initially imagine. For it is not just that such a principle or proposition must gradually come to acquire rather more colour and more contour, as non-dialectical and traditional modes of thought might typically put it at this point. It is rather that such a principle or proposition, as long as it is merely a beginning, as long as it is merely abstract, as Hegel would say, is also actually false. And the 'abstract' in Hegel does not mean quite the same thing as the concept of 'abstractness' in our ordinary mode of thinking. What is 'abstract' for Hegel is not simply the universal as such but, rather, what is isolated, the particular determination insofar as it has been detached, abstracted in the literal sense of the term, from the whole in which it belongs. And the movement of thought itself, as a movement towards the whole, is in a Hegelian sense a movement towards the 'concrete', understood in the sense of what has 'grown together', just as one of the determinations of truth for Hegel is that the truth is indeed essentially concrete.[16] In this connection, therefore, the abstract is the merely particular, that which remains merely isolated, and the 'beginning' is false precisely because it is abstract, because it is isolated, because it has not yet passed over into the whole, or because it has not yet 'come to itself'. Thus the relation between the development or execution of the task and its simple beginning is not like that between the final image and what appeared on the drawing board in the form of a pre-delineated schema. We are talking rather of the very process in which truth emerges for itself. These are the things which I wanted to get over to you today by way of introduction to the question of dialectic.[17]

LECTURE 5

3 June 1958

Ladies and gentlemen,

In our last session we made an initial attempt to grasp the concept of dialectical negation rather more closely, that is, to explicate the notion of dialectical contradiction. From what we have said, I believe that it is now already possible to dispel one of the most common and vulgar conceptions regarding the dialectic – the idea that dialectic amounts to an egregious intellectualization of experience and thereby also to a dubiously harmonious understanding of the world. The argument goes something like this. If we do undertake, with the dialectic, to grasp everything that is as a movement which arises from its contradictory character, if we submit everything that is to an intellectual schema and proceed as if the world in itself were utterly and entirely rational, then it is only on these assumptions that the world can be utterly and entirely 'constructed', as they say. But surely, it is claimed, this simply neglects the irrational aspect of things. As it happens, in a recent essay on Eichendorff, I was able to point out a particular passage where Eichendorff, who himself hailed from the broad tradition of German Idealism, had already charged the whole of post-Kantian philosophy, albeit in a rather summary way, with neglecting the darker and dissonant side of experience which can never be brought to full rational clarity.[1] In this kind of thinking, therefore, the dialectic is subjected to the kind of charge which a certain German tradition, and not the most noble one in my opinion, has frequently raised against the French spirit, and specifically the spirit of Cartesian thought. The reflections we have already pursued should enable you to see how inappropriate this approach actually is. For the Hegelian philosophy in particular, by virtue of its dialectical character – that is, through its recognition of the moment of negativity – is opposed to the idea that everything can simply be entirely construed or constructed by *ratio* in a seamless and unbroken fashion. We could express this in a very pointed way, and say that this philosophy is indeed an attempt to construe or construct reality, but precisely not as a seamless process. It attempts to do so in the breaks and fractures, and by virtue of the breaks and fractures harboured within reality itself. And if I may reveal to you here something of the fascination which the dialectic has always exercised upon me and my own intellectual efforts, and which it may also come to exercise upon some of you, I could almost say that this fascination springs from the way that dialectic somehow promises to square the circle – and not just promises to do so. For it does indeed claim to construe or construct precisely what cannot simply be exhausted in rationality – the non-identical, that which cannot itself be immediately construed – and thus to grasp the irrational by appeal to consciousness itself. I might also describe it, thereby turning a Hegelian trope upon a much more modern pair of opposites, as an attempt, through *ratio* itself, to rise above the opposition of the rational and the irrational.

The negative, as I pointed out last time, is not some kind of supplement to the positive claims of thought, something counterposed to thought merely from the outside. Thus the dialectical antithesis, the dialectical counter-thesis, is not something posited externally in opposition to the initial thesis, something which thought must also address. Rather, the essence of the dialectical process lies in the way that the antithesis is derived from the thesis itself, in the way that what is comes to be grasped as both identical and non-identical with itself. It is precisely because this moment of negation is harboured in the specific thesis itself rather than counterposed to it from without, and precisely because in order to grasp these moments properly at all we must not reduce or simplify things in advance, that the dialectic acquires that seriousness which I talked about in the last session. Perhaps we could also capture this seriousness by saying that dialectical thinking is a form of thinking which does not define or determine the particular by reducing it to its class or type, by subsuming the particular beneath ever more inclusive concepts. Dialectical thinking is thus an attempt to grasp the particular not by resorting to classification but rather by disclosing its own specific character, by trying to break it open, as it were, and thus reveal the opposition between particular and universal in the object of thought in each case. But subjective reasoning, and thus the supposedly all-governing rationality, is thereby also simultaneously exposed to its own opposite through the power of what is, of the particular which cannot be exhausted without remainder, of the non-identical, of what is other, of what can properly be brought to consciousness not by *ratiocinatio* – i.e., not by mere processes of inference – but only by attending or 'looking on'. In this sense, therefore, dialectical thinking is not actually a rationalistic form of thought, insofar as it is critically directed both against the opaque and unarticulated and against the limitations of every individual rational positing.

So that our reflections may not remain too formal, something which could hardly be avoided at the very beginning, this might be a good place to say something about the debate over rationalism. This debate – ever since the controversies which arose in connection with the philosophy of Jacobi[2] and later in the wake of Hegel's polemic against Schelling[3] – has continued to play a significant role in philosophical thought.[4] Thus on the one side we have rational thought in the usual sense, which was rather derogatively described by Hegel as the 'philosophy of reflection', a mode of thought which appeals exclusively to the usual logical forms – definition, classification, inference, specific conceptual articulations and distinctions, and all such features – and accepts nothing as genuine knowledge which is not couched and developed in these forms.[5] And on the other side we have all those philosophies which are commonly and rather crudely characterized as irrationalist in character, the last major and significant representative of which was surely the philosophy of Henri Bergson.[6] These philosophies basically defend a standpoint which Schelling was the first to formulate, claiming that the merely finite knowledge produced by 'the understanding', to express this in the language of German Idealism, does indeed remain merely external to its objects and reveals little of the actual life of reality. True knowledge, by contrast, is therefore one which sees the matter in question from within, as it were, instead of merely struggling to grasp and order it from without. But, in return, such knowledge appears to sacrifice those criteria of controllability, necessity, and universality which Western scientific thought had come since its Cartesian origins to regard as its highest criteria. I believe that this Hegelian talk, and this dialectical talk in general, about rising above certain fundamental oppositions – and this is indeed one of the most essential motifs of all dialectical thought itself – can be exemplified particularly well in relation to this so-called controversy over rationalism, a controversy which also finds its own place in Hegel's thought and is seriously addressed there. For on the one hand Hegel furnishes a most emphatic critique of all merely mechanical or classificatory thought – and I

believe I have already pointed out how the kind of tabulating mentality which has effectively come to prevail in scientific thinking today
was already expressly attacked in a passage from the *Phenomenology
of Spirit*.[7] But on the other hand he also fiercely attacks the kind of
thought which is 'shot from a pistol',[8] which aspires to grasp the
Absolute immediately or at a stroke, something which his erstwhile
friend and subsequent opponent Schelling appeared above all to
embody at the time. And one could specifically interpret the *Phenomenology of Spirit*, this first outstanding major work of Hegel's, as an
elaborate attempt to play each of these mutually contradictory
moments off against the other, ultimately allowing them to criticize
one another and be reunited on a higher level after all.

    What are we to say to all this, if we permit ourselves to consider
this alternative between very different philosophical approaches from
a rather greater distance? On the one hand, we must acknowledge
that thought does not actually possess any non-conceptual forms it
can appeal to, that since we have acquired the sort of classificatory
and definitional techniques that are developed in formal logic we
cannot simply leap out of these forms. And the claim of reason itself,
and thus the very meaning of 'reason' – in other words, the question
regarding a truly rational order for the world – cannot be separated
from this conception of reason as a conceptually perspicuous order
of knowledge itself. And thus in Hegelian philosophy as well we
discover that traditional logic – which Hegel of course criticized at
its most central point, namely the principle of contradiction itself – is
not simply displaced by dialectical logic. I believe it is extremely
important, if you wish to understand the dialectic properly in this
regard, for you to be quite clear that to think dialectically is not
somehow to think in a non-logical way, or somehow to neglect the
laws of logic. Rather, to think dialectically is to allow particular
determinations to point beyond themselves whenever they come into
contradiction with themselves, is thus to render them 'fluid' through
the application of logical categories. From this point of view you can
regard Hegel's entire *Logic* as a kind of self-critique on the part of
logical reason, the kind of critique which logic applies to itself. All
of the traditional logical forms are retained within Hegel's *Logic*. You
will find them comprehensively discussed in the third major division
of Hegel's so-called *Greater Logic*, in the 'Logic of the Concept'. But
at the same time Hegel shows with remarkable perceptiveness that,
while these structures of traditional logic, in their usual form, are
indeed indispensable, they cannot constitute the whole of knowledge
as long as they are taken in isolation or treated simply as so many
particular determinations.

On the other hand, what is generally described as 'irrationalism' also has a truth moment of its own. For it is a repeated attempt to bring home to thought precisely what has been excised by thought itself, what has been lost to actual experience through a form of reason which dominates nature and itself alike. It is an attempt to do justice within philosophy to all that has been sacrificed to the process of enlightenment. Irrationalism as a whole, we might say, shows a tendency to acknowledge precisely what has been obscured in the ongoing process of European enlightenment and effectively vanquished by the dominance of reason, everything that appears weaker or disempowered, everything merely existent that cannot be preserved in essential eternal forms and has therefore been dismissed as simply ephemeral, a constant tendency to vindicate a place for this even in the thought which has abjured it. And it is probably no accident, and not merely a correlation prompted by the sociology of knowledge, but surely something profoundly connected with the essence of these irrationalist philosophies if they have tended to be reactionary or restorationist in character – if for the moment I may use these words in a non-derogatory sense. In the sense, that is, that they somehow wished to lend a voice to all that has been sacrificed to history, though without thereby grasping the necessity of this sacrifice, or this defeat, within themselves. [Irrationalism thus reminds us][9] that, while human beings have been able to escape the blind compulsion of nature only by means of rationality, by means of the thought which dominates nature, and would sink back into barbarism if they were to renounce this rationality, it is equally true that the process of the progressive rationalization of the world has also represented a process of progressive reification – just as the reification of the world, the petrifaction of the world as an objectivity which is alien to human beings, on the one hand, and the growth of subjectivity, on the other, are not simply opposed to one another, are not simply contradictory, but are mutually correlated so that the more subjectivity there is in the world, the more reification there is as well, and it is precisely to this that irrationalism responds.

Once thought has grasped this fatal structure, which is nothing but the dialectic of the process of enlightenment itself, it cannot simply abandon itself to one pole or the other, and it certainly cannot seek the kind of wretched middle way that claims that we must somehow also find a place for the unconscious or the irrational alongside *ratio* itself. For an irrationality which is circumscribed in this way, merely tolerated by *ratio* in a kind of protected natural reserve, has indeed thereby already been consigned to destruction, no longer possesses any real power, is indeed impotent. And the desire of dialectic is precisely to refuse such impotence in thought, to insist that thought must also harbour the possibility of its own realization within itself. The conclusion which Hegel draws from the alternative here is not to pit the alleged powers of the irrational against the powers of the rational, as people tend to do today within the dismal administrative intellectual regimes of the present, which strive to bring everything, even the supposedly irrational, under conceptual bureaucratic categories, and thus neatly separate the class of rationality from that of irrationality. This wretched response is precisely what Hegel disdained, and he attempted instead to pursue what strikes me as the only possible path to take: by means of consciousness itself, by means of developed logical insight, or, if you wish, by means of enlightenment, to call enlightenment itself by its proper name, to expose in enlightenment itself those moments of reification, alienation, and objectification by rational means, moments which can otherwise be exposed only in an external and therefore powerless fashion. The task, in other words, is to take up the moment of irrationality into thought or *ratio* itself, as its own immanently contradictory element, rather than just playing this off against thought in an external way as an alternative 'worldview'. Or you could also put it this way: to comprehend for its own part the irrationality which eludes reason itself, and also, precisely through reason, to extend the critique of reason far beyond that attempted by Kant; to show that reason, insofar as it necessarily entangles itself in contradictions, repeatedly fails to do justice to what is not identical with itself, with what is not itself reason, and thus repeatedly miscarries. This is the very situation in which dialectical thought finds itself in relation to the controversy over rationalism,[10] and it strikes me as symptomatic of the appalling vulgarization of dialectics today that someone like Lukács,[11] who really ought to know better, has written a book entitled *The Destruction of Reason*,[12] which should never have seen the light of day. Here he simply brands absolutely everything that looks like irrationalist philosophy, including Nietzsche, and also an utterly misunderstood Freud, with the clichéd label of 'fascism', without realizing that a dialectic that does not also effectively incorporate the moment which is opposed to cognitive *ratio* essentially forfeits its own character and reverts precisely to the kind of mechanistic thought which the great pioneers of dialectical philosophy had so emphatically repudiated in the first place.

With reference to one particular passage from Hegel, I would now like to show you how inappropriate the usual charge of intellectualism raised against dialectical thought actually is. But before I do so, I should also warn you once more against one

misunderstanding which is so widespread that I cannot avoid
drawing your attention to it, in spite of its primitive character. This
is the misunderstanding which complains that philosophy intellectu-
alizes the entire world when it employs the means of reason, as if for
God's sake it could appeal to any other means. For naturally thought
in general, once it begins, must indeed be thought, cannot consist in
mere protestations, in mere enthusiastic effusions, about that which
is not itself thought; on the other hand, however, thought possesses
the remarkable and deeply rooted capacity within itself to call this
too by its real name – that is, to articulate that which is not itself
thought. And here is the relevant passage, drawn once again from
the Preface to the *Phenomenology of Spirit*: 'Thus the life of God
and divine cognition may well be spoken of as a disporting of Love
with itself [as theologians have indeed done]; but this idea sinks into
mere edification, and even insipidity, if it lacks the seriousness, the
suffering, the patience, and the labour of the negative.'[13] Once again,
in these remarks you can feel the distinctive atmosphere, the very
savour of dialectic, in a very striking way. For in a formulation such
as this you see how the standard separation between the sphere of
logic, which is marked by the concept of 'negation' or 'negativity',
and the sphere of real human experience, which is expressed by
words such as 'seriousness', 'suffering', 'patience', 'labour', has been
revoked. These categories are not strictly held apart from one
another in Hegel, as they are in classificatory thought, and, whenever Hegel comes to speak of contradiction, there too we encounter
that 'human' moment of experience, of suffering, of negativity, in
the sense in which we can suffer from a 'negative' condition or situation. This is because, in Hegel, that 'labour of the concept' in
which we are said to suffer is also always a labour of the subject – in
other words, is an activity and achievement of human beings engaged
in knowing. And this human activity and achievement involves not
only the intellectual sphere which has been divorced from the concrete content, but also the whole of experience, one could almost
say, the whole history of humanity. So that every process of thought
is also always a question of suffering or of happiness, and this whole
separation of thought from happiness, or of thought from suffering
– for the dimension of happiness and of suffering is indeed a single
dimension – must be revoked by a thinking which is fully aware of
its own historical conditions, conditions which are comprised in the
totality. In my little book on Hegel I once declared that Hegelian
philosophy is indeed life repeated, as it were, that in this philosophy
we actually do have our life again in the many-coloured show of
things.[14] What I wanted to say was that the thought process

presented in Hegel's philosophy as a whole is indeed an entirely
logical process, but at the same time a process which, by virtue of its
own logical character, also points beyond abstract thought and is
nourished on forms of experience with which we are all familiar.
And thus, if one could say that Kant's philosophy represents an
impressive attempt to salvage ontology precisely on the basis of
nominalism, we should have to recognize that all of the distress and
dissatisfaction occasioned by the loss of metaphysical meaning also
found its way into the logical exertions which Kant was obliged to
undertake, that this distress and dissatisfaction would indeed be a
condition of those logical exertions. And perhaps I can clarify my
own attempts at dialectical thinking in the following way. For the
essential task here, as I see it, is not to logicize language, as the positivists want to do, but rather to bring logic to speak – and this precisely captures Hegel's intention, namely that happiness and suffering
may be revealed as an immanent condition, as an immanent content
of thought itself, that thought and life alike may be redefined and
reinterpreted, that this task be undertaken with all possible rigour
and seriousness. And it is of course precisely this aspect which is
completely misunderstood as mere intellectualism in the standard
hostility to dialectical thought. But, in terms of traditional, and now
exhausted, thought, the dialectic naturally finds itself caught between
Scylla and Charybdis. Thus, on the one hand, it is reproached for
being unduly intellectualist, for logicizing the supposedly irrational
aspects of experience; on the other hand, every common or garden
logician will naturally respond to remarks like Hegel's by saying,
'Well, this is just emotional talk. What has thought got to do with
all this seriousness, pain, labour, or suffering in general? These are
completely different categories.' But the essence of dialectic lies precisely in this: that it tries by means of thought itself to undo that
separation of spheres which is pre-eminently reflected in the common
or garden cliché of the three faculties of thinking, feeling and willing.
And the celebrated notion of the unity of theory and praxis itself is
only the highest expression of this attempted revocation, if you like,
which cannot of course imply a mere restitution or restoration of
what was once single and undivided. It points, rather, to an immanent process of reunification, in and through separation, of what has
been divided.

But I shall continue with the rest of the passage we have been
discussing: 'In itself, that life [the life of God] is indeed one of
untroubled equality and unity with itself, for which otherness and
alienation, and the overcoming of alienation, are not serious matters.
But this in-itself is abstract universality, in which the nature of the

divine life *to be for itself*, and so too the self-movement of the form, are altogether left out of account.'[15] I should like to take this opportunity to clarify one or two particular expressions which are indispensable to an understanding of Hegel, and I cannot avoid pointing out here that these concepts, which are by no means easy to grasp in their precise logical meaning in Hegel, have nonetheless found their way into everyday language, although the actual influence or authority exerted by a philosophy and the general intelligibility or accessibility of that philosophy obviously have no direct relationship with one another. I am talking about the concepts of 'being in itself', 'being for itself', and 'being in and for itself'. Even if we have never heard of Hegel or the dialectic, we often say things like, 'in itself that's true', or 'that's true in and for itself', without expressly reflecting that in using such an expression we are already involved in a process. And while we may know how this process begins, it is hard to see exactly where it will take us. To talk about something 'in itself' is to talk about something insofar as it 'is' such and such, is not yet 'reflected within itself'. The concept of 'being for itself' is also relatively easy to understand if you take it quite literally: thus something 'for itself' here not only means something separated or split off from the whole – although this aspect of separation plays a very important part here – but also suggests what it does when we say, for example, that in himself this person is a scoundrel, but for himself, in his own eyes, is a decent and upstanding human being; that is, he doesn't reflect on what he is, he may not even realize his own untrustworthiness, but regards himself – through narcissism as the psychologists would say[16] – as a wonderful human being. Thus, for himself, he is a wonderful person, but in himself he is still a scoundrel – i.e., in terms of his objective behaviour, as this is actually revealed in his social role or conduct. The Hegelian philosophy – which indeed essentially addresses, like all dialectic, the way in which subject and object, the subjective and the objective, are also separated from one another – undertakes specifically to expose and explore this difference between being in itself and being for itself, although there are two paths it can take in this regard. Thus in the *Logic* the path leads from being in itself through being for itself and ultimately to being in and for itself, whereas in the *Phenomenology* one might say that the opposite path is pursued, as we begin from subjectivity, which then arrives at consciousness of itself, or being for itself, and solely through this consciousness and all of the reflection involved in it finally arrives at being in itself and being in and for itself. This contrast between being in itself and being for itself is intended with such seriousness that we can already recognize the really decisive objective motif, the objective dimension, at work here, the thought that human beings – and Hegelian philosophy is in its origins a humanistic philosophy – are not identical with themselves in the function which they objectively fulfil in society, and that their social role, to use a modern expression, or their being in itself diverges from the consciousness which they have of themselves, or their being for itself. And this disparity, this non-identity between human beings and their own world, which is indeed by no means yet their own, is itself the ground of that diremption, that suffering, that negativity which, as I have already suggested to you, can only be overcome through the labour, the patience, the seriousness, the exertion of the concept.

Thus you can see how the logical-metaphysical conception of Hegel is indeed directly associated with such emotionally charged expressions as 'seriousness', and so on, expressions which at least are saturated in actual human experience. Thus I doubt if you will now be that surprised if I challenge so much of your preconceived image of Hegel, and perhaps even shock some of you, when I say that the celebrated triadic schema of thesis, antithesis, and synthesis actually plays nothing like the role in Hegel's philosophy which it is commonly believed to do. And I would be more than happy if I could succeed here, from a whole variety of angles, in awakening a concept of dialectic which is liberated from the automatic responses typically encouraged in the context of examination questions. Of course, there is also something in all that, but as long as you imagine that we must have a thesis, a claim, a proposition, which we then externally confront with the opposite, before finally combining them both in a similar more or less external fashion, as long as you think in this way, then you will actually entertain nothing but the most external conception of dialectic. The seriousness of the dialectic springs precisely from the fact that it is not some such external intellectual game of juggling contradictions. For the contradiction itself springs from the thesis itself, and shows itself as such only because the speculative proposition itself is always at once true and false. And indeed Hegel himself mounted the most vigorous criticism of this standard manipulation of the concept of dialectic in terms of this triadic schema. The most important thing for you here is to learn what it really means to confront reality in a dialectical spirit, rather than in asking mechanically after the relevant thesis, antithesis, and synthesis in every possible context. And I should also confess right now that I always find the word 'synthesis' profoundly suspect, and, if I understand you rightly, I feel that most of you will also experience a certain sense of horror at the concept of synthesis.

The passage in Hegel which relates specifically to this issue, and which I would like to read to you now, runs as follows:

> Of course, the *triadic form* must not be regarded as scientific when it is reduced to a lifeless schema, a mere shadow, and when scientific organization is degraded into a table of terms. Kant rediscovered this triadic form by instinct, but in his work it was still lifeless and uncomprehended; since then it has, however, been raised to its absolute significance, and with it the true form in its true content has been presented, so that the concept of Science has emerged.[17]

You can see how this already suggests a critique of the kind of tabulating thought which in the era of the administered world today has indeed almost become the universal form of science in general, a form of thought against which language itself now obviously occupies a hopelessly defensive position. Under no circumstances, therefore, must dialectical thought even tempt us into forcing the objects of experience into such a schema. For to think dialectically is precisely to take individual objects as they are, to do so genuinely rather than in some limiting way; not to limit them or subsume them under their next highest concept, but to try and do justice to the life that prevails in the individual thing itself, that prevails in the individual concept itself, the life that was indeed regarded by Hegel as something contradictory, as something antagonistic in character. Hegel had already clearly recognized the danger that dialectic can degenerate into a mechanical device, although this is often what he has himself been accused of encouraging, and anyone who takes the actual trouble to study Hegel's major works, and especially the *Phenomenology of Spirit*, will find how little of this mechanical aspect is to be found there.

I should like to conclude for today with the following excellent formulation from Hegel: 'The knack of this kind of wisdom [the dialectic as an external method] is as quickly learned as it is easy to practise; once familiar, the repetition of it becomes as insufferable as the repletion of a conjuring trick already seen through.'[18] If I may give this thought a somewhat broader twist, it is this: where philosophy itself is concerned, all those claims to knowledge which can be foreseen from the moment that thought begins and thus inspire the reaction 'we know that already', which are fundamentally contained in advance within the generic concept that lies above them, are essentially worthless. And it may be regarded as an index of the truth, or an *index veri et falsi*, whether thought is capable of encountering something which is not self-evidently contained in the thought at the moment when it arises, which does not simply emerge from it all at once. There is no truth, one might almost say, which in this sense could be foreseen on the basis of the formulated thought, and it is probably the surest symptom of the appalling degeneration to which dialectic is exposed today, under the name of 'diamat', of the way it has now reverted to pure untruth, that ready-made phrases and slogans do spring forth as if in a conjuring trick and enable us to judge and subsume everything without undertaking the labour and exertion of the concept which is demanded by the dialectic. We could also express this by saying that dialectic has here forgotten what it intrinsically and essentially is. In other words, it has ceased here to be a critical theory and has turned into a merely mechanical process of subsumption. No form of thinking is immune to this. Even the principle of dialectic, opposed as it is to mechanical thinking, can revert to a conceptual mechanism once it is no longer genuinely dia-lectical – that is, once it forfeits intimate contact with its object and ceases to respond carefully and closely to that object. In short, nothing guarantees that dialectic itself cannot in turn become ideology.

LECTURE 6

10 June 1958

Ladies and gentlemen,

In our last session we discussed the problem of the supposed intellectualism of the dialectic, or what was once described as 'panlogism'.[1] And today I think I can draw out some further implications of that discussion which may help you to form a more definite conception of dialectic, and indeed to correct the idea of dialectic with which most of you will probably approach dialectical philosophy from the start. I would not wish to seem presumptuous here, but I imagine that most of you, insofar as you are not already 'professional philosophers', as people love to put it, will have this initial rather automatic reaction to the dialectic: 'Well, dialectic is surely a matter of thesis, antithesis, and synthesis.' Now I will not say that these concepts are completely irrelevant here, or that they have absolutely nothing to do with the dialectic. But, as far as these concepts are concerned, we must remember what dialectical theory itself has already insisted upon, namely that all propositions *in abstracto*, such as 'the truth consists in thesis, antithesis, and synthesis', possess no truth unless and until they are unfolded and developed. I would go further and claim we commit no great sin against the spirit of dialectic if we say that, as soon as such concepts are rigidly fixed, as soon as they are turned into a sort of manual for thinking dialectically, they become the opposite of what Hegel intended them to be. And indeed I can appeal directly to Hegel himself here. For this qualification regarding the significance of what is often called the 'triadic schema' – namely the three-step movement of thesis, antithesis and synthesis – is already expressed in the *Phenomenology of Spirit* itself, and indeed in words which will be able to take us much further. Hegel writes:

> Of course, the *triadic form* must not be regarded as scientific when it is reduced to a lifeless schema, a mere shadow, and when scientific organization is degraded into a table of terms. Kant rediscovered this triadic form by instinct, but in his work it was still lifeless and uncomprehended; since then it has, however, been raised to its absolute significance, and with it the true form in its true content has been presented, so that the concept of Science has emerged.[2]

I had already drawn your attention to this passage last time. And I would like to add a second formulation which may serve as a warning light against a particularly dubious use of dialectic: when this triadic schema is manipulated to produce the opposite of truth. Thus Hegel continues: 'The knack of this kind of wisdom is as quickly learned as it is easy to practise; once familiar, the repetition of it becomes as insufferable as the repletion of a conjuring trick already seen through.'[3] The thought here, therefore, is that even a method which is recognized *in abstracto* as the most advanced method of thought only produces falsehood when it is mechanically applied, that is, if the facts are simply subsumed under the method, if our experience or insight into the facts themselves fails to interrupt this subsumptive procedure. Paradoxically, we could say that the moment that dialectic becomes a kind of device, or a recipe, when it is manipulated as a method, then it is inevitably converted into untruth, and indeed in the strictly dialectical sense that it thereby comes into contradiction with its own concept. For to think dialectically is precisely to think through rupture, to think in such a way that the concept is emphatically brought to criticize itself in terms of what it attempts to cover, while the merely factical is measured in turn against its own concept. And the moment we retreat from this approach, when we no longer undertake what is described in another passage as 'the labour and the exertion of the concept',[4] the moment we believe we have the method securely at our disposal, then the method has already been falsified and distorted. And actually this is also a much more general experience, as we can discover again and again in the context of art. Kandinsky once formulated the same insight beautifully in his book *On the Spiritual in Art*, when he said that the moment an artist believes he has found himself, has finally discovered his style, then he has generally already lost it.[5] Here again you have a sense of the atmosphere of dialectical thought, something which is very important, for it involves a concrete sense of its opposition to the need for security about which I have already spoken to you.[6] It is one of the challenges of dialectical thought, and not perhaps the least, that in thinking dialectically we must avoid thinking like a certain kind of Kantian schoolmaster: 'Now I have the method, and once I have this, then nothing can surprise me any more.' Hegel vigorously rejected precisely this idea of method, where we can just carry on blindly and automatically, as it were, instead of undertaking the labour of thought itself at each and every moment. But these are actually relatively modest and straightforward insights, although it is really far more difficult to observe these insights in one's actual concrete thought than it is to entertain them in general terms. There is no guarantee, even when we try and think dialectically, that dialectical thought cannot fall into the embarrassing repetition of the conjuring trick which Hegel so vividly warns us against. And it is certainly most important, as a thinking individual, resolutely to resist any mechanical application of one's own categories – in other words, to reflect constantly upon these categories, to examine whether they are still indeed appropriate to the things which are being thought under them.

What is so impressive about Hegel in this connection, and what I particularly wish to bring home to you here, is that he does not merely content himself with identifying and polemically repudiating this mechanical application and ossification of dialectical thought. But, rather, as he invariably does with all other negative elements, Hegel also strives to grasp this specific phenomenon itself, attempts to derive even this aberration of thought, this reification and rigidification of thought, from out of the living process of thought itself. And this is entirely characteristic of dialectical thought generally, for the vital nerve of the dialectic is precisely to resolve all that is rigid, reified, ossified. But it does so not by simply confronting all that with what is allegedly vital and immediate but, rather, by making use of what has become hardened, recognizing what is sedimented here, the congealed life and labour as it were. Thus it only overcomes what has become rigid and ossified by allowing it to move by virtue of its own power, of the life that has been precipitated in the things and concepts which confront us in an alienated form. 'What is excellent, however, not only cannot escape the fate of being deprived of life and spirit in this way, of being flayed and then seeing its skin wrapped around a lifeless knowledge and its conceit.'[7] Here you can also feel something of the power of Hegel's language, although he has generally been deemed a poor stylist, as they say, in comparison with the allegedly excellent stylist Schopenhauer. And this is obviously because those who have more or less unjustly assumed the role of judges where linguistic ability is concerned imagine they can assess the language of philosophers by how far it directly accords with healthy common sense and ordinary spoken language, which is certainly not the case in Hegel. The power of his language lies rather in a remarkable kind of 'second' immediacy or sensuous vividness, for in the impressive conceptual architecture of Hegel's thought the concepts themselves are filled with such inner life, unfold so intensively and dynamically, that although they seem entirely abstract they nonetheless reassume all the colour and fullness of life within themselves and thus in this remarkable way also begin in sparkle. I do not think a genuine analysis of Hegel's language has ever really been undertaken. Such an examination of his philosophical language would not only be welcome in itself but could also illuminate the very deepest recesses of the philosophical content in Hegel. In a sentence like the one just quoted you actually find the essence of Hegel, where the idea of the bare skin from which the life has fled is directly applied to something as seemingly abstract as knowledge and consciousness. I have already spoken in our last session about Hegel's philosophy as a rather remarkable field of tensions, where the movement lies not in continuous transitions but in a tremendous exchange of energy, where thought leaps over from the pole of concretion to the pole of abstraction. In this way we pass from what is closest to us, what is most sensuous, to precisely what is most remote: instead of producing some middle term or connection between both, we see how the universal and the particular, the two extremes, touch. And again this is profoundly bound up with the very content of Hegel's philosophy, for it is indeed the essence of dialectical teaching that the universal is also always the particular and the particular the universal. Thus you can see how much the content of this philosophy has entered here into the boldness of such language. And in this context I might point out, for those of you who have studied German poetry in particular, that this approach to language may also help to shed entirely new light on the poetry of Hölderlin, in a way that has perhaps never seriously been considered before. Hegel continues:

> Rather we recognize even in this fate [that people believe they already possess the matter itself in the dead skin] the power that the excellent exercises over the hearts, if not over the minds, of individuals, as well as the constructive unfolding into universality and determinateness of form in which its perfection consists, and which alone makes it possible for this universality to be used in a superficial way.[8]

Hegel is saying something extremely profound here, namely that thought itself must assume such a specific objective form of presentation if it is to relinquish all merely arbitrary claims and contingent expressions of subjectivity, but precisely in assuming this kind of universality, this determinate conceptual form, it also inevitably courts the danger of becoming a recipe, of being reified and misused. In other words, the misuse which Hegel warns us about – the superficial application of the triadic schema – is by no means external to thought, for it is produced precisely when thought itself does what it must if it is to rise above the merely arbitrary *hic et nunc*, if it is to become an objective truth. In other words, the untruth that arises from such rigidification is inseparable from the objectivation which belongs to truth itself. We cannot have one without having the other – this is one of the most important dialectical principles there is. Thus one cannot acknowledge the power, the objectivity, the binding character of truth, without thereby constantly exposing thought to the danger of simply becoming independent as such, of forcing itself externally upon the matter itself, of being utilized in a blunt and mechanical fashion. In this warning against the mechanical use of dialectic you have an exemplary case of dialectical thinking itself, for the vital nerve of dialectic can be recognized right here: truth and untruth are not external to one another, are not simply opposed to one another as an abstract antithesis; rather, the passage into untruth inhabits truth itself, as its fate, as its curse, as the mark of the context of guilt in which it stands; and likewise the path which truth itself traverses – and truth is indeed a process – is solely a path through untruth. You can see, therefore, how dialectical thought responds even to such a warning against its own misuse.

This warning against the misuse of the triadic schema involves an insight which perhaps should not be forgotten as another fundamental insight of dialectical thought. This is the idea – which just gives a slightly different twist to what we have been saying – that there is no thought which cannot also become false as soon as we isolate it, and abstractness for Hegel is always a matter of isolating something and detaching it from the context of the whole. Hegel showed as much in the passage which I have tried to interpret for you, where he alludes to the idea of the world process as a kind of divine play. He says that, while this may be true in itself, it sinks into untruth, that is, into insipidity and indifference, if we fail to pursue this process itself in detail.[9] I think we can go much further here and say there is no truth whatsoever, not even the truest theory or even the theory of dialectic itself, which cannot also immediately become untrue if it is torn from its context, and especially if it is made to serve particular interests. There is nothing in the world, not the highest creations of philosophy or even the highest creations of art, which cannot be misused by clinging to them in isolation, and thereby holding people back from other things, deceiving people about other possibilities, generating false and untrue satisfactions, or creating spurious satisfactions. And if you expect me to suggest a practical application of dialectic here it would be precisely this: dialectical thought is extraordinarily mistrustful of any attempt to isolate and thus misuse thought. If any particular aspect of knowledge, any finite instance of knowledge – and any specific knowledge regarding the whole is always a particular instance of knowledge – acts as if it were the whole, is posited as absolute, it can readily enter the service of untruth and become an ideology. You can observe this most strikingly, of course, throughout the Eastern bloc, where the dialectic has been elevated to a kind of state religion. Although an honest and genuine attempt has perhaps occasionally been made there to render certain aspects of dialectical theory intelligible to people, the dialectic has long since functioned, as a religion of the state, to justify a praxis which only perpetuates the repression which the impulse of dialectic inspires us to challenge. But I would merely say that we should not draw the opposite conclusion that dialectic is untrue simply because such nonsense has been produced in the name of dialectic. For the dialectic shares with everything which has appeared as truth in history, and certainly with the truth which is embodied in Christianity, that it has been misused for every violent or shameful deed and for every kind of torture. I think it is a dangerous delusion to imagine that the galimatias commonly known as 'diamat' could actually tell us anything valuable about dialectical theory itself.

But here I should like to return to the question of the relative irrelevance of the triadic schema. You will easily be able to grasp this relative irrelevance after what I have said so far if you remember that the dialectic is not actually method in the traditional sense. Although I realize that this is not what Hegel himself literally says at this point, I believe this claim can indeed be defended in the spirit of Hegelian philosophy. What I mean is that the dialectic is not a mere procedure through which mind firmly secures its objective character. For the movement of dialectic is always also supposed to be at once a movement of the matter itself and a movement of thought. But if that is so, if the dialectical movement is a movement of the matter itself and can be accomplished by reference to the matter itself, then it springs from this that any form of dialectical reflection which is purely methodological – i.e., is externally foisted upon things – already violates the character of dialectic. This will perhaps become clearer to you if you grasp precisely why the usual conception of the dialectic as a game of thesis, antithesis and synthesis is so absurd and superficial. When the pre-philosophical consciousness hears of dialectic and of thesis, antithesis and synthesis, it thinks something like this: 'Well, you start by setting up some proposition or other, then you introduce another proposition which is the opposite of the first, but there is some truth to both of them, so then you have the synthesis. The so-called synthesis emerges once you have exhausted the framework of the two mutually opposed propositions with which you began.' I will not simply assume that you feel quite the same aversion towards the concept of synthesis that I have strongly experienced since my early youth. But the way all this is presented here is certainly entirely misleading. For the dialectical movement does not arise by taking an initial proposition and externally supplementing it with the opposed proposition. It arises when the contradictory moment is discovered in the proposition originally expressed, when it is shown that the proposition which initially presents itself to you in a fixed and con-gealed form is a field of internal tension, exhibits a particular kind of life within itself, so that the task of philosophy is in a sense to reconstruct this life within the original proposition. The synthesis cannot therefore be understood as the extraction of the common element in the two earlier propositions. Indeed, Hegel specifically describes the synthesis as the opposite of this, namely as a further negation, as the negation of the negation. Thus the antithesis, the opposite of the original proposition, which is spun from this latter, is qualified in itself, as a finite proposition, as untrue in turn. And, insofar as its untruth is further determined, the truth moment in the proposition which was originally negated thus reasserts itself. And the very essence of dialectical thought lies in the contrast between this kind of thinking, as I have here been describing it to you, and the purely abstractive kind of thinking preoccupied with logical extension of its concepts, which posits oppositions externally and then regards the common feature abstracted from both terms of the opposition as the result. That the triadic schema is not terribly impor-tant after all springs precisely from the fact that this schema is merely the subjectively abstracted process, a description of the subjective comportment with which we approach the matter itself, while this subjective comportment for its part is only one moment which Hegel then corrects through another which is described as a process of 'simply looking on'.[10] And this is the process of abandoning oneself entirely and unreservedly to the matter itself.

I am well aware that these rather formal considerations which we have just been talking about will hardly be able to satisfy you in this form, and I expect that you will naturally raise an objection which, as I can vividly recall, occurred to me too on my first encounter with dialectical philosophy. Why must everything really be a matter of contradictions? Are there really only contradictions everywhere? Aren't there also just simple differences? Is it not simply an arbitrary decision – and here we face the serious suspicion that concepts can easily become a straightjacket – is it not simply a violent attempt to contain or restrict reality by means of method, if we try and interpret everything that exists in terms of contradiction? In terms of internal contradiction, admittedly, but still a form of contradiction, whereas there is just an abundance of disparate qualities, as different from another as green and red and blue. And if we consider the beauty of the full range of colours, for example, would the attempt to read everything *partout* as a form of contradiction not basically involve a process of levelling, specifically of abstraction and homogenization?[11] This objection has often been raised in the history of philosophy, of course, and I think it would be a very bad idea if we simply tried to settle it with an elegant gesture rather than confronting it. The objection was first specifically formulated, and in a very acute manner, from the perspective of traditional Aristotelian logic, namely by the Aristotelian philosopher Trendelenburg,[12] who made this the basis of his general critique of Hegel in the first half of the nineteenth century.[13] And the objection was taken up again, in a quite different form, at the beginning of the so-called Hegel Renaissance in Benedetto Croce's book on Hegel.[14] This book can be said to have initiated the said renaissance, although in fact Croce approached Hegel with a slightly bad conscience, for rather like Trendelenburg he actually wanted to bring Hegel closer in a certain way to positivistic strands of thought, to what had formerly been described as the 'philosophy of reflection'. Thus the rebirth of interest in Hegelian philosophy which was begun by Croce remained somewhat problematic from the start.

Now, in order to put all of this into its proper context and perspective, I should probably also say something about what seems to me the most appropriate way for thought to proceed in general. For I would argue that it is certainly not the task of thought to try and bring everything that exists under one common denominator. Indeed, the need to do so has itself been challenged by the dialectic, and since in this regard – we might almost say – the dialectic has recognized the naivety of a philosophy which imagines it could possibly capture the full riches of experience in some sort of butterfly net, it might be said that dialectic has in a sense already reached the point where we can also raise very significant objections to dialectic itself. If the dialectic were in fact merely the kind of reductive thinking which tried to bring all actual differences under the formula of contradiction, then it would actually be equivalent to the attempt to explain everything by appeal to a single fundamental principle, the very thing which the dialectic repudiated in the first place. I believe that the role which dialectical thinking has to play, the significance which attaches to dialectical thought or philosophical thought in general, is to act as a kind of discipline or counter-force in relation to living experience. In a sense, therefore, we really think dialectically when we also specifically limit ourselves, for, if we perceive only differences, if we are aware only of variety, without discovering any unity in this difference and variety, we cannot perceive the contradictory character which is concealed in all this variety. For then thinking threatens in a sense to dissolve, to forfeit its own theoretical form, and, while we cannot turn theory itself into an absolute, we cannot have anything resembling knowledge without theory either. There is a paradoxical relationship there. If theory imagines that it has the whole within its grasp, that it is itself the key by which to explain everything, it has already fallen victim to the worst kind of hubris. Yet if thought entirely lacks this theoretical moment, this aspect of unification and objectivation, then we are basically no longer talking about knowledge at all, and we have effectively resigned ourselves simply to registering a more or less external, disparate and disorganized multiplicity of data. And it is precisely the need to work against this, without doing too much violence to the things themselves, which underlies the specifically dialectical approach. But this way of putting it is still rather unsatisfactory, for now you may say, 'Well, you are introducing the dialectic simply as a sort of cure for the soul, or for the concept, because it is healthy and advantageous for thought to have a method like this, something reliable to hold onto, although you do not really believe in it yourself and actually maintain there is no such thing as the Absolute.' And in fact I feel at this point that I am obliged to say something decisive about dialectical method and the concept of contradiction. The concept of contradiction is no more to be hypostasized than any other concept – that is to say, it is no more the key to the dialectic than any other particular concept – and that is because the dialectic actually consists solely in the relation of concepts to one another rather than in some absolute dignity bestowed upon any single concept.

But you still have a right to know why the concept of contradiction does indeed play a central role in the dialectic, and for what substantive rather than merely ancillary reasons this is the case. Thus I would begin by pointing out that, insofar as every finite judgement, by virtue of its form as a judgement, by virtue of affirming A is B, already claims to be an absolute truth, to be the truth itself, it comes into conflict with its own finite character, with the fact that no finite judgement, precisely as finite, can be the whole truth as such.[15] And if the concept of contradiction plays such a conspicuous role in the dialectic, if it is the concept which expects so much from the process of 'simply looking on', of giving ourselves over to the things themselves, if it is specifically described in the context of dialectic as the moving principle, then the reasons for this are to be found precisely here. The category of contradiction, or the origin of the modern doctrine of dialectic, derives in fact from the *Critique of Pure Reason*, and, if you wish to understand more fully the theme of these lectures which we have broached but not completely developed today, you would do well to take a closer look at what Kant calls 'the transcendental dialectic', either in the original itself or by means of one of the reliable secondary discussions of this text. The basic thought here is that, as soon as we try and extend the fundamental concepts of our reason, what are called our categories, beyond the possibilities of our experience, beyond the possibilities of sensible intuition, or in other words when we try and formulate infinite judgements, then we inevitably run the danger of positing mutually contradictory judgements each of which seems to be equally convincing. Such as the claim 'Everything that happens has a first beginning in time', or the claim 'Everything that happens in time involves an infinite series.'[16] And we can make analogous claims with regard to space. Or again: 'Everything that exists is subject to the law of causality', or again: 'There is also a causality of freedom – i.e., there is a point where the causal series is suspended.'[17] All of these mutually contradictory propositions arise when our categories, which in Kant's view function solely to organize our experience, begin to run riot as it were, to operate simply in a void, thereby claiming to possess an absolute truth through their own resources while they are actually valid only in relation to the phenomena with which they are confronted. Kant thus introduced the idea of contradictoriness into the context of knowledge in a new and indeed particularly emphatic way, for he argued that human reason inevitably becomes entangled in such contradictions. Since we cannot help but pursue our thought to the utmost, since the tendency to transcend the limits of finitude is also inscribed in the structure of our thought, we are constantly tempted to formulate such problematic propositions. And the fact that we can come to understand why these contradictions arise, and thus in a sense resolve them, does not really help us that much, as Kant himself points out in the *Critique of Pure Reason*.[18] And then, with Hegel, you may introduce a simple operation and argue as follows: 'If you tell us these contradictions are necessary contradictions which our faculty of knowledge is quite unable to avoid, contradictions therefore in which we constantly find ourselves entangled, and if your own supposed resolution of these contradictions does not ultimately help us, why not actually follow this path to the end, why not explore these unavoidable contradictions more closely, why not expose yourself to these contradictions which you claim are unavoidable? In short, why not try and reach the truth precisely through the movement of these contradictions?' And this challenge which Hegel raises is indeed based upon an essential epistemological modification of Kant's philosophical position, namely upon the fact that Hegel no longer accepts the tried Kantian opposition between sensibility and the understanding, between thought and experience, in the way this is somewhat naively and drastically insisted upon by Kant, for Hegel says that I basically cannot know how I can then arrive at something like sensibility at all, that there is nothing sensuous which is not itself mediated by the understanding, and vice versa, and therefore that this whole rigid separation between sensibility and the understanding – upon which the Kantian doctrine of the antinomies is based and which can in a sense protect me from becoming entangled in contradictions – cannot ultimately be sustained at all. And that is precisely because there simply is no sensibility without the understanding and no understanding without sensibility, and thus this movement of contradiction which Kant regards merely as a malfunctioning on the part of consciousness is actually one of the accomplishments necessarily prompted by the essence of spirit, and that is precisely why thought essentially moves and develops in and through contradictions.

LECTURE 7

12 June 1958

Ladies and gentlemen,

In the last session we began to address the objection which has been raised against Hegelian philosophy from fairly early on, and which is indeed a radical one. It is this: Why does this philosophy merely seem to acknowledge contradiction rather than simple difference? In this objection it is not difficult to recognize a rather more precise formulation of the problem which I have already mentioned in more general terms, namely the problem of whether Hegelian philosophy ultimately forces everything that exists into a conceptual straightjacket. Now you might say – and it would not be the first time it has been said – that this is a bit like the case of the emperor's beard, as we say – that is, making a big issue out of nothing. Perhaps the dialectic, in the strict form it assumed in Hegel, was just a kind of device which helped this philosophy to engage with history, but one which we could now relinquish without losing very much in the process. And under the influence of positivism in particular, there are innumerable cases where this has actually been undertaken by those who imagine that they can salvage or preserve something from Hegel in this way. Thus, according to one well-known formulation, we might say that Hegel the absolute idealist is also an equally great realist, that in reality all of the knowledge he has to offer, as Nicolai Hartmann puts it, comes from experience, a concept which is indeed particularly important in Hegel, and that what we find here is not so much a speculative or constructive dialectic as – to use a rather suspect expression – a 'real dialectic'.[1] If that were the case, we could simply spare ourselves the effort we are making here, and certainly spare ourselves the effort of engaging more closely with the two great systematic works of Hegelian philosophy, the *Phenomenology of Spirit* and the *Science of Logic*. We could then concentrate simply upon the so-called applied or material dimension of the Hegelian system, the most well-known and probably the most influential parts of which are the *Philosophy of History*[2] and the *Philosophy of Right*[3] and the most fruitful part of which is perhaps the *Aesthetics*.[4] But this approach cannot work for the simple reason that, if we actually ignore the strictly constructive form of Hegelian philosophy, it ceases to be philosophy at all, and in fact becomes nothing but a rhapsodic collection of various more or less significant material insights. But the celebrated 'spiritual bond' would then be just as missing here as in the standard practice of the positive sciences which this philosophy specifically undertook to challenge. In other words, without the rigorous and fully elaborated dialectic, we would simply turn Hegel into a learned and many-sided historian of thought in the style of Wundt[5] or, in the best case, Dilthey.[6] At the same time, perhaps even more importantly, we should thereby forfeit the very power which vouchsafed Hegel his insights in the first place. For with regard to Hegelian philosophy we may safely say – for all that it is a science of the experience of consciousness – that this philosophy owes its capacity to grasp reality as it did, namely as something essentially developmental in character, solely to the dialectical principle, and that without this dialectical principle in its pointed form everything that has remained of Hegel in the public consciousness – the idea of development, of dynamic process as the pre-eminent category in relation to all other concepts – would also inevitably be lost or become a matter of merely contingent observation. Of course, the fact that this philosophy necessarily postulates some 'spiritual bond' of this kind if it is to be binding is not sufficient to establish that the construction in question can actually be dignified as truly compelling. And, indeed, much of the critical discussion of the nineteenth century focused on this very aspect of Hegelian philosophy. Our task is to grasp this particular problematic very clearly, given that it concerns the core of the structure of this philosophy, rather than leaving the dimension of God or contradiction to itself and turning instead to the wealth of concrete insights it contains, insights which actually derive from that dimension anyway. For this core of the Hegelian philosophy – and this is the reason why I must encourage you to think through a whole series of far from simple reflections with me here – is indeed the principle of negation, or the principle of contradiction. The attempt has been made to interpret the Hegelian philosophy, above all and with particular emphasis by Kroner,[7] in his book *From Kant to Hegel*[8] [...][9]

In the last session we tried to take the bull by the horns and derive the Hegelian concept of contradiction or – to put it directly – the Hegelian concept of dialectic from the Kantian dialectic. Thus I would remind you that Kant's 'Transcendental Logic' falls into two parts, namely 'The Transcendental Analytic' and 'The Transcendental Dialectic', and that, for Kant, 'the dialectic' represents what would be called the 'negative' side of transcendental logic. In straightforward terms we can present the argument as follows: the *Critique of Pure Reason* attempts to show the possibility of universally valid and necessary knowledge, or, as Kant puts it, of 'synthetic a priori judgements', by analysing consciousness and demonstrating that such universally valid and necessary knowledge is made possible only by virtue of the constitutive forms of our consciousness itself. But the *Critique of Pure Reason*, precisely by being a 'critique', already reveals two things: on the one hand it wishes to exhibit the domain within which we are capable of such knowledge, while on the other hand it wishes to show where we are no longer capable of such valid and binding knowledge. Thus reason wishes to exercise a critique of reason itself precisely in order to prevent the latter from running riot, turning wild as it were, and presenting propositions as absolute, necessary and universal when in reality they are mere fabrications of the human mind. In other words, such a critique would not only serve to exhibit the necessity of metaphysics, it would emphatically reject metaphysics as well.

If I present this basic systematic and methodological conception behind Kant's *Critique of Pure Reason* to you in its full gravity, as I have just done here, some of you may already feel compelled to raise a question which, as tends to be the case with reasonable questions, you might actually drop once you have much greater familiarity with the matter at issue and thus also much less distance towards it. This is something quite simple and is a reflection which may have occurred to you in connection with those which led Hegel to his conception of dialectic in the first place. Thus you might say to yourselves, 'This is surely quite remarkable – reason is supposed to criticize reason, reason is supposed to assign to reason the limits within which it may now safely and confidently pursue its claim to universally valid and binding knowledge, and is supposed at the same time to cry: Halt, if you venture beyond this point, you will be talking nonsense, you will be creating fabrications, or at best producing assertions which in reality cannot be presented as theoretical knowledge claims, but only as normative or regulative principles for human conduct.' And you might also go on to say, 'But if as a rational being you assign these limits to reason here, is there not a sense in which you already raise yourself beyond these limits? And if reason claims to tell how far you may go and how far you may not go, does not this already imply that reason somehow stands beyond the limits which are set by reason itself?' From where does reason derive the right, we might also ask – and this is precisely how Hegel formulated the question – to subject knowledge to this critique, since for its part such a critique – a critique of the faculty of knowledge on the part of reason – is not itself an example of substantive knowledge or of material insight into any specific matters which are presented to us. On the contrary, it is nothing but a transcendental insight, as Kant calls it – that is, an insight which relates to mere possibility – but one which, according to Kant, is nonetheless supposed to possess absolute validity for the constitution of our knowledge in general. But if that is the case, then our knowledge must have within itself some kind of power which allows it to reach beyond the so-called possibility of experience. That is to say, it must be able to provide a kind of knowledge which does not itself depend upon given sensuous or material content, which in other words does not depend in the last instance on mere sensation. If this really quite simple argument is correct – one which can be expressed by saying, as Georg Simmel formulated it,[10] that to set limits also always means to step beyond them – then the distinction affirmed by the *Critique of Pure Reason* between a positive part, namely 'The Transcendental Logic', which exhibits the fundamental concepts of our experience, and a negative part, namely 'The Transcendental Dialectic', where we find ourselves entangled in contradictions, then the separation in question is actually no longer legitimate. And then that second part, where we are necessarily entangled in contradictions, also belongs as a positive part as much to the domain of knowledge as the first part also does. For if our reason, in reflecting upon cognitive reason as such, did not possess within itself the power to judge with regard to the unconditional and with regard to what is absolutely binding upon us, then it could not possibly pass those negative judgements which are indeed presented in the transcendental dialectic. In other words, reason must accordingly strive to take up precisely those contradictions, those antinomies, which are treated in the transcendental dialectic and incorporate them within itself as a positive element, to take precisely those points where reason comes up against and advances beyond its own limits and transform into an organ of knowledge itself. In other words, the critical role of reason and the so-called positive role of reason must be fused with one another – that is, the positive knowledge of what is must take up that critical and negative moment within itself. And the merely negative in turn must not remain merely negative but, rather, be developed to the point where it becomes a positive moment within itself.

That is in fact one of the most important aspects of the basic considerations which led Hegel to his radical formulation of the dialectic. In this regard I could perhaps just read you a rather fine passage from Kroner, who sums up these thoughts as follows: 'in his critique of reason Kant discovers the interdependence of the abstract and the concrete, of the formal and the material, of the rational and the empirical, of a priori and a posteriori thought, inasmuch as the concrete, the material, the empirical, the a posteriori here effectively reflects upon itself, analyses itself, criticizes itself.'[11] I might add here that the decisive concept for Hegel's considerations which go beyond the Kantian position is the concept of 'reflection'. And I should also like to make a couple of remarks which may help to clarify the decisive difference between Hegel and his predecessors in this regard. We are talking here about the concept of reflection [*Reflexion*]. Now 'reflection', in the first instance, simply means a 'mirror image' [*Spiegelung*]. In other words, 'reflection' in Kant initially signifies the way that our reason contemplates reason itself, relates as critical reason to the reason which stands before it. Now what Hegel essentially does, along with the other post-Kantian idealists – and this is what decisively distinguishes them all from Kant – is this. Instead of performing this reflection in an unconscious manner, as the British empiricists did, instead of letting reason simply look at itself in the mirror, as it were, they made this act of reflection itself, this faculty of reflection, into the very theme of philosophy. And the general claim that now emerges here is that this power which enables reason to know itself is and must be at the same time the power through which reason moves beyond itself in its finitude, and through which reason as something infinite finally comes to self-awareness. We could say that what we are talking about here is the reflection of reflection, as Schlegel once put it,[12] about the consciousness which has become infinite within itself, or infinitely reflected within itself, and is the presupposition of this entire philosophy. If you would like a simple definition – if I may use this term here – or a simple explication of the central concept of Hegelian philosophy which distinguishes this philosophy from that of Kant, namely the concept of speculation, then we may say that speculative consciousness, in contrast to simple or simply reflective consciousness, is one where this moment of self-reflecting consciousness has become thematic, has come to self-consciousness. Thus here, in the attempted analysis of knowledge itself, we already come upon what is ultimately the principal object of this dialectic itself, namely the distinction of subject and object which is already implicit in the peculiar internal doubling of reflection. For on the one side here you have thought as object, that which is being analysed and examined, as Kant says, while on the other hand you have thought as subject, the thinking which examines itself – or, if you like, the transcendental principle itself, the principle of the synthesis of apperception, the synthetic principle itself. And these two sides are thus intrinsically bound up with one another.

It is the entirely new and central role accorded to the concept of reflection which constitutes the organ of truth in this philosophy, and we shall see that this moment of reflection – and this is the answer to the question we have asked ourselves here – that this principle of self-knowing reflection is actually one with the principle of negation. The thinking of thinking – and here as so often in Hegel we find a renewal of an ancient Aristotelian motif, the νόησις νοήσεως [*noēsis noēseōs*][13] – the thinking of thinking itself in Hegel is actually nothing other than the fully developed principle of negativity. But allow me here to read a little more of the same passage from Kroner. Kant's critique of reason, he says, 'grounds the validity of the empirical on the synthesis of both moments [i.e., of the a priori and the a posteriori, of the formal and the material] in cognitive thought, in the knowing subject, the *identity* of which accomplishes the reciprocal supplementation of these two moments and renders it intelligible.'[14] In other words, it is the unity of consciousness – and the facts of this consciousness are precisely those which are brought together through synthesis in consciousness – it is this identity of personal consciousness that allows something like the unity of the world, the unity of experience, that allows identity, and in the last analysis also logical identity, to emerge for Kant at all. And Kroner then furnishes a clear and striking indication of that difference in relation to Kant which we have been talking about. For the critique of reason itself, he writes,

proceeds in a 'naïve' way in this regard insofar as its reflection remains 'merely' critical in character (and consequently, according to which way we consider it, remains either 'merely' empirical or 'merely' logical or analytic); to that extent the togetherness of the moments, the synthesis, is merely deduced for *empirical* knowing, but its *own* knowing is contrasted with empirical knowing as 'mere' reflection, as 'merely' formal knowing, and thus not really as a knowing, but only as 'mere' thinking, as a non-cognitive logic – i.e., a non-metaphysical logic. That is why this critique relates to metaphysics in a 'merely' negative fashion,

can see in metaphysics nothing but a self-contradictory form of thinking, a thinking which is therefore devoid of content, self-destroying
and nugatory – in the same way as empirical thought sees the contradictions which arise in metaphysical thought.[15]

What this means can be expressed as follows: on the one side, in
Kant, we have something like the form of knowledge or cognition,
on the other side we have the content; the content somehow happens
to reach knowledge from outside; the content itself – we could almost
say – is actually withdrawn from reflection. Kroner basically characterizes Hegel's position as follows: this whole separation actually has
something rigid about it. On the one side I presuppose that there are
certain forms, and on the other side I presuppose there are material
contents, and I decree somewhat arbitrarily that these forms are only
meant to be valid for those contents, but not valid in themselves. But,
in reflecting upon these forms, I already turn the forms themselves
into content, as it were, and thereby show that this distinction of
form and content, from which I begin, cannot possibly be conceived
as an absolute distinction, and likewise, in turn, the supposed contents – i.e., the data of sensation – cannot possibly be given to me
independently of my consciousness, independently of the identity of
thought. He says, in other words, that Kant had indeed already set
forth the principle of synthesis, the principle of transcendental synthesis or apperception, but he set it forth only in an abstract way,
and thus did not actually get beyond the unmediated oppositions of
form and content, of concrete and abstract, of a priori and a posteriori. And the task of philosophy is not simply to let these oppositions
stand opposed to one another in a dogmatic manner but rather to
develop these oppositions in and out of one another. But Hegel nonetheless follows Kant insofar as he does not simply deny the tension
which presents itself between these moments – the fact that form is
not merely absorbed into content, or that forms without content do
indeed get themselves entangled in such difficulties – all those, in
short, which Kant himself sets out in the transcendental dialectic. On
the contrary, Hegel recognizes this tension. But he also says that I am
not entitled to set up a kind of border or limit here, once I have
acknowledged and taken up into my reflection the fact that I find
myself in these difficulties when I attempt to move beyond the content
with these forms. Then I can no longer suddenly call 'Halt', but must
actually try instead to recognize these difficulties themselves as not
simply the result of an external misapplication of my cognitive
powers. Rather, I must try and grasp the very difficulties in which I
find myself as an endogenous principle of cognition itself, since I

cannot possibly evade them, since I cannot actually pass a single judgement, since I cannot express a single claim or proposition as a philosopher or theorist of knowledge without moving beyond the limit in question. For if I failed to step beyond this limit – that is, if I did not myself already possess some absolute cognition as one who expressly reflects upon reason itself – then I could never speak of this limit at all. The limit must be at once posited and transcended. And in this moment – that the limit is acknowledged in all seriousness as unavoidably posited but as one that must nonetheless be transcended – you have the simple form of logical contradiction which this thinking encounters once it no longer moves naively within the realm of either formal-logical or merely empirical knowledge, but actually becomes a philosophy of reflection – in other words, once it moves in a realm where the empirical moment and the formal moment can be recognized as mediated with one another.

This is an important point, for you can see here that Hegel does not simply cast formal logic overboard, as he has so often cheaply been accused of doing, and just philosophize away regardless, as if there were no such thing as the principle of contradiction. And to suggest that would be to get Hegel entirely wrong. In the first place, he acknowledges the validity of the principle of contradiction for the normal realm of knowledge established by 'the Understanding', that is, both for our normal empirical knowledge and for the field of formal logic, just as for any other form of thought. But when I relate as a reflective subject – that is, when I do not just focus direct attention[16] upon formal propositions or contents but, rather, think through the relationship between these moments themselves – then I actually find that the form in which they can be grasped is solely and precisely the form of contradiction itself rather than the form of blank identity. What is denied, therefore, is not the contradiction of form and content or any contradiction of this kind, for such contradiction remains in force as far as our finite and limited knowledge is concerned. But precisely insofar as this knowledge attains self-consciousness, or expressly reflects back upon itself, it comes to realize that contradiction, which it must deploy as a criterion of correctness, is at the same time the *organon* of truth – that is, it comes to realize that every particular instance of knowledge becomes knowledge only through and by means of contradiction. And this is the way in which this negative principle, this principle of contradiction, is actually derived from the Kantian doctrine of antinomies, as Hegel presents it.

You will rightly expect me at this point to provide some further clarification of these issues in terms of a specific model, as it were. I do not wish to disappoint this expectation, but I should also tell you that, in doing so, I would actually contravene Hegel's own practice in a serious way. For Hegel was always extraordinarily sceptical towards the concept of examples. There are a couple of passages in the *Encyclopaedia* where Hegel rather ostentatiously rejects the suggestion that he should provide examples.[17] Why Hegel should act in this fashion, why he should refuse to furnish examples – and it is especially difficult for pre-dialectical consciousness to understand Hegel properly in this regard – is not so hard to grasp, for the concept of 'example' always presupposes that we have a universal conceptual range or field at our disposal, something which is firm and reliable, positively given, a reified result, which can be exemplified in the particular case which it subsumes. But in Hegel this very conception of a universal logical field within which the particular is grasped is suspended, at least here on the level of the speculative concept. That is to say, there is here no universal conceptual field which includes so many things within it, for the universal conceptual field consists precisely in the life of the particular it grasps within it; it fulfils itself through the particular, it does not merely cover or include the particular but arises out of it. It has its life in the particular, and nothing particular can thus be regarded as a merely lifeless example which has been abstracted from it. And this is in fact what makes it so extraordinarily difficult, when one is required to think dialectically, to provide an example of the dialectic.

Nonetheless, while fully aware of these difficulties, I would like to try and offer you an example here, indeed a rather simple and elementary one, and, you may think, a rather shocking one. Let us take the proposition 'X is a human being'. The first thing we might say about this proposition, insofar as it subsumes Mr X under the logical species 'human being', is obviously that it is correct, assuming that we are talking about a human being as distinguished from, say, other biological species. But consider for a moment what this means, 'X is a human being'. *A* human, we have said. If in general you say 'X is a human being', as in the case of the usual logical form A is B, there is a certain problem in this, for the A that is supposed to be B here is not the whole of B. Rather, B is a universal, and the A is only a specific representative of the former. There is indeed an identity here, insofar as the particular phenomenon, the individual A, is subsumed under concept B, but nonetheless the identification involved is not a complete one. Now Hegel would say that what is formally implied here – that X is indeed a human being, though in expressing this in the logical form A is B you see that A is precisely not the whole of B but only a representative of B – actually has a very serious meaning.

For he would say – and this, I think, also reveals something of the rigour, of the remarkable freedom, of the almost playful superiority which dialectical thought actually involves – that, if I subsume the X under the concept of the human being, then the concept of human being includes everything possible which the individual X in fact is not. He would not simply content himself, therefore, with a primitive biological definition of 'human being', but would say instead, if we are talking about a truly vital comprehension of the human being as such, that we must think in terms of categories such as freedom, individuation, autonomy, the possession of reason, and a host of other things, all of which are already implicitly contained in the concept of human being as the objective character of the latter. And it is nothing but an act of arbitrariness to omit or ignore such categories in order to provide an operational definition of the human being as something which actually possesses these or those generic characteristics of a biological kind. We need only to listen attentively to the expression 'human being', I believe, to realize it involves more than just the *differentia specifica* that marks it off from the next nearest species – i.e., the anthropoid apes. And indeed, Hegel would say, if this emphatic dimension is always already involved in the concept of the human being – the moment that implies someone is rightly a human being, as I would put it – then the proposition 'X is a human being' is also at the same time untrue. For the emphatic moment which is involved here, even though it may not already have clearly emerged as such, is certainly not yet realized here and now in any particular existing being. One could almost say that something like a human being does not yet exist at all, as the emphatic concept of the human being objectively and intrinsically implies and understands this. In other words, the proposition 'X is a human being' is right or correct, as I said before, but is also false. And I believe that we need only to apply this proposition really seriously to any human being, to indicate that the individual in question is a human being, and we will realize this difference at once, will realize that the individual does not yet really do justice to the concept of the human being in the emphatic sense, the concept of the human in terms of absolute truth. And this, of course, presupposes that we already possess such an emphatic concept of the human being, ultimately the concept of a right and genuine human being, ultimately, indeed, the concept of a right and genuine arrangement of the world in general. When we say 'human being', the expression says more to us than the mere generic concept or species, even if we are subjectively unaware of this.[18]

I believe that I have perhaps shown you something at least of the climate of this thinking, something of what is really meant by the concept of dialectical contradiction. We could say that dialectic, insofar as it is a doctrine of contradiction, critiques the simple logical coherence of the world, for contradiction or absence of contradiction, which are of course correlative concepts, is precisely the logical criterion here. One can undertake to reduce the whole of logic to non-contradiction, and this has indeed been done. Now if we ascribe such a central role to the concept of contradiction, as Hegelian philosophy does, this implies something that I have already explicated to you in a very different context. It implies that we cannot just acknowledge the logical coherence of the world, cannot acknowledge without more ado that the world and our thought are identical with one another, that the world and thought essentially exhaust one another. Rather, we acknowledge precisely that they diverge from one another. And here we must confront the paradox that this divergence between thought and the world is in turn necessarily mediated through thought. Thought itself must therefore strive to grasp precisely what is not thought. And this paradox – that it must try and do what it cannot do – reveals itself in every particular judgement that thought makes, and refers that judgement to the whole, the connected totality, into which thought in its contradictory character must precisely unfold. We say in conclusion, therefore, that the Hegelian idea of contradiction follows from the emphatic concept of truth itself.

LECTURE 8

19 June 1958

Ladies and gentlemen,

In our last couple of sessions, and especially in the last one, I tried to show you why the dialectic is not simply concerned with specific differences – that is, with the specification of the individual object which is indeed in the final analysis an unavoidable condition of any knowledge – to show you, rather, why the dialectic is pre-eminently concerned with contradiction. And in this connection I also tried to unfold the principle of contradiction itself from within the heart of Hegelian philosophy. One could say that the recognition of difference represents a kind of utopia, or, rather, not so much the recognition of difference as difference itself. That the heterogeneous may coexist with the heterogeneous without each destroying the other, that one heterogeneous thing may leave room for the other to unfold as well, and that – we may also add – the heterogeneous may love and be loved, this would be the very dream of a reconciled world. Likewise it is the mark of a world wretchedly entangled in a context of guilt that whatever is in some sense unacceptably heterogeneous cannot be tolerated within this world. This intolerance of the heterogeneous is the ultimate mark of every totalitarian mentality, and here we may use the word 'totalitarian' in a multiplicity of senses. And the dialectic is the negative expression of a certain condition,[1] a thinking which answers to a reality where contradiction has taken the place of the happiness promised by difference – a thinking which strives from within itself, from within its own principle, to bring about its own demise. Now we could say there is an important conclusion which emerges from this, although it is one which has not always been accepted or rigorously drawn as such either within Hegelian philosophy or within the materialist version of the dialectic. This is the conclusion that dialectical thought itself responds to a negative condition of the world and, indeed, calls this negative condition by its proper name. I once expressed this idea straightforwardly by claiming that the dialectic is essentially and necessarily critical, although it becomes false the instant that it sets itself up as a kind of positive philosophy, or so-called worldview, and claims to constitute an immediate appearance of truth itself. Where Hegel is concerned, these issues are extraordinarily complex. For you may well object here that the Hegelian philosophy as a whole ultimately presumes to present nothing short of 'the absolute Idea', or the absolute identity, and to that extent surely incurs the verdict which I have just suggested with regard to every 'positive' interpretation of the dialectic as such. Nonetheless, I should like to believe that the power which effectively animates the Hegelian philosophy is actually very much the power of negation, namely a critical power at work in every specific moment, and that, in contrast to this the well-known affirmative moment of Hegel – which insinuates that in the totality subject and object are ultimately the same – essentially exhibits significantly less power and force than the negative moment we have insisted upon.

In response to the question why the dialectic is concerned with contradiction rather than simply with difference, I basically claimed that this is precisely how thought is capable of acknowledging its moment of non-identity, of acknowledging what is not the same as thought, without thereby abandoning itself to arbitrariness of what merely is – precisely how thought simultaneously retains the power to construe this dimension of the non-identical, to think that which for its own part is not actually the same as thought. What is usually described as 'logic' is indeed nothing other than the doctrine of absolute identity, and the heart of logic, the heart of all logical rules, is the idea that the signs or concepts introduced in the domain of logic are maintained precisely as identical with themselves. Logic is thus nothing but the fully explicated theory of the rules which arise from absolute identity exactly as this is preserved in logic at the expense of any content whatsoever, a content which – as Hegel has taught us – is always not simply included within these forms but also comes into a certain opposition to them precisely because the content is not itself form. One could thus almost construe the identity principle of logic entirely in these terms. And it is thoroughly to be expected, therefore, that the fundamental taboo erected by the discipline of logic is the principle of contradiction, namely the command – and it is a command rather than just a proposition – that, of two mutually contradictory propositions, only one can be true and that the laws of thought are violated wherever that is not the case. One might say that the priority of contradiction which prevails in the dialectic is actually nothing but an attempt to break the primacy of logic, understood as the realm of pure non-contradiction – to point out, that is, that the world is not simply mere thought, is not the mere operation of logical thinking as the world is presented to us in accordance with logical rules. In other words, the world is itself a contradictory rather than a logical world. The dialectic is a critique of the apparent logical character of the world, of its immediate identity with our conceptuality, and that is precisely why it makes the principle of contradiction itself, which is repudiated by logic, for reasons which I have tried to clarify for you in our last few sessions, into its very medium or *organon*. But this means not only that the world is not simply exhausted in our concepts but also at the same time that our concepts are not exhausted in that which merely is. In other words, the origin of the dialectic, which I initially developed for you from the side of thought, of form, of the subject, can just as well be unfolded from the side of the objective as well – as Hegel has also shown in considerable detail. If you would like me to convey to you in simple terms the experience which inspired dialectical thought itself, and which persists as a basic stratum, as it were, beneath the level of the logical and speculative moments we have just been discussing, then I would describe this experience simply as a recognition of the contradictory or antagonistic character of reality itself. In other words, it is that experience of diremption that effectively lay at the heart of the romantic age, the period to which Hegel also belongs. And the specific character of Hegel's response to this lies in the way that he did not attempt, within the context of this diremption, to assume the limited and one-sided standpoint of the individual subject simply thrown back upon itself and its own resources, but also in the way that he resisted the tendency – unlike the cultural classicism of the time – to smooth over this contradictory character of reality, or to resolve this situation, as the later Goethe did, by entering into some kind of understanding with this diremption. Rather, he took the bull by the horns in this regard, which is to say, simply put, that he pursued the thought that the reconciliation of a dirempted world could not arise through any resolution somehow located over and above the objectively self-contradictory character of this world, but only in and through this self-contradictory character itself. And the idea that this development, this driving force, and ultimately also that which strives for reconciliation, is something itself harboured within

the diremption, the negative, the suffering of the world, this idea is
equally, as an experience of reality, a sustaining element of the Hegelian dialectic. Just as, in turn, those things which we have been discussing – the idea that no concept is identical with its object – also
sustain and motivate the dialectic from the side of mere thought itself.
And what is so impressive about Hegelian philosophy, we might say,
is essentially bound up with the way in which these two roots of
dialectical thought – on the one hand the logical-speculative dimension, on the other the dimension of experience which I have expounded
with reference to the concept of diremption or alienation – are effectively brought together, so that their inner unity is ultimately revealed
within the dialectic.

If you now take what I have said about the rigorous necessity of
construing the totality by reference to contradiction and apply it to
this dimension of experience, you will uncover a 'speculative proposition' which certainly cannot be found in this form in Hegel himself,
although it may well preserve the truth of this philosophy more aptly
than any other particular proposition could do. I am talking about
the proposition that the world – and by 'world' here I mean the one
which the process of experience in Hegel is substantially concerned
with, namely the social and cultural or mediated world – is indeed
an internally contradictory world, but is also a system. Thus the
highly distinctive character of Hegelian philosophy and the dialectic
in general lies in the way it undertakes to construe a certain impressive unity while seeking this very unity in the moment of dichotomy,
that is, in the moment of contradiction. And this highly distinctive
character, this most paradoxical moment, is itself equally discovered
in that experience from which Hegelian philosophy arises, in that
experience of reality which is contained in the logical and speculative
issues which we have been discussing in our last few sessions. We can
also formulate it in this way: the world is construed as a unity, produced as a socialized totality which is internally unified down to its
ultimate particular features, through the very principle by which it is
also divided. And it is precisely here that the materialist version of
the dialectic is extraordinarily close to the idealist version, insofar as
the former attempted to grasp and develop that unified but internally
contradictory principle in objective terms precisely as the principle of
exchange which indeed harbours both the antagonistic and the internally unified character of a world governed by the process of exchange.

But I would like to come back to the well-known and popular
objection to the dialectic which accuses it of being an intellectual
straightjacket, a deductive system which attempts to derive reality
from purely conceptual considerations. From everything that I have

already said, you may now be able to appreciate and think through this complex of issues rather more clearly than was possible for you before. For this claim regarding the deductive or systematic character of the dialectic[2] is both justified and unjustified, just as we can indeed say that the world in which we live is a system, that it is thus internally unified, but also that it is profoundly dissonant and profoundly contradictory in itself. Indeed, from the perspective which I have suggested to you today, we can describe the dialectic as an attempt not merely to develop the logic of thought in its relation to objectivity but also, at the same time, to develop the logic of objectivity itself, and indeed as a logic which is not merely foisted on objectivity from the side of the subject but as one that belongs to the matter itself. In this regard, of course, it is true that Hegel appeals to an idealist conceptual framework insofar as, for him, in the last analysis, everything may be regarded as the product of subjectivity. In this sense Hegel thoroughly absorbed the most radical idealistic side of Fichte, and we would certainly be trivializing Hegel if we simply tried to eliminate this subjectivistic aspect of Fichte from his thought. And once the whole of reality has been grasped by Hegel in this sense as something generated by the subject, it is naturally possible for him to try and abstract as it were from the arbitrary influence of a limited and merely individual subjective consciousness. And since the subject is now recognized as the ultimate essence of objectivity itself, it is likewise possible to look for unity in the object itself, rather than grasping this unity simply as something which is constituted only through subjective-conceptual operations. But all that is relatively easy to understand, and I do not particularly wish to insist upon this point here. But let me remind you once again that the Hegelian philosophy is also indeed a philosophy of experience, that it therefore emphatically acknowledges Fichte's famous claim that philosophy must be the union of the a priori and the a posteriori, and not merely a doctrine of the a priori aspects of experience, as it showed itself to be in Kant.[3] In Fichte himself, this basically remained an ambitious programme, and in his thought you will look in vain for such a thorough treatment of experience.[4] But in Hegel the concept of experience is tremendously substantial in character, and it also expressly occurs in the original title of his first and most striking major work, the *Phenomenology of Spirit*.[5] And if you look at Hegel's *Phenomenology*, you will find that the concept of experience appears here in a most emphatic way, namely as the way that consciousness, in examining itself, also comes to experience itself as a kind of object, as the way that, in the ongoing process of this experience, in the ongoing experience of our own life for example, both the object that is observed and the subject that observes undergo change and modification in turn. If you take this idea of experience as seriously as I believe it needs to be taken in Hegel, and now that we have recognized the seriousness of the speculative moment in Hegel without incurring the sort of misunderstanding we find in Hartmann,[6] then perhaps we might say that the doctrine of the objective character of reality as a system, albeit at the same time a discordant system, is also in Hegel the fruit of such an experience. In other words, this doctrine springs just as much from an insight into reality as it did from the self-reflection of the concept in Hegel.

And I believe that we can now actually see that Hegel was the first to realize something that we may perhaps also express quite independently of the specific idealist implications of his philosophical system. And since I wish to provide you with a concept of dialectic which is also a rigorous conception of dialectic, albeit one which cannot be fully captured within the context of idealist theses which have become so problematic for us, I believe that further considerations on this very point may not be wholly inappropriate here. For I think that the experience with which Hegel is concerned here – to formulate this more precisely than I have until now – is the experience that the order of the world which we generally regard as the mere product of our concepts, as imposed by a subjective but coherent contribution of our own upon a more or less chaotic sensuous manifold in the Kantian sense, that this conceptual order is already harboured in the matter itself. Now you might reply that this is itself surely the most extreme form of idealism, a subjective idealism which essentially contains the whole of reality, where reality is the product of the subject. So it is no wonder if in turn it finds nothing in the object but what it has already placed in the object through the a priori features which provide the transcendental conditions of knowledge. But that is not at all what I have in mind here. And it is very important, if you are to understand the specific character of the dialectic, that you grasp the difference which I am particularly interested in at this point. For what we are concerned with here are the conceptual elements involved in the constitution of reality, and which belong to a quite different level, to a quite different dimension, than the conceptual elements of the scientistic order that we confer upon things. What we are basically talking about here – and this is a moment which is also involved in the materialist dialectic, even though, remarkably enough, it has never really been theoretically reflected upon as such – is the way there is actually already something conceptual in the fundamental dynamic of our existence, in the fundamental social dynamic of our existence, something which you might say has much less to do with knowledge than with the course of social processes themselves. I would like to leap ahead somewhat here and actually interpret the moment of internally antagonistic unity with which Hegel is also concerned precisely in terms of the moment of exchange which has been identified by the materialist dialectic as the relevant principle. For it is clear that this principle of exchange – which largely determines objective social processes and, far from being some special contribution on the part of the subject, actually lies in the matter itself – already harbours a conceptual aspect insofar as I can exchange something only where, and only to the degree that, I ignore the specific features of the objects to be exchanged and refer them to an abstract and common form – the 'form of equivalence' as it has been called – by means of which they become in a certain sense commensurable with one another. Thus the principle which governs at least the life of bourgeois society as a whole, the society with which Hegelian philosophy is indeed ultimately and substantively concerned, is objectively defined in itself by this conceptual aspect. For this abstractness in the relations between human beings – which ignores both the contribution and the needs of human beings in relation to the goods they produce, and which now retains nothing but the common form that subsumes these goods, that renders them commensurable and exchangeable in the first place – is precisely that character of abstract time which since Kant has also been profoundly grasped as the ultimate source of the so-called logical or metaphysical problems of constitution. You will see at once that this objective conceptual moment in the matter itself, which is vividly exemplified in the phenomenon of exchange, that this conceptual labour of the human species, as we may describe it, is something entirely different from that understanding of the conceptual which prevails in the contemporary conception of the logic of science and also in the Kantian philosophy, where the conceptual is actually nothing but an ordering principle that we confer upon things. And I believe that the decisive experience of Hegel is precisely the insight that the world which we know is not, as the idealist philosophy would have us believe, something chaotic which we ourselves first endow with some kind of form, and that the conceptual forms in turn, namely as a sediment of the history of mankind, are already contained in the reality we are attempting to know. But this presupposes that we grasp reality, as this is understood by philosophy, as something that is itself essentially marked or determined by human beings. It is determined not in the sense of the object of knowledge as abstractly and purely scientifically constituted by the transcendental subject but, rather, in the practical sense that the world philosophy undertakes to know is a world essentially mediated through human labour. The concept of spontaneity, of the generation of the original unity of apperception, which plays a central role in all idealist philosophy after the *Critique of Pure Reason*, in Hegel already assumes the form that the world itself, the world in which human beings live, is actually a world of labour, and that this moment of labour cannot be ignored, so that there is actually no 'nature' which fails to bear, even if it be merely negatively, the trace of human labour. And if you now ask for an interpretation of the Hegelian concept of mediation in terms of experience, a concept that I would certainly like to talk to you about today, we could say that what Hegel means by 'mediation', what he means by the claim that there is nothing under the heavens which is not mediated,[7] already signifies in Hegel that there is actually nothing human which is not determinately marked by the moment of human labour.

If you consider this thought concerning the objective determinacy of reality, which cannot be deemed a subjective contribution that might in turn be ignored, and pursue it a little more closely, you can also readily connect it with the charge that has so often been raised against Hegel in a superficial manner, namely that of fabricating a fundamentally constricting deductive system. I believe it is not the task of the philosopher, in expounding a philosophy which seems deserving of the name, to proceed apologetically in this regard, to say, for example, 'Well, the dialectic is not nearly as bad as the malicious critics of dialectic like to claim, for it also leaves room for the whole range of experience and God knows what.' Now I believe that it does leave room in this regard, and I have tried to show as much to the degree that was possible here. But I also believe that we must be extraordinarily careful not to make everything innocuous, or, as Hegel puts it, not to leave out the dialectical salt.[8] And I would far rather confess that dialectical philosophy, in both of its versions, actually does have something essential to do with the coercive character of a deductive system. Yet I would qualify this by insisting that dialectical philosophy does not simply do violence to a reality that is ever so green, ever so living, ever so immediate and spontaneous in itself. On the contrary, dialectical philosophy is the means of expressing – in concepts, in the medium of the concept – the coercive and restrictive character which reality itself possesses. We could really say of the dialectic that it 'outdoes the rogue' here.[9] In other words, the coercive construction which dialectical philosophy seems to expect from us is actually none other than the objective compulsion which a fatefully interlinked world exercises upon us. And in this regard we can now properly understand the wretchedness of that complaint about the straightjacket of concepts, once it is revealed as nothing but the cry 'Stop, thief!' Thus the dialectic is reproached for revealing the compulsive character of the world, while the compulsive character itself is thereby ideologically protected.

The irrationalism which opposes Hegel then turns into apologetics, whereas the denunciation of this compulsive character, even under the compulsion of conceptual construction, grants justice for what might be otherwise, for what is not already subjected to such compulsion, for difference in place of system alone. You could also express this by saying that without this compulsive character there would be nothing beyond mere facticity. Without theory – and the dialectic in this comprehensive sense is the very paradigm of what we may call theory as such – there would be no genuine knowledge, but merely observations of data. And if we stayed put with these observations, we would not only fail to advance towards truth, but we would thereby already speak with untruth, would think with untruth, precisely because those observations which act or present themselves as if they were a matter of mere immediacy, as if they were simply there, are all already mediated. That is to say, they also bear the social totality within themselves, and this is something that can only be revealed through the process of dialectical construction – i.e., through theory itself. Thus the systematic character of the dialectic would be precisely that of the system which constitutes reality, namely the dynamic of the system which in a sense develops as a kind of fatality, a system whose fatal character every individual can realize and exhibit at every moment in each particular case. In this regard dialectical philosophy is infinitely more realistic, is infinitely less guilty of spinning out some merely conceptual web, than those much more innocuous theories which proceed as if the world did not in itself possess a specific character and thereby precisely overlook what is decisive here, namely the compulsion which the world itself exercises upon us.

In the light of these motifs, as I have just described and developed them, you can readily understand how a theory which originally appeared so conservative, as if it wished to defend the world as a system, could also, in exhibiting that system at the same time in its negative character, become a starting point for the revolutionary conception of socialism which then directly referred back to it. Indeed, you can see precisely how these two moments interact with one another, and it would be a very interesting task to pursue how much, in their polemical extremes, in their specific repudiation of certain perspectives – such as a mediocre overly harmonizing conception of individualism – the two versions of dialectic, the Hegelian and the Marxist, both actually concur with one another. This is a task which has still to be undertaken, although it is imperative for the self-understanding of dialectical theory that this should be done properly.

I think I have now shown you the sense in which the systematic character of the dialectic must be understood as a critical concept. For while the moment of unity that is singled out by this system, and which leaves nothing outside it, certainly represents the moment of compulsion to which living human beings are subjected and from which they must strive to liberate themselves, this same moment of unity, as a dynamic and internally self-unfolding one, also has the potential to drive towards its own demise. Something like this was once formulated by Hegel himself, who perceived these things with a tremendous clarity and sobriety, when he argued in several famous passages in the *Philosophy of Right* that civil society, through its very own principle, necessarily created more poverty even as it created more wealth.[10] And perhaps I might also add here that the celebrated role which Hegel apologetically ascribed to the state finds its origin right here. For with a kind of desperate leap out of the dialectic, as we might say, Hegel introduced the state as a sort of umpire which is meant to bring some order to what would otherwise fall apart through the growth of internal oppositions in accordance with the very dialectic he has identified. But even here, as I say this, even as I claim, heretically, that Hegel has offered a kind of arbitrary or coercive construction here in order to preserve the positive character of his system, I should also add that even this passage, which looks at first sight like a *sacrificio dell'intelletto*, and one which indeed has always particularly irritated even mediocre and intellectually feeble critics, nonetheless betrays a most profound insight. For bourgeois or civil society, insofar as it tries to maintain itself as such under its own conditions, is ultimately driven in the final phase of its development to generate organizational forms of a statist or authoritarian kind, forms which no longer trust to the immanent play of economic forces but now attempt to stem this dynamic in a coercive fashion and return society to the stage of simple self-reproduction. One could therefore say, if we wish to express this in a very sober way, that Hegel's doctrine of the state and his conception of the fulfilment of absolute spirit in the state would be completely true if only it were presented to us specifically as a negative theory – that is, if it effectively attempted to show that civil society at its end, in order to preserve itself as such, necessarily reveals a tendency towards fascism and the totalitarian state, and that a civil society which remained faithful to its own system *ad infinitum* cannot actually be envisaged. But the momentous conclusion which is implicit in Hegel's philosophy of the state has, for essentially apologetic reasons, never really been drawn in any quarter.

That is all, for now, regarding the justification of the dialectic as a deductive structure which captures something to which our life is indeed subjected. But then again the dialectic is not simply a seamless or immediately deductive structure: it does not operate in terms of pure identity, and it does not try to derive everything seamlessly from a single principle or proposition. And precisely because it does not proceed in this way the central function of contradiction in the dialectic is understood from the perspective of the matter itself. In other words, in unfolding the matter in question as one that is internally contradictory, it also unfolds it as something that is dirempted, as something that is not identical with itself, and in this sense it is specifically a critical theory. Thus the dialectic also implies that the true philosophical concept must involve both the deductive element and the element of experience.

I would like to conclude by pointing out that the concept of experience, like all concepts in Hegel, is not to be understood in a primitive or immediate fashion. When I speak of 'experience' here, you should not think of it in terms of a narrowly defined sensuous experience, as this is presented in the so-called empiricist philosophers. For when Hegel speaks of experience he means something like the experience of consciousness, namely the way in which human beings who are aware of their thought, aware of the continuity of their life as a whole and of reality, also experience this reality as a whole, and attempt to realize what Hegel described in his *Propaedeutic* as 'freedom with regard to the object'.[11] That is to say, we may realize the sovereign freedom which refrains from violently imposing aspects of our own upon this reality, which opens itself up to this reality, which traces and responds to the object as it were.[12] This kind of responsiveness, of productive passivity or spontaneous receptivity, is really what the concept of experience, and in particular the concept of the experience of consciousness, means in Hegel as a specific attitude of thought. But what falls within this experience is social reality as an undiminished whole, and the one who undergoes this experience is the whole human being with every attendant faculty and capacity – and not merely a transcendental subject or, indeed, merely an experimental subject that simply registers sensuous data or particularities of some kind or other. Just as the concept of spirit in Hegel always involves the concept of experience, so in turn the concept of experience in Hegel acquires meaning only when you grasp it essentially and precisely as what we may perhaps simply call spiritual experience.

LECTURE 9

24 June 1958

Ladies and gentlemen,

If you reflect upon our interpretation of the dialectic as an attempt to do justice in thought itself to the non-identical, that is, precisely to those moments which are not exhausted in our thought, then it is clear that this very proposition involves a contradiction. For the identity of the non-identical, expressed as simply as I have just expressed it here, would be a false proposition. We are thus presented with a task. The dialectic could be interpreted in terms of this proposition as the effort to confront this paradox implicit in the predicament of thought itself. And it is evident that this difficulty cannot adequately be confronted in a simple proposition. And this is precisely what drives the dialectic to assume the systematic and ramified character that it displays as a whole. In other words, the paradox of the attempt which I have just described to you demands to be fully unfolded as such, and in a certain sense you could regard the dialectic as a single and very far-reaching attempt – through the unfolding of this contradiction – to confront a task which is given with the very claim to knowledge itself. Perhaps you can best understand the necessity of this thought if you clearly realize that the paradoxical approach which I have just been talking about is not some artificially confected paradox, but one that holds within itself the task of knowledge or cognition as such. For it is evident that thought or the process of knowing only really represents genuine knowing where it involves more than the mere consciousness of itself – that is, where it concerns itself with something other than itself, where it does not content itself with mere tautology. If we want to know something, then – if you will forgive the clever schoolmasterly tone here – we want to know *something*, and not just stay with the act of knowing. In other words, we want to advance beyond the domain of our thought. Yet, on the other hand, precisely in wanting to know this something, the latter itself also becomes a moment of our thinking, becomes itself knowledge, and also becomes itself mind or spirit. To know or to cognize something always resembles a process where something other or non-identical which confronts us is taken up into our own consciousness, is appropriated in a certain sense or made into something of our own. And this paradox – that knowing means translating something into identity, while yet relating to something which is non-identical, since otherwise there would be no process of knowing at all – this otherwise irresolvable paradox is precisely what calls for the labour of the concept for that process of both self-unfolding truth and self-unfolding thought which we understand by the name of 'dialectic'.

I believe we have now come far enough for you to be able to grasp the significance of this theoretical explication and interpretation of the dialectic. And from here we can proceed – not without a certain abruptness perhaps, but still illuminatingly I think – to a more specific discussion of the two fundamental types of dialectical thought which have been presented hitherto. I certainly do not wish to claim that these two types actually exhaust the entire field here, and I am well aware, for example, that there are certain powerful tendencies of an ontological kind today, and particularly in recent Catholic thought, which also strive to develop a dialectical philosophy.[1] I do not wish to go into this question here, especially since I have already presented you with some general claims about the relationship between dialectical and ontological philosophy, and which I can develop in more detail today and in the next session through some much more specific observations about the position of the dialectic in relation to the concept of 'being'. Thus I believe that I can justify my approach here in taking the two essential types of dialectic to be, firstly, the idealist dialectic, as this was developed and defended above all by Hegel, although the thought of Fichte and Schelling, and particularly that of Fichte, already exhibit strongly dialectical features; and, secondly, the materialist dialectic, which, in terms of its origin, is essentially connected with the name of Marx. Now if you clearly bear in mind the interpretation of the dialectic in general which I have presented to you here, you should already almost be able to derive both of these two principal types of dialectic directly from it – a temptation which I find it rather difficult to resist, and which I fear I shall not indeed be able to resist. For on the one side you find a form of thought, one type of dialectic where, of the two moments which essentially define the dialectic, the moment of identity is the predominant one, where every particular moment of identity is indeed challenged, where therefore, in other words, thought expressly brings out the moment of non-identity within identity in all of its own particular moments, but where a certain reconciliation is nonetheless effected as a whole. It is clear without more ado that this type of dialectic can only be the idealist dialectic, for the primacy of thought over being is indeed affirmed here. It is thus a kind of thought in which, in spite of all the non-identity in the particular moments, non-identity is ultimately turned into something identical within the whole. And since the dialectic always begins with reflection upon the knowing faculty itself, namely mind or spirit, we find that spirit – as the principle with which everything is ultimately posited as identical – becomes in this form of thought the dominant principle after all. If I may put this in a crude and rudimentary way here, the Hegelian dialectic as a whole, and regarded from a rather considerable distance, is indeed emphatically a philosophy of spirit – or, more than this, a metaphysics of spirit. In this dialectic, spirit is the Absolute. Everything that is ultimately reveals itself after all as a specific determination of spirit. In my own book on Hegel,[2] I particularly emphasized a different moment of his thought, namely what we may call the critical or negative moment. But I should tell you that this was already a specific accentuation on my part, insofar as the thoughts which I developed in my book are actually thoughts which you cannot simply take without more ado as an exposition of Hegel's philosophy, as things are intended at any given point by Hegel himself. Rather, this was an attempt to save Hegel, indeed to vindicate him, you may say, in some contradiction to certain central motivations of his own thought. For it is clear that, in a philosophical project such as Hegel's – in which the non-identical should be fully acknowledged, yet also ultimately be entirely resolved or 'sublated' in the principle of identity which is 'absolute spirit' – that in such a form of thought the dimension of the non-identical, namely everything in our experience which is not actually spirit, is not taken with complete seriousness after all. And I have attempted to emphasize just those moments in Hegel which, in contrast, do tend to bring out the seriousness of the non-identical, the seriousness of contradiction, in his philosophy. But a remark which Max Scheler[3] once made about Martin Buber[4] after hearing one of his religious lectures also applies to Hegel: 'serious, very serious, and yet not completely serious'. By this I do not mean to say that Hegel's philosophy is not to be taken completely seriously. I believe that I am hardly likely to court this misunderstanding. What I mean is that the thought of non-identity which Hegel himself so impressively acknowledged is not ultimately acknowledged with complete seriousness after all, so that the affirmative, consolatory and, if you like, apologetic moment ultimately prevails in his philosophy. And this is intimately connected with that aspect of his thought which was subjected to such penetrating criticism, albeit quite independently, by Kierkegaard and Marx alike.

Now for the materialist dialectic, in contrast – if you consider the points we have already made, especially the point that the dialectic is not a merely intellectual process, but a process of reality itself – that dialectical tendency to make the moment of non-identity, of contradiction, into the decisive factor does not imply that we must assert some final or conclusive identity of thought and being in the world as it is, that is, in the object of knowledge. You can also express this by saying that, in the Marxian dialectic, the experience which effectively shaped it and stands at the centre of attention – taking the expression 'experience' in the sense I attempted to develop at the end of the last session – is this: the world with which are concerned, the world with which humanity in general has been concerned to this very day, is an internally contradictory world, and that identity which the speculative concept in Hegel already claims in a sense to have at its disposal, and which is sought in the totality of the system, is something which would first have to be established, and the establishment of a form of reality free of contradiction is essentially a matter for human praxis rather than a matter for philosophy.

I believe that you can clearly see, from these two characteristics of the dialectic, how both these types of thought spring from the essence of dialectic itself. We can also derive them, of course, from the positions of the thinkers whom they reflected upon in turn, namely from the most advanced position that bourgeois culture has ever come to occupy. [From the standpoint of a general interpretation of the dialectic, as I have presented it to you, it is also clear][5] that, if the idealist dialectic finds itself in extraordinary difficulties in fundamentally emphasizing the non-identical while nonetheless affirming absolute identity as a whole, the concept of a materialist dialectic is also beset with the greatest and most serious difficulties, difficulties which belong in the same domain as I have just been presenting to you. If primacy is actually ascribed to the non-identical, namely to that which is not mind or spirit, in our knowledge of the world, then in a sense it is also extraordinarily difficult to grasp just how we are to arrive at a dialectic at all. For the dialectical principle itself, the principle of negation or reflection, is necessarily for its part a spiritual or intellectual principle. And as soon as one really tried to pursue, in all rigour, the thought that everything spiritual or intellectual is mere superstructure, that being radically determines consciousness, then it would basically be impossible to understand how we ever come to a dialectic. For then we shall have ascribed primacy to something which is precisely a *rudis indigestaque moles*,[6] to something which is precisely not intrinsically refracted in and through reflection, but is a mere immediacy. Thus the concept of a materialist dialectic leads to that difficulty which is bound up with the simplest meaning of the concept of 'dialectic', namely the difficulty that a conception of the world which essentially involves a movement of concepts, a *dialegesthai*,[7] a thorough explication of intellectual forms, is now in a sense hypostasized, as if it thus had nothing to do with such a thing. I cannot resolve this difficulty for you right here, but I wanted at least to draw your attention to it, above all because it is at this very point that we see how the materialist dialectic could begin to ossify into the kind of dogma or state religion which inevitably emerges when the thought no longer confronts its own immanent difficulties with full seriousness. But I should like at least to suggest to you where the resolution of this contradiction lies: the concept of dialectic which is in question is not a purely theoretical concept of dialectic at all, since the moment of praxis itself proves to be a determining factor, [even if it] does not by any means assume primacy – for the relationship between theory and practice in the materialist dialectic is an extraordinarily complex and involved one. But the idea of praxis is acknowledged with full seriousness here, and without taking the concept of praxis – namely the active transformation of the world – into consideration we cannot actually make sense of the thought that material relations or what merely exists could be dialectical in themselves. And, although this thought is not conceived by Marx as a purely contemplative or explanatory theoretical one, there is nonetheless a theory here. The question involves an extremely difficult structure. And towards the end of these lectures I hope to be able to explore this for you in fuller detail.[8] But I would like to draw your attention here to one thing at least: if we simply apply the concept of a philosophy, of some internally coherent mode of explaining the world, or even, as they do in the East, the concept of some type of science to the materialist version of dialectic, then we already run into the most tremendous difficulties and find ourselves specifically driven by these difficulties to perform the very opposite of all dialectical thinking, namely to turn an intrinsically dynamic form of thought which remains critical towards itself into something like a 'worldview' to be venerated.

I believe that I can now present you once again with the real difficulties which dialectical thought poses for us and at the same time try to elucidate certain distinctive features which may prove helpful if you attempt to think dialectically yourselves. For the task of any lectures which are intended to introduce you to the dialectic, apart from helping to facilitate the study of the most important dialectical texts themselves, must above all be that of bringing you to the very point where the difficulties actually lie, rather than concealing these difficulties with some kind of smooth conceptual derivation. The task is not to render such thinking innocuous, but to convince you of what ultimately motivates this thought precisely where it offers you the greatest difficulties. I hope that the distinctive features which I present here may help you a little in learning to practise dialectical thinking itself. The first of these difficulties lies in the way that part and whole must always be related to one another in dialectical thought. This is a claim that will strike a familiar chord with those of you who are studying psychology, for the theory of Gestalt psychology, which is the most widely established academic form of modern psychological thought today, also says much the same thing.[9] But the focus in that case is essentially on the domain of sense perception, and the priority of the whole over the part is tacitly assumed in this connection, along with the idea that the relation between the whole and its parts is generally harmonious in character, or at least is not in a relation of tension. I should also qualify what I just said in the sense that Gestalt theory does also recognize the moment of the non-identity of whole and part in its concept of a 'bad Gestalt', but the entire pathos of this scientific doctrine of the priority of the whole over the part is incomparably less antagonistic in character than it is in the dialectic.[10] I should like to say right away that the idea of the dominance of the whole over the parts was actually first expressed in the context of the dialectic by Hegel in the claim we have already discussed in some detail, namely that the whole is the true.[11] And then again by Marx in the material reversal or interpretation of this claim, when he argued that the totality of this society furnishes the key to all of the individual social processes and that independence cannot really be ascribed to these individual social processes over against that totality. But the dialectical conception of the relation between the whole and the parts is actually far more difficult than the very familiar claim that the whole is greater than the sum of its parts, for while, on the one hand, it is constantly demanded that the parts must be grasped from the perspective of the whole, and that the whole in turn must be grasped through the interplay of the parts, the dialectical conception also insists upon a relation of tension between these moments, between the whole and the parts, between the universal and the particular. That is why the effort to bring these two moments together actually proves to be extraordinarily problematic and extraordinarily difficult. The difficulty I am talking about here, and which I wish to bring home to you, is that, while the whole and the parts can certainly only be grasped in their relation to one another, we must recognize that the whole is by no means positively given when you have the part, and, conversely, that the relevant parts are by no means positively given when you think the whole. Thus you must constantly ask yourselves how you are actually to bring both these things together, for – as I believe I have already made sufficiently clear – the relation of whole and part in the dialectic is not one of mere subsumption. This is not a relation of logical extension where the parts would be contained within the whole in the way the segments of a circle lie within its circumference. Rather, it is a dynamic relation, one where both moments reciprocally produce one another rather than just being given alongside one another in a reified and, so to speak, timeless manner. And we may say in general that the dialectic in its entirety – to employ a Kantian distinction here – has extended the domain of the so-called dynamic principles to such a degree that what Kant presents under the title of mathematical principles, namely the logical principles, also comes to assume a dynamic character.[12] Thus we are talking about the problem – and this is one of the major difficulties with which the dialectic confronts you – of how I am already supposed to grasp the part by reference to a whole which is never completely given as such.

In order to show you how these things unfold with regard to the actual work of cognition, I could perhaps say something here about a controversy in which I was engaged over twenty years ago now with Walter Benjamin when he was writing his work on Baudelaire.[13] I am referring to the unpublished opening part of this work, and specifically to the interpretation of one of the poems from Baudelaire's cycle 'Le vin': 'Le vin des chiffonniers' [The Ragpickers' Wine].[14] At the time when Baudelaire was writing, the ragpickers were seen as extreme representatives of the *lumpenproletariat* and thus possessed key significance for the depiction of penury which plays such an important role in French literature as a whole in this period – you have only to think of *Les Misérables* in this connection.[15] In his interpretation of this poem, Benjamin had discussed a wine tax which was levied in Paris at the time and which forced the workers to go out beyond the town gates, outside the *banlieue*,[16] if they wanted to consume wine, if they could indeed afford wine in the first place. And there were some contemporary French writers who claimed – although this does not sound particularly credible – that these subsequently intoxicated workers defiantly displayed their drunkenness when they came back into the city precisely to demonstrate, in the spirit of an oppositional act, that they had managed to do something otherwise beyond their means, namely to get thoroughly drunk.[17] And Benjamin believed that he could specifically discover certain motifs of this kind in the cycle 'Le vin'. I would like to leave aside the question whether that is actually true or not. In looking through this material again recently,[18] in connection with these lectures, the details of Benjamin's argument struck me as rather more plausible now than at the time when we were involved in the original controversy. Anyway, the drift of his argument was to take the question of the materialist determination of reality as a whole – which, according to his theory, possesses a key role in Baudelaire's poetry as well – and trace it back immediately to specific events and experiences such as the wine business concerned, cheap drinking establishments, the rag merchants, and so forth. Now I did not wish, of course, to demote the significance of such individual experiences in this connection. But if you consider the idea of a materialist dialectic here, that is, of a theoretical explanation of social facts on the basis of specific material conditions, then it is obviously not enough for a theory of this kind to appeal to such unmediated data about the wine business, or the suburbs, however concrete that may appear, however tempting such concreteness may be, and however exciting and stimulating the thought of connecting such apparently vivid and concrete data immediately with the highest speculative categories. But this is the same tendency, the same temptation of dialectical thought which Hegel perceived in the work of Schelling, and the task of protecting thought from this was certainly not the least of those which Hegel undertook to fulfil in his polemic with Schelling. In this regard Benjamin was more of a Schellingian than a Hegelian. I attempted at the time to suggest to him that it was not enough, where the dialectical interpretation of poetic content is concerned, to identify individual motifs of material contradictions and material tensions of the kind we are talking about here. Rather, the materialist dialectic must constantly and under all circumstances acknowledge that the individual findings on which it is based are determined by the whole, that they are mediated by the totality of society. Thus it is that the individual experiences, however startling and however tangible they may be, never suffice in themselves if we wish to draw social conclusions of a theoretical kind, conclusions which concern the theory of society itself. For the individual moments, as experienced, must for their part be related to the structure of the social totality if we do not wish to resign ourselves to the mere description of particularly vivid data. And where we are interested in the relationship between Baudelaire's lyric poetry and the age of high capitalism – and this is indeed the first and still unparalleled case of a poetry which is wrested from the specific conditions of high capitalism – we cannot merely content ourselves with seizing on individual features of capitalist reality, as these appeared before the eyes of Baudelaire, and adducing them in order to explain the content of his work. Rather, we must try in this connection to derive the commodity character, which does indeed play a quite central role in Baudelaire, from the structure of society as a whole and then attempt to perceive the subjective reflection of the commodity form in this poetry itself, rather than contenting ourselves with individual motivations here.[19]

I should remark in passing that the distinction which I am sure you will all have heard of but is seldom analysed carefully and is generally also forgotten, namely the distinction between dialectical materialism and vulgar materialism, can be described quite precisely in this connection. And you can then perhaps understand what it really means to repudiate vulgar materialism. Thus it does not mean, for example, that vulgar materialism should be contrasted with some finer form of materialism. What it means is that, in attempting to explain certain processes or cultural and intellectual forms, or whatever, by reference to material conditions, we should not content ourselves with immediately introducing supposedly material motivations as the real principles of explanation. In other words, a vulgar conception of economics which imagined that it could derive reality from the so-called desire for profit, the love of money, or other affective predispositions on the part of capitalists, or simply from the so-called desire for profit, even if this is completely separated from any psychological motivations, would represent a vulgar materialist interpretation because it fails to refer to the totality of the society within which the individual desires of employers and workers assume their specific significance in the first place. That is to say, even if we assumed that all individual capitalists were angels – or, rather, saints – but were compelled, under the conditions of capitalism, to engage in economic activity, this would mean that, despite this subjective disposition, or despite the complete absence of the so-called desire for profit, nothing essential would change as far as the development of the social process as a whole was concerned. And I believe, I may also say, that many of the ready dismissals of the materialist version of the dialectic as it is presented to us today arise from this very point. For we no longer even make the effort to provide an explanation of social phenomena through their mediation by the totality but rather accuse the opposing view, namely the materialist theory, of real naivety in wanting to explain the world by recourse to something like the desire for profit, or, as people love to say, to base material motives and considerations. And once one has ascribed this meaningless thesis to the opposing view, then it is a really easy matter to point out that there are other noble and elevated motives to be found in addition to these rather base ones. Now if you really want to engage with the problem of the materialist dialectic, I believe the first thing you must do is to take the thought involved with full seriousness and dispel any notion that the world is simply being explained here on the basis of so-called lower motives, or that the striving for profit is being hypostasized as the fundamental characteristic of human beings as such. Rather, you should take seriously the thought of the social totality, of the objective spirit of capitalism, as the genuine principle of explanation here.

In response to what I have just said you may say: 'You are operating here with the concept of totality; you also say you cannot possibly grasp such a fact in its immediacy – so where do you get this totality from? Indeed Benjamin was probably quite right, the wine tax and other such things exist, there are quite specific individual tendencies on the part of individual groups who find themselves confronted with specific things, and, on the other hand we have your totality of society, something which as a thinker and researcher you cannot really grasp at all, which is merely a metaphysical thesis on your part.' This objection, incidentally, effectively lies at the heart of the most important critique which has ever been directed against dialectical materialism from within the perspective of sociology. I am talking about the critique provided by Max Weber, who did not in fact object – and this testifies to Weber's extraordinary perceptiveness – that materialism essentially failed to appreciate the significance of any higher goods or motives in society. Rather, his critique basically argued that the dialectic is a form of metaphysics, for in claiming that the particular can only be grasped from a total perspective, while it never tangibly possesses this total perspective itself as an actual given, it is always forced to bestow absolute significance upon certain concepts, to hypostasize these concepts, and thus ends up producing claims which are just as arbitrary as those of the metaphysics which the materialist version of dialectic was meant to challenge.[20] As far as the business of the sciences is concerned, the problem is then usually treated in a very banal manner. For it is said that the scientist or researcher must pursue the investigation, must gather, classify and organize the relevant facts, and then also draw upon something like intuition as a source from beyond. And if the celebrated spark of insight is granted, if the beautifully and efficiently arranged facts are subjected to this ray of illumination, then something like knowledge comes about. To discover the answer to this question, to say in this connection how the relation of whole and part must be configured if we proceed from the part while nonetheless requiring a whole which is not itself immediately given, this is actually the difficulty and the challenge which the dialectic presents at this point.

LECTURE 10

26 June 1958

Ladies and gentlemen,

In our last session I began to talk in more detail about the difficulties involved in the relationship of part and whole in the Hegelian philosophy, and about how these difficulties might be resolved. In this connection we discovered that the principal difficulty is this: the particular cannot just be grasped as the particular; rather, the particular must always also be grasped from the perspective of the whole; yet both logic and psychology in their current form claim that the whole is never adequately given, but only the parts. We were thus confronted with the problem of how we could anticipate the whole on the basis of which the individual parts must be understood. But in order to resolve this problem adequately – or at least to indicate how the dialectic responds to this difficulty, one which it cannot of course simply eliminate, for if it could there would be no problem of knowledge, the whole really would be immediately given, and subject and object would merely collapse into one – I must get you once again to consider something which will prove challenging as far as widely established habits of thought are concerned. And this is something that we also came up against in our most recent seminar on sociology.[1] For I would like to raise the question whether the whole actually does come afterwards, whether our experience does indeed begin with the parts and then gradually rise towards the whole. But please do not understand this in the wrong way. I am not speaking in the context of the Gestalt theory or the psychology of perception here – i.e., in the sense that some Gestalt or complex is already given while it is only subsequently, through reflection, that the individual parts are separated out. Rather, I am thinking about a much more comprehensive and authentically philosophical phenomenon, namely about how our experience is actually organized – that is, about how we actually come by knowledge in the first place. And here, it seems to me, as if the standard assumption of the logic of scientific investigation – that we first perceive parts, that we then order these parts according to similarities and differences, that we proceed to classify them and in this way arrive at a universal concept and finally a universal theory – is actually a construction on our part, one which is extraordinarily remote from the actual character of our knowledge or, simply put, from how we actually come to know anything. And there is indeed a question, which needs to be thoroughly explored in its own right, about how far what is called 'theory of knowledge' really does justice to what we effectively do when we know, and how far it more or less presupposes norms which are derived from the sciences and the specific claims to validity which they make, but which have relatively little to do with our living experience. Now science claims, of course, that it must be possible to transform this living experience, insofar as it is strictly valid, into scientific propositions. But there is also something extraordinarily problematic about this very transformation, and it has never actually been seriously undertaken, yet our living knowledge consists precisely of innumerable insights whose validity or whose truth – if I may put this more emphatically – we also accept, and indeed accept expressly as our own, as a truth proper to ourselves, even if such transformation into scientific propositions proves impossible here. What I am claiming is precisely that in a certain sense – and I am essentially speaking here, like Hegel, with an eye to our social and historical experience rather than to the specifically organized experience of the sciences – that in a basic sense we have more awareness of the system in which we live, that we possess a more direct experience in ourselves of the reality in which we are caught up, than we do of specific individual situations on the basis of which we might gradually ascend to a view or to a concept of the totality within which we live. And the particular or individual aspect, on its side, is just as much a product of abstraction in relation to the totality of our experience as the whole – and we must critically insist on this as against Gestalt theory – is also, in turn, a product of abstraction in relation to the individual moments which it encompasses. There is no immediate unity between the two, since the relation in question is a process. And the order which is pursued by science turns things upside down insofar as it would persuade us that the hierarchical classifications it produces, advancing from particular observations to universal concepts, is actually identical with the character of reality itself. This latter thought was first authentically expressed in Spinoza's claim that the '*ordo idearum idem est ordo rerum*',[2] a proposition that seems to me to be idealist in a dogmatic sense, and which we may come back to later in connection with Descartes and the critique which a dialectical perspective must apply to the Cartesian method, which is itself the prototype of scientific method.[3]

I am more aware of what kind of world I live in than I am of supposedly individual data. Above all, the moment of oppressiveness, of unfreedom, what contemporary sociology describes with such a neutral expression as 'social role', namely the orientation of the individual to some particular function – all of these, you may say, relatively abstract things manifest themselves to consciousness in an incomparably stronger fashion than, let us say, specific situations such as parliamentary procedures or the current business climate, or whatever other social situations we care to consider – the team situation, the family situation, and so on. Of course, you may respond here by saying that, from the ontogenetic point of view, if you wish to speak in psychological terms, the paradigm for these relationships must generally be sought in the institution of the family. But, even if you would really prefer to foreground the genetic aspect here over against the philosophical aspect, we should still have to say that even a little child does not presumably behave like a little investigator, rising from the experience of a concrete threat on the part of the father to the notion of more general threats. Rather, the child will first experience something like threat as such, namely anxiety, and the supposedly concrete aspect of the specific situation – that father is angry – will only gradually emerge from this. But it is surely the case, if we leave aside these genetic moments and focus upon relations within a fully developed society, that what is actually immediate here, what we first of all perceive, are the general relations much more than the particular relations in which we are involved – rather as a dog, for example, will generally react by specifically wagging its tail when well-dressed people enter the room, will act less excitedly when less well-dressed people come in, and will even start to bark if someone like a tramp appears at the door. I believe that human experience generally organizes itself in such a way. Indeed, in this regard I am deeply convinced that the difference between the human being and the animal is not nearly as emphatic as idealist philosophy would have us believe in order to flatter our narcissism and encourage us to submit to the most unlimited moral demands.

If this is so, if in a certain rather tacit sense – in contrast to the organized approach of science – we actually become aware of the whole before we become aware of what is more specific, and if what we describe as specific experience is itself already a product of reflection, then we could find a formulation for the dialectical procedure, one which also serves to reveal a particularly dangerous moment of dialectical thought, and specifically of Hegel's thought. For we could say that the task of dialectical thought is to restore the naivety, the kind of perception of the world that we enjoyed before we allowed ourselves to be stupefied by a wholly organized form of thinking; that the task of dialectic, therefore, is to overcome in and through reflection those moments of separation and objectification that have been posited by reflection. I have just suggested that this is a dangerous thought, and indeed when I speak about this danger it is precisely Hegel that I have in mind. For in the work of Hegel – for whom this thought, as I have just expressed it, plays a very significant role – it assumes a particular form on account of his affirmative view of the world, that is, of his belief that spirit effectively wins through, that spirit is absolute and ultimately the only substantial reality. Thus by means of the dialectic the naivety which is more or less prior to reflection in the sense of the merely affirmative, in the sense of the mere acceptance of given relations, of given positive perspectives, of given religions, effectively comes to prevail – something which finds problematic expression in Hegel's claim that speculative philosophy makes common cause with religious belief against reflection. And this formulation can be found in these words in Hegel.[4] But it is clear that, if we renounce the fundamental conception of identity which prevails in Hegel, as I showed you in our last session, and replace it with the concept of an open or fractured dialectic, then that kind of demand falls away. But this is surely not the least significant of the motivations behind the dialectic: that thought – in reflecting upon itself, in becoming aware of itself as a means of breaking up and dividing the content of experience, as a dominating moment of pre-formation – nonetheless attempts to dispel the guilt, or at least to prepare the way for this, which thought itself has actually produced.

I have said that we first effectively become aware of a certain pressure or oppressiveness, that we thereby become aware of the totality before we register more specific aspects, and that situations in this regard may be just as abstract as the whole. And you may well respond that this is merely a relatively vague and unarticulated form of experience which should not simply be equated with the task of acquiring knowledge, that is, with a genuinely responsible claim to knowledge. I would, of course, admit the justice of this objection, and would claim that the specific significance which theory possesses for dialectical thought is to be found precisely here. That is to say, theory is really the attempt to explore that consciousness of the whole, which is always already there beforehand, and the ensuing specific individual forms of givenness, which are themselves mediated in turn through the whole, and to do so in such a way that they may enter into a certain concordance with one another. And here I shall try to formulate the dialectic for you as a kind of programme, a kind of suggestion which you may, God willing, attempt to try out for yourselves if you wish to think dialectically. Thus, on the one hand, dialectical thought must always try and measure up the data with which it is concerned against theory – that is, it must not simply and naively accept them as they initially give themselves out to be but, rather, attempt to render them transparent with respect to that whole which is mediated through theory; on the other hand, dialectical thought must equally keep theory open to those specific experiences by which it is nourished and sustained, and in this regard must equally avoid becoming something merely rigid and definitive.

When I try here to elucidate the significance of the whole, or that moment which goes beyond the organized, causal-mechanical and classificatory conception of knowledge, there are two things which need to be said: firstly, that we are dealing with a dialectical moment – and once again I am here translating an important and extremely involved motif of Hegel's in terms of the simple processes of our own activity of knowing – which is precisely only a moment; it is not the whole, therefore, and you should not imagine that knowledge in its entirety consists of such theoretical anticipations, consists of mere theory. If it did consist in this, it would in principle be that which it may always become – something from which it cannot indeed be protected a priori by any power whatsoever – and would simply degenerate into a system of delusion. Furthermore, I would warn you against pursuing something which many, including Richard Kroner, have taken at this point to be the essence of the dialectic, namely the temptation of identifying this moment of a comprehensive whole – which is not yet actually present to me as something securely given – with the wretched concept of 'intuition',[5] quite apart from the fact that this concept of intuition is only really justified, to the extent that it is justified at all, precisely as a moment in the process of knowledge, not as something exclusive in its own right. In this context, however, I am not really talking about the kind of articulated philosophy of intuition that was developed by Bergson, where the concept of intuition is transformed and differentiated to a degree that what I am about to say is not altogether applicable. What I wish to do is to prepare you for the kind of arguments you will repeatedly encounter as an automatic response whenever you claim any knowledge which goes beyond what we already have in black and white terms and can readily carry home with us. For then you will hear something like this: 'Ah yes, that's the moment of spiritual intuition, enormously stimulating', people will say, if they are feeling friendly. But this response also generally betrays a certain hostility: 'enormously stimulating', but also rather childlike, for although the serious scientist or researcher needs something like this, and there can indeed be no science without such intuition, the whole point of science is to turn these intuitions into small change as rapidly as possible and to ensure that everything runs utterly smoothly in the systematically organized context of knowledge. I do not particularly want to go into the question as to how far such intuitions are involved in the process of knowledge. But I do believe that to say something 'occurs' to us testifies to a living experience still at work in us. If nothing strikes us or occurs to us, this generally means we are being stupid, that we have no relationship to the objects of our experience, and what is called a merely logical intelligence – one which does not involve that aspect of unanticipated insight – is a form of intelligence which simply turns upon itself without enjoying any relationship to the matter itself. But even disregarding all this, it is quite false to take intuition as a specific source of knowledge *sui generis*, as a special perspective opposed to other forms of knowledge – and I would also say that this was actually Bergson's most serious error in his critique of merely reflective thinking, a critique which he shared with Schelling and indeed with Hegel. It is a strange paradox that Bergson himself – who tirelessly denounced the tendency to divide everything up into categories and principles of order, to think in terms of compartmentalized little boxes and rigid, mechanical and merely classificatory concepts – should then have packed the kind of knowledge he held to be truest into a little box of its own and treated it as if it were something utterly separate from the process of knowing in its totality. I believe that this view of intuition is completely mistaken. For what may rightly be described as intuition, if the concept is to mean anything more than it does in the jargon especially favoured by composers of operetta, is a kind of knowledge which lies in the unorganized and – if I may express this for a moment in psychological terms – preconscious level of experience, which is then illuminated, as it were, by the ray of reflection that emerges at a certain moment at the surface of consciousness. At this moment of emergence it assumes a certain sudden, abrupt or, if you will, desultory character. But this desultory and disconnected character – which belongs, as the logical positivists would argue, to those despised concepts which are described as intuition – springs not so much from the way that these insights have allegedly fallen from the heavens as from the way – and this is undoubtedly what Bergson actually meant even if he did not express it so clearly – in which it properly captures those moments where living experience or living cognition breaks through the crust of reified and pre-formed conventionalized concepts and perceptions. This is therefore where we really come to know something, where our thinking is fulfilled, instead of simply feeding off the already given and socially approved view of the object. Then we come to a kind of encounter, a kind of explosion, and out of this conflict springs that sudden and illuminating character of what is called intuition, and which has so often been described to us. But as far as the process of knowledge itself, or, if you like, the origin of intuition, is concerned, this is by no means so abrupt. For behind it there actually lies that whole fabric of experiences which transpires in us, and only transpires in a really living way where we are not compelled to think in a purely controlled manner, where we still preserve something resembling our freedom of consciousness, where our thinking is not already simply directed by the norms which it is supposed to observe.

That is what I wanted to say about the concept of intuition in the spiritual sense. To say that the concept of intuition itself can only properly be given a dialectical meaning is just to say that the unexpected character of intuition is really nothing but that sudden reversal from ossified and objectified concepts into living knowledge which occasionally arises when the concepts from our not yet thoroughly organized or pre-digested experience emerge for reflection. Intuition itself is thus a way in which the object comes to move precisely through the movement of the concepts which lies behind it. This movement certainly does not need to unfold in terms of pre-formed concepts and, from the psychological point of view, is by no means identical to the *clara et distincta perceptio* with which it is generally equated. But I would like to say once again that theory as well as intuition, precisely by virtue of the dialectical character which I have attempted to describe for you here, may not be arrested in turn, for the self-contradictory essence of the object of knowledge is also naturally at work here too. Thus all theory is open and – to return to the problem with which we began – theory is not to be conceived as something finished either. That is a further difficulty, if not perhaps such a flagrant one as that we have previously been discussing. On the one hand – to emphasize this once again for you in a rather

pointed fashion – I can only come to know the particular insofar as
I also have some knowledge of the whole and measure the particular
against this knowledge of the whole; on the other hand, however, this
whole is never given to me as something finished or complete either.
And as soon as I try and use the whole as something finished and
complete, as soon as I simply draw conclusions from it, as they say,
then it already turns into something false. And the whole in turn – as
I suggested to you in contrast to the image of a circle and its segments,
must be derived, in any dialectical theory, from the movement of its
parts, and not from some abstract overarching concept.

And in fact it strikes me as the decisive symptom for the decay of
dialectical theory – there where it is declared to be the prevailing
view, namely in the countries of the Eastern bloc – that this dialectical
moment is just what has been lost from view. For here the dialectic
has actually ossified into a system or a list of theses of a more or less,
and indeed generally more, rigid kind, from which the particular is
simply derived, and on the basis of which, above all, the particular
in every case is judged. Thus if we consider the entire later work of
György Lukács, who must undoubtedly be credited in his earlier years
with reawakening a real sense for dialectical thought in the materialist version of dialectic[6] – we can observe at every stage just how
dialectic in its most dogmatic form has prevented him from reaching
genuine dialectic at all, so that we are confronted with a host of value
judgements spun out of rigidified concepts simply adopted from the
dialectic. We may take a single structure as an example here: Lukács
has a theory regarding the ascent and decline of the bourgeois world,
and, as far as the relationship with art is concerned, the works produced by bourgeois culture in its ascendant phase are supposed to be
valuable and outstanding in character; but where bourgeois culture
in its decline is concerned – and for Lukács this begins very early,
with Flaubert and impressionism – everything is simply condemned
as inferior, very much in the spirit of any old party secretary of the
SED [Sozialistische Einheitspartei Deutschlands – the Socialist Unity
Party of Germany]. Here Lukács completely forgets the category
which he once emphasized so strongly himself, namely that of the
social totality; he completely forgets that society continues to develop
internally, and forgets above all what he once so dramatically insisted
upon, namely that the proletariat – as the class which is opposed to
the bourgeois class by its exclusion from the privileges of culture and
by a series of other factors – cannot now by any means be regarded
as the most progressive class from an intellectual or cultural point of
view. Thus everything that is substantial, intellectually and culturally
speaking, has been played out in the context of the development of

bourgeois society. And however critical we may be in relation to bourgeois society, this critique, as far as cultural and intellectual matters are concerned, only really has a relevant object insofar as it explores the internal dynamic of this bourgeois spirit within which the development of society as a whole in a certain sense is also refracted and revealed. But, in failing to follow this through, Lukács ends up pronouncing judgements which were typical of the kind of high-school teachers from whom my generation, when we were about fifteen, precisely tried to escape, and ends up proclaiming Walter Scott to be a great writer while presenting Joyce and Kafka as agents of monopoly capitalism. I think I have therefore shown you, in rather drastic but not I think entirely unjust terms, how the ossification of theory, and specifically of dialectical theory, in terms of a living relationship to the object which it would know, proves to be just as false and fateful as any approach which clings immediately to what is supposedly simply given without grasping its relationship to the whole.

But let me say more here about the specific difficulties which belong to dialectical thought, and thus pursue my intention of bringing you face to face with the concrete problems of such thinking. I believe that a further challenge presented by dialectical thought – one which will certainly present difficulties to those among you who have been educated in the context of the prevailing logic and theory of science – is precisely that thinking of this kind does not proceed step by step, unlike the thinking for which the natural sciences provide the classical model and which we typically encounter in traditional and practically oriented science. Thus, grotesque as it may seem, it is precisely dialectical thought, where the various moments are much more intimately connected with one another than they are in the traditional form of thought, which is constantly reproached for being unscientific, in the sense that it lacks the requisite systematic character. What underlies this objection is the fact that there is no absolutely 'first' principle for dialectical theory. One could rather say – and this is a critical issue – that Hegel's theory acknowledges an absolutely 'last' principle from which everything flows, namely the fully developed totality, the fully developed system. But it is certainly true that dialectic knows no 'first' to which everything else would have to be reduced, and thus the dialectic also lacks that pathos of reduction for which truth, as I once put it, is a merely differential determination or, rather, a merely residual determination: what is left over once we have deducted all the costs incurred in the process of cognition. On this banal conception, what is left as the net profit of cognition – I am being deliberately basic here – is an absolute first, purified of every contribution of merely subjective conceptual labour and conceptual artifice. Hegel has shown us that an 'origin' is not the truth, that an origin, on the contrary, becomes a deception the moment it is taken as the truth. It is a deception because it is not an origin at all, and everything that claims to be an absolute 'first' is already mediated within itself. But this already challenges a view which all of you, and I myself, have absorbed with our mother's milk, as it were, quite irrespective of whether we encountered it in a specifically philosophical form or not. I am talking about the Cartesian doctrine of the *clara et distincta perceptio*, the view that individual absolutely clear and distinct and mutually independent cognitions constitute the foundations of our knowledge, and that only what can be reduced to such moments can properly count as knowledge. In a German context, due to the influence of Hegelian and idealist philosophy generally, this idea has never become as prevalent as it has everywhere else. And sometimes, indeed, one might regret that this conception, as a moment of truth, has not been more strongly represented, for it is really only through a critique of this idea, and only once we have properly appreciated what a *clara et distincta perceptio* is, that one can actually make the transition to dialectic in its full significance. Sometimes I have the rather uncomfortable feeling that you are following my dialectical reflections all too readily, because the resistance which arises at this point in the whole of the civilized Western world and rests precisely upon a certain Cartesian outlook does not in Germany exert anything like the traditional power that it enjoys there. And in this respect I would like to say that one can almost arrive at dialectic too easily, and that is probably none too beneficial for the cause of dialectic. Anyway, with regard to *clara et distincta perceptio*, we must object that there is no such ultimate and absolute instance of givenness purified of any mediation, whether it be pure consciousness or some pure sensuous datum. The proof of this forms the very content of the *Phenomenology of Spirit*, and I wish to introduce this basic thought of the *Phenomenology* into our general presentation of the dialectic here. I hope I shall find time to sketch enough of the overall argument of the *Phenomenology* for you to see how this fundamental motif is developed and elaborated there: wherever thought believes it has now reached an absolute point of rest, this absolute point of rest is once again dissolved, until this quest for something absolutely reliable, something that no longer moves within itself, finally reveals itself as a delusive image of knowledge.[7] Truth, as we learn in the course of the dialectic, is by no means something given and is not something fixed, as Hegel puts it.[8] Rather, truth itself is involved in a process, and the object we find before us is itself caught up in movement; and, inasmuch as the object is in movement, it is not a distinct or unambiguous object. Or let me say, more precisely, that it is not *only* a distinct object. That is to say, we also require a certain distinctness and determinacy in the object – and here the Cartesian moment asserts its rights – we also require insight into specificity, into the object just as it stands before us in its particular contours. And it is precisely by examining this firm and determinate object closely and carefully in its determinacy that we discover it is not such a firm and determinate object after all. It is through the micrological insight which immerses itself in the particular that what is rigid, what is seemingly distinct and determinate, begins to move, and it is this which also exposes the Cartesian claim to critique.

You should not forget that this claim derives in fact from dogmatic rationalism. If we think in a philosophical way and work in the positive sciences at the same time, it is quite remarkable to see just how many notions that once played a particular role in the history of philosophy but have long since been effectively criticized or at least heavily qualified by subsequent philosophy have still remained extremely influential in the context of the individual sciences, which allegedly proceed in a much more rigorous and serious way than we philosophers are thought to do. And among these notions which have been dispelled by philosophy we find this idea of *clara et distincta perceptio*, which repeatedly turns up in barely concealed form in the demands raised by the rational and positive sciences. Here we should simply remember that this demand – that an object must be given to me in an absolutely clear and distinct fashion, and quite separately from others, if I am to possess valid knowledge of it – effectively already supposes, and this is the dogmatic moment of all perception, that the world does in fact possess this character of distinctness and determinacy. That is to say, we can only arrive at this *clara et distincta perceptio* in the first place if the objects of knowledge are indeed static, distinct and clearly delimited in themselves, if they are so isolated from all others that they can be separated from the whole and can be treated as individual objects without violating their intrinsic truth. In other words, it is effectively postulated – for the sake of science, basically for the sake of a mathematical ideal, in order that we can construct a systematically organized science – that the objects of my knowledge are already such that they present themselves to me adequately under these categories. Now this is not only a dogmatic claim, for we do not know whether the world is actually organized in this way, but critical reflection on the question of knowledge, and especially Hegel's examination of this question, has shown in detail that this character of objects, which must indeed be assumed if we are to perceive objects *clare et distincte*, does not exist in this way at all. For objects are dynamic and contradictory in themselves and, precisely by virtue of this contradictory character, are actually bound up with all other objects as well. That is why any knowledge which would proceed in a genuinely rigorous manner, which does not simply reserve philosophy for the Sunday sermon while operating with 'healthy common sense' throughout the working day, will not attempt to salvage the demand for *clara et distincta perceptio*.

LECTURE 11

1 July 1958

Ladies and gentlemen,

Before I continue with our discussion of the difficulties which dialectical thinking presents for us, I would like to forestall certain possible misunderstandings and clarify in more detail a couple of points which I may have presented in an overly crude or cursory a fashion in the cut-and-thrust of the argument during the last session. And perhaps a more differentiated account of these things will also provide a further opportunity for me to introduce you rather more deeply to the character of dialectical thinking with regard to a specific problem. I am still talking about the theme of our last session, namely the relationship between the whole and the parts. In the first place, I feel I was probably guilty of some inaccuracy when I referred to the concept of role in order to show how much this concept has effectively and increasingly established itself within contemporary social science, especially under the influence of the theories of the American sociologist Talcott Parsons.[1] In this connection I said that we could principally and immediately recognize the priority of the whole over the part above all in that essential part of our life – i.e. in our work – where we essentially feel ourselves as dependent upon society, but not indeed so much as real parts, that is, as beings that are also reliant upon themselves, since we have already been assigned a role by society itself. With regard to this thought, I do not wish to take anything back here, and I certainly stand by it, but it should be said that the term 'role', as encountered in modern sociology – in contrast to the way it is used in Sartre's *L'être et le néant*,[2] for example – is generally meant to signify the opposite, namely the specifically individual forms of behaviour that we assume in a particular society.[3]

But this terminological correction also effectively brings us to a substantive problem. In the last session, as you will probably recall, I said, rather drastically, that we encounter a kind of priority of the whole over the part in our own experience inasmuch as we perceive social pressure more readily than we do the so-called specific situation in which we find ourselves. And in this connection I had expressly objected to the inductive logic which prevails in the sciences, according to which we advance from particular experiences step by step in a more or less continuous manner until we come to an experience of the whole. Here, too, I would not wish to retreat from the impulse or idea which I have already expressed to you. Nonetheless, I think that the comparison was somewhat misleading insofar as I cannot speak in the strict sense – and the psychologists among you will surely confirm this – of an experience of the whole as a whole without also having an experience of the parts, and vice versa. For neither of these concepts can even be imagined, let alone be thought, without the other. This already furnishes a little model for dialectic. We only really know about the whole as a whole insofar as we perceive or conceptually recognize this whole in relation to parts over against which it presents itself as a whole, and in turn we also only know about the parts as parts insofar as we are able to relate these parts to a whole, such as the visual field, for example. Without this reciprocal relation of opposition, the concepts of whole and part simply forfeit their strict significance. Here therefore, in a quite elementary sense, you can evaluate the truth of the dialectical claim that categories such as these which contradict one another, such as the concept of the whole and the concept of the part, are reciprocally mediated by one another. The point I was trying to emphasize for you in our last session, however, could probably be characterized more rigorously and appropriately by saying that what we initially perceive is neither whole nor part, but a sort of third alternative that is extraordinarily difficult to capture in words. This is what my old teacher Cornelius[4] used to describe as a 'confusion inside a confusion', a concept which is not devoid of a certain objective irony insofar as the concept of 'confusion' already presupposes its opposite. You can see, therefore, just how difficult it is to get any firm hold on what is at issue here. Neither the whole nor the parts are initially perceived as such in an articulated fashion, and what we perceive in the first instance is 'something in general' – something antecedent in a sense to the distinction of whole and part, whereby the priority of the parts over the whole to which we supposedly rise, as affirmed in the usual logic of science, falls away, as does any dogmatic notion of internally and thoroughly articulated forms or *Gestalten* which we are supposed to perceive without any awareness of the parts also being given to us. I should add – in order to avoid misunderstanding – that these fundamental reflections do not specifically relate to the psychological-genetic question as to what we first encounter empirically in terms of our sensory apparatus or our psychological processes. Rather, what we are concerned with here is the question of constitutive priority, that is, of whether we must proceed in each case from some 'first', or whole, in order to be able to produce meaningful judgements. And, as far as this question is concerned, the question regarding the psychological-genetic origin of our ideas is not of course the absolutely decisive one. But I hope that you can also see for yourselves, on the basis of these reflections, that actually we can no more speak here of a priority of the individual parts than we can speak of a logical priority of the whole.

What I should like to discuss here is a difficulty which you may be entirely unaware of as such, but one which makes itself felt all the more tenaciously in the ways all of us tend to think. For even if we are not philosophers, even if we have not been corrupted, as it were, by philosophy, we are still of course thoroughly imbued with all kinds of philosophical conceptions, and it is just these conceptions, which we unwittingly bring to things, that require critical reflection in order to be rethought or rearticulated, far more so indeed than the so-called naive or immediate experiences that we have. This effectively disguised philosophy with which we all grow up, and which is constantly and implicitly knocked into us, as it were, in the course of our scientific and scholarly development, teaches us that genuinely reliable knowledge is that which derives from some absolute 'first' ground or source, quite irrespective of whether this 'first' to which it is ultimately referred is alleged to be an absolute *datum*, a mere given that cannot supposedly be thought away, or behind which we cannot go, or whether this absolute 'first' is presented as pure thought, as Idea, as spirit, or whatever else, which is accorded such absolute priority precisely because it mediates everything particular or individual and constitutes its possibility in the first place. Now if you consider this thesis of an absolute 'first', which is also identical with the entire traditional conception of philosophy – and it is no accident here that philosophy is indeed known as πρώτη φιλοσοφία [*prōtē philosophia*], *prima philosophia*,[5] or 'first philosophy' – and if you reflect explicitly upon the procedures which you employ yourselves in the various areas of scientific knowledge and expertise, I think you will repeatedly discover that you spontaneously believe you do have some such ultimate point of reference as an absolute, reliable and indubitable criterion of truth at your disposal. But it should be clear that this need to have an ultimate point of reference or repair at our disposal is emphatically connected with that need for security with which our knowledge as a whole is intimately bound up.[6] And, from a philo-genetic perspective at least, this knowledge is indeed grounded in our attempt to overcome that anxiety in the face of the overwhelming power of nature which assailed us in archaic times. In this way we strive to appropriate what confronts us as alien, attempt to make it our own and understand it in a certain sense as part of ourselves. This orientation is still at work in every form of what I call the 'philosophy of origins', for the immediately given – that is, the facts of our consciousness – to which we appeal as an ultimate point of reference are indeed precisely always facts of our consciousness, and are supposed therefore to be specific to us, to be our very own, while spirit or consciousness, as the ultimate legitimating ground of all beings, is also a conception on our part, and one that effectively represents an ego which has been metaphysically magnified and inflated into a kind of absolute. When we come to consider and evaluate the various basic types of metaphysics – such as materialism and spiritualism, idealism and empiricism, or again idealism and realism, rationalism and empiricism – we may draw certain consequences from this perspective. For wherever some such 'first', some such absolute or ultimate principle, is proffered, we are effectively dealing with idealist thinking,[7] quite irrespective of whether the theories in question present and understand themselves as idealist or exactly the opposite. Thus this 'first', to which we refer whatever befalls us, whatever is not ourselves – that it may become our own, become such an absolute first – is at the same time always identified with 'ourselves', irrespective of whether we think this self as an empirical person or as a transcendental form, or eventually, as in the metaphysics of speculative idealism, whether we think of ourselves in terms of 'absolute spirit'. As soon as I provide some such ultimate or original principle, what we actually discover is spirit's claim to exercise power over everything that is, for this ultimate principle is itself always something that has been conceived by spirit, and to that extent even in dogmatic materialism – namely in a materialism which is not dialectical – we shall uncover an idealist moment insofar as it believes it possesses an absolute and original principle from the resources of pure thought.

The pathos of dialectical philosophy itself, whatever specific form this philosophy takes, is directed against just such an absolute and original principle. And the greatest challenge, given the intellectual habits with which we have been inculcated, is surely to relinquish this notion, to abandon the idea that we can appeal to such ultimate truth, and to content ourselves instead with what – for a philosophy of origins – must appear and be devalued as something secondary, tertiary, or merely derivative in character. Now this order of evaluation is basically turned on its head by dialectical thought, and indeed already by Hegelian thought, even though, as I have often pointed out to you, the ultimate priority of spirit is nonetheless affirmed within the total context of the Hegelian dialectic. One could say, ultimately, that Hegel remains dialectical precisely insofar as he is at once idealist and non-idealist. But just recall for a moment what I have already explained to you about the Hegelian philosophy in a quite different connection – namely that it does not proceed from a single claim; that it does not, for example, equate the starting point itself with which it begins, and which is also variously presented in Hegel's different works, with the truth; that, on the contrary, it sees truth only in the whole, as he puts it, in the process, in terms of its interrelated moments; that it regards the origin, or the supposed Absolute, as actually the poorest and most absurd thing conceivable. If you bear all this in mind, then you will see that the challenge with which dialectic confronts us is actually that of recognizing truth in the process, in the entwinement, in the constellation of moments rather than in an attempted reduction to some such original principle. And this is significant for the position of dialectic in relation to the two major currents of philosophical thought with which Hegel found himself confronted, and which remain directly relevant for what is described as the contemporary philosophical 'discussion', however pointless such discussion may often appear to be.[8] For the sake of your own strategic orientation here, as I might almost put it, we can say that dialectic cuts in two directions at once: on the one hand, it works against ontology and, on the other hand, against positivism. And, indeed, it creates a specific difficulty for dialectical thought that it cannot comfortably be accommodated within this currently prevailing albeit regressive alternative.

But first I think it is necessary for me to take the bull by the horns today and say something more decisive about the position of dialectical thought in relation to ontology, and indeed preferably in Hegel's own words, lest some of you suspect that, as an opponent of the ontological restoration we see around us today, I am just making an arbitrary appeal to Hegel for support here. This is all the more necessary since, at very different points within the ontological currents of contemporary philosophy, we can also observe various attempts to reclaim Hegel as an ontological thinker.[9] Heidegger himself had

already announced a similar approach in his early work on Duns
Scotus, which indeed contains a kind of heartfelt declaration of sym-
pathy with Hegel,[10] and Heidegger's later work *Holzwege* or 'Forest
Trails' also contains an elaborate and somewhat cautionary interpretation – somewhat reminiscent of the discussion of the two Sophists
in the *Gorgias*[11] – of the 'Introduction' to the *Phenomenology of
Spirit*, and especially of the title Hegel originally intended for the
work (which one critical edition of the book would happily restore).[12]
And similarly, in very different places within the reconstruction of
Thomistic or Scholastic ontology in general which has been undertaken today, we repeatedly find attempts to incorporate Hegel in
some way,[13] attempts which are anything but contemptible since they
clearly betray a dissatisfaction with any static or rigid form of ontology, but which are also extremely difficult to combine with Hegel's
own philosophical intentions. It is true that Hegel's philosophy, at
least in one work, and perhaps his most impressive, namely the *Logic*,
does begin with the concept of 'being'.[14] And it is also true that there
is a sense in which we may regard Hegelian philosophy with some
justification, since logic and metaphysics are here supposed to be the
same, as an explication or interpretation of being as a whole, where
'being' is expressly understood dynamically, namely as 'life', as my
friend Herbert Marcuse[15] has tried to show in his own book on Hegel
and ontology.[16] But I nonetheless believe that such a characterization
of Hegel, although it may be correct *formaliter*, is ultimately incompatible with the essence of Hegelian philosophy since it would itself
inevitably exhibit that character of abstractness, namely that form of
universality and particularity which is specifically criticized by Hegelian thought.

But I would also like to introduce a terminological observation
here which may prove helpful to you in your own reading of Hegel's
texts. For the concept of the abstract in Hegel is by no means
restricted to what we generally understand by the term 'abstract'.[17]
The abstract in Hegel is not merely that empty universality in contrast
to the specific individual contents which go to make it up, although
this concept of abstractness is not absent from Hegel either. And in
our next session we shall read a passage from the *Phenomenology of
Spirit* where this very concept of abstractness is in question. But if
you recall that, for Hegelian philosophy, the merely a-conceptual, the
'this-there' which is not yet aware of its own mediation, the τόδε τι
[*tode ti*],[18] is just as empty and indeterminate as the emptiest and
most generic of concepts, then you will understand that the concept
of the abstract in Hegel may sometimes signify the very opposite of
what it means in ordinary speech: namely that which is merely

isolated, which is not yet reflected-into-itself – where through this reflection-into-itself, through this unfolding of its own indwelling contradictions, it would know itself in its relation to the whole. The non-conceptual, the isolated particular which has been arbitrarily broken off – as this forms the content, to a considerable degree, of the positive sciences – is therefore just as exposed to the verdict of mere abstractness as is the empty universal concept. Thus the uniniti-ated and as yet uninstructed reader is confronted with the astonishing paradox that precisely what we are used to regarding as concrete – namely the individual data, the individual facts with which our knowledge begins – very often appears as the abstract, whereas 'the concept' in the specifically Hegelian sense, namely in the sense of the particular or individual which comes to comprehend itself, then effec-tively bears the attribute of the concrete.[19]

In this sense it may therefore be said that such a general charac-terization of being as we have just mentioned – even if this is for-mally correct, even if we might say that the entire conception of being in Hegel is precisely that of an internally dynamic and indeed internally contradictory totality – is also false insofar as every such isolated proposition, every such isolated claim, is itself false. And what Hegel would fundamentally hold against ontology – any phi-losophy of being which now believes it possesses the Absolute in the concept of being or in being itself – is not the thought that being is indeed a dynamic totality but, rather, that such a determination of being is one-sided insofar as it remains unfolded, is not rendered explicit. But since for Hegel the explication of concepts, the process through which these concepts become conscious of themselves, is for its part an element of their own truth, such an abstract determina-tion of being, however correct it may initially appear, however correct in itself it may also be, it is nonetheless inadequate for itself, that is, according to the measure of its own reflection-into-itself, and thereby precisely false. But this thought, which should now be clear to you after all that we have already discussed, leads in concentrated form to a range of formulations in Hegel which are so trenchant that we cannot fail to recognize the pathos of this philosophy: it is directed against the idea that philosophy should find its absolute in such an abstract, isolated and hypostasized concept as that of being as such.[20]

I would just like to offer you a couple of examples one after another to show how this critical motif is developed by Hegel in a particularly concentrated way. Thus at that point in the *Logic* where 'being' is identified with 'nothing', Hegel writes: 'In its indeterminate immediacy it [being] is equal only to itself...'[21] In other words, once 'being' is expressed in its immediacy, it contains no moment of non-identity.

> It is pure indeterminateness and emptiness. – There is *nothing* to be intuited in it, if one can speak here of intuition; or it is only this pure, empty intuiting itself. Just as little is anything to be thought in it, or, it is equally only this empty thinking. Being, the indeterminate immediate is in fact *nothing*, and neither more nor less than nothing.[22]

But I think I should also add something else here in order to clarify this point. One must always read Hegel in a very differentiated manner, and above all with a constant readiness to think through all the possibilities harboured within a concept, just as Nietzsche later wished his own readers to do.[23] Now you might be tempted to read this passage merely as a logical treatise, as if it meant to say simply that the concept of being, precisely in its complete abstractness and lack of content, in its immediacy, passes over directly into the concept of nothing, as you may see for yourself in any standard manual of philosophy where the first stage of the Hegelian dialectic is being described. But you would fail to understand this passage properly if you did read it in this way. For the prevailing tone here also gives us to understand that the concept of being itself – if it is deployed without going beyond it, that is, without releasing the process contained within the concept of being itself – is nugatory as a concept – that is, as a medium of cognition or as the ultimate substrate of philosophy.

In other words, the assertion that 'being is nothing' bears a double face for Hegel. On the one hand, it signifies precisely what I have just suggested to you, namely that the abstractness of the concept of being means that it cannot be distinguished from the concept of nothing and passes over into its own opposite. That is what you may call the logical-metaphysical side of the concept, and the famous claim that Hegelian philosophy is a logic and metaphysics in one can perhaps nowhere be better understood than here in this connection. On the other hand, however, you should also bear in mind that a proposition such as 'being is nothing' is also a critical proposition which tells us that, as long as we talk simply about being without actually unfolding the life of this concept in its own meaning, then all our talk of being is worth nothing at all, and the Absolute we believe we have within our grasp is nothing but a mirage. Again, I have certainly not been reading anything into Hegel here, as I can clearly substantiate with reference to a passage from the *Encyclopaedia* which I shall now read out for you. The point here is to show that what this doctrine

represents is less an ontological quality of being than the deficiency
of any philosophical thought which simply terminates in being. Thus:
'When *being* is expressed as a predicate of the absolute, this provides
the first definition of the latter' – namely the absolute beginning as
understood by a philosophy which seeks the beginning or first principle, as understood by *prima philosophia*. Thus '*the absolute*' – or
that which is utterly 'first' – '*is being*. This is (in the thought) the
absolutely first, most abstract' – i.e., which still lacks its fulfilment
through a process of explication – 'and most impoverished [*dürftig-
ste*] definition.'[24] And, by specifically introducing the notion of
'impoverishment' at this point, Hegel also clearly shows that he is
criticizing the use of the concept of being, however necessary it may
be for the subsequent process of dialectical unfolding. That is, he is
telling us that he regards a proposition such as 'The absolute is being'
as false. But since this proposition provides the very form of a philosophy of origins, which itself necessarily underlies every ontological
intention, it also implies a repudiation of the possibility of ontology,
of that which today is so often invoked in its name.

To conclude, I shall read you another passage from Hegel, one
which is expressly directed against Jacobi,[25] whose philosophy of
immediate intuition indeed roughly corresponded in his time to the
meaning of the philosophies of origins of our own time, insofar as
the latter are developed from the idea of categorical intuition. And
you will see how much this critique of the concept of being amounts
in effect to a critique of any kind of ontology. Hegel writes:

> With this totally abstract purity of continuity, that is, with this inde-
> terminateness and emptiness of representation, it is indifferent whether
> one names this abstraction 'space' or 'pure intuition' or 'pure thought.'
> It is altogether the same as what an Indian calls Brahma, when for
> years on end, looking only at the tip of his nose, externally motionless
> and equally unmoved in sensation, representation, phantasy, desire,
> and so on, he inwardly says only *Om, Om, Om*, or else says nothing
> at all. This dull, empty consciousness, taken as consciousness, is just
> this – *being*.[26]

You will know that it has become common these days to return to
the standard orthography of Hegel's time and write *Sein* as *Seyn*,[27]
or being as 'beyng', and thus effectively to remove the concept from
the realm of discursive thought and turn it into a magical word that
is precisely meant to designate the Absolute in an immediate fashion.
There is no doubt, so I am convinced, that Hegel has no other word
or expression for this 'beyng' than precisely 'Om, om, om'. That is

to say, he would actually see here nothing but a reversion to mere mythology or an abandonment and betrayal of all that Western civilization has effectively struggled to achieve in the course of its conscious development. And any attempt to present Hegelian philosophy as genuinely compatible with such 'Om-philosophies' strikes me only as a sophistical attempt to cover one's own questionable manoeuvres with the authority of a thinker whose substantial concern is essentially the substance of reason, and who is here being harnessed for philosophical purposes whose substance is, rather, the renunciation of reason itself. That is all for now regarding the question of Hegel and ontology.

But here I should also like to say something about the relationship between Hegel and positivism – and this may perhaps prove the most difficult point to grasp in this context. For if my experience of the cultural and intellectual climate to which the young in particular are exposed today is not entirely mistaken, I believe that a kind of bifurcated thinking prevails, or is at least latently present, among the younger generation in this connection. Thus you may effectively say, 'Well, of course, metaphysics, that's basically ontology, where there must be some eternal values, or an Absolute or an absolute principle of some kind, and if there is no such thing, then we are left with nothing but mere facts – that is to say, there is actually nothing but what the positive sciences ascertain in their methodical way, and anything else must be shunned as illusion.' But it is precisely my innermost purpose in these lectures to show you the problem with this alternative: either metaphysics, on the one hand – and metaphysics amounts to a rigid doctrine of being and of invariant eternal values – or science, as an exclusive orientation to what is the case, and *tertium non datur*; to show you that this rigid alternative is itself the expression of the reified consciousness of today, which demands official documentation for every thought, which requires us to ask of every thought: Excuse me, but where exactly do you belong? If you are metaphysical, you must be concerned with being; if you are scientific, you must be concerned with positive facts – and *that is that*. But this very way of thinking in terms of set and rigidified alternatives seems to me to embody the fateful character of the contemporary state of consciousness in general. In these lectures I should like, in however modest a fashion, to do my part in breaking the power of this idea in you, in helping you to see that avoiding an orientation to 'being' certainly does not mean falling into an obstinate cult of the scientific facts. Again, on the other hand, when we are overcome by a *tedium scientiae*, when we are no longer satisfied simply with registering facts, we are not necessarily or unconditionally forced to seek nourishment from some preordained metaphysics of being which is conveniently served up for us. But, if you are to work your way through and beyond this alternative, you must resist the conviction that all this is somehow already prepared for you, that these two alternatives are there waiting for you, and you just have to decide for metaphysics or for positivism, rather like choosing between Adenauer and Ollenhauer in an election.[28] Rather, you must recognize that this is precisely how reified thought itself, how the power of the administered world, has effectively compelled our own consciousness to think in terms of such pre-given alternatives. And that is why it is so important for us, I believe, to distinguish dialectic just as vigorously from positivism as from that impoverished parody of metaphysics represented by contemporary forms of ontology. But please do not understand this to mean that dialectic is distinguished from positivism essentially by taking the dish of facts which is served to us by the special sciences and then spicing it up with the sauce of faith, of meaning, of some higher principle. Likewise, it strikes me as a boundless misunderstanding of any consciousness that cannot find nourishment in mere facts to imagine that every thought which goes beyond a mere *factum* just amounts to saying, 'Well, yes, this all has some kind of meaning. Everything is arranged for the best, and we just have to be satisfied and content with it as it is.' On the contrary: what goes beyond mere facticity in the eyes of dialectic, what bestows on dialectic its metaphysical right to life, is the very opposite of this – it is precisely the rebellion against the idea that the world of facts to which we have been bound, and which is utterly meaningless, should have the last word in our existence. Dialectic is the attempt, precisely in and through the critique of this world of facts which holds sway over us, to perceive the possibility of something else, without this world of facts itself being in the least transfigured by us in the process.

As it turns out I shall not be able, today, to explore the relationship between dialectic and positivism in any detail.[29] But I would just like to say to you here today that the difference between dialectical and positivistic thinking should at least be evident to you by now. Dialectical thought is distinguished from positivist thought in that it is anything but 'natural' in character. What I mean is this. If we do think dialectically, this cannot mean that, faced with the temptations of metaphysics, we simply cling instead to a kind of ordinary human 'common sense' or turn to some kind of self-styled Common Sense Philosophy. It is rather the reverse, and here I come to another challenge which is posed by dialectical thinking. The challenge of dialectical thinking, at this point, consists essentially in this: you must cast overboard the established habits of thought with which you are so familiar and take upon yourselves the labour and exertion of the concept, and indeed in this very precise sense, that you come to recognize how everything which is given to us so 'naturally' that we have no doubts about it is not for its part something natural. For you will recognize it as something already 'reflected-within-itself' or – expressed in materialist terms – as something which is already socially mediated within itself, and what presents itself to us as nature is thus in truth 'second nature'[30] rather than first nature. Thus you will recognize that, specifically in order to allow a damaged and oppressed nature what belongs to it, we must not allow ourselves to be blinded precisely by that semblance of naturalness which a rigid world of conventionalized perceptions requires us at every quarter to accept. And in our next session I shall say something further about this, and about the critical intention of thought in contrast to the uncritical and merely accommodating posture of positivism.

LECTURE 12

3 July 1958

Ladies and gentlemen,

In the last session I had begun to say something about the relationship between dialectic and positivism and, indeed, specifically from the perspective of the double contrast between dialectic, on the one hand, and any philosophies which appeal to some 'first' ground or principle, on the other. And in this connection, with a certain interpretive violence of which I am well aware, one may also regard positivism as belonging among such philosophies, insofar as positivism of every sort finds its absolutely first principle in the data provided by experience, whether in those of consciousness or in so-called protocol sentences. However, I feel duty bound here to say at least that such an identification of positivism with a philosophy of origins is not entirely correct, or, to put this more broadly, the identification of empiricism with any 'metaphysics' in the usual sense is not entirely just. For, while it is quite true that a certain first principle is indeed assumed in this context, namely the principle of just such a 'givenness', the principle is not specified in substantive terms. Thus where the ontological and, in a narrower sense, idealist or rationalist philosophies also believe they can positively specify the first ground or principle – whether it be as spirit, consciousness, transcendental synthesis, being, or whatever the ground or principle in question may be called – the positivist and empiricist positions do indeed claim that the given, or the facts, provide their ultimate point of reference as far as all genuine knowledge is concerned. It lies in the nature of the case here that the concept of such facticity itself does not specify or anticipate its own determinate character. For it is a mere general concept which can in the event be specified in terms of different or changing content as the case may be. And this also explains why positivistic forms of thought cannot actually be identified directly with what I call a philosophy of origins, and indeed why – in the context of the contemporary debate – these forms of thought regard themselves as emphatically opposed to the ontological tendencies of the present time. You might say that it would seem rather absurd and far-fetched if I now attempted to indicate, and even with some precision, the position of dialectic in relation to positivism – for it is surely quite obvious that dialectic is anti-positivist in character, and that it was the entire positivist trend of Western philosophy, as this has spread throughout Europe since the death of Hegel, which specifically brought speculative dialectical thought itself to an end, at least from a historical point of view. And I would not contest this claim, yet the relationship between dialectic and positivism is actually by no means as straightforward as such reflections suggest. If I may remind you for a moment that the problem of dialectic, from one point of view, is not that of starting from some preconceived totality but, rather, to explore the 'windowless' power of the whole – to borrow an expression from an older form of speculative metaphysics[1] – at work within the individual givens of experience in each case. And it is precisely in this lack of any pre-given or entirely conclusive highest concept that there is actually an inner affinity between dialectic and positivism, and indeed I have often found in my own work – when I have drawn the appropriate conclusions from these reflections and approached individual phenomena in a 'micrological' way, as I have already expressed it, without bringing them under their higher or generic concept in advance – that I am reproached as follows: 'Well, there is basically no difference at all between positivism and what you are doing here.' And there are some grey areas here, which have also been reflected historically in certain strands of dialectical thought which I would not exactly describe as 'positivistic' but which nonetheless involve a certain tendency towards sceptical relativism, something which is indeed deeply related to positivism, as you may see particularly clearly from the Anglo-Hegelian School in the case of that extraordinarily significant dialectical thinker Francis Bradley.[2] And I gladly take this opportunity to draw your attention to the two great works of Bradley, his *Appearance and Reality* and his *Logic*,[3] which in a specifically speculative and philosophical sense are probably the most radical and original contributions to the theory of dialectic which have been made since Hegel. These works offer extraordinarily subtle and difficult investigations which demand considerable attention and patience, but I can assure you that the substantive wealth of these reflections amply reward such patience.

But to return specifically to the relationship between dialectic and positivism, I would remind you above all, since we are concerned with substantive issues here, that in a certain sense dialectic is precisely what the movement of phenomenology perhaps unjustifiably claimed to be: an attitude other than the 'natural attitude', an attitude which already approaches everything which is regarded as a given, as a fact, with a certain scepticism, an attitude which tends to seek out the hidden powers of the whole behind what appears to us, behind what we encounter as given. The distinction between essence and appearance is indeed utterly constitutive for dialectical thought itself, as we can already see from the way that concepts come to move only by entering into a process of reflection; that is to say, this reflection brings out in the concepts themselves a substance, as it were, which was not actually intended in, and indeed was concealed in, their merely initial appearance, in their apparent or surface meaning. And if I often speak in these sessions about the different forms of resistance to dialectic, and try and make you specifically aware of them in order to facilitate your access to dialectical thought, I believe we are dealing with a particularly widespread form of resistance at this very point. This is the suspicion that attaches to dialectic of being all too clever, of being a kind of secret wisdom, the suspicion that we are simply never satisfied with what is actually and specifically given to us, and the suspicion, above all, that the objective moment of dialectic would actually deprive human beings of everything that they subjectively believe about themselves, everything that they take to be their real interest and concern. Now dialectic does indeed involve this moment, and it would also certainly be a serious mistake to deny this and thus render dialectic innocuous. But if for quite different reasons, for reasons that are grounded in social experience, we have once come to see that the world in which we live effectively weaves its veil not through any particular lies and intrigues but by through its own immanent law-like character, and repeatedly generates appearances which contradict what this world actually is, then we shall generally come to share this mistrust, then we shall no longer be able simply to accept the given, the positive, which is presented to us above all by the special sciences as the ultimate legitimate source of certainty – no longer able to accept it precisely in the way it is presented here. This very capacity to doubt what is given to us appears increasingly – under the tremendous pressure of the 'givens' within which we exist today – to be slipping away from human beings. And if we can speak of a certain transference or extension of ego-weakness into the process of thinking itself, then I would see this precisely here, where human beings capitulate before the so-called givens without displaying that very mistrust which, from the perspective of conventional conscious-ness, of the mere acceptance of the world as it initially presents itself, cannot fail to create the impression of something artificial and all too clever which does violence to the way things are. I believe that it is far more appropriate to concede this, far more appropriate to claim that, in an entirely alienated world – a world that exists entirely θέσει [*thesei*] rather than φύσει [*phusei*][4] – what we need is precisely this arguably unnatural exertion on the part of consciousness if we are to break through the surface of second nature, than it would be to try and introduce dialectic simply as a kind of sound common sense. Of course dialectic does have a good deal to do with sound common sense, and the steps it takes in each individual case are always steps guided by rational reflection. As I have already attempted to show you, it is not as if there were another kind of source of reason, a speculative source, which would itself be separated by a gulf from the merely reflective rationality of the 'understanding'.[5] But, on the other hand, I emphatically believe that the dialectical mode of think-ing is distinguished from the ordinary use of the understanding pre-cisely because it refuses to be satisfied with the givenness we have described, because it properly begins its work exactly there where the given confronts us most inexorably, where dialectical thought attempts to penetrate what is opaque and seemingly impenetrable, and to bring all this into movement. And if I were not afraid that some of the natural scientists among you will tell me that scientific analogies from the mouth of a philosopher of dialectical persuasion always have something fatefully problematic about them, then I would say that dialectical thought is always involved in something like an intellectual version of atomic fission, although I would certainly not claim any-thing like the celebrated status of the modern natural sciences for the efforts and exertions of dialectic, which as we know has no such brilliant results to show as the creation of the atomic bomb.

I said to you that the specific position of dialectic in relation to positivism already lies in the way that the givens which furnish the ultimate point of reference for the positivist view, and which standard positivist epistemology typically describes as 'the immediately given', are recognized for their part as something which is mediated. In other words, dialectical thought shows that the ultimate point of reference to which our claim to knowledge appeals as a solid and secure pos-session is not an ultimate point at all, but something that generally presupposes in turn what it purports to produce from itself. I have tried to develop this thought in a very emphatic fashion in the third chapter of my *Metacritique of Epistemology*[6] and would draw your attention to that discussion here. For there you will find a detailed attempt to show that, through their interconnection, the particular categories of what is called the theory of knowledge – which are supposed to constitute the objective world in the first place as this is understood by the traditional epistemological projects – for their part presuppose that same objective world, namely existence in space and time, just as no existence in space and time can be thought in turn without those categories. I cannot present these developed dialectical reflections properly in the context of these short introductory lectures. But instead of that I think at least I owe you one or two specific indications of what I mean here in terms of the argument between dialectical and positivist thought. And since the content of dialectic, both in Hegel's *Phenomenology* and in the work of Marx, is indeed essentially a social content, and since I know that many of you are particularly interested in questions of social science, I believe it is particularly fitting if I just take some examples from this domain – forgive me if I give 'examples' here, for I know I should not really do so, but it's a hard life being a dialectician[7] – and specifically from the positivistic side of the social sciences, and in part from what is known as 'empirical social research' insofar as this aims to gather information about the opinions and forms of behaviour of individuals and even of statistically defined social groups.

Thus in an investigation into the community of Darmstadt, for which I was responsible in the later stages of the enquiry,[8] it emerged that a substantial proportion of the population harbour a specifically hostile attitude to the municipal authorities of the city, and it turned out that extraordinarily negative judgements were routinely expressed with regard to municipal officials and employees. In this connection one would initially be driven to think about specific experiences which people have had in relation to the municipal authorities in this sort of city. And in the context of any rather purblind investigation, that is to say, one which has still to be enlightened about itself – and the significance of dialectic for empirical social research, it seems to me, is essentially that of casting some kind of light on otherwise purblind approaches – one would just have said, 'Well then, in Darmstadt that's how it is: it's an old official sort of place and an old administrative centre; the people here have had a good deal of contact with bureaucracy and have had a lot of negative experiences in the process, and this is expressed in the rather hostile attitudes which we have discovered.' But a dialectical thinker would not be satisfied with this illuminating thesis at such a point, for here he would at least ask whether this negative attitude of the population towards the public employees in a particular city or area is actually derived from specific experiences and specific factors connected with the place in question. That is, he will raise the question whether we are not rather dealing here with what American sociologists would describe in terms of 'generalized attitudes', namely with the way that people may already bring such a negative attitude to bureaucracy in general and then apply this generalized perspective in their judgements concerning public employees, namely the judgements which had been identified in our particular empirical study. Perhaps I can tell you here about the somewhat remarkable way in which I came to entertain this kind of suspicion, for this may also reveal something to you about how the relation between empirical social approaches and dialectical considerations actually works. I am very familiar with a particular work which deals with a completely different area, a study in the sociology of literature which is concerned with a novelist who was not in fact German. The author of the study showed that, in the novel principally under discussion, we find that a specific opposition within the petit bourgeois world is at least suggested here, even if it is not developed in expressly theoretical or sociological terms, namely a certain antagonism between lower- and middle-ranking public employees and somewhat freer, more independent individuals who did not receive anything resembling a regular salary.[9] In the eyes of those who have a somewhat freer and more independent existence – small innkeepers or artisans, for example – the officials frequently appear as parasites who do not have to exert themselves nearly as much as they themselves do, and who can also look forward to the security of a pension at the end of a not especially laborious life. In the eyes of the officials, on the other hand, those who have a freer existence, on account of the greater earnings they could potentially make, appear as a distinctly enviable group in several material respects, and also as one that is not nearly as accustomed to the virtues of order and reliability as they themselves are. I remembered all this in connection with that other study, and so I found myself asking whether this immanent opposition between two groups, namely the public employees and everyone else within the middle and lower-middle class, might not also find significant expression in people's attitudes precisely in an area where the group of such employees was in relative terms rather large. And the conclusion which I drew from all this was that I directed the investigation, or rather attempted to redirect it, by ensuring it also included a question, or complex of questions, which could determine firstly whether the people under discussion who had expressed negative judgements about public employees in the city at issue had in fact come into any significant contact with these employees, and secondly whether they had specifically negative experiences if and when they did so. Now where such techniques of empirical social research are concerned we do not ask an abstract question like 'Have you had negative experiences', but we enquire after specific negative experiences, for it is only when such specific reports are available that we can check on whether anything is really behind it. I am proud to say that in this case things actually turned out as I had anticipated, for there was a complete discrepancy between the negative judgements about public employees and the actual experiences involving such employees. In other words, we were dealing here with an externally motivated ideology – and indeed, I might add, one which involves society as a whole. For this is a sort of opinion which somehow hangs in the atmosphere of society as a whole, which people in certain numerically significant groups absorb and which affects the 'experiences' which they have. In other words, the 'givens' which we encounter here, in this case the negative attitudes about public employees, which a purely positivistic sociology would simply register, analyse and interpret, are revealed once again to be a function of an entire social process, or that what is individual, particular and concrete actually shows itself as dependent upon the totality [. . .][10] And of course this general mood or attitude towards state employees would not exist if it were not built up from numerous individual cases of such hostility. There is a kind of interaction in play here.

Another example may help to show you the outstanding social-theoretical significance which attaches to what is known as motivational analysis in the field of empirical sociology. For it is only through motivational analysis, that is, by discovering the motivating ground for such negative judgements, that we can even begin to break through the context of delusion surrounding the merely given. I may refer here to another investigation – one conducted in the context of industrial sociology[11] – where we came across a particular kind of hostility on the part of workers who were employed in a specific industrial plant. In considering the investigation of merely subjective opinions, that is, in examining the information concerning the merely subjective data of the hostility, we did not stop there but also simultaneously examined the objective data directly connected with the industrial plant itself. And it emerged that the workers' superiors within the plant acted in an uncommonly reasonable, humane and sympathetic way in the context of the general situation; but it also emerged that, for quite specific reasons, the overall organization of the plant, which was somewhat old-fashioned, exerted continual pressure on the workers, and it turned out – to put the matter briefly

– that the superiors, or the people towards whom the workers in question had reacted with hostility, were simply 'character masks',[12] to use a Marxian expression, and that the hostility had nothing to do with the actual people themselves. Thus, if the workers developed a certain hostility to these people, this was because they had thereby simply transferred an objective relation – the structural relation with their superiors along with the specific relations of production operative within the business – to these individuals, although these individuals themselves were only 'masks' of the functions they performed. What we are dealing with here is a process of extraordinarily far-reaching significance, to which I wished at least to draw your attention *en passant*, namely the process of personalization. And some insight into concrete dialectical operations here may help you to avoid falling victim to this mechanism of personalization yourselves. What is meant by 'personalization' in this context is simply this: the greater the power of objective relations becomes, and above all the more anonymous the relations of power and pressure in which we are caught up become, the more this alien and anonymous character itself becomes unbearable. As a result, if we fail to reflect closely upon these things, we experience an ever stronger tendency to project what in reality is due to such objective circumstances precisely upon personal factors, upon the characteristics of particular human beings or particular groups of human beings. And here I would voice the thought that the racist delusions of National Socialism was able to exercise the extraordinary influence that it actually did only because it responded to precisely this need – that is, because it burdened specific vulnerable human beings and vulnerable human groups with responsibility for sufferings and misfortunes which in reality were anonymous in character and utterly unbearable for that reason. From the psychodynamic perspective, this process also possesses a number of other advantages, for it is much easier to project one's own aggressive affects upon specific persons than is the case with more objective or material relations. But if we naively rest content with registering what people in general happen to think, then we ourselves fall victim to that delusive mechanism of personalization which I have attempted, at least in outline, to describe for you in my preceding observations.

I may also mention, as a third example, something which I already encountered in America, for when I intervened in just this sense by introducing dialectical considerations into the supposedly spontaneous running of the sciences I certainly had my difficulties, even if I also enjoyed some modest triumphs. Thus I challenged the notion that people took pleasure in particular 'hit songs' specifically on

account of the songs themselves; and when I considered the particular
preferences and rejections which were identified here, or the relevant
'likes' and 'dislikes', as they are called in the jargon of American
'communication research', and attempted to relate them to the objective givens, it turned out that the songs people like most are the ones
that are played the most and with which they are most familiar, while
the songs with which they are not so familiar and which they do not
hear so frequently are generally rejected by them.[13] And when we ask
in turn why these particular songs are played so frequently, we also
discover that certain subjective qualities and preferences are involved
here. What you find in this connection is an extraordinarily complex
system of reciprocal relations which is rather the opposite of the
straightforward or immediate givens with which so-called opinion
research is generally concerned. For opinion research is indeed usually
interested in discovering, for administrative or commercial reasons,
what people are for or against, as the case may be. And if we simply
stop here, with this 'for and against', then we only help to weave that
veil around the so-called givens of which I spoke to you at the
beginning.

The positivistic social scientists among you will probably object at
this point that all of the thoughts I have developed for you here are
for their part entirely compatible with positivism, and that I could
have presented these same thoughts in investigations which would
have to be conducted along more or less positivistic lines if they were
to prove conclusive. Now I would not actually deny this, and would
like to repeat here that dialectical thought is precisely not a kind of
intuitionism, is not some form of thinking that is entirely different in
character or kind from the thinking which is ordinarily practised in
the logic of the sciences. It is simply that dialectical thought, in contrast to such thinking, is expressly self-reflective in character. In other
words, dialectical thought is thought that sheds light on itself, as I
put this earlier, rather than proceeding in a rigid and purblind fashion.
In other words, I do believe that the transition to dialectical thought
is necessarily implicit in every so-called positivistic investigation that
is internally consistent and truly self-aware, just as we discovered in
our recent seminars on sociology that a sociologist such as Weber,
who saw himself at least as entirely positivist in orientation, found
himself driven to certain dialectical formulations under the impact of
the data which he himself undertook to explore and develop, even
though these formulations were quite incompatible with his own
·position regarding the theory of scientific knowledge, incompatible
with his own philosophy so to speak.[14] But I don't wish to stop here
with this all too convenient point. For above all I want to remind

you and bring home to you that when, in the investigations I have mentioned, we keep referring back to the social whole, or society in its entirety, in relation to a more tangible, determinate and specific social field, we are dealing here with something other than a mere hypothesis. The reason for this is simple: in the case of a hypothesis it must be possible for you to test the principal content by recourse to some *experimentum crucis*, so that you can in turn convert this hypothesis itself into a kind of scientific given. But in all of the examples I have provided for you here this is certainly not the case, for society as a whole, or even the prevailing ideology as a whole – that which lies in the general atmosphere, as it were, that which brings human beings into a certain decisive relationship to public employees, to their superiors, to hit songs, as the case may be – this is something that you cannot actually grasp in the same way that you grasp the individual and specific attitudes to these phenomena, attitudes which you can not only identify empirically but which you can even measure and quantify as such. In other words, what theory, what the knowledge of society as a whole which precedes such an empirical investigation, brings to this sort of investigation is indeed a certain power which sets the results of such an investigation into internal motion, yet it is not itself a given like the givens which are themselves discovered in the process. Rather, it is more like a centre of forces which for its own part largely eludes the precise and unambiguous mechanisms of verification and falsification. One must also add that the significance of this recourse to the general structures of society or the ideologies of society as a whole, or whatever it may be, certainly does not lie in the idea of simply opposing some further particular instance of knowledge to those particular instances of knowledge that we have already criticized in this connection. On the contrary, the point is just to grasp and describe the social tendency within which these particular instances of knowledge can be grasped for their own part. Such a procedure therefore cannot for its part simply be redeemed here and now, for indeed its essential intention is not to be redeemed through observational data, through the firm and reliable declaration 'Yes, now we have it, this is society as a whole.' Rather, its significance is solely that of grasping the factual data themselves in their movement, even though this would precisely contradict the positivist conception of the formation of hypotheses.

You may say in reply, 'How then do you actually operate with such concepts, and what is the path which justifies you in using them, assuming that you wish to avoid falling into merely arbitrary conjecture or into a kind of airy speculation?' And here precisely I think I have another opportunity to show you in an extremely tangible and striking way what I have tried to describe for you in very general philosophical terms with the concept of negativity or contradiction. For the path which leads us to these reflections is a twofold one. In the first place, I must in a sense already bring something with me from without. Thus I believe that it is an essential part of any dialectical thinking to be a thinking which is always both within its object and also outside of its object, for the movement which we perceive in the object also always presupposes some knowledge of what transpires outside of the object in question – that is, some knowledge of the wider context and connections in which the object itself stands. If I do not recognize that we live in a society in which, for example, the relation to one's superiors in the context of work has a determinate objective structure, and involves a determinate aspect of perpetual pressure which already shapes in advance every personal relationship, then of course I will never even come across the thought that one's superior is to some extent a character mask of the function which he or she has to perform. But secondly, on the other hand, the path which actually leads me to set the merely empirical observations into dialectical motion is none other than that through which the individual givens that I have before me turn out to be contradictory or problematic within themselves. To formulate this in a very blunt and thus rather primitive and inadequate manner: in the first place, there is a contradiction between the remarks of those who were questioned in the Darmstadt investigation ('I regard all public employees as idle, as a bureaucracy which fails to take our pressing needs seriously') and the fact that the people who spoke in this way either had had no particularly bad experiences with public employees or had actually had no experience with them at all. This contradiction, which I here encounter in the so-called given itself, thus compels me to go beyond the given and to introduce something more comprehensive and universal in its place. In this connection you will have noticed that, in this very example, and in a number of others, I have certainly spoken of society as a whole, yet you will also have noticed that the kinds of substantiation I have offered you in this regard are by no means as abstractly all-embracing as the concept of society as a whole implies. This means that I am driven here to adopt the perspective of an immanent contradiction between the public employees on the one hand and independent forms of social existence in specific social strata on the other, something which itself then finds expression in that contradiction between experience and opinion. And it would then be another further and much more complicated step which would go far beyond the rudimentary reflections which I introduced earlier, if we were to proceed from here, on the basis of this contradiction, to address questions concerning the structure of society as a whole. Or to go further: the path which has brought us to regard the tensions within a particular industrial plant not as something conditioned by personal factors but as something which is conditioned, on the one side, by the objective relation to superiors in the particular plant and, on the other, by specific conditions of production which determine that relation in the plant in question, this path is actually none other than this – that the contradiction between the judgement of the respondents regarding the supposed unfriendliness or maliciousness of their superiors and the objective insight into the actual character of these human beings and of the process of production itself is what has brought us to qualify those supposedly ultimate givens which we first encountered when we simply questioned the respondents in the course of our investigation. All this, of course, is in a profound sense pre-philosophical, or is not dialectical in the radical sense, for the path and progress of dialectic consists precisely in challenging every concept of facticity, of immediate givenness, of particular observational data, such as I have just used here. But since indeed we have interpreted dialectic not as some heteronomous form or structure which is simply contrasted with science as such, but rather as science which has been raised to its own self-consciousness, it was perhaps still useful to show you how particular scientific work is driven by its own immanent dynamic to approach the perspective of dialectic, and thereby to clarify for you the difference between positivism and dialectic.

LECTURE 13

8 July 1958

Ladies and gentlemen,

It seems to me that the best way to demonstrate the specific difficulties which dialectic presents, and what I have called the challenge of dialectical thinking – now that I have initially illustrated this challenge for you with a few models regarding the question of 'first' principles – would be to confront really dialectical thinking with the classical rules of the game which – we may claim – to a considerable extent have undoubtedly underpinned scientific thought to this very day. And without question these are the four rules which can be found at the beginning of Descartes's *Discours de la méthode*.[1] Now you may say that we are already talking here about an essentially rationalist form of philosophy, but I am not particularly interested at this point in exploring the question of rationalism versus empiricism, a question which also implicitly arises in connection with the four Cartesian rules. Rather, I would like to talk to you here about these Cartesian rules in terms of the spirit of scientific method generally, for which, as I would ask you for the moment to accept, they are crucial far beyond the context of specific differences between rival schools of philosophy. I might also just point out, in this connection, that the very distinction between rationalism and empiricism is by no means as rigid as it tends to appear in the context of standard examination questions for example, for if you read Bacon[2] and Descartes together, you will find whole tracts of text where you would not easily be able to tell which of the two was the author, and this is because the spirit of science itself is here revealed far more emphatically than the spirit of any particular philosophical school, and indeed the spirit of science is, principally speaking, the spirit of method.

The famous Cartesian demand, which furnishes the first of his rules, is the demand for *clara et distincta perceptio*, that is, for 'clear and perspicuous', or – better – 'distinct' perception or cognition, where Descartes's formula is specifically intended to apply to all possible objects of knowledge. For at this point Descartes does not make any distinction, for example, between the things of sense perception and mental representations or the intellectual realm in general. For the thought expressed here refers in an extraordinarily broad sense to all objective knowledge as such. I shall just read out the formulation precisely as he presents it. First of all, Descartes traces his rules back to a certain resolution or decision which he tells us he had already made.

> And as a multiplicity of laws often furnishes excuses for evil-doing, and as a State is hence much better ruled when, having but very few laws, these are most strictly observed; so, instead of the great number of precepts of which Logic is composed, I believe that I should find the four which I shall state quite sufficient, provided that I adhered to a firm and constant resolve never on any single occasion to fail in their observance.[3]

I would immediately draw your attention to the role which is played by 'resolve' here, by an act of will – by what later philosophy would describe as 'subjective positing'. These rules in their entirety are concerned more with ensuring that we proceed rigorously in the spirit of mastering nature, and that we deploy our intellectual powers in an internally rigorous and coherent manner, than they are with allowing thought for its part to respond to its object, to the matter itself. And it actually seems to me that the defining characteristic of rationalism is much more readily to be discovered here than it is in the usual and vulgar distinction between rational and sensuous forms of knowledge. You can already see here that the central thought is that method is essentially determined by the will to establish order in a rigorous manner through the exercise of our mental capacities, and where, by contrast, the thought of passivity, the thought of responding and cleaving to the matter itself, recedes from view in a rather remarkable fashion. And if I may anticipate for a moment, one could say that dialectic is ultimately the attempt, in a manner that also effectively corresponds to rationalism and the rationalist tradition, to release the power of rigorous thought itself, but to do so in a way that may also bind this power by confronting it with the essence of the objects to which our cognition actually relates. That would be the key difference at issue here.

With regard to the rules he had decided upon, Descartes writes: 'The first of these was to accept nothing as true which I did not clearly recognize to be so: that is to say, carefully to avoid precipitation and prejudice in judgments, and to accept in them nothing more than what was presented to my mind so clearly and distinctly that I could have no occasion to doubt it.'[4] Now if anyone were to ask you in general terms what the sciences which you pursue effectively require of you, I believe you would come up with something not so different from this, and I am certainly far from wishing to belittle the significant motivations that are implicit in this fundamental Cartesian principle, namely those which are directed against the merely dogmatic acceptance of things which I have not been able to recognize for myself as an autonomous thinking human being. Thus when it is said that I should try to set aside all prejudices, this is of course also clearly directed against the theological authority which has been exercised over human claims to knowledge and appeals to certain dogmatically defined propositions without ever submitting these propositions themselves to any rational reflection. The expression 'precipitation', I might observe in passing, is also very characteristic of this form of thinking. I should not think in a 'precipitate' kind of way, that is, I should allow myself time in this regard. An eminently bourgeois perspective this, one which still found expression in Keller's remark 'The truth will not run away from us.'[5] But I should also like to point out that there is much more involved here than can immediately be seen in these apparently innocuous words, which already basically imply that truth and time are not supposed to have anything to do with one another. I am supposed to think without 'precipitation', that is to say, I should calmly carry on thinking until the timeless core of truth presents itself to me. This does not involve the thought that truth itself could have something like its own time, its own tempo, something that is also required of me – although any thinking person knows that thoughts actually do have a tempo of their own, that it is very difficult to combine certain kinds of extension or elaboration of thought with the intensity of thinking; nor does it involve the audacious thought that thinking itself may not be able – in an essential and constitutive sense – to allow itself any time in this way, that it must be precipitate, precisely because it must happen now, or, as someone once said, only a hundred years hence.[6]

I only mention these things here to remind you that, with major philosophers such as Descartes, and naturally this is especially true of Hegel, we often come across formulations which seem so self-evident that we simply read past them, but which actually involve infinitely more if we only grasp them in terms of their 'specific difference' – that is, when we are able to recognize the particular significance they possess precisely within the structure of thought in question, and which often lends them a quite different power, and a quite different intention, than is the case if we just read them as are without already relating them to the heart of the thought to which they intrinsically belong. In the study of philosophy itself we also discover, as I have tried to show you with respect to dialectic in general, that you can really understand the individual moments only if you really understand the whole, that you can therefore understand something like this Cartesian rule in the deeper sense only when you already recognize the pathos, and also above all when you appreciate the polemical import of Cartesian philosophy as a whole. But if we just simply read such propositions, as we just simply read something without presuppositions merely in order to understand it, we cannot actually understand anything. For with regard to philosophy – and I am almost tempted to say with regard to anything whatsoever – there is actually no such thing as presuppositionless knowledge. And I cannot help pointing out to you that we have therefore already to some extent done violence to the proposition that I have just read out to you. For it naturally already involves a certain prejudice for its own part. The good Descartes would be horrified to hear the way in which I am encouraging you to interpret his work, and would say that he wishes to be understood purely in terms of the order of his thoughts just as he presents them to us, and that to import anything else into them would actually be a case of prejudice. Nonetheless, these formulations about avoiding 'precipitation' or 'prejudice' cannot be understood in philosophical terms unless you also bear the whole of Descartes in mind. And I would say that the whole art of philosophical understanding and philosophical reading consists in this: that you do not simply read what lies written in front of you – although you must of course do that – but also learn to read what is written precisely in its own specific gravity, as it were. Thus if you read the opening of Spinoza's *Ethics*,[7] and the definitions he provides there, with the conviction which Spinoza, along with the other rationalists, specifically encourages in you, namely that you need only to grasp these definitions in order to unfold the whole of the *Ethics* in a purely deductive process, then you will probably find, if you are honest with yourselves, that these definitions of 'substance', 'mode', 'attribute', etc., also strike you as exceedingly arbitrary, and that you do not really know what is at stake here. But if you consider this definition of substance which stands at the beginning and are able to

relate it to the original context, where Descartes's doctrine of the two
fundamental substances had already given rise to innumerable difficulties, where it no longer seemed possible to assume that these two
substances could even interact with one another – in other words,
that what we are really dealing with now is an attempt, through the
power of *ratio*, to reunify a world which had been broken apart into
the 'Inner' and the 'Outer' through the exercise of philosophical
reflection – then this knowledge will also allow these definitions
which you encounter at the beginning to assume a completely different meaning.

But I would just like to add, in connection with the famous Cartesian definition we have been discussing, that 'clear' knowledge here
means that the object itself is completely 'evident' to you, that something is '*évidemment*' such and such, as he says. In other words, it
means that the state of affairs with regard to which you pronounce
a judgement is truly so, that it stands immediately before your eyes,
without your having to rely here upon anything other than that which
presents itself to you with such uncontaminated 'evidence', while all
knowledge that is 'distinct', as the term is usually translated, refers
to the precise difference of the object which you have before your
eyes with respect to any other object. If I have already emphatically
attempted to show you that dialectical thought stands in contradiction to the notion of any absolute 'first', we can concretize that
epistemological insight specifically in relation to this apparently self-
evident demand which we naively accept in our own attempts to
know, unless of course we have been infected by philosophy. For what
is said to be either sensuously or intellectually given to me with absolute clarity, in kind of 'self-givenness', and with absolute distinctness,
in absolute distinction from anything else, effectively amounts to an
absolutely ultimate point of reference, something behind or beyond
which we cannot go, because its self-evident character – this is the
very meaning of self-evidence – consists precisely in the fact that no
such further recourse is required. For any such recourse would also
have to appeal in turn to cases of self-evidence – there is no other
criterion of truth – and you have here therefore reached an absolute
foundation, as traditional logic would assure you, beyond which you
cannot possibly go.[8]

Now dialectic puts this claim into question. Yet dialectic does not
put it into question – and this is entirely characteristic of dialectical
thinking – by demanding, as you might maliciously be tempted to
imagine, that we think in an unclear and confused way instead of
thinking *clare et distincte*. I will not deny that there are practitioners
of dialectic whose thought sometimes turns out like this, but you can

believe me when I say that the task of dialectical logic is certainly not to encourage or to produce such thinking. Rather, we can perhaps best express the point this way: only if we first take the Cartesian demand with extraordinary seriousness and observe it with extraordinary strictness can we come to realize that it does not possess that absolutely binding character which it ascribes to itself. And this would actually be the dialectical path to take. The dialectical understanding of an object would be distinguished from a more primitive approach by 'taking a closer look at things' – as the people I am happy to belong to like to put it – or by staring intensely at the object, I would almost like to say, until it becomes clear that no such thing as that absolute clarity which Descartes expects of the object is ever actually given. You will find, therefore, if you appeal to some pure sensuous certainty on the part of consciousness, a certainty from which all further knowledge depends and upon which you then try and build up the world of things, that this very givenness, in accordance with its own meaning and character, requires something like sense organs. Thus you cannot possibly grasp the concept of optical perception, which traditional theory of knowledge postulates as the immediately given, as a form of immediate givenness, if this is separated from the organic constitution of the eye and everything that is connected with it. You cannot conceive of anything visual unless the relationship to the eye, and thus to the body, and our sense organs, is also involved in this visual character as a kind of immediate knowing. On the other hand, the theory of knowledge tells us, you must first determine the character of the body as a functioning complex, as a regular law-governed condition for any possible sensuous perception. You will find, therefore, when you really try to hold fast at this point purely to the sensuously given as the ultimate ground of justification, that it is already mediated by what it is supposed to give rise to in the first place. And likewise in turn, of course, you cannot speak of sense organs without this moment of primary sensuous givenness. Thus the moments which are involved here, even in this elementary example, do not stand in a relationship of something primary and something secondary; rather, they stand in a reciprocally conditioning kind of relationship. And if we wished to express the truth about sensuous knowledge here, we would not assert either that 'sensuous knowledge is knowledge through the eye' or that 'sensuous knowledge is primarily a sensation of colour'. Rather, the truth would involve revealing, would first only properly be expressed by revealing, the interaction and entwinement of relations that is at work here. But once you reach this point, you will have to conclude that the demand for *clara et distincta perceptio* is itself dissolved as soon as it is strictly observed.

During the last session, in attempting to contrast dialectic and positivism, I said to you that dialectic also contains a positivist element within itself, namely the micrological element, that is to say, the moment through which it immerses itself in the smallest details. And here perhaps, in relation to this model which I have just mentioned, you may be able to see a little more precisely what I am trying to get at. For if we abandon ourselves to what is individually given, if we obstinately stay with the given until it gives itself up entirely to our gaze, then it ceases to be such a static and ultimate given and reveals itself as a dynamic process of becoming, as I have just tried to show with the example of the reciprocal production of moments in the case of sensuous givenness and the corresponding sense organ. This is where the dogmatic element of Descartes lies, as you can discover through these reflections – and I believe this is the real criticism of his rules, although it can only be developed in the first place by following these rules through. The dogmatic element which underlies the Cartesian conception, even though this conception strikes us as self-evident, is the way that the objects of our knowledge, or even truth itself, come to assume in themselves the form we bring to them through the method, namely through the demand that we should be able to know everything in a clear and distinct manner. The rule that only what we clearly and distinctly know is true for us is indeed required to preserve our knowledge from error and confusion, but this rule does not itself possess an ontological meaning, as such philosophers always assume. That is to say, it does not say anything about whether the very matter that we know *clara et distincta* is something that is unambiguous in itself or something that is clearly and absolutely distinguished from everything else. Once you have brought out this moment, namely that the object in itself, if I only look upon it properly, is intrinsically dynamic, and that what seems rigid, if I only attend to it long enough, begins in a certain sense to teem, like something beneath a microscope, it also follows from this that its distinction and differentiation from other adjoining and related objects, which is required by the postulate of distinctness, is by no means as simple as this has seemed for traditional thought to be. Rather, insofar as the object reveals itself beneath the gaze of knowledge in its functional and dynamic character, it transpires that the object is not just the same as itself, that it is always also something more and other than itself, is already a relation to what is other; and thus, while it is indeed distinct from other things, it is however not absolutely distinct from them. Now the error which is involved in the Cartesian rule is this: the rule tacitly treats the order of concepts traditionally demanded by extensional logic – the classificatory concepts which tell us that 'this is this and that is that' – as if it were really the order which knowledge itself must essentially address. Thus, while it is true that without this method we would fall victim to chaos and confusion, we must nonetheless drive this method in turn to the point where we approach the object itself, so that thought may do justice to the matter in question rather than simply to a self-sufficient form of order. One could actually say that dialectic as such is an approach which enables us to distrust the tendency, or which should arm us against the tendency, to conflate the order that we impose upon the object for the sake of our own peace of mind with the character of the matter itself, an approach which should encourage us to confront this order with the object in an insistent fashion until we arrive at a form of knowledge where our own subjective forms of knowing may genuinely concur with the essence of the matter itself.

At this point you will ask: 'How then are we actually supposed to think?' I believe you will not expect me to present you with some kind of anti-Cartesian *Discours de la méthode* and tell you what the correct way of thinking should look like. Any such attempt – as I think should be obvious by now – would itself simply stand under the sign of that superstitious belief in some uniquely saving and beneficent method which we specifically wished to dispel through the reflections we are pursuing right now. But we are of course not entirely defenceless with regard to the objections which are typically raised against a kind of thinking which does not immediately submit to the diktat of these powerful ordering schemata. For we also recognize a demand for unity with regard to theoretical experience. And the path which leads to knowledge is neither that of capricious insights nor that of some abstract coherence in the organization of individual moments. Rather, we are talking about the unity involved in the development of theory. We can perhaps elucidate this best by indicating how even thinking itself is not actually a *tabula rasa* – i.e., that thinking is not something that we bring to the matter in some ultimate or merely general way, that it is not indeed, as people like to say, 'pure' in character. For, in such purity, thinking is first perverted precisely by the demands of a method which is supposed to be entirely independent of its subject matter and which first undertakes to remove all substantive moments from the instrument methodically employed. But thinking itself, the manner in which in fact we concretely think as living human beings, is actually by no means separated off in this way but is, rather, something entwined with the

whole process of our experience. And I would say – if I presumed to
offer you any positive instruction here about what one should think
– that thinking which genuinely comprehends things, in contrast with
one that merely orders and classifies them, is a kind of thinking that
measures itself against the living experience which we have with
objects. It is a thinking which acknowledges the moment of conceptual order which it must naturally retain – for I cannot indeed think
without concepts – but continually confronts that moment of conceptual ordering with the living experience that I actually have. And
out of the tension between both these moments – between conceptual
order and that pre-conceptual experience from which concepts themselves have also nonetheless always sprung – such thinking, in a
process of constant reflection upon both the matter and thought itself,
eventually leads us out beyond a thinking which simply subsumes
things beneath its grasp in a merely external fashion.

This is the approach which would actually have to counter this
Cartesian postulate. Some of these issues may become even clearer
to you if we consider his second postulate. The second rule instructs
us 'to divide up each of the difficulties which I examined into as many
parts as possible, and as seemed requisite in order that it might be
resolved in the best manner possible.'[9] In the first place I would draw
your attention to the quite everyday experience that the way in which
we actually resolve difficulties does not invariably lie in referring
what is difficult back to what appears simple. Basically this idea
already betrays something of that hatred with regard to the differentiated, to the all-too-complicated, which has accompanied Western
subjectivism and rationalism like a shadow in a rather remarkable
manner. The more the world becomes rational, the less I am really
allowed in a sense to think about in the process. That is to say, everything must now ultimately be reduced to wholly simple, wholly
thoughtless, wholly incomprehensible elements, although such a
demand completely forgets that, if all that remains is really just what
is most simple and most elementary, the object itself, whose complexity is what I wish to understand in the first place, has already slipped
through my fingers, so that I have then actually failed the object, that
I am now left with nothing but the trivialities into which I have
broken down the object. On the other hand, that which actually
attracts my attention, as a potential object of knowledge, that to
which such knowledge is actually addressed, that which constitutes
the salt of the object, has already been removed in this way and is
actually no longer to be found. Of course, it is also true that I cannot
manage without any analysis into more elementary aspects. Indeed,
I have already talked to you in some detail about the dialectic of

whole and part, and wherever I am confronted by some whole in its mere immediacy, without further articulation, I cannot simply rest content with this whole. What I have specifically attempted to grasp with the concept of micrological thinking, namely the persistent attention to a given object, already implies in a certain fashion that the wholeness with which an object of knowledge is presented to me is itself resolved into elements,[10] and the movement into which what is alleged to be clearly and distinctly given is resolved lies precisely in this: that the whole in question shows itself to consist of parts, though not simply as a mere sum of parts to which it might be reduced but rather – and this is decisive here – in such a way that these parts themselves constitute a reciprocal relationship, and stand in a dynamic relation to one another, so that the whole can no more be grasped by simply adducing the parts than it can by simply acknowledging and resting content with the undifferentiated whole itself, rather than analysing it with regard to its individual features.

Here you can see particularly clearly that it is problematic to transfer the ideals of natural science to the realm of philosophy because, in this respect, the latter – and I would like to put this somewhat cautiously – seems to lag far behind the natural sciences themselves. And I should also like at least to venture the thought here that the difficulties of mutual comprehension that beset philosophy and the thought developed by the natural sciences – a difficulty which appears to have become insurmountable precisely since Hegel – is connected with the fact that the philosophical reflection which the natural sciences have devoted to themselves does not actually do full justice to what the natural sciences do. That is to say, the natural sciences, since the time of Hegel, have not attained the requisite level of reflection, for natural philosophy – or what we now describe as such – generally amounts to little more than an abstract presentation of the rules and procedures involved in the thinking of the natural sciences, whereas the real task would precisely be to comprehend and explore these modes of procedure themselves. A rule like this Cartesian one which requires us to analyse everything into its elements derives of course from the realm of the mathematical natural sciences – that is to say, it is a rule which is essentially connected with the analytical treatment of conic sections, which seeks to express them in terms of equations and thus ultimately to reduce them to their constituent elements. But if I have rightly estimated the character of the natural sciences here, then they are by no means so ontologically convinced that everything complex and complicated must be capable, in itself, of being reduced to simple elements. Rather, natural science regards that very process of analysis into constituent elements, and

on which of course it relies, only as a model – that is to say, only as
an attempt to secure the object in question within the ordering categories of consciousness, without thereby claiming that this simple
and elementary dimension is itself simply identical with the essence
of the matter. The philosophers, on the other hand, who are always
concerned as we know with the essence of things, proceed as if the
ordering concepts which the natural sciences have to employ were
already, in themselves, an intrinsic order of things. That is to say, they
proceed as if the whole were simply composed of parts, whereas in
truth the whole and the parts reciprocally produce one another in the
manner which I have tried to present to you in some detail.

All I have been trying to do in the course of these remarks is to
show you that the rather wide-ranging reflections about the relationship between the whole and the parts which we have pursued in the
context of dialectical logic do have certain consequences, that they
are not simply philosophical speculations; on the contrary, they imply
something for the method of actual knowledge, namely that this
apparently self-evident demand for the reduction of what is complex
into its constituent parts does not possess the universal relevance or
absolutely normative character which is ascribed to it in Cartesian
philosophy, for example, and that, in order to grasp these parts, their
own dynamic and reciprocal relationship must equally be taken into
account. And this gives me an opportunity to remind you here of a
dialectical moment which we may have somewhat neglected until
now, but which will afford you a rather better idea of the particular
relevance which dialectical thought should possess, not as some sort
of abstract philosophical system but rather in the context of living
knowledge itself. For it is characteristic of dialectic, I would like to
say, that it does not ultimately recognize the separation of philosophy
from the particular sciences. It belongs to the defensive posture which
philosophy has felt driven to adopt through the development of
science over the last couple of centuries that philosophy has come to
believe that it must assert itself as a realm which is beyond and independent of the sciences. Philosophy has found itself remarkably
impoverished as a consequence, as we can so emphatically see today
from that metaphysics of being which ultimately ends up in mere
tautology. But this also really reveals a kind of impotence of philosophy with regard to knowledge, something which must certainly be
overcome if philosophy is to present itself actually and seriously as
more than a mere 'Sunday' metaphysics or a mere taxonomic system
of some sort. If a philosophy really is one, this must mean that
the philosophical motivations themselves enter into the material
dimension of substantive cognition, instead of simply surrendering

the material knowledge of things to the individual sciences, or even to the treatment of the formal sciences. And if I am critical about the role of 'definition' in philosophy, that cannot mean that speaking as a philosopher in my lecture from four till five I assure myself that definition is indeed a problematic matter, but then go into the law seminar, for example, and simply define the concepts which are employed there, whatever they may be. For what is required, on the contrary, is that knowledge regarding the relationship between thought and thing, or regarding the problem of definition itself, that all of these matters must really also be introduced into the cognitive procedures of the individual sciences. And this is to say that philosophy, to say that dialectic, if it is to have any genuine sense at all, is by no means innocuous, is not a matter of 'mere' philosophy which is simply occupied with itself. On the contrary, the reflection to which philosophy exposes our so-called natural consciousness – that is to say, our unnatural and conventional consciousness – also intrinsically requires that we rethink in a fundamental sense its own attitude and response to the knowledge proffered by the individual sciences and that, as ones who reflect upon our own work, we now also bring the knowledge derived from philosophical reflection to bear upon such particular forms of knowledge. And I would say that this movement, this critical movement, of thought is specifically what the individual researcher or investigator can really learn in the first place from the practice of dialectic, and this is the key thing here.

LECTURE 14

10 July 1958

Ladies and gentlemen,

In the last session we discussed the dialectical criticism of the principle which demands analysis of a problem into its most basic elements. It is evident that I certainly did not mean to suggest that we should somehow avoid analysing an object; on the contrary, we must do so, for every kind of attempt to determine what is given simultaneously implies a certain limitation or qualification, and to that extent indeed already inevitably involves emphasizing certain moments, while the mere identification of an abstract totality is not just inadequate but ultimately not even possible. If I try and apply the dialectical mode of thinking here, I could almost say that any attempt to grasp a whole at all, by denominating it in some way, already includes an analytical aspect, insofar as we do not simply stop or rest content with this totality but relate it to certain conceptual determinations which cannot, in any immediate sense, be simply the same as the whole, but must rather bring out some specific moments of the latter. Having said this, I think I may be able to make even clearer to you what I was really driving at with this critique of the analytical method. For it is essentially a critique of the fetishism of ultimate 'elements'. From a certain perspective, we may say that dialectical operations of thought do not signify alterations in the intellectual processes we actually perform in knowing something so much as alterations in the interpretations we furnish in this regard. In a specific sense, dialectic is nothing but the critical attempt to resolve the philosophemes with which – unless and until we think and intervene here in a really radical way – we tend to rationalize and in considerable measure to misinterpret our own activity of cognition. The essential thing I want to say here is that we should not believe that we have already done justice to the matter itself just because we have accepted the necessity of analysing a whole in order to comprehend it. We should not believe that our cognitive demands – for which a whole is not immediately given but is accessible only as mediated through conceptual operations and thus necessarily as differentiated into particular moments which have been conceptually discriminated in terms of characteristic unified features – have already fully determined the matter itself. I think it is especially important to recognize this with regard to the process of knowledge today, for specifically in our contemporary situation, subjected as we are to the demands of administrative and bureaucratic thought – demands which today make themselves felt even within the most subtle stirrings of spirit – there is an enormous temptation to identify the analytic process of knowing which we perform with knowledge itself. It is as if we considered the process of the division of labour – from which indeed the analytic resolution of the process of knowledge into its elements is directly derived, as the late Franz Borkenau has shown[1] – and conflated this expression of the division of labour – i.e., a specific way of organizing the process of knowing – with a determination of the matter itself, so that we imagine that these moments of our knowing, expressing the division of labour, are simply the same as the determinations of the matter we are attempting to know.

I believe I can clarify this with a concept which will be familiar to you from the practice of the sciences, and especially those sciences which somewhat emphatically describe themselves as empirical sciences. The concept to which I want to draw your attention here is that of analysis into specific factors, and especially into laws. We encounter it repeatedly, for example, in the work of someone like Mannheim,[2] who is hardly unaware of epistemological-theoretical issues, but even in that of Marx, when they distinguish universal factors from particular ones, as though the universal factor would exercise its own effect, while certain specific effective forces or specific effective laws, as they are described, would also additionally come into play. We meet with this kind of procedure, which distinguishes between universal factors and additional more specific factors in this way, wherever one attempts in a broad sense to identify such things as motivations or causal relationships within the domain of the social sciences. But there is no question that we thereby easily succumb to the temptation to hypostasize the products of our mechanisms of abstraction, of our ways of conceptually organizing the material, treating these products as if they were essentially the same as the matter itself. Thus when it is claimed – to choose an example from Marx's theory – that something like the relationship between classes provides an explanation for social processes, and we then further take account of the specific conditions which arise from free wage labour and the exchange of labour power as a commodity within capitalist society, it looks as if, on the basis of this conceptual schema – firstly, that the world has until now been a world of class struggle; secondly, that we live in the particular period of capitalist society – we can derive two series of factors as it were, the universal factors and the special factors, and all we need to do is to bring these together in order to explain the phenomenon in question. And if I express it in this way, it may perhaps strike you as so naive and absurd that you cannot really understand all the effort I am making to criticize this mode of thought here. But I would seriously ask you not to under-estimate the temptation which always arises from the imposition of such organizing principles whenever you are expected to provide some conceptual organization for the relevant phenomenon which is under investigation. There is something uncommonly seductive about this procedure for the scientific investigator who undertakes to clas-sify the material that presents itself, who is indeed required to compare his or her findings, to bring the same things together under the rel-evant concepts, to distinguish different things in terms of different concepts, just as we learn to do in the practical context of scientific research. But in truth it is naturally otherwise, for the dynamic laws to which modern capitalist society is subject, for example, are not a) universal laws regarding classes and then b) further laws regarding the specific form of the currently prevailing relation between classes. Rather, the fundamental fact here is that society until now has been riven within itself, has not been identical with itself, that society bears a certain dynamic within itself, a quite specific sort of dynamic, which comes to manifest itself historically, or which finds its concrete his-torical expression in the class relations that prevail in capitalist society – that is, in a society of free wage labour where the exchange principle has unfolded in universal form. It would be quite wrong to try and discover, over and beyond this determination, some further universal law to which the phenomena in question would be subject, for this universal factor itself is mediated through the specific situation in which we exist and, in a sense, manifests itself only in a specific form. Here too we must attempt to think this through in a properly dif-ferentiated manner. Thus it is entirely meaningful to say that there has always been such a thing as exploitation, such a thing as the appropriation of other people's labour, such a thing as exchange, and where indeed the weaker party always draws the short straw in the process of exchange; but it is not the case that this invariant factor which has always existed and which still exists should be regarded as something in addition to its merely logical form of specification, for it has developed in precisely this specific form. In other words, if we are really serious about the concept of the self-developing movement of the matter itself, which is indeed, after everything we have heard, a fundamental requirement of dialectical thought, then the notion of some such invariance independent of the concrete forms which it assumes in the course of development effectively loses its meaning. Thus we can say that all this applies to a world where there are classes and where there is exploitation, but it is not as if there were certain general laws for this, and then in addition there were also specific laws which apply to the current situation. Rather, it is the essence of these laws themselves that they unfold into the laws which hold for the current situation. Of course, it is also quite possible, and this is a problem which is very important for all material dialectic, for the content of dialectical thought, that certain elements of the past may continue to survive in a particular historical situation. Thus to a considerable extent it has come about in Europe, in countries such as Germany and pre-revolutionary Russia which are said to have developed rather late, that all sorts of feudal remnants have persisted within the context of the bourgeois principle, and where in turn quite particular forms of class relations are also expressed. But then they are not representatives of some more general class relation with respect to the particular class relation which currently prevails. Rather, they simply represent a stage of previous historical processes that have survived.

Perhaps I can use this opportunity to say a few words about the position of dialectic with regard to the concept of 'development' more generally. And this brings me directly to a question which perhaps possesses a certain significance for the way we construe the idea of development itself. Dialectical thought, which works in terms of contradictions and reversals, is necessarily opposed to the notion of an even or simply continuous development. That the processes in question – and here we are talking above all about historical processes – are internally contradictory, that they consist precisely in the unfolding of contradictions, is what already excludes the idea of some even and seamless progress, just as it excludes in turn the idea of social stasis or invariance. In relation to historical reality it may specifically be one of the deepest insights open to dialectical thought that it need not regard the non-simultaneous character of what has lagged behind yet still persists simply as an obstacle upon the smooth path

of historical progress. Rather, it is capable of recognizing what for
its own part resists or cannot comfortably be accommodated within
this so-called progress and grasping it in terms of the principle of
development itself. If the idea of dialectic does indeed possess a temporal core, as we have tried to show here, this means that it is also
essentially a dialectic of non-simultaneous aspects, namely a dialectic
which must also try to understand, in terms of ongoing temporal
development, precisely what has, if you like, proved unable to keep
pace historically speaking. Thus if we can observe certain reactionary
currents within the petty bourgeoisie, currents which then came to
play such an extraordinarily significant role in the emergence of
fascism itself in Germany, we shall not be able to regard these persisting elements simply as vestiges or remnants within the historical
process. Rather, we should have to confront the paradoxical and
eminently dialectical task of deriving what has lagged behind precisely – if I may express this in a very extreme fashion – by reference
to the movement of progress itself. In other words, the path of progress involves a process in which certain human groups find themselves dispossessed, groups which certainly belong, in terms of their
origin and ideology, to the realm of bourgeois society, but which now
suddenly forfeit the material basis of precisely this bourgeois existence to which both their history and their ideology points. Thus
these human groups, which are acquainted with a materially and
ideologically preferable form of life, or have experienced the possibility of such a life, and which in comparison with the past can expect
nothing good, rightly or wrongly, from further changes in society, are
turned into *laudatores temporis acti* by the path of progress itself, by
the process of historical development – that is, into people who seek
salvation in the past and whose consciousness is turned backwards
to earlier phases of development. And this regressive tendency of their
consciousness is then very easily combined with the strongest social
forces which for their part negate the usual conception of progress,
since this conception of progress is a bourgeois one in the genuine
sense, one that is bound up with notions of liberality and individual
freedom. These forces, for reasons which we cannot go into here, like
to appeal specifically to authoritarian forms of rule, and here they
are able to use this regressive feature on the part of certain very large
groups which have come to depend on them. To this extent we might
say, therefore, that precisely the most reactionary aspects of National
Socialism – such as the notion of 'Blood and Earth', the racial theories, and all these things which are connected with a spurious cult of
origins – in a certain sense were themselves actually functions of
dynamic social change, of social progress, if you want to put it that

way, namely of the increased power of large-scale industrial production. And the task of a dialectical theory of society must always
consist in refusing to regard what has not kept pace, what has lagged
behind, in a simply static fashion – that is, as something which has
simply lagged behind, which is now opposed to change and movement. For if the extremes are indeed as reciprocally mediated as I
have attempted to make clear to you, then the static and the dynamic
dimensions[3] are themselves mediated with one another here; that is
to say, the supposedly static sectors of society must actually be derived
from the dynamic trajectory at work. I think it will be useful for you
to grasp this point clearly, and it will enable you to form a very precise
idea of the difference between dialectical and non-dialectical thinking
here. A non-dialectical sociology would say something like the following, as Mannheim and others[4] have indeed actually said: 'On the
one side there are certain dynamic, mobile, and progressive groups,
namely those involved in finance capital, and to a certain extent in
industry, especially manufacturing industry and the like, and then, by
contrast, there are also static, regressive and conservative groups,
such as the peasantry; and society simply consists in the way the static
and dynamic factors yield a kind of mixture.[5] And the results of these
static and dynamic factors then constitute the history which we have
to accept as ours.' This conception is fundamentally superficial and
undialectical, for what it fails to grasp is not so much the eminent
degree to which the dynamic process of history also bears elements
of the past within itself – everyone will concede that – but rather and
above all the reverse: the fact that the static and persisting aspects
are actually functions of dynamic principles.

    I might perhaps also draw your attention to another phenomenon
in this connection, that of the family. The family is indeed a natural
form of association, one that actually contradicts the universal principle of exchange. In other words, the things which individual family
members accomplish for one another within the family cannot
simply be expressed in terms of exchange relations. You find this
above all in circumstances where in a certain sense the family is still
actually involved with the material process of production, namely in
the country, where the peasant family still functions as labour power
and where in fact to a considerable degree these very small economic
units are able to maintain their life at all only because – from an
objective-economic perspective – the labour of the family is under-
compensated. It is very easy to say that the family is like an island
of irrationality, of merely natural growth, of mere traditionalism,
within an otherwise thoroughly rationalized world, as if in the shape
of the family the feudal past still somehow reached into our world,

as indeed in an emphatic sense there is something feudal about the concept of the family. However matters stand in this regard, here too it would be a superficial view of things to believe that the family has persisted simply as a kind of remnant within an otherwise fully developed exchange society. Rather, we must ask ourselves how it is actually possible that the family should survive at all in spite of the constantly increasing degree of rationalization. For the moment I would like to ignore the fact, as various sociologists – such as Schelsky[6] or, with a somewhat different emphasis, Baumert[7] – have shown, that the family itself is currently undergoing a process of restructuring and effectively forfeiting more and more of its natural and, if you like, its pre-capitalist features. But even in the context of these modifications the family as such still retains a pre-capitalist in character. The answer to this question, it seems to me, does not really lie in the notion that something like the family possesses a kind of greater resistance in this regard – and indeed one may question whether such a power of resistance is really so great within any individual family – and anyone who knows anything about psychology also knows how problematic the unity of the family is and just how much material for potential conflict for everyone involved the family invariably brings with it. Rather, in order to understand this archaic and anachronistic character of the family which has survived within our own society, it seems necessary to bear in mind that our society, for all its rationality, itself remains irrational. That is to say, it continues to stand under the law of profit rather than one which prescribes the satisfaction of human needs, and this same irrationality also causes or compels society to maintain certain irrational sectors within itself, for at the point where the bourgeois principle of bourgeois society would be fully realized, would be utterly and completely rationalized, there bourgeois society – we might almost say – would cease to be a bourgeois society at all because there would then no longer be any place for precisely those moments which provide the motivation of economic activity in this society. Thus insofar as a progressively rationalized society is still bound to the irrational and arbitrary control over the labour of others, it is thereby also necessarily and inevitably dependent upon the survival of irrational institutions of the most various kinds. Thus while, on the one hand, these institutions are indeed an anachronism within bourgeois society, they are, on the other hand, also required by bourgeois society itself, and we may suspect that the more purely and completely bourgeois society realizes its own principle, the more it will require such irrational institutions as the family, the only one that I have specifically emphasized here. We could also point to other and in our time probably much more powerful and influential institutions in this regard.

You will perhaps have seen from this that the notion of analysing something into its constituent elements may prove extremely dangerous, even in simply conceptual terms. Thus were you to analyse our society, for example, into elements, starting with the larger economic units, then taking the smaller economic units, then the smallest and not wholly rationalized kinds of association such as the family, and then all other possible institutions, you might conceive of society as a whole as a sort of map which is made up by the way all these moments fit together. But such an image of social reality would be literally false, for society is not composed out of these elements. Rather, these elements for their own part stand within a highly complex self-conditioning functional context, for which I have attempted to develop a brief schema for you here. And you will perhaps have seen from this schema that this context is actually better described as one mediated by social antagonisms than as one of 'wholeness' – as people love to say – or as a so-called organic social context. For, if there is such a thing as society, it is far more like a system than an organism, albeit a system of disparate moments, a system which is essentially self-contradictory in character.

The next rule of Descartes that we wish to consider is one that concerns continuity. This third rule 'was to carry on my reflections in due order, commencing with objects that were the most simple and easy to understand, in order to rise little by little, or by degrees, to knowledge of the most complex, assuming an order, even if a fictitious one, among those which do not follow a natural sequence relatively to one another.'[8] The last qualifying remark clearly betrays an emphatically rationalistic motif here, namely the notion of 'assuming' a certain order as a kind of working hypothesis. In other words, in order to render something like a scientific order possible, one must presuppose that a seamless and continuous form of order already characterizes the object to be known. For, if I did not make this assumption, I would not really in all conscience be able to build up any scientific order at all. In this regard Descartes still shows the kind of impressive honesty which is peculiar to the earliest and to the final phases of such a development, for he clearly expresses the 'as if' character of this assumption here, whereas subsequent philosophers, beginning with Spinoza, and not excluding my own Hegel in this respect, would far rather ascribe directly and dogmatically to things themselves that which Descartes still quite openly describes as a rational ordering principle.[9] After what we have heard, I think we can now see that the path of gradual, step-by-step and continuous knowledge cannot claim unconditional validity as such, at least if our reflections on dialectical contradiction are to the point. The step-by-step procedure is one we are familiar with in the natural sciences and in the traditional forms of applied science, above all when the science in question deals with an object which has been so deprived of qualitative features, so reduced to qualitatively indistinguishable moments, that the determinations of the object itself are irrelevant to us here in comparison with the determinations that we confer on it through our ordering principles. But given what we have tried to show about the contradictory character of the object of knowledge itself, we hardly need to say that such continuity cannot actually be presupposed. And, from this point of view, from the perspective of the question of continuity and discontinuity – which is incidentally the fundamental problem, or one of the fundamental problems, of Leibniz,[10] one of the greatest rationalist philosophers – the principle or the problem of dialectic would be not simply to insist upon the moment of discontinuity but, rather, to connect the moments of continuity and discontinuity with one another, namely to grasp continuity and discontinuity themselves as reciprocally mediated.

I have already put it to you that our society is more of a system than an organism, and that it is nonetheless an antagonistic society. Perhaps this alerts you to the dialectical problem that I would particularly like to draw to your attention in the present context. On the one hand, the theoretical task of dialectic is specifically to comprehend the whole or totality, and knowledge is not possible without the idea of a totality; yet, on the other hand, this totality itself is not continuous in character, is not a logical totality within a seamless deductive context. Rather – to put it bluntly – the totality is internally discontinuous in character. And the dialectical response to the problem which arises here is none other than to recognize that the unity of the society we live in is actually constituted through its very discontinuity. In other words, the dissociated and discontinuous moments of the object of knowledge, insofar as they are related to one another as contradictions rather than being simply disparate from one another, come precisely through this relationship which they all make up together to crystallize specifically into that whole which should properly constitute the object of knowledge here. It follows from this moment of discontinuity, incidentally, that our initial cognitive approach, the point where we decide to begin, is in one sense a matter of indifference for dialectical thought, for we do not presume, of course, that we can develop everything from an absolute 'first' in some purely continuous fashion. Rather, it is the power of the whole, of which we have spoken already, which makes itself felt as it were in the same way in every individual moment. We might say, if you like, that everything is equally close to the centre, which is why any truly consistent dialectical thought can begin from what looks like the most obscure and ephemeral of phenomena, and indeed this is often the best course to take since it is precisely those things that have not yet been saturated by the official categories of thought which may lead us most readily into the concealed essence of the whole, far more so than if we orient our thought in terms of established and already approved categories.

We may also express this by saying – and this brings me to a 'material' critique of traditional thought – that the problem of the 'position of thought towards objectivity'[11] becomes a moral problem in the light of the question of continuity or discontinuity. For the idea that the object of knowledge is itself something wholly coherent and consistent that may be logically explicated without remainder always involves the notion that what is articulated in such meaningful and consistent terms is effectively something positive. But if we are really in earnest with our critique of the existent, that is, if we take the thought of the antagonistic character of reality itself really seriously, then we are specifically bound to exhibit the discontinuity that characterizes the existent. And we are thereby driven to lend this character of separation and discontinuity to our own thought as well, but to do so in such a way that the unity and interconnectedness of what we are actually dealing with is revealed precisely through this discontinuity, precisely through this internally mediated contradiction, in the matter itself. There is absolutely no question that productive thinking today can take the form only of one that works through breaks and fractures, whereas any thinking which is simply oriented in advance to unity, synthesis and harmony can only serve to conceal something which thinking is called upon to penetrate, for it then inevitably contents itself with simply reproducing, or even reinforcing, the façade of what is already there in the medium of thought. And if your own thinking – as long as your approach has not entirely been shaped in advance by standard scientific expectations – feels a certain resistance against what can commonly be described as 'pedantry', then I believe this cannot simply be regarded as the typical attitude of the youthful enthusiast who still needs to learn the importance of discipline. There is something such as intellectual discipline, of course, but the intellectual discipline which people would instil in us usually amounts to a kind of hostility to things of the mind, that is to say, ends up by stunting or emasculating the productivity of thought – namely the relation of thought to its object – and encouraging it instead to submit to certain regulated procedures. But in truth there is no rule for thought other than that of freedom towards the object, as Hegel calls it.[12] The discipline of thought is simply that of measuring itself against the matter itself, of doing as much justice to the matter itself as it possibly can. It is not that of imposing upon itself, qua method, a rule which prescribes how it is to proceed, and then on the basis of this so-called demand for method ultimately renouncing thought itself, for to think in the richest sense is invariably to think in a way that is not methodically regulated.

I have no intention here of encouraging an arbitrary appeal to entirely fortuitous hunches or insights. I simply wish to emphasize how thought must be capable of its own freedom, must along with freedom towards the object also possess freedom within itself, and cannot therefore just relinquish itself, so to speak, before the object but must continually seek out relationships of some kind with the object, relationships in which alone thought can find itself contented. Thought which is no longer capable of this will never be able to disclose its object. The pedantry of thought is the way it fails its relation to the matter itself, fails it for the sake of securing what one already has, for the sake of the small security of the private person, of the small individual. And, as with the security of small private property, this form of pedantry is exposed to inflation to an especially high degree. In other words, it will always forfeit exactly this; it will always show itself most wretched just where it believes it must maintain its current value. Thus I believe that it is really essential to intellectual health, if you are already engaged in disciplined scientific or academic work or wish to become so, that you always continue to retain a critical attitude to the moment of pedantry that attaches to the exclusively step-by-step procedure. For of course this step-by-step procedure immediately threatens to paralyse the productive power of thought. Wherever thought actually rouses itself – and I beg you not to think I am being sentimental here – it is able to soar rather than simply proceed step by step. And a thought which can no longer soar is no more a thought than one which can do nothing but soar. And to this extent I think the Platonic notion that 'enthusiasm' is a necessary moment of knowledge and of truth itself[13] is not just a passing expression of a philosophical mood, a mere expression of intellectual style, but does indeed capture a necessary moment of the matter itself. When thought simply proceeds step by step, advancing in the smallest possible steps, it cannot avoid endlessly repeating what it has already known. Where thought can leap beyond what is merely given to it, what it already knows anyway, and remains fully aware of this leap, it is able to go beyond what merely is and thereby precisely reveal its character as the merely existent.

I am well aware, at this particular point, that I may encounter certain objections on your part, although I also hope that I have said enough about the positive moments of 'continuous' forms of thought to protect myself in this regard. But I believe that precisely here, where we come to the really sensitive point at which dialectical thought is especially liable to provoke resistance, I should be prepared to speak in more detail, in our next session, about the specific nature of this resistance.

LECTURE 15

15 July 1958

Ladies and gentlemen,

In the last session we spoke about the Cartesian demand that our intellectual procedure must be careful not to leave out any steps, and I attempted to show you in what sense this Cartesian axiom is actually incompatible with the approach of dialectical thought. Now Hegel was certainly not the first to express specific resistance to this procedure, and indeed a very important French conservative philosopher, de Maistre,[1] had already parodied the old Baconian critique of idols,[2] which was revived during the eighteenth century, and spoken in this connection of the '*idole d'échelles*'[3] – that is, the idol of the ladder, the notion that we must always proceed step by step, that thought is never allowed to take off, which basically implies that thought may not run ahead of itself, that thought may not bring anything to bear beyond what it already has anyway. We could almost say, echoing the paradox of the flying arrow, that the rigorously applied Cartesian demand for an entirely seamless and continuous form of thought would inevitably end up in pure tautology.[4] But it is not so much this which strikes me as essential here, although objectively speaking it seems to me to furnish an emphatic critique of any thought which can only proceed step by step. Rather, the moment which dialectic rebels against – at least dialectic as I believe I may understand it, and indeed as I think on closer inspection it was also deployed by Hegel himself specifically in the *Phenomenology of Spirit* – is the coercive character of thought. We have the concept of what is logically 'compelling' – namely an operation which leaves nothing out, where there is no possibility of escaping the conclusion – and we have what psychology describes with the concept of the 'compulsive character' – namely a human being subjected to forms of ritualistic behaviour, inflexibly bound to the notion of order and incapable of genuine freedom – but there is nonetheless a remarkably powerful affinity between these two concepts of compulsion, between merely logical compulsion and the psychological compulsion to ritualistic behaviour – as we may observe, for example, from Ludwig Thoma's *Die kleinen Verwandten*,[5] a play which I saw when I was very young and which made an unforgettable impression on me. In the play, a station inspector from Grossheubach pays an unexpected visit to relatives of his, academics by profession, who are on the point of finding a suitable husband for their young daughter. They now make fruitless efforts to get rid of their provincial relative lest he endanger the delicate marriage project, but he keeps on insisting that everything must be identified in its proper 'category'. I have never forgotten this image of someone who has to bring everything under a stable category, and, when I later came to read Kant and his deduction of the categories,[6] I was never completely able to dispel that image of the station inspector from Grossheubach. I will not try and decide here whether this is Kant's fault or my own.

This implies a particular kind of obligation on the part of dialectical thought, and one which probably accounts for the resistance to such thought that we shall discuss in more detail here. For dialectical thinking is obliged to show a specific kind of mobility, namely a refusal to be nailed down precisely to that particular point, to be confined or compelled to remain at that particular point, where the chosen object or form of argumentation currently finds itself. This already became clear to me at a time when I was still far from relating these dialectical reflections, relating dialectical philosophy itself, to the actual practice of own thinking with the radicality that I hope I shall gradually be able to achieve. At the time I had published a considerable number of theoretical pieces on musical questions,[7] but I immediately realized that these theoretical reflections on music, which still obeyed the principle of immanence, namely the principle of immanent and thus above all technical critique, thereby ran the danger of assuming a narrowly specialized or even academic character; and a Viennese friend of mine[8] once told me that a certain kind of strictly technical immanent analysis always reminded him of the way they approached art in Horak's Music School, an institution of great strictness and pedantry which nonetheless succeeded in maintaining sub-branches in many parts of the city.[9] Now I wanted to avoid the danger of thinking in the style of Horak's Music School, so I experimented by producing reflections and considerations on music which I described in both a literal and a metaphorical sense as 'Music from the Outside'.[10] I understood this in the literal sense of not hearing music as it sounds in the concert hall or the opera house, for example, but rather of hearing what an opera sounds like if we fail to return to our seats after the interval and then simply perceive all this noise from outside – of seeing what this noise tells us from outside; and I had the feeling that this brings out a side of music that we otherwise overlook, and what struck me here, in more general terms, was that we can really say something about a phenomenon only if, in a sense, we also look at it from the outside rather than solely from the inside, that is, if we also consider it within the social context in which it stands.[11] And I believe, as if in obedience to that famous 'darkling aspiration',[12] that I was not just seeking to combine the view from outside with the view from inside in order to produce a so-called synthesis of both. For I was already vaguely aware that, while these two perspectives do belong to one another and stand in a certain tension with one another, they cannot be collapsed together; and, when I talk about the mobility of thought with regard to the phenomenon, what I mean to say is precisely that one must consider the phenomenon both from within, in terms of its own demands, its own origin, its own principles, and also indeed from without, in terms of the functional context in which it stands, the side which it turns to human beings, its meaning it specifically assumes for the life of human beings. And I may remind you that it is quite conceivable, and indeed highly likely, that works of art of the greatest stature – works which in themselves are anything but mere ideology and are actually, as Hegel would say, a form in which truth appears[13] – can nonetheless become ideology through the role which they assume within the prevailing cultural industry today. Thus you can perhaps see that it makes good sense to pursue these two perspectives, the immanent and the transcendent approaches, independently of one another in a certain way, and simply trust that, if our thought penetrates both aspects deeply enough, the relationship between them will reveal itself after all – a trust which, I must admit, I have never been able to relinquish to this day. This double-edged character of thought, which must therefore be at once within the matter and outside of it, and which is also involved in the method pursued by Hegel in the *Phenomenology of Spirit* – this very double-edged character of thought expresses something essential to dialectical thought, and it is only for that reason, and not for the sake of some passing *aperçu*, that I am talking about this idea of the mobility of thought here today. For dialectical thinking does indeed imply the unremitting effort to bring together the universal and the particular, the *hic et nunc* and its concept, while remaining aware that there is no immediate or unmediated identity between these moments and that, indeed, they diverge from one another.

I would say that the epistemological-dialectical place of what I have called the mobility of thought, in contrast to all merely inductive or merely deductive intellectual procedures, is precisely the attempt of thought – now abiding with itself, now moving beyond itself – ultimately to bring the knowing subject that approaches from without together with the movement of the matter itself. This is something which is necessarily involved in the dialectical method. And, if we distinguish these things, if we refrain from seeking any blank identity between them, if we are able, on the contrary, to alternate these genera, as it were, if such alternation is the very colour of dialectical thought, this does not simply spring from an artistic nature which is incapable of thinking in any other way. It is because this is actually the colour of dialectic itself, the colour of a kind of thinking that unites identity and non-identity. But it is clear that, specifically with regard to this aspect which I have just described for you so suspiciously, as I might put it, so suspiciously precisely because so seductively – it is obvious that the strongest possible resistance will instantly be provoked. When it is claimed that this is a privileged form of thought available only to those who are particularly fitted for it, one that certainly cannot be translated without more ado into a universally binding method, this is the most innocuous form of resistance that I have mentioned. The much more widespread suspicion regarding the mobility of thought arises from the charge that such thought effectively avoids responsibility, that it is a slippery and unreliable form of thinking which eludes our grasp, which we cannot hold down, and thus really evades any firm decision about what is true or false. If we remember the fundamental reflections about 'the true' and 'the false' which we have already presented, the first thing to say is that even this, which I have just expressed in a rather crass manner, is actually not so inapplicable to the concept of dialectic. For a single individual judgement, taken in isolation, is indeed neither absolutely true nor absolutely false, and the truth is actually nothing but the path that leads precisely through the falseness of our individual judgements. All the same, given that philosophy and science always also play a part in the power struggles between individuals, groups, states, classes, nations, and so on, a certain suspicion is naturally appropriate at this point. For if our thought is only 'mobile' enough, if we relinquish real argument rather than just refusing to be bound by it in a rigid manner, as we suggested here, then we may be tempted to do what Socrates, the ancient practitioner of dialectic, was specifically accused of doing: τὸν ἥττω λόγον κρείττω ποιεῖν [*ton hētō logon kreittō poiein*],[14] or 'making the weaker word appear the stronger', like the nimble and well-oiled wrestler who can defeat his stronger and simpler opponent, or like the clever talker who knows precisely how to cheat the peasant out of his cows. Now this ancient objection to the sophistical appearance of dialectic, which I mentioned by way of anticipation right at the beginning of these lectures,[15] is not to be taken slightly, and we cannot of course deny that dialectic, and especially certain dialectical forms of argumentation, can indeed degenerate into this kind of evasion we have mentioned. You will repeatedly discover that the more differentiated our critical intellectual reflections become, the less rigidly they unfold, the more variables they thereby take up into themselves, the more they must also forfeit stringency in the traditional sense, and the more they are thereby exposed to the danger which I have just outlined for you. And it is specifically philosophical discussions on the highest level which generally prove especially vulnerable to this danger. In the first place I would say that this danger can only really be allayed by that freedom with regard to the object which Hegel asked for,[16] in the sense that any practice of philosophy, and especially critical philosophy, is legitimate only as long as it is reflective about itself, and that also means as long as it does not demand to be in the right. We could almost say, with due exaggeration, that the renunciation of this demand is a criterion of the truth of thought itself, that in a sense thought must set itself in the wrong, though in a way that convicts the very demand to be in the right of its narrow and limited character.

But this on its own is hardly enough, for I believe that what strongly emerges here is precisely what I described a couple of sessions ago, in a way that may well seem paradoxical and surprising to several of you, as the positivistic element in dialectical thought[17] – an element, incidentally, which in a sense was also emphasized by Benjamin in his vindication of induction in the Preface to his work *The Origin of German Tragic Drama*.[18] The only way of meeting the chronic danger of that μετάβασις εἰς ἄλλο γέγος [*metabasis eis allo genos*][19] which is involved the 'mobility' of thought, it seems to me, is an extraordinary obligation to expose ourselves to the object in its specificity. Thus, if we are talking about particular epistemological questions, I would say that it is a false argument, or a false kind of dialectic, if we tried to direct the discussion by claiming that specific motifs which have already been subjected to criticism in this connection nonetheless possess a good, useful, respectable or positive function for their part within the totality of the form of thought in question, for in that case we should simply keep to the original epistemological problematic. The path of dialectic, which attempts to move beyond the specialist and highly circumscribed perspective of logic and epistemology, would be one which did not content itself with simply identifying the point which requires criticism and then declaring: 'Look! There is a mistake in the reasoning here, you have got yourself entangled in contradiction – the whole thing is therefore worthless.' Rather, the next step would be to show why, within the constellation of such thinking, the relevant mistakes and contradictions inevitably arise, what has motivated them within the movement of such thought, and thus how far they reveal themselves, in the total context of thought, to be significant in their own falsehood and contradictoriness.

This is actually the most important thing one can learn about the discipline of dialectical thought. Since dialectical thinking does not start from any rigid concepts, from a rigid system, from any rigid givens, but is eminently required to abandon itself to the matter itself, it can only really avoid the danger of that relativism, that arbitrariness, that spurious flexibility of which we have spoken if it takes that obligation towards the individual object not more loosely but indeed more seriously than the usual sciences and our usual habits of thought typically do, if it immerses itself in individual problems with an incomparably greater seriousness than conventional thinking ever allows.

Now if you ask me here for some kind of rule for how to proceed in this regard, for how to accomplish this, you will only embarrass me, for I can offer you no such general rule, and that would indeed be to demand too much of dialectical thought. All I can say to you, where dialectical thought is required to explore any specific object, is that we must expressly reflect whether we have tarried long enough with the latter, whether we have looked at it so closely that it begins of its own accord to come alive, or whether we have contented ourselves merely with the conventional cast, as it were, with the stereotypical pre-given concepts, of the thing in question.

I would like to take this opportunity to point out that I have no intention of simply recommending dialectic to you here as the best method of thinking. 'Dialectical thinking is indeed the best' – this is a slogan but it is not the truth. Dialectical thought as such can of course be misused for any conceivable mischief in the world just as much as any other form of thought, and if it possesses any advantage on this level I would say it is this: precisely as a method of mobility and continual self-reflection, it may involve a moment that makes us

rather more alert and sceptical in relation to such misuse or in relation to the obtuseness of traditional thought than is generally the
case. The suspicion which dialectic encounters at this point, the
general suspicion with regard to the mobility of thought is itself
grounded in social factors. Such mobile thinking is generally identified with relativism, with a refusal to acknowledge anything determinate or firmly established at all, instead of seeing that the movement
of such thought proceeds precisely by taking what is determinate and
firmly established even more seriously. This is exactly the domain
where the dialectical approach is accused of being essentially
ungrounded, of offering us nothing established to hold onto, of rep-
resenting a form of thought that only ever deprives us of something
without giving anything back. The tacit assumption here is already
the affirmative one that thought, rather than abandoning itself to the
matter itself, is supposed to fulfil a particular psychological function:
to set us on firm ground or to warm our hearts, just as sentimental
heart-warming literature does. And what is commonly described as
a *Weltanschauung* or 'worldview' – which can never be distinguished
too strongly from genuine philosophical thought – is indeed intimately related to the sphere of heart-warming literature, even where
the content of such literature assumes the form of Buddhistic pessi-
mism. That matters little in this connection. And it is already quite
wrong to demand that philosophy give us anything at all in this sense.
For it is we who must give something to philosophy, namely everything, our entire conscious experience, and we must be prepared to
enter into rather questionable kinds of speculation, while recognizing
that, in return for what we give in this regard, we may well not receive
back what is commonly expected of philosophy.

This approach naturally arises from the circumstance – if I may
introduce a sociological excursus here – that the more rural parts or
agricultural sectors of the population must usually pay the price of
progress in that universal advance of rationalization which indeed
increasingly undermines the merely direct connection of human experience and thought to the realm of nature. These parts of the population, therefore, rather than radicalizing the idea of progress itself to
the point where they too would receive justice for themselves, tend
to lay the blame on this principle of mobility, as if the itinerant
pedlars were to blame for the increasing poverty of the peasantry,
selling them pitiful wares for a pitiful return. I am not sure whether
such pedlars still exist today, but I think it would be better for us
philosophers to confess that we do have something of the pedlar
about us than to sport old-fashioned costume and betake ourselves

to the mountains in the style of the settler who still knows all the train times, as Degas wonderfully put it.[20]

That is all for now regarding the charge of groundlessness. The assumption that thought should always stand on firm ground, that it must never be deprived of such ground under any circumstances, is essentially bound up with that notion of a given absolutely first principle, of the primacy of such a ground or principle, which we have already criticized. Dialectical thought must confront this issue. There is no such ground for philosophy, at least not for philosophy today, any more than contemporary society can still be grasped on the basis of its supposedly natural foundations, any more than agriculture is still crucial for contemporary society. For here the truth itself is a dynamic truth, where the primordial moments, as they say, do still also appear as moments, as moments of the archaic, as moments of memory, or however you want to describe them, but not as something to which any higher substantial meaning could be ascribed from the metaphysical, moral or logical point of view. The core of thought, that which is actually substantial in thought, that which allows it to show its truth and makes it more than merely empty talk, this core is not the unshakeable ground on which it stands, nor is it some reified detachable thesis to which we might point and say: 'Well then, there it is, that is what it has to say, there it stands, it can do no other, God help this thought.'[21] These are all notions about the content of philosophy, which have sprung from considerations of conscience, from the need to show our colours, which generally suggests that the only true and responsible thought for those who profess it is one which can be called to justify at every suitable opportunity by the relevant boards and commissions. In other words, all this effectively implies the denial of that moment of intellectual freedom which provides the essential climate for the dynamic exploration of philosophical thought. For the core or substance of thinking is the latent power from which thought is ultimately drawn, the light which falls upon things through thought, which is not itself thing-like, not some reified object to which one then has to swear allegiance. This is the *'idole d'échelle'*, for which truth ultimately depends on the demand that thought must be able at any and every moment to justify the ground on which it stands and the reified core that forms its content. Whereas we have to recognize that this substantial moment is something that stands behind thought, a source of power rather than something like a thesis, something we could just repeat or take into possession merely by a process of checking or control. I have no wish to impugn the notion of methodical control, and I think you will already have recognized that the conceptions of dialectic which I am trying to unfold for you here really have nothing to do with a kind of wild and unbridled thinking which has simply forgotten everything that critical philosophy has developed in the way of methodical control. Dialectical thought cannot possibly proceed in this way since it emerges strictly from critical thought, is itself nothing but philosophical critique brought to its most acute point of self-awareness. But I would specifically like to remind you that the concept of philosophy which we are trying to develop here is not a merely isolated or specialist one but one which is meant to be significant for the vital concerns of your own work, and thus I would like to point out that this concept of methodical or intellectual control, which certainly plays a very important role with regard to dialectical thought, has itself undergone considerable changes over the course of time. Now the idea of such methodical control, and indeed with potential reference to all individuals and all questions, namely to everyone who shares the faculty of reason, was originally intended to liberate thought from all dogmatic tutelage, was simply designed to prevent human beings from submitting to arbitrary claims of any kind. It was directed above all against certain fundamental theological arguments which appealed to miracles, and the possibility of rational or empirical control was most emphatically asserted in this regard. But today the concept of intellectual control has largely – I will not say absolutely, but largely – reversed its original function. For today it effectively amounts to preventing a non-conformist form of thought – thought which cannot simply be translated into a step-by-step approach to knowledge, namely into a development of what is already given – a form of thought which cannot just be reproduced by anyone whatsoever and at any time whatsoever. The principle of the gradual acquisition of knowledge basically amounts to the idea that we can only ever think what is already known with constant variations, as it were, in a process of infinitesimal transition to the new. And this idea negates those fractures in truth and knowledge which are rooted in the fractures of the world itself and which furnish the content of genuine knowledge as such. In view of the danger that I seem to be contradicting certain 'democratic' rules of the game where knowledge is concerned, I should perhaps say here that even in the *universitas litterarum*, in the republic of the learned, the notion that everyone must check every thought, at least in their own professional field, that the truth or dignity of an intellectual achievement must be judged in each case by the number of positive recommendations that have been garnered from professional colleagues, strikes me as extraordinarily problematic. For the consciousness to which we actually appeal here as a criterion of truth is for its part a consciousness that has already been shaped by the mechanisms of social accommodation, and one which tends in many cases to excise what is actually essential to thought. But of course there is also no guarantee that a non-conformist thought is necessarily true, for, precisely through the kind of intellectual control which has now become universal, everything which escapes it tends in turn to assume an apocryphal or rather far-fetched character, and indeed in extreme cases, such as that of the originally highly gifted and recently deceased psychoanalyst Wilhelm Reich,[22] may ultimately come to appear paranoiac or even fraudulent. In our current situation we are actually confronted with a very grave antinomy: on the one hand, thought is consumed in the blind repetition of what exists and is known anyway, namely in conformity, and, on the other, thought which eludes methodical control thereby runs the danger of becoming uncontrollable in any sense and effectively falling into delusion. And this tendency is surely not the least innocuous of those symptoms of intellectual dissociation and collective schizophrenia which we can observe today in so many areas of our life, and one that deserves, it seems to me, to be taken with extraordinary seriousness.

The truly new, by contrast, is thus always a qualitative leap, to use Hegel's language[23] – a qualitative leap not in the sense of a kind of thought which leaps anywhere, but in the sense of a leap which is produced by persistent exposure to the object itself. And, expressed in these terms, this approach stands in inevitable contrast, in extreme contrast, to the adoption of some quite new or quite different standpoint. When I spoke earlier about the mobility of thought and, if you like, defended this mobility, I should perhaps add, in order to protect this especially vulnerable thought from misunderstanding, that 'mobility of thought' here does not mean a constant readiness to change what is generally described as a 'standpoint'. Rather, it refers to a self-reflective change in the approach of thought, depending on whether it has to relate to the context in which the particular stands or to the particular itself. But the essence of philosophy – and I believe that the important philosophers specifically since Hegel are actually all agreed on this – seems to lie precisely in the repudiation of anything like the concept of a standpoint, although this is exactly what defines the popular notion of philosophy as a kind of worldview. Thus, in place of some such externally introduced standpoint, what is involved here is actually the compelling movement of the matter itself, something which is also captured in the Cartesian doctrine of a gradual advance from one point to another. The movement of thought, the dynamic moment of thought, is also contained in that

Cartesian axiom which we criticized earlier. If I omitted any reference to this positive aspect here, that is because I regard this as almost self-evident. Descartes himself also knew, of course, that knowledge is essentially a process rather than a merely immediate kind of recognition. It is just that he could only grasp the movement of thought which he saw and articulated – and this is precisely the bourgeois aspect which strikes me as untrue here – in the image of what is static and rigid, and the symbol of the ladder which appears in this connection, and which was mocked by de Maistre, is itself the sign that even what is dynamic appears only in congealed form here. This dynamic itself appears as if it were thing-like and immobile, as a freezing of movement into something static, and this has somehow always been inscribed in philosophy in the most remarkable fashion, even in its most dynamic representatives from Heraclitus through to Hegel. And if there is one decisive sense in which dialectical thought must move beyond Hegel himself, then it is surely here at the very point I have described.

LECTURE 16

17 July 1958

Ladies and gentlemen,

Today I would like to turn to the last of the Cartesian postulates and its relation to dialectical thought, namely the postulate of completeness, and thus the problem of system. This is a problem which has certainly not received sufficient attention in the course of our reflections so far, although there is no question, if we take the idea of the power of the whole in the particular with the full weight and seriousness it deserves, that the idea of system as ultimately the sole guarantee of truth cannot be eliminated at least from the Hegelian conception of dialectic. And here I would just like to draw your attention to the question which we shall have to consider very seriously during these last sessions, and one for which I shall certainly not be able to offer you any straightforward solution. The question is this: What happens to the concept of dialectic once the concept of system has become seriously problematic? The fourth of Descartes's axioms and his last rule 'was in all cases to make enumerations so complete and reviews so general that I should be certain of having omitted nothing.'[1] Now I believe that, if you want a really vivid idea of what should properly be understood by 'rationalism', a vivid idea of that moment which the subsequent and especially Kantian critique of rationalism described as its 'dogmatic' element,[2] you can recognize this in a nutshell, and in very concrete form, in this particular proposition of Descartes, and without actually having to mull over those general features which are said to characterize the basic philosophical schools. For this demand already betrays an entirely dogmatic assumption which does not actually appear intelligible at all. This is the assumption that – in order really to possess that completeness which Descartes regards as the authentic criterion of binding truth – you can be quite sure that all of the elements which you are dealing with and have to reckon with are also in fact completely known to you. But this assumption is actually valid only under very specific conditions, such as those which are perhaps most obviously provided by mathematics. Now I do not wish to get involved in fundamental questions of mathematics here. And I believe since the introduction of set theory in particular that things are by no means so simple in the realm of mathematics either – at any rate, even from the mathematical point of view we can say that this axiom of completeness can tacitly be assumed only where we are dealing with definite manifolds. Furthermore, we may say that, in general, the pursuit of knowledge can follow this procedure only if it has a guarantee that, apart from the elements involved the axiom of completeness, no further elements will emerge for knowledge, or if it has decided, arbitrarily as it were, to cut off the possibility of any further elements emerging and has thus contented itself in advance with the order of what is already there. In other words, if you apply the axiom of completeness beyond the extremely narrow mathematical domain in which it was conceived, then you are dealing with a reification of knowledge in a precise sense which I can perhaps clarify for you with this example, now that we have already employed the concept of reification rather frequently. For here we find a third term, as it were, that intrudes between knowledge itself and the object of knowledge, a sort of order or principle which is arbitrarily imposed upon the matter itself from the side of the subject, a kind of schematism, we might say, which disturbs the immediate experience, the immediate relationship, of knowledge to its object, and which, if you like, actually arrests that relationship. Thus this principle of completeness, which is indeed clearly identical with the principle of an all-embracing system, can meaningfully be applied only when it has already been decided, through an arbitrary cognitive act, that our knowledge may reach this far and no further, that a certain order can then be established in material which has been 'prepared' through this regulated conceptual process. If you do not enter this qualification, if you do not therefore observe this demand for completeness, then the axiom of completeness actually becomes a mere dogma. That is to say, it is assumed as a binding truth that the knowing mind could be certain in and of itself, in an almost magical way we should have to say, that all the elements whose unity it is supposed to establish, and which knowledge is supposed to encompass, are also in fact already given to us in a complete and seamless fashion.

If you like, you can regard the efforts of post-Kantian German idealism, and paradoxically even the efforts of Hegel himself, as an attempt to resolve this dilemma, to confront this extraordinary difficulty, in the following way. The material that presents itself to be known – which we cannot initially be sure is capable of being incorporated within a fully systematic context – is itself spun out of consciousness, as it were, and the attempt is made to deduce from consciousness that in which such order is subsequently supposed to be exhibited. Thus in a certain sense the radical intention of German idealism – of resolving objectivity entirely into subjectivity, or, more precisely put, of resolving all that exists entirely into the absolute character of spirit – could find its justification precisely in terms of this systematic requirement, that is to say, in the requirement which is stipulated by Descartes here in a merely dogmatic manner: the idea of justifying this kind of completeness through the constructive process of knowledge, through the way the theory of knowledge itself is grounded, namely the idea of determining knowledge itself as something which in a sense is entirely independent of what would simply be out there, as something which takes up everything into itself for the simple reason that it ultimately produces everything out of itself. But then this gives rise to the difficulty – as we are thrown from Scylla to Charybdis as it were – which is what knowledge is really supposed to mean, what we can really be said to know, if the sum of knowledge as such is nothing but the sum of what is already known. In other words, the question is whether this strictly realized identity does not actually transform all knowledge into a single tautology, and whether by thus merely repeating itself it does not actually frustrate what it set out to achieve, namely the knowledge of something with which it is not itself identical. Hegel also tried to resolve this problem, as I have already suggested to you, by asserting the non-identity, the persisting distinction of subject and object, in every individual moment, and by making this specific contradiction, namely the non-identity of the judgement and the thing which it intends, and thus the inevitable failure of the individual judgement which affirms such an identity, into the motor which drives the individual judgement beyond itself and thus ultimately constitutes the system itself in a comprehensive sense.[3]

I do not wish to go into this idea any further here, but would prefer to say something to you about the way in which dialectical thought should proceed if it remains critically aware of the problems which arise at this point, and if it no longer dogmatically stipulates the completeness of all the elements involved in knowledge. Since we can never be sure of the completeness of our knowledge if we cannot say whether new elements of knowledge will not constantly emerge in what is already given – for every object harbours an infinite wealth of aspects, and there is no need to add anything new here precisely because the matter itself offers infinite newness in every moment – how are we to respond if we are not to proceed in a simply non-conceptual manner, if we are not simply to surrender in a bluntly empirical way to everything new in each particular case, if we do not actually wish to renounce knowledge altogether? Now I would say that, while we should not strive for completeness of knowledge, neither should we of course simply isolate our individual cognitive acts, merely registering things in a static and thus unconnected form which lacks any relationship to the whole. And dialectic is a trick – if you can forgive me this looser mode of expression – or perhaps at least an attempt to square the circle which this problem presents to you – just as dialectic as a whole is essentially the attempt to resolve the paradox of identity in non-identity not just by coming to a stand-still here but by unfolding and advancing through these elements. I would therefore say that the authentic task of philosophical thought is to furnish certain models rather than trying to embrace everything, rather than yielding to the chimerical demand not to leave anything out, something which is closely related anyway to that pedantic petit bourgeois need for absolutely continuous step-by-step conception of thought which I described for you during the last session. Philosophy should effectively be concerned with constructing models, and, if I expressed this last time by saying that the substance of philosophy, the substance of thought, lies not in its supposed theses or its individual propositions but in the source of illumination which stands behind this thought and falls upon the individual objective moments in each case, this also applies to what I am saying to you at this moment: this source of illumination, this cone of light, falls in fact upon individual and specific objects which it brings out – here, if you like, it indeed resembles positivism – but does so in such a way that the cognition of the particular thing also casts light, or is reflected in turn, upon all other objects which there are. In contrast to the merely limited sort of 'correctness' which is involved in procedures of identification and observation, I would say that the criterion of philosophical truth lies in how far it is capable of moving from something specific already known to us to shed further light upon a range of other things – lies in how far the activity of knowing is driven onwards from this centre of cognitive force. It is this cognitive intention, which allows illumination to transpire from the perspective of particular knowledge, rather than mere subsumption under a cover concept which has effectively been shaped by an administrative mentality, that seems to me to be the essential concern of philosophy.

Perhaps it is worth pointing out that what I am saying to you here, and which may strike some of you as rather audacious, can in a sense also be found in the theories of knowledge defended by two of the most influential thinkers of the previous generation, who were also aware that, while the traditional conception of system was indeed inadequate, the mere subsumption of the individual under general concepts, namely the mere classification of what happens to be given, was certainly not sufficient either. I am thinking of two thinkers who have very little connection with one another in terms of their influence and their explicit intellectual positions, but whose teachings I would like to touch upon for a moment here precisely in order to show you that what I have just formulated for you in a very extreme way is not some impulse that has fallen straight from heaven, as it were, but is something that is already very clearly prefigured, at least as a potential, in the context of contemporary thought. I am referring here to the concept of 'ideal type' in the work of Max Weber and to the concept of essence developed by Edmund Husserl and subsequently extended by the phenomenological movement to specific material areas of experience. Now the concept of ideal type in Max Weber is an attempt to manage without system – and indeed Max Weber possessed no system. And you will not find a general overarching concept of 'society' itself in the entire theory presented in his *Economy and Society*. Nonetheless, Max Weber felt the need to move beyond any merely isolating form of scientific observation, and his conception of *Verstehen* or 'understanding' is itself an anti-positivist concept, and one which was also criticized by other sociologists.[4] For indeed to 'understand' something already means that we have not allowed it to stand simply as a factum, as a mere factum, since, precisely by understanding it, by discovering meaning in it, I render it intelligible in relation to something else, something which it itself is not. Now it is in this connection that Max Weber introduces the remarkable concept of 'ideal type' which is then supposed, once it is concretely developed, to indicate the universal context in which the particular falls, without thereby claiming that this relationship actually exists. For this is supposed to be a purely heuristic device – that is, it is supposed to allow individual phenomena, such as individual forms of economy, to be compared with capitalism as an ideal type and thus to be conceptually articulated in turn. And once the ideal type has fulfilled this organizing role, and perhaps even been refuted by the facts, it can be relinquished or can now just 'go', like Schiller's famous Moor once he has done his duty.[5] And the number of ideal types is in principle infinite, for I can form as many ideal types as I wish, according to Weber. The purpose of such types is solely the practical scientific one of providing a means of organization.[6] You can clearly see here how he attempted to deploy a type of thinking which comes extraordinarily close to the concept of model I have introduced in this context. It is just that he did nonetheless basically retain a certain positivist conception, since for him the universal, in relation to the particular, is ultimately nothing but an abbreviated expression of characteristic features, and he completely fails to see how the universal essentially inhabits the particular, which is precisely what we have been trying to grasp here in specific epistemological terms. Thus this ray of cognition, which sees what is ultimately essential in the phenomenon, becomes a merely ancillary operation in which no trust is actually placed, something entirely without substance, since its object, the encompassing universal itself, is supposed to be without substance, and the model in question is relinquished after all. In other words, the concept of model as a weighty epistemological category is effectively replaced in Max Weber by a pre-dialectical model of knowledge which reflects the perspective of traditional logic.

And we find something comparable, if you like, in the phenomenology of Edmund Husserl, at least in this regard, for there are indeed countless other facets to phenomenology which cannot be considered here. For Husserl believes that with an individual object I am able to intuit its essence, its pure *quidditas*, that which makes it precisely what it is, through a process of leaving out the effectively contingent aspects of the object, and that I can do this without referring to a multiplicity of objects of the same kind and without abstracting the element they have in common. And he quite rightly realized that the concept which allows the individual thing to be illuminated, which allows us to grasp it in its essential character, to grasp it precisely as it is – that this concept is not the same as the ordering concept under which a series of objects can be encompassed in terms of a merely formal unity. It is just that Husserl too, like Weber, shrank back from the decisive step towards dialectic insofar as he also remained oriented to traditional logic, insofar as he effectively conceives what I intuit in and through the individual object – the essence that is illuminated for me, the model, as it were, in which the individual object appears to me – once again as nothing but the universal concept of that object. He had no other notion of essence itself than the universal concept under which individual objects can be grasped, and simply believed that, in a mode of cognition that resembles a model, this universal reveals itself to me in and through the particular. But this universality for its part was still understood in terms of the usual classificatory logic, with the result that his own theory of essences got caught up in the greatest difficulties, since this universal, the ordering class concept in which the individual moments are included, is of course precisely what I can never intuit out of the individual thing.

If you consider for a moment this concept of model which I have tried to suggest to you here – the attempt to let the illumination of particular moments cast its light upon other things in turn – and if you try to think this concept further, you will immediately recognize an essential feature of these models which philosophy undertakes to develop (and I must confess here that everything that I do in the way of philosophy, every word that I publish, is not some attempt to deal exhaustively with a certain field but solely an attempt to develop models which could indeed cast a distinctive light upon an entire field, a light that also alters and determines that entire field in a particular way. And in all of my own contributions, whether they are good for anything or not, I always orient myself very strictly by this concept of models). You will recognize that this concept of models only possesses any meaning if it successfully forfeits its mere isolation, if it really also points beyond itself, if in some way it redeems the claim that the particular that has been illuminated here is itself something universal. And the question of how we redeem the claim of particular and specific cognition to a certain universality, that – I would say – is the specific problem of knowledge which dialectical thought must confront today. But if we do not wish our individual models simply to stand side by side in an isolated and unconnected manner like so many little pictures[7] – which was once a critical objection to phenomenology, and one could also say the same for Weber's idea types – this cannot be accomplished by bringing these models under some overall concept, such as a 'worldview' or a general 'position', or again by gathering them into some supposedly systematic form, by fitting them into a system. I would say that the requisite communication between them is best accomplished not by bringing them all under a common denominator, but by sinking subterranean passages, as it were, or by somehow opening doors into these subterranean passages from each individual instance of knowledge. In this way these models can connect with one another, indeed connect subterraneously, as I would like to put it, without this interconnection being imposed upon them by the arbitrary demands of organizational thought. The interconnection here must emerge out of the complexion of the matter itself, and is something over which the thinker has no actual power;

and I would almost say that it is a further criterion of truth, an indication of the wealth and binding character of knowledge, whether this communication of the individual models is produced in and through itself, as it were, or can only be produced in an external superficial manner. If I once wrote that it is a genuine indication of trustworthy work that draws forth its requisite quotations spontaneously, as it were, that it tempts them to come forward of themselves, this is precisely what I was trying to capture.[8] Thus I would say that the interconnection of thought, the interconnection of knowledge achieved through such models, which actually accomplishes what earlier ages had once expected from the idea of system, that such interconnection displays the character of a labyrinth rather than that of a system. And I once formulated a claim which those of you who have read these things must surely have found rather shocking or at least highly thought-provoking, and it is this: 'True thoughts are those alone which do not understand themselves.'[9] And it is very easy just to say, 'Well then, it's also obvious from such philosophy that it cannot actually understand itself.' Now I would not deny anyone their delight in such an *aperçu*, but I wanted to express very clearly precisely what I have just been trying to bring out for you here, and I would ask you to take what I am saying as an interpretation of that earlier claim. And perhaps you will also see here that such claims are not actually *aperçus*, although they may initially strike you like that – and not merely pointed remarks either, for they occupy a very precise place within a continuous line of thought. For I wanted to say that actually only those thoughts are true which communicate with other thoughts by virtue of their own intrinsic gravity, while those thoughts are not true which are captured in a superficial general concept, which are merely classified and subsumed under an abstract universal, and thus can already only be determined as a 'particular case' or mere example of a universal, whereby they naturally lose the very salt which makes knowledge into genuine knowledge in the first place.

If I may perhaps use an analogy from literature to suggest what I mean by that distinctive labyrinthine character of knowledge which seems to me to be quite indispensable today for knowledge which really is such, knowledge which is interconnected but not systematic, then I believe that Kafka's novels – or indeed Kafka's work as a whole – actually possess in this regard a very precise epistemological function, while I may also note in passing, for those of you with a specific interest in literature, that Kafka's works, by virtue of their close affinity to parables, cannot be assimilated into the category of works of art. What I mean is that, if you read Kafka attentively, you will not

be able to shake off the feeling that all these novels and stories communicate with one another in some kind of way, and this not on
account of the single personality that supposedly stands behind them,
or of a single pervasive mood – and in Kafka's honour we should
point out right away that there is no such thing as a 'mood' in his
works – or even of some 'worldview' they allegedly contain, for these
novels are far too significant in themselves even to think of expressing
that kind of content – this is all so much nonsense, the sort of thing
you can read in the wake of Brod and Schoeps, for example.[10] What
we actually encounter, on the contrary, is a remarkably coherent and
internally connected world which nonetheless eludes any attempt to
grasp it as a unity, and which appears in a multiplicity of facets to
which this thought returns again and again. And it is this labyrinthine
element alone which allows knowledge to address the infinite character of living experience without either truncating it or blindly
submitting to it, and which represents one of the impulses of the great
form of the novel generally. And if we wished to write a logic, an
epistemology, of the great novels, which God knows would be an
important thing worth doing, then we could also discover a labyrinthine form of communication between particulars in the work of
Balzac[11] which is very similar to that which I have pointed out in
Kafka. And if I may introduce a completely different kind of writer
from our own time here, then I would say that the work of Heimito
von Doderer in its general structure is entirely pervaded by this labyrinthine character.[12] Allow me simply to add here that this labyrinthine dimension indeed has something essentially to do with the
structure of society as the ultimate object in question and also as the
ultimate constitutive subject of knowledge itself, for in fact we live
in a society in which everything effectively communicates with everything else in a specific functional context, but where this intercom-
municative context itself is in a certain sense irrational, that is to say,
is by no means transparent. For it manifests itself in a particular kind
of compulsion where one thing finds its way to another without the
overall concept of the whole, the system which everything obeys, ever
clearly revealing itself as such. What I mean is that our thoughts,
without reflecting upon themselves in terms of their universal determinacy, are necessarily driven beyond themselves and almost always
lose what they actually intend by allowing themselves to be reduced
to a generic universal concept. I have already spoken about the
concept of intuition in extremely critical terms at an earlier point in
these lectures.[13] If the notion of insight is to tell us anything over and
beyond the purely subjective character of particular kinds of thought,
if 'insight' is to mean more than the fact that we just suddenly 'see'

something, then I would say that it always actually signifies just this moment when a thought is not produced on the basis of the relevant abstract generic concept, but where it is related, I would almost say, as an individual thought to a concrete object, while also pointing beyond itself and releasing the power which allows the individual moments to hang together in their subcutaneous and actually hidden structure.

But I would now like to turn to the concept of system which is effectively implied by Descartes's axiom of completeness. And the first thing I would like to say to you, in order to bring the discussion regarding the concept of system in relation to its contemporary form, its contemporary manifestation, is that the philosophical conception of system itself, in terms of its inner structure, has already undergone decisive historical change. And I think it would be well worth investigating the various transformations to which the concept of system itself has been subjected. I don't exactly want to begin with Adam and Eve, and will therefore restrict myself here to modern philosophy, to the history of philosophy since Kant. And in this context it looks as if what the concept of system is basically meant to do, in the face of the sheer multiplicity and irrationality, the sheer opacity and contingency of things, is precisely to secure the moment of unity; and this minimal but necessary unity of thought which can assert itself against this otherwise overwhelming sense of contingency is what precisely Kant understands by system. In those significant philosophies which developed in response to Kant, and in the most extreme degree in the philosophy of Hegel, who has inevitably furnished the thematic angle of orientation for these lectures, we find that the claim of systematicity is immeasurably extended in comparison to that starting point. For what we see here is ultimately an attempt to develop the entire abundance of reality itself, the abundance of everything that exists, out of the pure concept – in other words, out of spirit. And since this[14] is posited in identity with spirit, since spirit generates everything out of itself, there is a sense in which spirit thereby also has everything at its call and is thereby the master of everything that it is. Thus everything now stands within and nothing is left out of that complete context that was already postulated by Descartes. Yet this context – and this point reflects one of the deepest impulses of post-Kantian philosophy – is no longer the somewhat reified context which was conceived by Descartes in accordance with a definitely mathematical schema. For the context in question here, by contrast, is that of the self-production of the whole. In other words, the system is complete not in the sense of bringing everything that exists under a single denominator, as it were, but rather by attempting to produce everything out of itself, out of this Kantian point of unity, namely out of the synthesis of apperception, so that 'system' is now the comprehensive totality of productive spirit which is certain of itself, or the native realm of truth as Hegelian philosophy describes it.[15] Now, if we can speak with some justification of a backward-looking development, or a certain regressive movement, on the part of bourgeois thought, this also applies to the concept of system itself. In other words, once the original claim of identity philosophy had collapsed in the course of post-Hegelian thought, we find that the concept of system effectively goes to the dogs, if I may put it that way, for it now returns to what it was before, namely to being merely an organizational schema. Systematicity now means nothing but the attempt to classify everything as completely as possible, to leave nothing at all out, and in the end, as we can typically see in the contemporary situation, the concept of philosophical system or the system provided by each individual science in fact just becomes a mould or frame, as it were, for administrative purposes, a procedural outline, in short a schema, in which everything that could possibly come before the bureaucrats of thought will find its appointed place in order to be efficiently dealt with. In our next session we shall say more about this specific development, and especially about the characteristic problems, the philosophical problems, which this poses for dialectical thought, and in this connection we shall also give particular attention to the now popular notion of a 'frame of reference'.

LECTURE 17

22 July 1958

Ladies and gentlemen,

In the last session I had begun to say something about the relationship between dialectic and system. And in this connection I have kept our final sessions for the really central question that besets any dialectical method, and that is the question whether we can still hold onto the idea of a dialectic at all once we have surrendered the concept of system. This question is an extraordinarily serious and difficult one, and no one should regard it as something already decided; and I myself certainly do not regard it as so. But first I should like to pursue this relationship between dialectic and the concept of system a little further in terms of a problematic that has already emerged within the context of philosophical systems. You will recall, as I pointed out in the last session, that the concept of system which effectively characterized the rationalist forms of Western philosophy after Descartes first emphatically appears in Kant as the attempt to develop the minimum range of utterly binding and necessary insights from a single unified point of view; and indeed the concept of unity and that of system are essentially equivalent for Kant, which is to say that the systematic structure of philosophy in Kant is actually nothing other than a demonstration of the unity of consciousness and the connection between the given contents or facts of consciousness and the unity in question. And post-Kantian idealism subsequently tried to move beyond Kant, in a certain sense with considerable rigour, by recognizing the incompatibility between this concept of self-sufficient systematicity and the notion of an arbitrary and contingent manifold that is merely furnished from without. It thus attempted to elevate the concept of system to the level of the totality – that is to say, to develop all of reality on the basis of thought in a completely immanent or seamless fashion without leaving anything whatsoever 'outside'. And the most impressive attempt of this kind is precisely Hegel's dialectical system which endeavoured for its part not merely to derive the accidental or contingent, namely what is not peculiar to consciousness, from consciousness itself, but even to determine the very form of contingency as a moment of necessity.

This conception of system fell into disrepute during the nineteenth century from two different quarters. On the one hand, it sprang from the positivist side of the natural sciences, which eschewed the a priori constructions of the Hegelian philosophy of nature in particular, along with Schelling's philosophy of nature, a critical development which eventually came to embrace even the minimum of a priori elements still preserved in the Kantian table of categories or the Kantian system of principles. On the other hand, the concept of system also fell into disrepute for a philosophy which was oriented above all to history and to the category of 'life', an approach which emphasized the incompatibility of systematic logical constructions with the irrational facts, as they were called, which could not themselves therefore be reduced to the realm of consciousness – a development which in a way already begins with Schopenhauer, even if his own attitude to the concept of system certainly remained ambiguous.[1] Such criticism then found its culmination in Nietzsche's influential dictum about the disreputable character of system.[2] After all this, the official or academic forms of philosophy found themselves in a rather difficult and precarious situation as far as the concept of system was concerned, for while on the one hand they were reluctant to renounce the notion that philosophy is the queen of the sciences and that it is possible to unify or to construct all knowledge, all science, from a single unified perspective, they were also of course unable to withstand the force of the critique which had been concentrated upon the concept of system from both of these poles. And this gave rise to certain compromise solutions such as that provided by the rather complex and involved philosophy of Dilthey, which can indeed be described as a kind of positivistic secularization of Hegel with the concept of system now removed. Then there were others who attempted to reduce the concept of system once again to the more modest dimension that it had enjoyed in Kant, while fashioning it in such a way that it could also embrace the full range of the modern natural sciences. This was the solution which was favoured by the representatives of the Marburg School such as Hermann Cohen and Paul Natorp.[3] And there were, finally, other neo-Kantian currents, such as the Southwest School of Windelband and Heinrich Rickert,[4] which sought to attenuate the concept of system by reducing it to a set of general principles, so that in effect it simply became a way of 'housing' the sciences.

If we consider the history of the concept of system more generally, we can specifically trace the process of resignation or, perhaps better put, the process of the rise and subsequent resignation of the modern form of metaphysics. Such thought describes an arc which culminates in Hegel before declining into either eclectic or more modest forms of constructive philosophy. The doctrines of Rickert, for example, are particularly characteristic in this regard for, while he polemicized against *Lebensphilosophie*, the 'philosophy of life', and dedicated a critical book to this subject,[5] he nonetheless felt so threatened by irrationalism that he declared that a system should resemble a 'house' where a whole and living human being – Goethe's name naturally being invoked here – could indeed dwell.[6] This is already of course a highly suspect formulation, for it proclaims system itself merely as a home for any content that it may possibly accommodate, thus renouncing the claim to comprehend the whole truly as a whole and effectively contenting itself instead with a merely organizational form of thought. One might therefore imagine that the concept of system had thereby been silently interred and that any systematic structure had been reduced to that entirely formal domain where it may successfully be maintained without internal contradiction, in other words to the domain of pure logic. And, indeed, logical positivism claims to provide just such a conclusive and absolutely rigorous systematic logical structure, namely a deductive system in the proper sense, which in a quite unconnected way now stands over against an extreme form of empiricism in an even more radical and modernized manner than before. But it is nonetheless worth noting that, in spite of this remarkable history, the concept of system has lost nothing of its attractiveness and that, while any philosopher who undertakes to furnish a system of philosophy today already thereby cuts a rather ridiculous figure – for surely only someone who does not know the world can even entertain the idea of trying to capture the whole world in such a butterfly net – the concept of system nonetheless survives in a certain sense all the same.

Perhaps I can take this opportunity to point out to you that any conception of the history of mind or spirit, and not only of the history of spirit but of actual history as well, which somehow imagines that historically surpassed forms of thought would thereby simply disappear, would be all too innocuous. What we find, rather, within the persisting irrationality of the whole, is that these forms which in truth, in terms of their own claims, have already been overcome and are now literally obsolete still continue to exist, albeit as we should have to say in a certain decayed fashion, and which haunt our transformed world like poisonous substances and create all kind of mischief in the process. And in terms of the historical dialectic we can find some very good or, if you prefer, some very bad reasons why the ultimately very stringent critique of the concept of system has never actually succeeded in completely eradicating the idea of system, and above all the need for system. So, just as before, there are still things that resemble systems, albeit in an extremely resigned form, whether simply as an organized way of sheltering the most general scientific principles we need or, alternatively, as a suitable basis upon which everything else can then be constructed.

I believe that I have already said enough to show that the concept of the whole or the totality, in terms of the role which it plays in dialectical thought, is intrinsically incompatible with this conception of the whole, interpreted as the highest or the lowest common denominator as the case may be. But especially in the contemporary situation in which we find ourselves, where certain systematic approaches also appear to appeal specifically to those of an emphatically scientific orientation, it seems appropriate that I should say something about the concept of system in the new form which it has now assumed. For the positivists themselves speak of a form of thought which allows them to accommodate everything, to assign everything its proper place, without having to endorse any specific theory. Rather, it seems we could almost say that the less any constructive theoretical power effectively determines the individual moments in question – and thus the more the 'spiritual bond' between particular findings disappears – the greater the need appears for some abstract protective structure where everything else can be accommodated, a kind of totality or accommodation which lacks the moment of conceptuality, of comprehending and understanding, of meaningfulness itself. For these systems in the most recent style are nothing more than organizational schemata which are measured in terms of whether they are capable of capturing everything without leaving anything 'outside', and without anything turning up that they would not already know how to file away. I believe that the contemporary appeal of such systematic or pseudo-systematic structures is not accidental, that it is connected with the way in which the world is experienced by human beings today in a new and – I would like to say – negative manner precisely as a closed world. Not indeed a closed world in the sense that this was understood in the philosophy of the High Middle Ages, where revealed dogma effectively coincided with the most advanced level of consciousness, but a closed world in the sense that absolutely everything that is possible within experience is already regarded or experienced by human beings as something pre-formed by society, that the experience of anything new in a serious or emphatic sense is effectively excluded, that the world is moving back, economically speaking, towards the level of simple self-reproduction and is neglecting the tasks of enhanced reproduction – a movement which, at least as a tendency, has actually been confirmed by many economists today.[7] Thus this is effectively a world of experience – we might say – where there is no longer really any 'frontier', where there is no longer anything as yet ungrasped, where everything is already perceived by human beings as something that has been organized in advance. And the need for systematic structure that arises in this new situation is then simply that of finding the conceptual forms which correspond to this pre-organized character, which are already foisted upon everything that is, namely through the phenomenon of the *'bureaucratisation du monde'*,[8] through the phenomenon of the administered world. It is characteristic of these systems of the most recent style that they essentially furnish enormous procedural plans or arrangements where everything is expressly assigned its preordained place, that in such systems there is therefore no room for anything whatever which might transcend them. The great systems of the past, on the other hand, specifically drew their power from the way that the transcendence that belongs to consciousness, the transcendence that belongs to spirit, itself a secularization of the divine spirit, has here assumed immanent form in relation to all that is actual and particular, from the way these systems thus attempted to comprehend even what is not spirit as something that is spiritual nonetheless, to comprehend what is not spirit as more than it is. This tendency on the part of the older systems to lend a kind of meaning to what merely is by grasping it within the context of the totality is something that has completely vanished today. All that we encounter now are effectively gigantic bureaucratic plans which encompass everything within themselves and where the decisive criterion is simply the idea of a seamless fit between everything already contained in them.

Thus these systems provide the very opposite of those dialectical attempts which have exercised such influence on philosophy since Fichte. Such systems are exclusively concerned with pure non-contradiction, and insofar as this non-contradiction is not secured through the content of experience it is transposed precisely to the merely methodological level – that is to say, to the merely procedural level. This means that the categories must be selected in such a way as to establish a seamless continuum between the different sciences that deploy them. Here I am thinking above all of the system developed by Talcott Parsons, namely the structural-functional theory of society[9] which is currently playing such an extraordinary role as a kind of cover theory for empirical research not only in North America but now perceptibly, so it seems to me, in Europe as well. The decisive methodological idea here is to project a system of categories which will permit us to grasp all of the individual sciences within the realm of the so-called human sciences, or the social sciences in the broadest sense of the term, basically in terms of the same categories. He specifically demands this for psychology and sociology, and it is not difficult to show that he also expects much the same with regard to economics and sociology, and that sociological criteria of successful and unsuccessful functioning operative here are essentially derived from Keynesian economics.[10] We must adopt this critically – and I think it is important to draw your critical attention to these things precisely because I believe there is nothing more dangerous for contemporary consciousness than a false sense of security, and because I believe that the greatest temptation for us today is not so much that of extravagant intellectual flights as the desire for protection or security. What I basically mean to say to you is this:[11] one of the specific theses of Parsons's theory is that we should develop categories which will allow us to formulate sociology and modern psychology – which is also how he regards analytic depth psychology – in much the same kind of terms. As a conscientious scholar, of course, he certainly acknowledges that we cannot simply assume continuity between psychology and sociology without further ado – and indeed, as is well known, this difficulty had already been encountered by Max Weber, who, while he also constantly insisted that his sociology was not itself a psychology,[12] was never really able to separate his own concept of 'understanding' decisively from the concept of psychological empathy. But in this regard I think we must say even more radically that, in the context of an antagonistic society, the laws which govern society and those which govern the individual are widely divergent from one another. That is to say, from the substantive point of view, that social laws are purposive-rational ones which are defined by the process of exchange, as Max Weber and indeed to a large extent also Talcott Parsons recognized, whereas the sphere which we characterize as that of psychology in the genuine sense specifically embraces those dimensions in human beings which are not simply exhausted in such rationality. If we do not fear being accused of putting this in too banal a fashion, we might even say without really violating the truth too much that psychology in the emphatic sense is always concerned with irrational phenomena, in other words, with all those phenomena which arise wherever particular individuals withdraw from the demands of rationality upon them by society as a whole, a rationality which is actually no full or satisfying form of rationality anyway, and develop within themselves psychological symptoms and complexes which signify the opposite of those demands – in other words, for reasons which are grounded in the development of society itself, namely on the basis of the simple fact that society depends upon the way it constantly expects various forms of sacrifice and renunciation from the individual, but without ever really making good on this sacrifice and renunciation for which it actually promises some rational compensation. And it follows from this intrinsically contradictory structure of society itself that the psychological constitution of particular individuals and the laws under which particular individuals are to be grasped are the very opposite – we might almost say – of those laws under which the social totality as a whole itself stands. And if, instead of acknowledging this contradictory relationship between the laws of psychology and the laws of sociology and defining it in more concrete terms, we attempted to abstract from it, thus presenting us with a third and higher universal level which is binding for the sphere of sociology and for the sphere of psychology alike, we would simply end up with something wholly abstract and attenuated that could do justice neither to the concrete requirements of sociology nor to those of psychology. Thus the demand for continuity of concept formation and application in systematic domains of this kind finds itself fundamentally compromised from the very start, for it is itself already contradicted by the substantive structure of the moments or by the structure of the contents which it is supposed to be addressing.

In these critical reflections you will encounter once again the same dialectical issue which we have emphasized throughout these lectures, namely this: in contrast to merely subjective reason, to mere method, to the idea of forms externally applied by the subject, we must bring out objectivity as an independent moment, must emphasize that every kind of categorical form which is not developed as much through contact with the object in itself as it is by reference to the classificatory or other logical needs of organizational rationality will thereby inevitably violate the truth. I am speaking about types of system which are highly characteristic of our time, and which, as I predict, will soon emerge in even more encompassing forms – that is to say, the more the administered world also comes to be reflected in what we can describe as a sort of administrative logic or administrative metaphysics. Now these structures typically proclaim a remarkable kind of neutrality, something which is expressed in Parsons's system, for example, by the way the concepts of 'functional' and 'dysfunctional' are employed as the sole criterion in relation to a specific structure of society, as the criterion for the truth or untruth, the legitimacy or illegitimacy, of the structure of society. The sole question is whether such a social order functions or not, where the tacitly assumed criterion of functioning is the ability of the order in question to maintain or preserve itself, even if this transpires at the cost of terrible sacrifices, even if the self-maintenance of such a systematic social order proceeds at the expense of the interests of human beings themselves. Thus all we are basically concerned with here is the logical form of identity, is the fact that such a structure maintains itself as such, and precisely though this identity of the system with itself – irrespective of what it actually relates to, namely the human beings who are included in it – the neutrality which is supposedly preserved here is revealed as a mere appearance. For this kind of thinking, which seems to be nothing but a means of conceptual organization, effectively becomes a form of apologetics for the actually existing social order, quite irrespective of how this order relates to the interests of human beings. The 'harmonizing' tendency of such neutral thought, which arises from the way its own categorical forms help to make contradictions invisible, thus ends up serving the apologetic needs of the existing order. In other words, the actually prevailing social contradictions are not registered by such thought, and the latter thereby ends up justifying the existent as such and effectively offering recommendations about how the continued functioning of the existent may be secured. It is not recognized that the very contradictions which are underestimated by the systematic categorical framework deployed also drive beyond the existing system and could lead towards one that is quite different. I might point out here that the widespread positivist notion of a neutral form of thought, in contrast to one supposedly based on more or less arbitrary value systems and particular standpoints, is itself an illusion, that there is no such thing as so-called neutral thought, that generally speaking this alleged neutrality of thought with regard to its subject matter tends to perform an apologetic function for the existent precisely through its mere formality, through the form of its unified, methodological and systematic nature, and thus possesses an intrinsically apologetic or – if you like – an inherently conservative character. It is therefore just as necessary, I would say, to submit the concept of the absolute neutrality of thought to thorough critical reflection as it is to do the same for concept of thinking in terms of 'standpoints', with regard to which we have already heard some particularly hostile observations on the part of Hegel.[13]

In this connection I would also like to say a few words about that specific form of the concept of system which we repeatedly encounter in the most advanced Western form of positivist thought, and specifically in the social sciences, and which is also invariably invoked when we attempt to construct some kind of whole in contrast to the mere registration of individual facts. This is the well-known concept of a 'frame of reference', as the Americans call it, which could be rendered in German as *Bezugsystem* or *Koordinatensystem*, a 'relational system' or 'coordinated system', to which the individual data can then be related. It is precisely in the context of positivistic empirical research that we constantly encounter the question regarding the appropriate 'frame of reference', and we are constantly told that some such relational system is indispensable. And for positivist thought in particular it often seems as if the possession of such a frame of reference, to which we can refer the data that have been collected and classified, relieves us of further contact with the content itself, with the gathering of the material itself, and as if the real intellectual and scientific achievement consisted in this process of subsumption, this coordination of the accumulated data in such a frame of reference. I believe that this conception is quite mistaken. It seems to me that the notion of a 'frame of reference' actually dissolves that continuity or interconnection between facts and thoughts which I have already tried to clarify for you a little in terms of dialectical categories, and thereby transforms it into a purely technical matter, or a sort of dogmatically arrested perspective. It is typically the case, when such a frame of reference is demanded, that the latter is not supposed to require any legitimation – that is, no one insists that the frame of reference itself be specifically justified, either in theoretical terms or even in terms of the material to which it is applied. It is rather that one just needs to possess a 'frame of reference' if one is somehow to accommodate the relevant data that have been collected in such a relational system. In this way the dialectical relationship between the factical material and the so-called relational system, or the conceptual dimension, is effectively broken in favour of the mere subsumption under categories. And that is not the worst thing either, it seems to me, for what is really problematic here is the fact that this frame of reference itself has an arbitrary character to it. In other words, it is as if we are encouraged to devise just the kind of organizational schema that will accommodate as much as possible and possesses certain advantages of logical elegance, although it is not itself actually derived from a theory or from the concept of the object in question and could basically just as easily be replaced by another schema. It is actually thus, in the literal sense, an act of intellectual administration, a sort of procedural schema which is forced upon us in the bureaucratized world of spirit as it is in the realm of bureaucracy more generally, without ever actually being legitimated in relation to the matter itself. And so we often see how apparatchiks of every kind, the producers of memoranda who know how to apply to the right 'foundations', and all those people who are principally interested in presenting their 'ideas' in the most skilful manner in order to secure some financial reward or some particular position, generally show a remarkable gift for fitting the individual things which concern them into such a 'frame of reference'. And while this may well create the impression that it is indeed the whole which has been comprehended, that the whole was indeed in question here, what we are actually dealing with in this connection is simply a presentational schema rather than a schema of the matter itself. But it should be obvious that such a schema is inevitably rigid and formalistic in character precisely because it accommodates everything so readily and is designed to encompass everything within itself.

But, in addition to this, the idea of a 'frame of reference' also seems to me to have a very sinister aspect to it. For precisely because such a frame of reference, abstractly 'ready-made' or 'factic', is externally applied to the facts it is supposed to grasp like a solid or palpable thing, it becomes something like an article of faith, however vacuous or nugatory it may be. Whenever in the course of a discussion with sociological colleagues we encounter the question: 'Well, what is your frame of reference?', you can generally be sure that the meaning behind the question is this: 'Just come clean, and tell us what your theoretical ideas are, and admit that perhaps the framework of your views about society involves certain ideas which do not fit in with the schema of this society itself, and even endanger it.' The reification of social or philosophical understanding which is implicit in this concept of a 'frame of reference' thus also has a very precise social function. For it helps to make our thought appear solid and reliable, helps to reduce it to a rigid underlying relational system that can easily be labelled in terms of one of today's readily available 'worldviews' or 'ideologies', as people like to put it – and that is precisely what strikes me as sinister in this connection. It is very interesting to note that the only function which has remained over from the idea of system here is that of a formal sense of security, that system here is no longer really meant to signify, as it did in the idealist period, that thought is at home everywhere, that thought comes to itself in and through the world, that thought returns to spirit as its home.[14] Rather, thought now finds security by escaping into forms of conceptual organization where, provided it is clever enough to decide on the most suitable frame of reference, relatively little can ever disturb it. And if a spurious metaphysics and a spurious logic of science effectively complement one another in an almost demonic fashion today, I believe that this is nowhere more evident than at this very point. In other words, the idea of a 'frame of reference' is the scientistic form of the new need for security and is also worth much the same.

I think I have thus shown you something of the relevance which, to my mind, still seems to belong to dialectical thinking in our contemporary situation. On considering the developments which I sketched out at the beginning of our session, you may well think that dialectical thinking has also now finally descended to the underworld, that the speculative moment of such thinking and all the other related things which have fallen victim to decisive criticism must effectively spell the end of dialectic itself. And I have no wish to gloss over the situation here. As far as the 'technological' development or the 'stream-lining' of thought is concerned, the idea of dialectic has indeed been left behind, rather as Valéry suggested that the practices of the poet or artist seem to have been left behind by the white-coated experimental scientist who operates his array of flickering instruments without ever getting his hands dirty.[15] Yet I believe that dialectical thinking alone – in its anachronistic features and, if you like, in its powerlessness before the overwhelming tendencies of current reality – is capable of disclosing the dimension of untruth involved in those seamless and stream-lined categorical forms that are increasingly coming to prevail today. For this dimension of untruth can no longer be recognized at all within the framework of the currently existing scientistic approach itself, precisely because thought no longer acknowledges any 'frontiers' here, precisely because there is no longer anything that in some sense remains outside this fatal structure of immanence. In other words, it seems to me that dialectical thinking alone is capable of calling the administered world by its proper name, even if it looks very likely that the administered world will swallow everything up into itself, that for an unforeseeable length of time this overwhelming power may well efface the kind of thinking for which I have been attempting to furnish certain models here. But I believe it is also part of the historical dialectic that, under certain circumstances, precisely what is anachronistic possesses a greater contemporary relevance and significance than that which can claim to be most relevant and significant today, at least on the surface, namely in terms of what functions best within the given forms and structures.

LECTURE 18

24 July 1958

Ladies and gentlemen,

I concluded the last session by trying to show you precisely how dialectical thinking stands in contradiction to the essentially administrative mode of thought which prevails today. And if I now continue to speak about one of the particular difficulties which dialectical thought presents for us, this is perhaps because it touches upon that aspect of contemporary consciousness which is most obviously marked by such administrative thinking. I am talking about the tendency to think in simple alternatives, to model thought on the research questionnaire, to encourage the kind of thinking which in totalitarian states expects people to produce the relevant papers to show whether they are Aryan or non-Aryan, proletarian or non-proletarian, right thinking or dissident, or whatever it may be. The world in which we live tends to determine the fate of human beings under the rubrics of precisely such narrowly defined classes, just as we now witness something like a cruelly ironic fulfilment of the idealist thesis of the identity of thought and being insofar as all possible categorical forms, all possible merely organizational forms which derive from the realm of administration and have been foisted upon the human world, are turning into powers – and indeed into fearful powers – in the real life of humanity. It is the kind of thought which can be characterized in the old words of the German cabaret singer who asked 'Are you for, or are you against?'[1] And whenever you get involved in political or other discussions, you will almost always encounter this tendency to force people to declare quite unambiguously whether they are for something or against it. I will not consider here how far the concept of 'engagement', which has become so popular today, is basically identical with such thinking in terms of alternatives. I sometimes harbour the suspicion that this is indeed so. In Germany there is naturally a specific background to this administrative mentality, one which probably has something to do with the German Protestant tradition, just as it was characteristic of the German situation, which dialectical thought was destined to challenge, that a certain 'inward-ness' was also curiously combined with that administrative mentality. This is something that actually still awaits adequate analysis, and the circumstance in question accounts for the extremely compromised character of the concept of inwardness which is involved here. Anyway, I can clearly remember how violently, even as a child, I rebelled against the saying 'He that is not with me is against me'.[2] For this already seems to imply – under the ethical pretext that we have to decide rather than remain lukewarm – that we are forced to assume certain alternatives or certain decisions which in reality are not derived from the authority of autonomous thought at all, and where we must appeal instead to the concept of 'decision' and accept something externally prescribed for us in a heteronomous fashion. Thus we have no other choice but to decide between one sample on offer and another, between two such alternatives, and the concept of free decision which is postulated here is already effectively negated once we are confronted by these possibilities.[3] This is typically the form in which heteronomous thought is imposed upon us under every conceivable imaginable pretext as the only conceivable kind of thought there is, just as we would really have to describe the regres-sive thought which prevails today principally as a reversion to heter-onomy, as indeed Paul Tillich very perceptively argued over a quarter of a century ago now.[4]

But the particular difficulty which the dialectic presents for thought in general at this point is this: the dialectic itself cannot simply become the opposite of an Either–Or. In other words, dialectical theory and dialectical thought cannot be read in terms of a Both–And. And I imagine that you will recognize both the difficulty and the provocation of dialectical thought very clearly in this regard: it is neither an Either–Or, like the aforementioned choice between pre-established alternatives, nor a Both–And, like a weighing up of mutu-ally conflicting possibilities between which we are supposed to discover the middle way. It is the historical fate of the dialectic which hails from Hegel that its central concept, that of mediation, has been misunderstood in the very sense I have just tried to point out for you. For people have imagined that to think dialectically is basically to think that there is something good and also something bad about every conceivable thing, and this has therefore eventually dragged dialectic itself down into the ubiquitous broth of conformist consciousness, thereby reconciling it with that well-meaning relativism which claims that there is something to every position, while also claiming the opposite, namely that everything that exists has good and bad sides as well. Now I will certainly not deny that this motif is also involved in the distinctive perspective of dialectic, which attempts to do justice to objects in all their complexity, and indeed there is a specific moment of humanity here insofar as this attitude of Both–And at least negates the assumption that consciousness must exercise some kind of judicial function in the face of what confronts it by strictly separating its objects into the sheep and the goats. But once we have acknowledged this motif of dialectical thought, we must certainly not ignore the other dimension, the insight that what is described as 'mediation' in the dialectic is not a middle way between extremes. Rather – and this seems to me to be the really decisive thing here – we must recognize that dialectical thought itself can move only through its extremes towards that moment with which it is not itself identical. In other words, if I may express this in a phoronomic fashion, dialectical mediation is not a mean between opposed terms, for it is only produced by entering into the heart of the extreme, and it is precisely by driving this extreme to the uttermost point that we become aware of its opposite within the extreme itself, in accordance with the logical structure which I attempted to explicate for you right at the beginning or at least in the first few sessions of these lectures.

What we are talking about today is not the logical aspect of this movement through the extremes but rather the ethical aspect of thinking, if I may put it that way. Thus when we attempt to point out the historical limitation or the questionable character of some progressive phenomenon or other, we do not do so by contrasting the more even and moderate side with the more advanced or progressive side of the phenomenon and qualifying the former as superior. Rather, we are critically compelled to drive those questionable moments themselves in the direction where they might genuinely be corrected, to promote self-reflection with regard to the phenomenon in question and, where possible, to encourage its further development in a clearer and more consistent form than it had formerly exhibited. To be honest, I am speaking rather *pro domo* here, for I have repeatedly found when I felt compelled in my aesthetic writings to exercise decidedly critical judgement regarding certain avant-garde phenomena that, while this met with a kind of problematic enthusiasm among the public, it met with a kind of disappointment among my avant-garde friends, as if I had finally come to see reason and was now prepared to defend the claim 'Thus far and no further' – something that I would actually regard as a completely undialectical proposition.[5] There is no power in the world which can arrest the movement of critical thought, and if dialectic itself has ever been tempted in certain contexts, as in its critique of so-called 'reflective thought', to abort the process of critical reflection, this is surely its cardinal sin and the very moment which implies that we cannot simply stay with the Hegelian dialectic itself.[6] But, if critical thought fully engages with a progressive phenomenon, this cannot mean invoking an average and wholly familiar expression of human reason in this regard. It can only mean the attempt to reveal the higher potential of the phenomenon whose inadequacies are in question by bringing its own principle ever more powerfully to bear. Or to express this more substantively: if we must constantly recognize a dialectic of enlightenment, namely a dialectic of rationality which compels us to acknowledge all the sacrifice and injustice which the path of enlightenment has brought in its course, this should not mean and cannot mean that we try and return to something before this enlightenment or that we cultivate protected 'nature parks' of irrationality. It should mean and can only mean that we also recognize the wounds which enlightenment has left behind as the moments where enlightenment itself betrays its own imperfect character and reveals that it is actually not yet enlightened enough. And it is only by pursuing the principle of enlightenment through to the end that these wounds may perhaps be healed.

This is the distinctive position of dialectical thought which is indeed difficult to grasp, and extraordinarily difficult to occupy and maintain consistently, a position which refuses to think in terms of simple alternatives but equally refuses any facile reconciliation of these alternatives. I should like at least to clarify what I mean with reference to a specific model. When I express these things in a rather general way, as I have been doing here, it may well seem quite clear to you, or at least to those of you who have followed me up to this point. But whenever concrete thought is involved, and particularly whenever concrete methodological arguments are involved, you will repeatedly discover that this proves much more difficult than it all sounds *in abstracto*. Thus it seems to be an almost ineradicable intellectual disease in Germany that we typically adopt a dual perspective with regard to the social sciences. On the one side, we have those who say, 'Of course, we have to think in a radically sociological and empirical way, to think in a historicist manner, and there cannot really be anything firm or solid here, for all that is clearly relativized through insight into the dynamic character of things.' On the other side, we have those who defend the view that every social science or every science that takes human beings as its subject matter must be oriented towards what people love to call a 'set' of firm or supposedly eternal values – or a *Reihe* [a range or series] of values, as we might say in German. Only recently, when I gave a lecture in Munich on 'Individual and Society',[7] a young academic, hailing from sociology I believe, informed me that I would either have to think in radically sociological terms or I would have to provide an anthropology, and that we would get nowhere without one or the other. And if in response one tries to unfold the rather more complex and differentiated dialectical structure which I am attempting to present here, people immediately tend to assimilate this conceptual approach to a relativistic historicism or to a form of thought for which in the final analysis there is no such thing as the concept of truth. I would be more than happy if I had at least managed in these lectures to disabuse you of this assimilation or identification, and to make something clear to you that I can only really formulate here as a thesis: that I am just as emphatically opposed to relativistic sociology in the style of Pareto[8] or his imitator Mannheim[9] as I am to the ontological anthropologies of today, whether we are talking about Scheler, Heidegger or Gehlen, and that the model of thought which I am attempting to outline for you here is precisely one that refuses to recognize this very alternative. In other words, dialectical theory holds fast to the idea of truth. A dialectic which was incapable of bringing the measure of truth to bear so rigorously and persistently upon every claim to knowledge that this latter would dissolve in the face of it would already lack the power without which no dialectical process could ever be grasped at all. And the idea of truth is already involved in the insight into untruth, namely in the critical motif that is the decisive dimension of dialectic, as its necessary condition. The notion of exercising critique without thereby capturing the untruth of the matter in question is meaningless. Yet the concept of truth which is called into play here is not something transcendent to the phenomena themselves. This is precisely what the dichotomous consciousness of the present finds so hard to grasp, namely what is at stake in dialectic as a whole: that, while the theme of truth is ineluctably and unconditionally posited and intended in this moment of critique, in the moment of thought which cannot but press onward, the truth in question cannot itself be fixed and reified as something beyond the phenomena. Rather, the truth must be sought within the life of the phenomena themselves, and the individual phenomenon must be questioned with regard to itself, with regard to its own internal consistency, if it is to be convicted of its own untruth.

Perhaps I may express this in analogy with a theological mode of discourse and say that the dialectical concept of truth is a negative concept of truth, just as there is a negative theology.[10] If Spinoza proclaimed the celebrated proposition 'verum index sui et falsi',[11] we would declare that 'falsum index sui et veri',[12] that there is no tangible, positive or thing-like concept of truth such as could be vouchsafed only by the assertion of an immediate identity of the order of things and the order of things. On the other hand, the power from which all insight into untruth lives can only be the idea of truth – it is just that we cannot lay claim to this idea itself as something given, for it is more a source of illumination by which determinate negation or insight into determinate untruth may transpire, as in the saying from Pandora which I recently adopted as the motto for something of mine: 'Destined to see illumined things, not light.'[13] In other words, dialectical thought cannot accept the traditional distinction between genesis and validity either. It cannot endorse the radically psychologistic conception, or the psychologistic view in general, that every kind of truth is reducible to its point of origin, that truth itself is displaced once we have got behind it and uncovered how it has arisen. Here I would expressly appeal to the insight of Nietzsche, who rightly objected to the traditional idea that what has come to be can never be true – in other words, that what has emerged can never be anything other than what it has emerged from.[14] But if you accept the dialectical conception that I have tried to develop for you in contrast to any philosophy of origins – namely that what has emerged is or may be qualitatively other than that from which it has emerged – then we can relinquish the belief that the truth of some spiritual content is necessarily compromised or disqualified through reference to its genesis. On the other hand, we must recognize something else in turn: that the hypostasis of any truth without regard to the process in which the life of truth consists, in which it emerges, in which it expires, in which indeed it finds its own content, that any such hypostasis of truth in contrast to its emergence – in other words, the absolutization of validity in contrast to genesis – is just as false as the relativization of truth in terms of mere genesis. And here too any dialectical analysis must effectively demolish the alternative into which it would otherwise be pressed, must comprehend this alternative itself as merely apparent, as a product of a reified form of thought, rather than allowing itself to be subjected to such an alternative in the first place.

And something analogous holds in another context, if I may touch on this at least in a passing or cursory fashion – for it is obviously impossible at this point to provide a full analysis of all the categories involved. All I can do is introduce them here and try and elucidate them in the light of some of the fundamental reflections we have developed. Thus something similar holds for the whole complex of issues surrounding the so-called concept of value, a concept which for its part actually arises in philosophy only when its intended object is itself no longer substantial – that is to say, when the given order of existence is superseded by rigid and administrative concepts which are then specifically set up before us as norms or values or even as guiding conceptions. On one hand, the notion of supposedly value-free thought, as emphatically defended by the positivist conception of science and as epistemologically formulated by Max Weber, already strikes me as extremely problematic precisely because the very distinction between true and false is, if you like, a value distinction. Unless I ascribe priority to the true over the false in some way or other, unless I maintain something like the primacy of the true over the false, then that concept of the objectivity of thought upon which the notion of value-freedom specifically insists must forfeit its meaning. On the other hand, however, it is just as dogmatic to swear by certain values supposedly enthroned beyond all history, and then, like Scheler,[15] introduce an external criterion defined in terms of these rigid values, and in relation to which all content is measured. This leads precisely to the kind of anachronistic thought where criteria such as *Bindung* or 'bonding' are brought to bear *in abstracto* upon social situations and structures of behaviour which, in accordance with their intrinsic character, cannot possibly be measured against such a criterion in this way. Thus we see that, here too, the task of dialectical thought is not to mediate between concepts of this kind. It would be merely comical to say, for example, 'Well, there are indeed no eternal values, but there are certainly relative values with respect to each particular epoch, and within the epoch in question we must keep to the values which specifically hold for this epoch.' Now I do not think that I need to present the comical aspect of this approach in further detail, which is hardly diminished by the fact that there are innumerable philosophies which actually imagine they can successfully deal with the so-called problem of historicism in this way. The solution to this problem, it seems to me, lies in the recognition that a genuine analysis of the concept of value itself leads us to its conditions and its inadequacy, while it is equally clear that the concept of value-freedom cannot strictly be realized either. Thus a form of thought which understands these categories themselves in the process of their constitution will not simply negate one of these concepts in favour of the other but will rise above this alternative and thereby specifically attempt to appropriate those normative moments which are generally grasped by the concept of value only in their abstract and reified form.

I have already said that the relevant criterion, or the only possibility which dialectical thought acknowledges as such, must be immanent in character. And I believe that it is precisely here, if anywhere, that genuinely contemporary thought can learn something absolutely decisive from Hegel's thought – namely from his demand that thought must not bring any external criteria to bear upon the matter, which was indeed the characteristic approach of the time, but rather abandon itself to the matter itself and derive its criterion solely from the latter precisely by simply 'looking on', as Hegel himself puts it.[16] And this is the decisive moment of the dialectic: that the object to which dialectical thought addresses itself is not something intrinsically featureless which acquires determination only through the way in which we impose a categorical network upon it. Rather, the object in question is also already something determinate within itself; in other words, there is no object, precisely insofar as it presents itself to us as something determinate, which does not also already harbour thought, does not harbour subject, within itself. In other words, at this point in the dialectic there is a moment of idealism, namely the reference to subjectivity as something mediated, a moment which must also be retained, however critically or sceptically we otherwise resist the general claim of idealism to grasp or produce the world out of itself. On the other hand, this approach is not idealist in character, for the moment which I have just described as subjective is itself precisely only a moment, and the underlying concept of subjectivity itself in this connection is something abstract, is an abstraction from those living subjects, those living human beings, whose thought belongs to the determination of the oppositions in question. And precisely on account of this abstractness, on account of this untruth, if you will, this moment cannot itself be turned into something absolute either, cannot be turned into something which simply exists 'in itself'. For the subject is just as inevitably mediated through the object as the object in turn is also precisely mediated by thought.

In this connection there is one other thing that I would just like to say here. The prevailing form of thought typically proceeds in a dichotomous fashion: on the one hand it undertakes to gather facts, while on the other it says, 'Of course, we also need some kind of value system to organize the facts, for otherwise we shall never be finished with them.' Yet there is also an arbitrary and contingent moment inscribed in such dichotomous thinking – even and indeed especially so when it presents itself in a highly absolutist or dogmatic manner – and it is this: the act of evaluation, or whatever it is that appears to transcend the relativity and contingency of the merely given with which I am engaged, is inevitably referred back to some 'standpoint' or other, and the choice or adoption of this standpoint itself is implicitly treated as something which is effectively contingent. I am talking about the way someone will pursue their investigations as a scientist, for example, and then say, 'But as a Christian I also have to assess the facts I am dealing with in the light of my norms', or, 'Speaking as a socialist I must assess them in this way', or again, 'Speaking as a German', or whatever it may be. Perhaps you will forgive me, ladies and gentlemen, if I offer you some rather crude and banal intellectual advice here, but in the course of these lectures you may rightly learn to be sceptical about all statements which involve the words 'Speaking as ... I think ...' The moment that you say 'Speaking as ... I think ...', you have yourself already relativized the truth you are about to claim as an absolute truth in adopting this form of words, and thus effectively fall short of your own intentions. And, what is more, you thereby confirm and strengthen that social schizophrenia of thought which splits up human consciousness in such a way that individual consciousness may function precisely as scientist, as citizen, as Christian, as private person, as professional person, or as whatever else. I am well aware that this phenomenon of social schizophrenia that I have just described is itself of course grounded in the functionalized character of modern professional life and ultimately in the unfolding economic tendencies of our time, and that this cannot therefore be changed merely by an act of will or a philosophical edict. So I harbour no great illusions about the effect of my sage advice in this regard. But if we reflect on these things, if we no longer naively go along with them, if we draw them within reach of philosophical critique, as I have attempted to do here albeit in a rather fragmentary way, then I believe we may move beyond these habitual ways of thinking. On the other hand, it is quite clear to me – and what is a poor dialectical thinker to do except to show the difficulties, to show how far we are actually imprisoned, how far thought is walled in on every side? – that any appeal to the whole and undivided human being, indeed to the undiminished human being fully capable of genuine acts of cognition, also has a rather powerless ring to it. And it remains the case that the insight which the specialist possesses with regard to a particular field, a field which he or she really understands something about – and this holds for poetry just as much as for medicine – is generally superior to that possessed by someone whose undiminished humanity actually depends on never being exposed to the discipline involved in any concrete specific field.

In short, dialectical thought refuses to provide intellectual recipes. I have often said as much *in abstracto*. I believe I have shown with reference to certain models today just how little the dialectic has to offer in the way of recipes, how little it can provide for anyone. And I believe that, unless you can renounce the idea that thought should 'give' you something, as they say, unless you are prepared instead to give something to thought, namely to give yourselves to it, then you should eschew dialectical thought altogether. I would strongly recommend anyone who cannot do these things to stay with traditional forms of thought which are not only generally accepted but also provide a rather comforting sense of security which anyone who engages with dialectical questions must abandon.

When I speak of renouncing the usual sense of security, this immediately brings me to the position of dialectical thought with respect to the prevailing logical forms of thought, and I must also say something to you about this here. The most important question that arises in this connection is the issue of definition. And it is most curious to note that, while very significant philosophers such as Kant, Hegel and Nietzsche have emphatically eschewed the concept of definition, standard intellectual practice in countless areas of thought has continued to insist upon definition – and indeed not only in the context of the natural sciences but also in the field of jurisprudence, in contemporary forms of mathematical economic theory, and in numerous examples of what we may perhaps call 'hyphen-philosophies' – that is, philosophies which are concerned with logistical methods. And all this in the belief that, once we have firmly and cleanly defined a certain concept, we are thereby absolved of all further worries and now stand on absolutely secure ground. This sense of security is a deception, and one of the tasks of dialectical thought, among others, is to shatter the deceptive confidence of this faith in definitions. I would just like to make some brief observations here about the problem of definition and then offer some related comments about the problem of certain other logical forms, in the hope that you may at least find it helpful to recall some of this when it comes to your own concrete work. A 'definition' is basically a way of determining concepts by reference to other concepts. It is astonishing to see how widely and unreflectively this procedure of determining concepts through concepts is generally regarded as obligatory today, without people even realizing that it involves us in a kind of infinite regress which undermines the very sense of security that one wanted to ensure in the first place. But in addition to that I would like to remind you here of the elementary logical fact which may not actually be as familiar to some of you as it ought to be to all of you, namely that we can in principle determine concepts in two ways: either through other concepts or – and for didactic reasons I remain entirely on traditional logical ground here – by pointing to the states of affairs which are brought together by the concepts in question. And traditional logic specifically tells us that every concept, insofar as it is reduced to other concepts, ultimately requires a final 'fulfilment' where we can directly indicate or point to the thing or state of affairs which is intended by the relevant concept. Thus, to point out the obvious, you cannot define the concept 'red' but can only show what is meant by the concept 'red' by presenting various shades of red before the eyes of those to whom you are trying to explain the concept and allowing them, within the parameters of the psychology of perception, to grasp the feature common to all these individual perceptions of red under the concept 'red'. In other words, we can define concepts or we can determine them 'deictically', to use the technical epistemological term, and this already indicates the limitation of the usual concept of definition. The primacy which is accorded to definition today harbours a kind of archaism, a regress to the sort of thinking which predated the critique which first emphatically showed that no truth can properly be derived from concepts alone, that truth can only be fulfilled. But this produces a whole series of consequences for the position of dialectical thought in relation to the practice of definition itself, something I would like to talk to you about in our next session.

LECTURE 19

29 July 1958

Ladies and gentlemen,

In the last session we had begun to address the problem of definition, and, as you may recall, I had specifically drawn attention to the difference between two possible ways of determining a concept, namely the deictic approach, which refers us directly to object intended by the concept, and the definitional approach. This distinction belongs, of course, to traditional epistemological theory, and you may justifiably ask what such an elementary point is doing in a series of lectures about the dialectic, although I must confess that I am not always sure that the principles and assumptions of traditional logic and epistemology are always as present as they should be to those who would specifically like to develop a dialectical logic, so that we cannot perhaps completely dispense with the occasional recapitulation of such issues. But, however things stand in this regard, I mentioned this distinction precisely in order to introduce you to a whole series of expressly dialectical problems. For it is quite evident that recourse to the deictic approach is only possible, can only really be accomplished at all, in a very small proportion of cases, whereas with more complex concepts, which are embedded in a much broader context, such deictic reference is impossible, and that not only because it would presuppose an endless regress but because quantity here also springs over into quality.[1] Thus if we had to show by direct reference to the object itself, let us say, what 'class' or what 'society' is, and both are concepts which reflective investigation cannot do without, we would certainly find ourselves at a loss, not simply because it would require an endlessly mediated process in order actually to show people what class is, but also and pre-eminently because these concepts themselves are so complexly structured, because the categorical moments are so predominant here, that we cannot get away simply by referring or pointing to the object or state of affairs in question. And as a rule these are precisely the concepts which – as philosophers, and especially Hegel and Nietzsche,[2] have objected – effectively elude definition because they involve a historical content which cannot be reified or tied down, as it were, which cannot be straightforwardly related to other concepts without those concepts forfeiting all determinacy in the process. This problem arises directly wherever the relationship between dialectical thought and concepts in general is concerned – and this whole complex of issues involved in 'definition' is very difficult to separate from the complex of issues involved in the question of the 'relationship to conceptuality' as such. Thus, while concepts cannot be sworn to a determinate content in such a way that everything else that it brings with it is thereby simply excluded from the concept itself, our concepts must still possess a certain determinacy *sui generis*. And from this perspective – and you will have seen how I have always attempted in these lectures to introduce you to what dialectic actually means from a fresh perspective each time – you can look upon the dialectic, if it may here be regarded for once as a method, as a way of thinking which expressly does justice to this distinctive character of the concept, since it refuses either to treat the latter as simply vague and indeterminate or alternatively to arrest its movement by an arbitrary recourse to definition.

I would indeed generally encourage a certain scepticism on your part regarding the whole procedure of definition, not merely for the kind of epistemological reasons which have become sufficiently evident in the course of these lectures but also, if you will permit me this *metabasis eis allo genos*, for moral reasons. I have been able to observe, on repeated occasions, that, when someone insists in the course of a discussion that 'It is necessary to define this concept before we can really talk about it', this involves a wish to evade responsibility, as it were, for the concept in question, and that the impulse behind this insistence on defining concepts rather smacks of the sophistry which imagines that it can evade genuine reflection on the matter and responsibility for the issues involved by manipulating all conceptual devices available. Thus if you are engaged in a discussion about the entire complex of guilt regarding the concentration camps, and someone tries to postpone the discussion by saying, 'Before we can discuss the concept of guilt at all, we must first be entirely clear about

how we actually define the concept of guilt here', there is already
something unspeakably obtuse and even malignant about this in view
of the fact of Auschwitz, namely a certain tendency to conjure away
the thing itself through the seeming intellectual freedom and scholarly
sobriety with which we aim to ensure a well-grounded judgement
about the issue involved. And I believe this leads to something else:
the generally accepted and frequently defended view that we first
bestow meaning on concepts precisely through definition, that concepts are in effect therefore arbitrary subjective products that do not
really stand up. That which appears to us, in the concepts with which
we generally operate, as a vague horizon of associations is not, or at
least not entirely, something contingent, something merely constituted in and through the subject, but something which is always also
harboured in the concept itself – certainly not unambiguously contained there, certainly contained there in a potentially aberrant form,
and certainly exposed to all kinds of potential misinterpretations and
merely subjective interpretations. Nonetheless, it is a nominalist error
to believe that every concept we employ is a *tabula rasa* which can
be transformed into a richly furnished table only by virtue of our
definitions. If that were really so, then all meaningful speech, indeed
language itself, would be impossible. And you will repeatedly be able
to observe how those who speak *ex cathedra* in a scholarly or scientific capacity are still by no means inclined to entrust themselves
simply to that other language, the language of definitions, as if its
concepts already involved or provided something meaningful in itself.

This aspect of language, namely the way that concepts always
already bring something to us that we do not ourselves first produce,
something which we must already accept, as it were, along with
language itself, this is precisely what is inhibited by the need for definition. The concept that has not specifically been defined, namely
the word itself that is initially acknowledged just as I receive it,
brings a greater wealth of the objectivity which it intends than the
definition which effectively excises what the word contains in order
to serve the idol of security, the indubitable concept which henceforth stands at its disposal. Now the art or task which the use of
concepts in any dialectical method sets before us is precisely to preserve what is contained in every concept rather than to excise it or
to conceal it through arbitrary posits and stipulations of our own; it
is to become aware of this content as such so that it may emerge
from its initial ambiguity and problematic vagueness. But this comes
about not through definition but by virtue of the constellation into
which our concepts are drawn. And this brings us back to our
earlier insight that the concept of truth is not fulfilled in relation to

any one particular moment of cognition, that no particular cognition can redeem its whole truth since each refers back and relates back to every other.

I think I can illustrate what I am driving at here by reference to a relatively simple kind of experience, something to which I also alluded in my piece 'The Essay as Form', a text that is particularly relevant in this connection.[3] I am referring to the situation of someone who wants to learn a foreign language without participating in the blessing or the curse of regular instruction in school or other institution. I imagine that such a person will broach a text in the foreign language with a certain enthusiasm, even though he is probably familiar with only a rather limited number of concepts, with the auxiliary verbs or a range of other plastic expressions, for example. But, once he has read a certain word thirty times, its sense will become clear to him from the specific context in which it appears; he is eventually able to extrapolate its meaning in further contexts, but he will also probably be capable in the end of appreciating an even greater wealth of meaning when the word is transformed in the context of varying constellations, something that is generally closed to us if we simply look up the relevant word in a dictionary. You only need to try looking up some concept or other in the dictionary, and then looking up the same concept in a thesaurus, to appreciate all that the concept in question involves, and what it does not immediately involve, to see how much this life of concepts fully unfolds within a constellation rather than in isolation. On the other hand, we must also say of course that, while the concept only assumes determinacy through the varying constellations into which it enters, and only reveals its life in this process, the concept also changes at the same time. In other words, the particular value that any concept assumes at each new position – if we are not dealing simply with relatively primitive and undifferentiated terms that are drawn from the world of things – amounts to a transformation of the meaning which the word enjoys in a different position. And the crucial thing where an appropriate relationship to language is concerned, it seems to me, is that we have both aspects at the same time: on the one hand, with the precise view of the concept, or I would almost say with an obstinate insistence on the concept, we become as precisely aware as possible of what it intends, while on the other hand we also become aware of the transformation which the concept undergoes. In this way we grasp the concept as both internally determinate and susceptible to transformation. Concepts are not arbitrary in character: they already possess a kind of firm core, and in a sense the change they involve transpires in relation to this firm core, but at the same time they actually possess no static content and constitute a process within themselves. Every concept is indeed internally dynamic, and the task is somehow to do justice to this dynamic character. And here it is often enough language itself that will have to furnish the canon for the appropriate use of concepts.

I do not want you to misunderstand me here: these critical observations on the practice of definition are not meant to encourage an arbitrary approach to concepts – for what I have been suggesting to you here, I would like to say, is precisely an attempt to become aware of the concept itself in a much more binding way than is available to mere definition. Nor is it my intention simply to impugn the practice of definition as such. And realizing how easy it is to turn such thoughts into nothing but a series of taboos or warning lights, I would not wish to frighten you away from definition in principle[4] – and not only because I worry as a result that the jurists and economists among you would soon encounter serious difficulties in the academic context, something for which I would not like to bear responsibility. For I believe that definitions can play a part in philosophy – and indeed specifically in philosophy with emphatic claims – and even must play a certain part in this context. But then such definitions, I would still argue, are radically different in kind from the verbal definitions which are generally required in the business of the sciences where the reification of things accomplished by science takes precedence over the experience of the thing itself.

Perhaps for the sake of clarity, although I would not like you to imagine that I am ascribing too much importance to this particular example, I could offer you a definition which I myself once deployed in *Minima Moralia*, and which may show you what I am trying to say with these observations, and what I really understand by a definition. For there I claimed, in short, that art is 'magic which is delivered from the lie of being truth'.[5] If someone does not already know what a work of art is – if we may assume there are people who are unresponsive to art, and there are such people, as we know – then a definition such as this will certainly not tell this person what it is, and if the concept of art is not already bound up with a host of other living ideas in the mind of such a person, then this definition will certainly provide no further help.[6]

[Thus if we wish to clarify for ourselves, without already possessing any idea of art,][7] precisely what art is, [and are then informed:] 'Well, art is magic delivered from the lie of being truth', this definition will naturally leave us high and dry. But unless I am deceived here, I would argue there is a higher sense in which a definition such as this is superior to the more standard and widespread definitions of art, such as the notion that art is a sensuous form or structure which lies beyond the world of immediate practical ends and purposes but is simultaneously experienced as meaningful in itself, and other similar approaches. And it is superior to these precisely because a definition such as the one I have proposed can prove illuminating for someone who already has some conception of art, can suddenly intensify all of the elements involved in a way that transcends any merely static or two-dimensional conception of what a work of art is, and thus reveals something of the immanently dynamic character of what the work of art as a process actually ought to be. Whereas I would say that other more static definitions, such as the one which I have just mentioned, which is by no means the worst of them, are essentially flawed because that feature of 'lying beyond immediate ends', for example, can only properly be grasped, can only really speak to us, if we clearly recognize the dialectic of the useful and the useless in a world that is disfigured by utility. [Definitions such as this therefore] can only become genuinely meaningful once we fully acknowledge this moment. And something similar, for example, also holds for Walter Benjamin's definition of fate as the nexus of guilt among the living,[8] a statement which naturally [will be of little help to] anyone who is not already aware of fate, of those moments of blind necessity and menace that are necessarily involved in the thought of fate, of the interconnected character of events – all those things which come to gather round such a definition as if it were a magnet. And I would say that the sense and point of definitions, of philosophical definitions – i.e., of definitions in a higher intellectual sense of the word – is precisely to generate such magnetic fields without arresting the movement of concepts. In other words, these definitions serve expressly to release the life that is already harboured in the concepts themselves, to release the power that is still preserved in them, to release these concepts as so many fields of force. And if it is precisely the task of dialectic to transform what is given in reified form, to transform the merely existent, into a force field of this kind, then we might even describe [definition][9] in this higher sense as the instrument par excellence of dialectical thinking; and perhaps the reason why dialectical thought is especially allergic to the vulgar use of definition is precisely that it violates what philosophy must achieve at the end by placing what can only be a result and a process right at the beginning.

Perhaps I can also say something else here about these definitions which I have been encouraging you to reflect upon and which, as I hope to show you, do not just crop up in the writings of dialectical thinkers by accident, as it were, but are fundamentally bound up with the nature of their thought. For an essential moment and distinctive feature of these definitions is their very concentration: the highly pointed character of such formulations brings them into specific tension with the extensive character of the actual process which they present for us. And this specific contradiction which they embody, the contradiction between something inconceivably extended and something inconceivably intensified, is the flame, so to speak, through which this kind of dialectical definition is able to perform its illuminating role. In other words, such definitions are not to be taken *à la lettre*, as if these were mere conceptual determinations; rather, I would almost like to say, what we need to recognize here is the gentle moment of implicit irony which lies in the way the very formulation intensifies the most extensive content in terms of some proposition which essentially narrows that content without thereby being taken for the matter in its entirety. Rather, the sole purpose of this intensification is to bring out the life implicitly at work in the matter itself.

The stylistic ideal of dialectical definition would thus be a Tacitean one,[10] and this type of definition is infinitely [preferable] to the sort of mere conceptual determination and manipulation of concepts which is deployed in framing research projects, for example. Definition as this is usually understood – the type of definition which flourishes today in particular – is what is known as operational definition. And although I do not regard it as my task in these lectures to examine the contemporary positivist conception of logic, I would still like to say something, especially for the sociologists among you, about this operational concept of definition. It is certainly the case, whenever we work with the kind of reified methods which are effectively modelled on the procedures of the natural sciences, that we cannot simply dispense with definitions in the usual sense. And the point of my remarks here is not so much to disabuse you of this necessary tendency as to encourage you to reflect upon these modes of procedure, which may well have their τόπος νοητικὸς [*topos noētikos*][11] within the accepted practices of the special sciences, but not to ascribe some absolute status to them or not to confuse them with the source of truth. An operational definition is one where the concept in question is determined by the operations undertaken to secure the applicability of the concept in relation to some specific material. Thus if you were ever to carry out an investigation into social prejudice – God help you! – you would find yourselves in the position of having to present your experimental subject with a series of ten propositions, for example, and you would be expected to identify the occurrence of specific prejudices by applying a quantitative method to these propositions as an interrelated totality. You will define the relevant prejudice simply as a mathematical value within the numerical analysis of the responses provided to each proposition, so that someone who scores a numerical value of +5 in relation to specific propositions, for example, is regarded as a prejudiced individual, while someone who scores −5 is regarded as an unprejudiced one. You will thereby naturally have ensured that you do not get into any awkward difficulties with your investigative procedures – that is to say, if you encounter any criticism, you can always claim that what you understand by 'prejudice' in such an investigation is precisely the state of affairs which has been mathematically determined in this way.

But I would argue that this procedure is vulnerable to criticism in a higher sense, and would like at least to indicate some of the reasons behind such criticism. The point of a definition in the philosophical sense would have to be this: that the determination of a concept sheds a kind of light, as I like to put it, that it allows us to see what actually constitutes the life of this concept, what effectively stands behind the concept in question. In other words, a genuine or productive definition would have to be a synthetic definition; it would have to furnish something new beyond what is already contained in the concept, would relate it to something new that has not already been thought, and by virtue of this very relation would bring what we already know to speak. But this synthetic moment is what is excised in principle by an operational definition, such a definition is in effect nothing but [....],[12] or, to put it bluntly, is effectively a tautology – that is, it is defined solely in terms of the means used to determine it, and thus actually says nothing at all over and beyond what it is directly applied to.[13] And, in the second place, we would have to say, as I already suggested in our criticism of the concept of definition, that the concept is treated here as if it were simply a *tabula rasa*, that is, as something which actually brings nothing at all to us in its own right. Thus the concept is exposed instead to a kind of arbitrary determination on our part, and it is indeed one of the best-known paradoxes of all non-dialectical thinking that, the more such scientistic and non-dialectical thought claims to attain to so-called objectivity, the more its determinations reveal themselves to be merely subjective in character. The passion for objectification always effectively leads to the predicament where everything that properly belongs to the object, everything in which the object itself has an essential and constitutive part, is stripped from the object and in a sense now located solely within the subject. The older forms of positivism [that of Hume, or also of Mach and Avenarius][14] also clearly admitted as much and thus developed an essentially rather subjectivist theory of knowledge, whereas more recent forms of positivism exhibit tremendous virtuosity precisely in denying this latent subjectivist moment, although they fall victim to it all the more emphatically. In other words, if you define 'prejudice' as the behaviour of an individual who provides the answers A, B, C and D to propositions 1, 2, 3 and 4, such an interpretation would only be meaningful if you already possess a theory which goes beyond these propositions, which also situates the statements which constitute the definition, irrespective of the quantitative relationship through which the definition is arrived at, in a certain theoretical context – which could develop, for example, a social-psychological model for individuals who respond in precisely this way rather than that because they exhibit a rather specific if nonetheless complex kind of character structure. If you do not proceed in such a way, you actually falsify the life which also inhabits a concept such as 'prejudice', if in God's name you wish to employ this concept for once, and if you continue talking about prejudice in this case you fail to capture what the expression 'prejudice' intrinsically signifies.

The problem I have been talking about here is by no means simply an innocuous one, and by no means simply an epistemological subtlety, as it might initially appear to you once we proceed to employ operationally defined concepts in this way over and beyond their operational definition, which is what always happens, which is what also happened, for example, in *The Authoritarian Personality* at this particular point.[15] In other words, you will repeatedly find that, once a concept has been operationally defined – and this not merely through some intellectual error but for reasons which are deeply rooted in the matter itself – what such [a quantified value] of prejudice effectively means already gets smuggled in, even though the operational definition would actually exclude this use of a concept beyond what is strictly defined by it. And if we proceeded in this way in the context of *The Authoritarian Personality*, which I cannot exactly [regard] as a masterpiece of dialectical logic, this was perhaps justified by the fact that the individual statements which were employed for the operational definition of the prejudiced character, for example, were framed in terms of a basically coherent theory, so that meaningful extrapolation was at least possible in this case. But it strikes me as highly doubtful whether the same could be said for the great majority of similar social-psychological investigations.

I pointed out earlier that the problem of definition is basically one with the problem concerning the position of the dialectic with regard to universal concepts. And here I come to an objection which has repeatedly been raised against dialectical thought, and which I imagine is also still familiar to several of you. You have [learned] from these

lectures, and especially from our critique of definitions, that purely
isolated universal concepts are [not] really defensible, and, insofar as
you have not fully grasped the motivating impulse here and failed to
see beyond the surface of what I have been saying, it may well strike
some of you, in spite of my best efforts to prevent this, as if this
simply amounts to the relativizing of our concepts. And those of you
who make this assumption will then easily be able to say, 'There we
have it, you constantly impugn universal concepts; you say we
shouldn't hypostasize them, shouldn't arbitrarily restrict them,
shouldn't arbitrarily tie them down, but you yourself also need these
universal concepts all the time, you cannot possibly dispense with the
universal. And if you even attempted to do so, then you would simply
– as Paul Tillich once put it to me – end up saying nothing beyond
"that there" and would no longer be justified in making any meaningful or comprehensive assertion about anything.' So I would like
to repeat emphatically here that of course dialectical thought cannot
dispense with universal and comprehensive concepts either, and
moreover that such thought constantly employs concepts characterized by an extremely high level of abstraction. It is even the case, in
contrast to the positivist perspectives adopted in the social sciences
in North America, for example, that dialectical thought is all too
easily accused of deploying overly general and sweeping concepts, of
clinging to the concept of society 'itself', for example. Whereas critical sociological thought would never permit us to use the concept of
society 'itself' as a whole but would recommend instead that we stick
exclusively to concepts which can be empirically substantiated,
namely concepts which move in a kind of intermediate realm in this
regard, which certainly possess a certain theoretical power in relation
to what is immediately conceptualized through them, but which can
effectively be replaced in turn with givens, without going beyond this
realm in any essential – i.e., qualitative – sense. But to this we must
reply: the whole argument here is not about whether we can deploy
universal concepts or not. Dialectic is not a form of nominalism, but
nor again is it a form of realism. For these twin theses of traditional
philosophy – the notion that the concept enjoys substantial being in
relation to the individuals which it grasps and includes, and the
alternative notion that the individual is substantially real while the
concept is merely a *flatus vocis*, or simply 'empty sound and smoke'
– these two conceptions must both be subjected to dialectical critique.
In other words, for dialectical thought, there is conceptual being
solely in relation to some determinate factical being, and likewise
there is factical being only as being that is mediated through cognition, and cognition cannot be thought otherwise [than] as conceptual

cognition. Neither of these two moments, therefore, can simply be exchanged in favour of the other; both must be grasped in their necessary reciprocal relationship. As separate they must indeed be distinguished from one another, cannot simply be identified or collapsed with one another, but neither of them can be turned into an absolute either. The point here – and this is all I want to say to you about this controversy today – is not to insist, given we are using some universal concepts or other, that we must now say B because we have said A, that all conceptual existence ultimately belongs in a [Platonic *mundus intelligibilis*],[16] where [the investigation][17] of the most universal concepts assumes a kind of ontological priority in comparison with the other essentially inferior realm. Thus we are already forced to adopt an ontology simply by employing concepts at all, for everything which is not ontology would then be just pure nominalism, would be reduced to a pure 'there, there'. It is precisely the task of dialectical thought to overcome this divergence, this external and unmediated disparity between these two logically possible extremes, which itself finds particularly drastic expression in the external juxtaposition of the schools of ontology and positivism which we see today. The position we adopt with regard to concepts is neither an attempt to legitimate them by recourse to a realm of highest and absolute concepts independent of any actual beings nor an attempt to legitimate them by treating them merely as an external cast or dissolving them into the things they encompass. Rather, the task of philosophy is specifically to display the interdependence of these concepts in each case, to display both the unity and the variety which is involved in them. But to say that this B is derived from that A, to say that when I use any general concepts I must also use the highest conceivable universal concepts, to which I [must then ascribe an absolute dignity in the sense] of the [proposition] 'If you say A, you must also say B' – all this seems to me to be an element of the kind of fettered thought which dialectic is expressly called upon to challenge. It seems to me to be an expression of that compulsive character of thinking which demands that once a thought is moving in one direction it must always continue in this same direction in order finally to lay hold of something Absolute, whereas due reflection on this very movement actually reveals instead that there is no such absolute 'First' and no such absolute 'Last'. But I would emphatically ask you to remember in all of this that our concepts can affirm this kind of partial substantiality that I have talked about only as long as we refuse to treat them as mere products of the process of abstraction, as long as we recognize that they always already mean something in themselves, mediated as they are [by] history, and that, in being possessed of such meaning in themselves, they are also necessarily related to one another.

I have expended a considerable amount of criticism upon phenomenology, and perhaps some all-too-destructive criticism at that. But today I would like to do [justice] to phenomenology after all and point out that it was a merit of Husserl's, but also of his successors, that with their attempt to provide an objective analysis of the meaning of concepts they actually strove to grasp this moment we have been talking about here – strove not simply to [inject] meaning into concepts [in subjective] constitution by recourse to mere [intuition] but [to grasp meaning as] something which already inhabits them in each case.[18] But they then fell into the mistake of fetishizing this objective moment of objective meaning of conceptual content in turn, of arresting it, of turning it into something that enjoys a kind of absolute existence in itself – in other words, the mistake of not fully grasping the dialectic of universal and particular [...][19]

LECTURE 20

31 July 1958

[Ladies and gentlemen,
    In the last session we saw how dialectic is essentially concerned with the conceptual determination of its object and, at one with the philosophical tradition in this regard, establishes an interconnection between the universal concepts involved; but it also][1] recognizes a feature of these concepts which exhibits a certain freedom in contrast to traditional logical procedures. For dialectic knows that it is bound not to any process of definition but to the matter itself, to the life at work in the concept. Insofar as such conceptual determination does not appeal to definitions, it can only emerge – as I think I have indeed already pointed out to you – through the configuration, through the reciprocal interaction into which these concepts are drawn. The way in which these concepts can only properly be determined in and through this interaction with one another reveals [not only][2] the insufficiency and inadequacy of each individual concept on its own but also the essentially relational character of them all. On this view, therefore, in the higher sense, there is no such thing as a partial individual truth. Now, ladies and gentlemen, of all the challenges which the dialectic presents for ordinary consciousness, the notion that no such individual truth can actually be assumed, that on the contrary there is truth only in the constellation which the quite specific individual instances of knowledge come to make up, is the hardest challenge posed by dialectical thought in relation to the usual conception of thought. And it is also precisely this dialectical challenge which is most strongly resisted by that need for security which in its backward

and regressive form possesses such extraordinary significance for our position with regard to knowledge today.

Without wishing or being able to eliminate this *skandalon* for you in any way, I believe you will still see that we are not dealing here just with a wild claim on the part of an excessively self-reflective philosophy. Rather, we are dealing with how philosophy at this point suspends something which appears so self-evident, which has become almost second nature to thought, which has now exerted its influence over an inconceivably long period of time. For the idea that we can lay hold upon an essentially stable and reliable truth first in individual concepts, and then in the highest generalizations and in highest fields of scientific knowledge, is itself nothing but the projection of the social division of labour upon knowledge as such and ultimately upon metaphysics. In other words, the particular contributions to knowledge which have been facilitated through the necessary specialization of human experience in terms of highly specific roles and professions, and without which the progress of civilization itself would not even be conceivable, have been hypostasized into a very limited conception of intrinsically stable truth. It then comes to look as though the individual field, along with the conceptual apparatus bound up with it, were something that essentially existed in itself, while the interconnection of the concepts involved, of the areas of knowledge, and finally of the spheres of social production as a whole is treated in this regard merely as a result of the interplay between these individual moments. What is actually primary thus comes to appear as something secondary. It is indeed no accident – and I am not sure whether this particular fact in the history of philosophy has ever been emphasized as much as it surely deserves to be – that the specific philosophy in which the claims of limited particular truth, and above all the claims of a limited form of concept which has been specifically developed and scrupulously distinguished from all other concepts, and the claims of definition itself, were first expressly defended, namely the philosophy of Plato, is the same philosophy in which the concept of the social division of labour first expressly appears as an issue of political philosophy and in which the order of ideas, the order of concepts as such, also appears in a direct relationship to this division of labour. You will encounter something rather similar in what is called Plato's psychology – and the term 'psychology' is quite inappropriate here – with the division of the highest faculties of the soul as pure concepts which are distinguished from one another in turn by reference to the different functions exercised within a city state organized in terms of the division of labour.[3] The much earlier philosophers, by contrast, especially the ancient Indian thinkers but also the early pre-Socratic metaphysical thinkers, captured the moment of the particularity which belongs to the individual concept and to individual knowledge in their conception of the interdependence of all beings. But this conception, which was permeated of course by mythological notions of a single overarching fate, was challenged, and in a sense quite rightly challenged, by the criticisms of Greek enlightenment and showed itself to be unsustainable in the face of more rigorous knowledge. It effectively declined as a result and now survives in an impoverished form only in a kind of salon metaphysics – like that of Hermann Keyserling[4] – or in certain doctrines which basically belong in the realm of cultured dilettantism like those of C. G. Jung, for example. And this degeneration of philosophy into a sort of salon gossip, on the one hand, is the counterpart of the scientistic conception of philosophy, of its transformation into a purely specialized enterprise, on the other. In truth, however, concepts do not simply become vague when they take on various meanings in specific constellations, for they are actually vague precisely when they function in a purely isolated way. And they assume genuinely determinate character only in the context of such constellations, namely the kind of determinate character and particular value which I attempted to clarify for you last time when I compared this with the process of reading stories in a foreign language without a dictionary constantly to hand.

In this connection I drew a comparison from the realm of language, and it strikes me in retrospect that this was not exactly accidental. For you can or ought to see at this point that, for philosophy – or, as I would prefer to say, for any kind of knowledge that could properly be regarded as 'scientific' knowledge in accordance with the older Hegelian use of the word *wissenschaftlich* – you can see that the presentation [*Darstellung*], namely what we generally call the specific language or describe with that appalling expression as the 'style' of the work, is not merely an addition which certain more or less aesthetically cultivated philosophical authors externally provide for their thoughts in order to prove their distance from the vulgar understanding of things which otherwise prevails. On the contrary, we must recognize that any thought which is fully aware of the consequences and implications of the dialectical approach, any thought therefore that is in earnest with dialectic, requires an emphatic form of presentation. We must recognize that it is not possible here – as it is in the reified approach of the special sciences – to present a fixed content in a way that separates form and content and allows this content to be expressed in a fashion which may in a sense be described as arbitrary and irresponsible. Rather, it is the very fact that the content here is not fixed in this way, that the content first finds its meaning through the context into which its individual moments enter – namely through that whole which I have been trying to clarify for you – [which requires presentation in an emphatic sense. This circumstance implies that the whole] necessarily becomes a means of grasping the matter itself, becomes a category of cognition. [And this] finds expression in the way, on the one hand, the vigour and accuracy with which the linguistic formulation captures the individual aspect that is intended in each case is precisely what leads the concept most effectively into the overall context, while, on the other hand, the construction of the whole bestows a specific meaning on the concept right down to the grammatical construction of individual propositions, realizes through the medium of language that concretization of the concept, that concretization of concepts in a specific context, which as I have already suggested is precisely what breathes something of that life into concepts which definitions would dearly like to instil but in truth merely serve to expel. In other words, we must recognize that philosophy, insofar as it is not concerned simply with the communication of a fixed and finished content, insofar as, on the contrary, it consists essentially in the conceptual self-reflection of the matter itself, is constitutively bound up with its mode of presentation. It is not some quirk therefore – as I tried to show in more detail in my little piece on 'The Essay as Form' – if philosophical writers who are to be taken seriously are as serious about language as we have become at least since Schopenhauer, who was the first to address this stratum of philosophy explicitly. And, similarly, it is an undeniable measure of the ossification or abandonment of the inner dialectical movement of thought when the latter ceases to be concerned with the specific form of its linguistic expression. You can recognize something of the kind in Scheler, for example, where the irresponsible journalistic tone belies the ontological pathos of this philosophy, or again in the later Lukács, whose total indifference to matters of linguistic expression corresponds to that simple repetition or duplication of a dogmatically ossified doctrine which is also quite appropriate to the content of his thought.

I would just like to say something else about the problem of presentation here, namely that it is only the process of presentation which allows thought to go beyond the merely pre-given character that a concept already brings with it. I have attempted to show you that the concepts I employ as such already have a certain content, that they are not simply counters, that they are, rather, something which I must in a sense obey. Insofar as I offer a resistance to these concepts through the process of presentation, insofar as I employ them in such a way that they express precisely that and only that which I want to express with them, there is a sense in which I challenge the blind power of what they bring with them, and this facilitates that communication between the mere opaque objectivity of conceptual meaning and the subjective intention in which the life of these concepts actually consists. But the distinctive feature of presentation in the medium of language lies in the way that this contribution of subjectivity, which transpires wherever presentation lays hold of its concepts in an emphatic sense, is not in turn an arbitrary matter, does not simply spring from the mere caprice or particular taste of the singular individual, but itself contains in turn a moment of objectivity which is first mediated through subjectivity over against the rigid and merely pre-given objectivity of the concept. I am talking about the objectivity which is involved in the way that the concept must grasp what it is meant to grasp as precisely as possible – and this is an essential function of presentation – while the demands which I make upon my object through the process of presentation are demands which spring not from some merely subjective caprice but effectively arise from the discipline of language itself. Thus insofar as I follow the postulates of language, insofar as I take up the concept by virtue of language, and indeed attempt thereby to realize my subjective intention, I still do so in such a way that, through the subject, I also bring out that objectivity which is indeed necessarily involved in the logic of language and the rigour it demands. I would say that this is the epistemological function of presentation – and this is how I would like you to understand it – of those definitions which are only true as long as we already have a grasp of the matter itself, as long as we constantly insist that all philosophical questions are essentially questions of formulation in a higher sense. The problem of formulation furnishes the specific perspective, the specific site, as it were, where what we can call the dialectic of subject and object is effectively realized in the context of philosophical argument.

   This brings me to the question of the relationship between the dialectic and specific logical forms, an issue about which I would like to say at least something here. For in our discussion of definition and individual concepts we have already been talking about one of these fundamental logical forms. The two other fundamental logical forms, as you presumably all know, are the structures of judgement and inference. What we mean by a judgement, if I may start by offering you the standard account – and in fact we sometimes have to employ such definitions in order to be able to challenge them in some way later on – what we mean by a judgement in the context of philosophy[5] is a linguistically formulated assertion with regard to which the question of truth or falsity can meaningfully be raised, while what we mean by an inference is a relationship of propositions or judgements whose validity is supposed to consist in the interdependent relation between them. I believe – and maybe I can repeat this today at the end of these lectures, in order to make it a little easier for some of you who have found this otherwise difficult to follow – that perhaps the fundamental thing, the simple and elementary thing, from which the process of dialectical thought begins is this: while it is indeed the case that, without judgements – or, to use the traditional language, without the syntheses accomplished between a subject or subject concept, a predicate concept and a copula, namely the 'is', where 'A is B' furnishes the fundamental form of a judgement – there is no such thing as knowledge in an emphatic sense; it is also the case that the judgement itself or every singular judgement is problematic in character. And it is this contradiction which perhaps provides the most drastic motive of all for dialectical thinking: if we do not make judgements, in other words, if we do not subsume certain givens or other under certain concepts or other, then no knowledge is possible; further, and above all, we can advance beyond mere tautology only if by means of some judgement we [place] something which is into relation to something else with which it is not itself immediately identical – that is to say, if we perform a certain act of identification. We can only make objects our own, we can only admit them 'into the native realm of truth', as Hegel puts it,[6] inasmuch as we identify them, namely identify them with ourselves – that is to say, make them the same as ourselves, make what is unknown into something that is in a certain sense already known to us. And it is perhaps one of the most painful experiences we must encounter when we engage in philosophy that, while our entire pathos in this regard, our entire labour and effort, is dedicated specifically to the task of expressing what we do not already know, what is not already present for us, we nonetheless find ourselves driven again and again to express what it is we wish to express by rendering it the same in some sense – that is, by reducing what is new to what is already known, what is already given. Thus every kind of theory, with regard to what it essentially intends, comes to assume that distinctively deadened, rigid and reductive character which makes the conclusion of any particular philosophical work into such an awkward and difficult business for the individual who had to undertake it – an experience which you will find expressed most vividly by Nietzsche, if memory serves me right, in the final aphorism from *Beyond Good and Evil*.[7]

I have thereby already also anticipated the negative moment that is involved in the notion of a judgement. And I might add that this negative moment also has in fact a very precise logical place of its own, for there is something untrue even in this simple act of subsumption which I must perform if I am to arrive at something like truth, at the idea of truth itself. We were already agreed – if I may presume as much after providing you with this definition – that, in the first instance, a judgement is precisely something to which the question of truth is in principle applicable. On the other hand, it is also the case that a certain double untruth is involved in every judgement as long as you take it simply as an isolated judgement. If you say 'A is B', this always necessarily implies, on the one hand, that A is identified with something with which it is not entirely identical, something under which it falls with respect to some moments or features, whereas it remains distinct with respect to others. Otherwise we would simply be stuck with the proposition 'A is A' rather than 'A is B', and that is a purely analytical proposition and would therefore not be a judgement at all in any emphatic sense. On the other hand, however, it is also the case that the predicate concept too, under which the subject concept is brought, precisely through its incomparably greater range or extension with respect to the individual instance which I bring under it, cannot possibly be identified with the individual thing in question. In a strict sense an individual thing is not identical with its concept but falls under that concept. In other words, you will have recognized at this point the paradox that the very form through which the concept or the idea of truth springs, and without which it would be meaningless to speak of truth – for nothing that is devoid of apophantic form, that is to say, nothing which is not a judgement or a complex of judgement could be described as true[8] – that [this form] is at the same time, in its very essence, also necessarily afflicted with untruth. And, seen from this perspective, dialectic is actually nothing but a desperate effort to heal this untruth in the form of truth itself. Thus dialectic is the attempt to arrive at truth through the form of its own untruth.[9]

You could also pursue this in another way precisely by looking at the theory of judgement, about which I have been able to offer you only these rather desultory remarks today, specifically from the perspective of subject and object. For, on the one hand, what you are engaged in here is what is described in the traditional language of philosophy as 'synthesis': you are relating and bringing together moments which were not previously connected with one another in just this way. For synthesis, namely this relating of diverse moments which thought accomplishes, is indeed precisely the necessary subjective side that is involved in any judgement. On the other hand, the truth claim implied in the judgement itself depends on the ineliminable assumption that there is precisely something in the state of affairs affirmed in the judgement itself which actually belongs together. Thus, when you judge 'two plus two is four', the very sense of this judgement is impossible without the synthesis accomplished in consciousness insofar as the latter enacts the multiplication, namely insofar as it duplicates the concept 'two' as such. But the proposition is true only if there is actually also something in the matter itself such that two plus two is four. Now of course you may say, 'That is all very well, I have two moments here: on the one hand I bring something together, on the other hand there are two things that are already connected with one another; so on the one side there would be the mere "form" of the judgement, and on the other side there would be the "matter", as phenomenology describes it, namely the state of affairs itself which is judged.' And yet, ladies and gentlemen, we have to say – and here once again I can offer you a glimpse, as it were, into the hidden life of the dialectic – that the issue is by no means so simple and straightforward. For, while it is certainly possible to distinguish these two moments and say 'if you do not have both these moments, then there is no such thing as a judgement, then there is no such thing as the truth of judgement', it is nonetheless impossible even as you distinguish them to separate these moments clinically from one another as if with a scalpel. You cannot say, 'This is the mere form in the judgement, and that is the mere content in the judgement.' For unless you accomplish the aforementioned synthesis qua subject, you cannot be conscious of the state of affairs that is being judged and which underlies [the judgement][10] in question. And unless, on the other hand, the synthesis relates to such a state of affairs, that is, unless it finds support in the material itself, it cannot arise at all. In other words, the subjective or 'noetic' side of the judgement, as the phenomenologists call it, [and][11] the objective or 'noematic' side of the judgement do not stand opposed to one another specifically as form and content, respectively, but are reciprocally mediated one with the other. You may say, therefore, that the dialectic of subject and object, the reciprocal self-production of the subjective and objective moments can actually be recognized even in the situation of a judgement which appears so formal-logical in character.

And now, ladies and gentlemen, you will perhaps allow me in these final minutes, standing on one leg as it were, to say something else to you here, something more fundamental, about the relationship between dialectic and logic, something that goes beyond what I said to you earlier on when I pointed out that dialectical thought invariably presupposes the validity of the logical forms themselves, even though there is also a sense in which it must also go beyond the validity of the latter. For you may say, 'Through our categorical system, through the structure of those categories which we gather together under the name of logical categories, we have foisted a kind of net over the entire world. And without this net we cannot know anything at all about the world.' And it is absurd to assume that there is some immediate consciousness of the truth which would not in itself simultaneously presuppose this net, would not in itself presuppose these logical forms, and it would not really be difficult to show even the most extreme defenders of intuitionism, such as Henri Bergson,[12] that, even when they attempt to deal solely with their intuitions, in actuality these very intuitions continue to involve the whole logical apparatus. At the same time, however, what I have just tried to make clear to you in a rather drastic way in the context of our analysis of the judgement also holds for absolutely everything that is logically mediated, namely that this logical apparatus is inadequate to the life of the matter itself, and not inadequate in the merely rhetorical sense in which conventional souls love to declare on Sundays that logic cannot do justice to the world and that – on Sunday at least – feeling is all that is left to us. Rather, it is inadequate in the more rigorous, precise and unsentimental sense that the same logic which first allows us to know the world simultaneously shows itself, in terms of its own meaning and object, as always also false, as also always internally contradictory. Now inasmuch as the dialectic specifically grasps these things of which I have spoken to you today, of which I have been speaking throughout these lectures, inasmuch as it reflects upon these things and expressly tries to bring them to consciousness, it is effectively attempting to square the circle, as it were, to carry off the feat of Münchhausen, and, while I admit that it is highly questionable whether this can successfully be achieved, it perhaps still represents the only chance that the claim to knowledge possesses at all. For dialectic is the attempt to break out of the prison of logic, to break free of the compulsive character of logic – in which indeed the compulsive character of society is comparably reflected, just as the primordial form of a judgement is that which condemns to death – but certainly not to break out in a merely declamatory archaizing way, somehow imagining that we can appeal to a pre-logical dimension as the immediately true and substantial, although the latter would thereby be consigned to a realm of chaos. Rather, the course of logic must be challenged by appeal to its own means, challenged therefore by bringing logic itself – concretely in relation to all of its determinations – to an explicit consciousness of its own insufficiency, allowing it to disintegrate through its own power. And the power which accomplishes this disintegration, this negative power of the concept in the Hegelian sense, this essentially critical power is indeed in truth identical with the concept of truth itself. This is ultimately the heart of every form of dialectic, insofar as dialectic itself can still be conceived in philosophical terms and not just inevitably and invariably in relation to praxis. This attempt to remedy the injustice of logic with its own means, as it were, or, if you like, to help do justice to nature by recourse to the moments involved in its own organized domination, and in the first place to do it justice in the context of mind or spirit – this, I would claim, is the central motive which ultimately inspires dialectical thought itself, without which such thought cannot be understood at all. And in this regard, precisely in the spirit of Hegel's *Logic*, it calls upon that power which stands against truth, namely the power of untruth. This disintegration of traditional logic by logical means is brought about not by some external critique of these logical means but solely by an immanent demonstration that, in each case, measured by their own standards, they are inadequate to the truth.[13]

I may point out in passing that similar considerations apply to the forms of inference. I believe that a reformulation of the dialectical critique of the forms of inference would be an essential task for a fresh account of dialectical logic, something which, in the sense I have in mind, has never been accomplished as yet. Remarkably enough, however, we can certainly find the rudiments for such a critique of inferential procedure in the phenomenological tradition, which in many respects of course actually represents one of the most advanced epistemological positions of modern bourgeois thought. And, while I may have touched upon this aspect in my *Metakritik der Erkenntnistheorie* [Metacritique of epistemology], it has not yet been developed as fully as it demands to be[14] – which is why I specifically wish to remind you of this here – phenomenology could also be understood in a certain sense as a critique of inferential procedure. To begin with, I would like to describe the motivation behind this critique precisely as we find it in phenomenology itself. Now phenomenology certainly commits the mistake of believing that we are actually dealing with immediate intuitions even when in truth we are talking about arguments, that is to say, about kinds of inference. It seems to me that this mistake has indeed been sufficiently established, and I feel it is almost superfluous to insist upon it any longer. Yet the underlying phenomenological impulse here is none other than to show – with regard to specific cognition which grasps its object, which is appropriate to its object – how the relationship to other cognitions is not a matter of earlier and later, that cognitions of whatever kind do not actually stand in merely inferential or formal-logical relations to one another. In accordance with our earlier critique of the idea of a first ground or principle in philosophy – or indeed of a final ground or principle, for both are essentially correlative – one must also claim that any hierarchy of propositions, namely any relations of priority in which one would found or be founded in turn by another, is not ultimately compelling. And if you consider for a moment that the theory of inference – if we ignore the issue of induction here – is in fact essentially formal-logical in character – i.e., basically aims to show how various propositions are contained in one another – then the hierarchical relation of major and minor premises becomes doubly problematic. For it is by no means easy to see why any one of the propositions which are conceived as containing one another should enjoy an absolute priority over any other. Insofar as phenomenology specifically attempted to furnish descriptions [in place of logical] inferences and arguments, it also gave expression, without being clearly aware of this, to the notion that formal argumentation in comparison with the reciprocal constellation of thoughts has something arranged and artificial about it, something which it is precisely one of the tasks of philosophy itself to remedy. I would say, therefore, that, while any philosophy which does justice to its own idea must certainly avail itself of argumentation in a critical sense,[15] it should be directed not towards argumentation itself but towards the dissolution of such argumentation. And Georg Simmel's observation that anything that can be proved can also be disputed, and that only the unprovable is indisputable, actually possesses a stronger meaning than it was supposed to have in the specific context, namely that of a psychological relativism, in which Simmel himself originally defended it.[16] If I may simply remind you for a moment how thin and arbitrary are the arguments that are generally introduced in philosophical writings as intermediate concepts between what we might call the 'theses' in question, and how much, even in Kant for example, that which serves the specific domain of argumentation actually reveals itself merely as a kind of architectonic bridge, as a device for sustaining the overall systematic structure, then you will clearly understand what I mean by the dissolution of argumentation in this context.

This too – and here I come back to the issue which I actually wanted to talk about in our session today – is essentially a question of presentation. And, speaking for my part, I would say that the particular kind of dense and concentrated expression which I strive for, with perhaps questionable success, is not somehow designed to do away with argumentation – one cannot do that anyway, and you could easily produce a hundred arguments from writings of my own

– but rather is designed to challenge the traditional distinction between thesis or assertion and argumentation, and thus the traditional form of inferential reasoning, for those reasons of principle which I have tried to present for you. And if the relationship between thoughts is indeed to be conceived not as a hierarchy but as a constellation, then methodologically speaking we must recognize the demand that every thought is equally close to the centre, that there are really no such things as bridging concepts, or theses, and conclusions derived from them. For every individual proposition is imbued with the power of argument, of reflective thought, as well as the power to grasp the matter itself with precision, and the ideal of philosophy, which cannot indeed be redeemed by thought, would be to express in its very form that philosophy is concerned not with assertions and demonstrations but solely with a truth which presents itself in the construction of the whole, and where every word, every proposition, every syntactic structure must in a sense bear the same responsibility as any other. When I said to you that dialectic is in a certain sense a critique of the pedantry of thought, this is an example of what I mean. And I believe that, if you are in earnest with dialectical thought, then the form of presentation you adopt, insofar as it effectively dispenses with the traditional approach which claims to demonstrate certain assertions, is a good indication of whether you are actually thinking dialectically, namely whether the content intended in the thought and the enactment of the thought itself attain that identification which is called for.

I am quite aware, ladies and gentlemen, that this lecture, perhaps more than any other, has proved something of a patchwork, as is effectively unavoidable, especially if one undertakes to engage with the dialectic without being an idealist. Dialectic here is a form of thought which speaks of constellation, of interconnection, of the whole, even while it cannot claim any confident grasp on such a whole, for it has indeed nothing simply at its disposal – [where one cannot say] as in Hegel that subject and object, by virtue of the process they undergo, are ultimately one and the same. And in presenting such a philosophy – and especially given the inadequacies which freely improvised spoken lectures inevitably involve – all we can do is emphasize that fragmentary character which is perhaps the only form in which dialectical thought is possible today. And to that extent, here at the end, I also discover something like an ideology for the inadequacies of what I have been saying to you. But I would not like to let you go, in conclusion, without at least giving you something even in withholding it from you – [inasmuch] as I would like you to consider the question whether such an assumption of identity [can

be avoided at all], or, as I might perhaps express it, [whether] something like knowledge is possible at all without the assumption that
subject and object are ultimately not wholly unlike one another,[17] or
whether in forbidding the thought of such a possibility in a radically
completed enlightenment we do not thereby perhaps forbid ourselves
knowledge itself, and then through this very enlightenment fall back
into the darkest form of mythology. This is a hard nut that I leave
with you to crack, but the vacation is indeed also a long one, and
perhaps you will be able to engage effectively with this problem for
yourselves. For the rest, I would simply like to thank you for your
attention throughout these lectures, which have often proved something of a rough road, and sincerely wish you a most enjoyable vacation, in the hope at least that I may see many of you again for the
lecture series on aesthetics in the next semester.[18] My thanks to
you all.

ADORNO'S NOTES FOR
THE LECTURES

Sum[mer] Sem[ester] 1958

Introduction to Dialectics[1]
General Plan

Themes

4
8
<u>10</u>
12 hours

1. Introduction: the standard objections to dialectic
2. The concept of dialectic
3. Idealist dialectic: the positions of thought with regard to objectivity
4. Idealist dialectic: the experience of consciousness
5. Idealist dialectic: objective logical movement

<u>– 8</u>

6. Dialectical models: sense certainty
from the Phen. of   master and slave
Spirit   unhappy consciousness
                                     essence and individuality, ethical life 300–307
                                     also: conscience
                                     absolute freedom and the Terror

9–10 Dialectical models from the Logic
        Being nothing becoming
        Quality and quantity

Transition from being to essence
    Critique of traditional logic
11. Resumé of Hegel's method
12. Transition to mater. dialectic: Phil. of Right a. Hegel's theory of the state
                                           b. Marx's critique of Hegel's Phil. of Right
13. Concept and problem of a materialist dialectic
    The conceptual mediation of society – an open dialectic
14. The dialectical construal of history as a history of class conflicts
15. The dialectic of exchange relations as central issue
16. Dialectic and ideology
    –18|
17. Dialectical models:
    Overproduction
    Elucidation of society by critical destruction [*Destruktion*]
    Dialectic of the concept of freedom
    Dialectic in the very concept of materialism
    Dialectic of concepts – the state and politics
19. Aesthetic dialectic
20. Our own concept of dialectic
21–22. Our own models

22.IV.58[2]

Lecture: Introduction to Dialectic
8 May 1958.
Dialectic in ill repute, suspicion of sophistry and intellectual exaggeration.
It contradicts the prevailing positivist approaches of today in double sense.
Against sophism: subjective dissolution of truth not the aim

dialectic since Plato is

rather ^ the attempt to save objectivity of truth
by taking up subjective and negative elements

Today:

into truth itself. Idea of a truth without apologetics.
adequation theory of truth in itself already bestows right on what exists. The pathos of the word truth.
Truth not in time but dynamic character of truth itself.
The essence no mere result Phen. 15 and Phil. of Right [?] 31
Dialectic not subjectivistic but just as much also objective.

Thus: the movement of historical forces, even into the most elevated forms of spirit.
Not a method of having right on one's side in a dialogue, but an attempt to grasp the objective contradictions of reality.
From the outset in acute opposition to the contemporary philosophies of being, which already proceeded undialectically from the start.

13 May[3] Beginning
Double character:
Dialectic is the move-
ment of contradictions
in thought and the
matter. Method and
non-method. Allusion
to idealism = identity.

cf. Phen. 24[4]

Also: the mere

Philosophy expressly insists
on being right,

Against the concept of an absolute first, unchanging, original principle.
Read out Phen. p. 14 + interpretation
p. 16 especially penetrating

Re exaggeration: meaningless notion that philosophy, the very concept of which implies the most concentrated intellectual attention, could dispense with this intellectual moment. Truth lies in the extremes. Only what is supposedly exaggerated, what rejects the ordinary superficial appearances, has any chance of approaching truth. On the other hand, dialectic recognizes the given, the immediate, what cannot be resolved into spirit, precisely as one of its own moments.

Dialectic, it is said, is the doctrine of the universally mediated character of everything that is, or, as the Phenomenology of Spirit puts it, of becoming, and this also implies

though the victor still senses a certain unease.

22. Beginning of L. Reflect. on the quotation: The true is the whole.

Mediation in no way external to the matter

More on this after Easter.[5]

the concept of an immediacy that re-establishes itself at every stage.
Transition: the seriousness of dialectic, i.e. the fact that no stage may be omitted, involves this very moment:

On the controversy over rationalism. We cannot charge the thinking which reflects upon rationalization with this latter.

Against the notion of the seamless intellectualization of the
But the negative is no mere supplement, but is not simply to be made good,[6] but must be world through the dialectic. ^ Hegelian philosophy especially, epitomized no mere subsumption under a higher concept. The concept not the [X] by the whole. insofar as it criticized purely subjective ratiocination before the power of what is, has brought out this opposed moment in the most emphatic way.　See Phen. p. 13, seriousness, pain, patience and labour of the negative

Examination of the triadic schema. Against the merely external aspect of opposition. The old mistrust of the concept of synthesis –

Phen. p. 33 | 34 against this p. 35 below
Alleged straightjacket of concepts thus not the case. Relative irrelevance of the triadic schema. In strictest sense dialectic not a method in sense of a subjective procedure, but precisely the opposite, a pure looking on, a self-abandonment to the matter. Most typical objection to dialectic: it recognizes only contradiction rather than simple difference. The concept of

negation of the negation. The negated preserved in the negation.

Model: formal and material
X is a human being.
Human being involves an idea, the whole, what is right.
The concept of man
Humanity not yet fulfilled in any human being! Freedom, autonomy X = human being is false.

this involved in universality.

The proposition is true and false at the same time: contradiction.
When we say: human being we mean more than just the species.

not to impoverish but to discipline contradiction is not to be hypostasized. ^ It simply means that every finite judgement, in claiming, in accordance with its form as judgement, to be the whole truth, comes into conflict with its own finitude, which cannot possibly be the whole truth.

Finitude the content, the matter of the judgement. Contradiction of form and content. The category of contradiction is derived from the Kantian doctrine of the antinomies, must be developed from that perspective. The category becomes a universal one

The notion of 'beyond experience' thereby loses its meaning. once the Kantian separation of form and content, once the rigid and unmediated

character of these paired Kantian concepts is relinquished. Idea of contradiction follows from the emphatic concept of truth itself.

Contradiction is basically the criterion of logic.
Dialectic as theory of contradiction criticizes the simple logical appearance of the world, its dissolution in simple conceptuality, and

likewise the identity of our concepts with what is.

For the beginning on 19.VI.58: Why contradiction, rather than merely difference?

Difference is utopia, dialectic not a worldview, but critique.

Goethe's answer the non-identical, that which cannot be dissolved into spirit.

Logic = absolute identity, contradiction its criterion.

Dialectic as critique of the logical appearance of the world, of its dissolution in terms of our concepts, and likewise of the identity of concepts with what is.

From the perspective of the matter itself: the antagonistic character of the world. The fundamental experience: the world is at once system and antagonistic in character.

13 May.

Re dialectic as straightjacket: dialectic said to be a deductive system, an attempt to unfold reality purely from the conceptual realm.

That is both right and wrong. On the one hand dialectic does indeed seek to develop the 'logic' of real existence, though not as a logic imposed by the subject but as a logic of the matter itself. In other words, the logical compulsion of dialectic is the logical compulsion of society itself, its systematic character is that of the system which constitutes reality and which unfolds as if it were a kind of fate. For the theory of dialectic we are defending, the concept of system is a critical one. On the other hand, however, dialectic is specifically not an immediate or seamless deductive structure. It does not operate with pure identity, does not derive everything seamlessly from a single principle. That is precisely the function of contradiction.

E.g: developed form of exchange society, growth of wealth and poverty etc.

without theory there is actually no knowledge but merely observations.

Some brief comments on the relation of Hegel and Fichte.

Dialectic is the attempt to do justice in thought to the non-identical, to that which cannot be dissolved in thought, and this contradiction, the identity of the non-identical, is the vital element of dialectic.

The paradox of this attempt drives us to unfold it as such, i.e. to recognize that this cannot be accomplished in a simple judgement.

19 June 58[7]

Reference here to the two possible versions of dialectic, the positive, i.e. idealist dialectic, and the critical, i.e. materialist dialectic.

That is, the side of identity and the side of non-identity. In Hegel there is indeed spirit, not so in M. But thereby – without mediation – the concept of dialectic itself in difficulties.

Dialectic presents a series of difficulties for traditional modes of thought.

1. Whole and part must constantly be seen in relation to one another. The part must already be grasped on the basis of a whole that is never entirely given to us; this is precisely what is falsely understood as 'intuition'. 24.VI[8] More on concept of intuition. the whole, in turn, is not to be conceived as something finished, but must be derived from the movement of the parts rather than from a higher general concept. That is, it cannot be derived from theory, the later Lukács for example and the abstract concept of ideology.

precisely this is the case

E.g. mater. interpretation of literature mediated through the totality. Controversy with Benjamin. This is the precise value of theory, which stands in for that whole.

NB. the anti-positivist moment

means in real terms: the apparently ultimate data

– 4 – are all mediated through society as a whole.

no clara et distincta perceptio: the object intrinsically dynamic,

2. There is therefore no step by step procedure as there is in the

not unambiguous.   especially the

natural sciences and in traditional ^ practically oriented

dialectic implies discontinuity. Against breaking everything down into elements, step by step, completeness.

simple and complex

science. Dialectic attacks the traditional concept of an

NB H's scorn for 'being'

absolute 'first' of any kind. Dialectic is not ontology,[9]

not 'natural' reflection.   The mobility of thought, the

^ nor is it positivism.   being within and being without

Answer: knowing where we want to get to   tendency

3. Dialectic eludes the simple alternative, the

without cheaply [?] mediating, not a maybe, or a both / and

Either–Or, or classifying, compartmentalizing thought. Acute

The anti-positivist aspect.
Core issue: refusing to
accept the façade.

Suspicion of evasion [?]

'Leaps' – those of

method – reality.

Thinking in fractures =
refusal to harmonize everything.

e.g. sociology = anthropology

opposition of dialectic towards the standard forms of thinking today. No recipes, no schemas. New seriousness of the Hegelian demand to abandon oneself to the matter itself.   This is precisely the anti-subjectivist aspect.
Not even of itself.

4. Dialectic does not begin with definitions ^ The concepts already appear | phenomenology | (see Essay as Form) owe their form to the context ^ and also change in their internal composition through the movement of thought.
The foolish aspect of definitions as an avoidance of things.
Exemplification through the concept of the individual in relation to the concept of society, a concept which involves both the identical and the non-identical. The need to analyse this double concept of involvement with regard to the individual.

5. Concepts must be considered in their mutual configuration rather than taken in isolation.
Reasons for opposing the arbitrary character of conceptual definitions, attempt to do justice to the life of the matter itself in terms of the concept. This naturally involves a critique of the usual separation of subject and object, i.e. of the assumption that the

How are we then
to think?
Inspiration? Amateur-
ish appeal to hunches?
Answer: through the unity
of the thoughts which express
the matter (contra the usual
analysis in terms of parts)
Models instead of
Completeness.

The truth in this identical motif: the S itself is an abstraction, a moment.

object is characterless in itself and acquires any categorical determination solely through the subject. In this sense, all dialectic, including the idealist dialectic, is opposed to traditional theory of knowledge.

Characterization of dialectic.
A form of thought which does not recognize the separation of phil. from the sciences,
i.e. which brings phil. motifs into substantive questions of knowledge,
e.g. phil. critique of definition: the reluctance to define.

For the lecture of 12 June 58[10]

Kroner *ad vocem*: contradiction.
Identity is contradictory within itself
substantive rather than merely formal truth.
Kroner 331–332
How is transcendental logic possible if insight into formal conditions of knowledge is not itself knowledge?
To set a limit is to transgress it
Kroner's dialectic 333

For 26 June

Problem involved in anticipating the whole.
Critique of the notion that the whole emerges later: the individual as much a product of abstraction as the universal

Scientific order has things upside down.
I am aware of the world we live in <u>prior</u> to any supposedly individual data.
It is only the theory of knowledge, rather than knowledge itself, that imagines otherwise.
Task of restoring naivety in and through reflection
(an essential motivation of all dialectic).
What is sensed first is a kind of pressure.
In relation to this the situation is just as abstract as the whole.
Theory must attend to this experience.
Specific role of theory: to express experience in terms of rigorous thought.
No intuition: the knowledge that points beyond the facts is latent, already present without organized form, and is driven on by rigorous thought.
What intuition is seems is the opening up, the actualization of potential knowing – becoming aware of something, and this is precisely theory.
But this nothing absolute as such, rather it is open.
Always related to its own contradiction, hence <u>not</u> fixed in form.
The whole not envisaged as <u>finished</u> in character.

2. No step-by-step procedure as in the natural sciences and in traditional practically
   oriented science.
   Discontinuity. Relative arbitrariness of approach.
   Related to positiv. in this.

No absolute 'first'. The origin is not the truth but deception.
Here from the other side: ontology and positivism.
Against clara et distincta perceptio, for such an ultimate, absolutely given principle is not the truth,
is not actually given, but involved in a process.

Related to something else, hence not absolutely
distinct.

The object dynamic in itself, thus not unambiguous.
The dogmatic aspect of the Cartesian demand.

How are we to think?[11]

| Not inexactly, but <u>more</u> exactly,
| this is what dissolves fixity.

Insistence

Defence against arbitrariness. Insight not abstract coherence

| Thought no *tabula rasa*, nor 'pure'
| but a moment of experience

but unity of theoretical experience.

Against <u>analysis into elements</u>.

This is unavoidable but only a <u>moment</u>; the elements are not absolute.

Presentation substituted for the matter itself.

The whole not simply composed of the parts but self-producing.

E.g. universal and specific laws.

Natural science: model

Clarify through the concept of <u>factors</u>

Against <u>seamless</u> transition. | from the other side |

problem of intellectual discipline

freedom of thinking

unfreedom of method

Its correlate is freedom towards the object.

Productive thinking is discontinuous, thinking in terms of fractures, otherwise a harmonizing fiction.

not pedantic. The poverty of system. Simmel. ~~System, if substantive, as a home~~

Mobility of thought, within and without. ~~Otherwise untrue:~~

idole
d'échelle.

Suspicion involved here: evasion, (social) relativism

The core of thought is source of its power, not method

Answer: determinate character of particular knowledge and tendency.

In dialectic the particular is <u>more</u> binding than in traditional thought.

Taking up an immanent position – but not as a 'standpoint'.

Integrated, not a system

Dialectic neither ontology nor positivistic.

Against <u>completeness</u>. Models preferable to exhaustive coverage.

Parsons

ident. presupp. of completeness

Centres of power

Against 'frame of reference'. Arbitrariness. Over-sophistication

<u>Ontology:</u> Hegel on 'being'.

Dialectic not 'natural', reflection. Resistance to this.

<u>Positivism:</u> the apparently given always (socially) mediated.

Core issue: refusal to accept the fetters.

3. VIII. 58   Models for the mediated character of the given

1) Relation to public employees (Darmstadt)
2) Role of manager as mask
3) Preference for musical hits: songs that are most performed.   NB the regression involved here.

Objection: as a hypothesis this is compatible with positivism.
Response: 1) Not a hypothesis, since it is not provable through an experimentum crucis.
2) The totality involved here cannot be grasped as a pure given.
3) Meaning as such attaches not to the particular instance of knowledge but to the mediation of the immediate.
4) The path that leads to this is negative, e.g. by showing that those performing objectively managerial roles not necessarily ill-disposed, that public employees not actually known in person. Max Weber.

15. July 1958[12]

Summary: idol[e] d'échelle.

Against the compulsive character in thought, 'category', everything in its place.

Mobility.

'Music from without'.

Meaning of mobility: immanent (coherence)

transcendent (place in the whole)

It is precisely this double character which expresses the non-reductive nature of dialectical thinking.

Suspicion of this mobility, of evasion.

μετάβασις εἰς ἄλλο γένος [metabasis eis allo genos], old objection to the Sophists.

In contrast, obligation of taking a stand where

thought in each case

is responsible, unfolding its transcending character.

The suspicion of this mobility as relativism is socially grounded.

Settled place, ground, against the 'groundless'.

This must be developed; there is no firm ground, only the self-moving truth.

The core, the substantial aspect, of thought is the latent source of power from which it is drawn, not a method that can be applied at every step, not a reified 'thesis' that can be extracted as such.

The changing function of <u>methodical control</u>:

    once an anti-dogmatic moment which refuses to be overawed.

    later the suppression of non-conformist thought.

    constancy = what is actually already familiar, infinitesimal transition from one

        thing to the next.

    The new is a qualitative leap.

Binding character of the particular. Taking up an immanent position, not a 'standpoint'.

2

18. VII.[13]
<u>Completeness:</u>

Dogmatic aspect here. The assumptions of identity philosophy.
Postulate holds only for definite manifolds.
Elsewhere completeness cannot be anticipated, unless I proceed in purely
classifying terms in relation to finished already assembled material, i.e. where
experience has already been arrested.
Hence: completeness as such not be sought.
Task of – philosophical – thought: to furnish models, instead of
trying to encompass everything + ensure that nothing is left out. 'Source of light'.

Criterion of truth:
how much is brought
together.

Process of irradiation, not subsumption.
This motivation in Weber's 'types' for example + in Husserl's
                                        insufficient in both cases on account of alliance with

non-subsumptive approach.   traditional thought
| In opposition to both 'theory-less' positions: | in W: heuristic principle in H: identified
But ^ not unconnected, not isolated.   with the universal concept.
Communication of all thoughts with one another, not to be brought under a
single denominator, but various paths to explore.

More labyrinth than system. 'True thoughts are those alone which do not understand themselves'.

> i.e. those driven beyond themselves in their own movement without being bound to the concept above them. This is the epistemological significance of an 'insight'.

Here a brief history of the concept of system. | Change undergone by the concept of system. in Kant: that which is not merely rhapsodic, unity.

Once the attempt to develop concreteness from thought itself. Hegel.

Major and minor figures. Regius

Today an expression of resignation. A shelter already in Rickert, a place where everything can be housed.

Empirical researchers in particular, and positivists, promote the new concept of system which permits them to accommodate everything without thereby committing themselves to a single theory.

The world appears as 'closed'. Regress to simple reproduction. No frontier. Immanence.

The influence of Talcott Parsons.

Deceptive appearance of compatibility in this connection.

This already highly questionable. No common system of categories for sociology + philosophy; and this follows precisely from the antagonistic character of society.

3

Mere semblance of neutrality.   Objectively speaking there is no neutral
                                irrespective of how thought sees itself.

The logical form of seamless identity becomes a substantive
ideal: the concepts of functional + dysfunctional.

Critique of the concept of 'frame of reference'.
It is the precise correlate of merely chaotic facts.
The continuity of thought is reified into a technical device, or into a dogmatically fixed view.
Arbitrary system of organization legitimated by the governing ordering principle

> Apparatchiks, authors of memoranda
> can always produce frames of reference.

rather than by truth.
Such a relational system is inevitably rigid.
Becomes an apparatus of control: what is your frame of reference? =
                                    Answer: it's in the thoughts themselves,
                                    not external to them.
Do you not harbour serious reservations?
                                    Ability to accommodate them. Frame of reference
Role of security in formal sense.   as new form of protection.

Historical function
of dialectic today:
        its resistance to administrative mentality.

Dialectic not a matter of simple alternatives. Hence its opposition to administrative thinking.

Refuses the imposition of Either–Or (the Protestant force of conscience).

'He that is not with me is against me'. Heteronomous moment in this.

But not mediated as a middling kind of 'perhaps', as a 'both and also'.

Movement through the extremes. Against the misunderstanding of bourgeois reason that everything has 2 sides to it.

Point this out with reference to the alternative: either sociology

or [xxxxx] ontological anthropology.

Cite Feuerbach here: not against but beyond.

Tendency to subsume dialectic under I.

But neither is right.   It holds fast to truth, not 'everything is conditioned', rather the untrue is conditioned.

But there is no static truth.

The spurious origin

Against unmediated dialectic of genesis + validity.   diminishes truth.

Refusal of 'speaking for myself as ...' Against philosophy as a 'standpoint' and relativism. Both

Against the philosophy of value and value-free thought.

are the same.

Remedy: Hegel's demand to surrender to the matter itself.

The object not devoid of qualitative character but determinate, the S[ubject] is involved, the truth moment of idealism, the S[ubject] which alone is crucial according to traditional thought is itself an abstraction, a moment.

4

Dialectic does not start with <u>definitions</u>, not even that of itself.

The demand for clear concepts implies that concepts can always be

~~Detetis~~ Foolish aspect of the demand for definitions as

determined through other concepts. | warding off things. 'Debt'.

The archaic, pre-critical aspect here: hypostasis of the concept.

Against this: 1) Clear determination of concepts.

2) The historical moment of concepts which eludes definition.

Concepts not fixed <u>in themselves</u>, but involved in a process.

Task of dialectic is not to arrest them for practical purposes,

Language as canon:

but to grasp this process, e.g. the family.   linguistic [?] expression type

Possible to <u>end</u> with definitions – i.e. those in which the power of unshackled theory is

preserved – but not to begin with them. E.g. my definition of art as magic [xx] purified of the

illusion of being actual.

I must also already know what art is – Tacitean ideal. NB concentration as such.

Against operational definitions

1) Their tautological and repetitive nature. Not synthetic

2) Moment of arbitrariness with respect to the subject matter. Holding fast to

the prejudice.

3) The problem of extrapolation.

Dialectic cannot dispense with general concepts.

<u>Position on concepts:</u> Hence the objection: I must therefore have a

general conception in advance. Not so: to say A is not necessarily to say B.

1) Thought is not a *tabula rasa* of concepts; it already receives them as concepts which <u>in themselves</u> intend something substantive, and employs them as such.
Truth of phenomenology: it attempts to do justice to precisely this.
Untruth   ..   ..   : it turns this objective moment into an absolute; it arrests the concepts, overlooks the way that they are transformed in the context of thought, the way that subjective intention becomes involved in them. They undergo change of themselves.

Begin here on 31.VII.58

5

2) They owe their form to the way they are specified in a particular context. Only apparently vaguer: as isolated concepts. In truth, <u>more specific</u> by

Through presentation thought goes beyond its merely

the place they occupy.   pre-given character. Subjective contribution.

At the same time something which is itself objective.

Model of the s–o dialectic within knowledge.

→   This is the epistemological function of presentation.

Some remarks on dialectic and logical forms in general. Dialectic as an attempt to break out:

to outwit logic through itself.

Indicate the 3 basic types.

The concept of a <u>judgement</u>.

‖ Analysis of necessary untruth in the copula. (Develop this and provide outline
‖ for the following session.)[14]   Judgement always an abstraction from what

the subject is <u>not</u>, and to that extent <u>false</u>.

But no truth without judgement.

State of affairs <u>and synthesis</u>.

Model of a logic without judgement music, art in general

Here truth is <u>mediated</u>.

Judgement: the judgement pronouncing death as model here.

Concept of inference.

Dawning awareness of its inadequacy.

Inferential method assumes a hierarchy based on proximity to the origin.

Its questionable character revealed by the tenuousness of bridging concepts.

In dialectic everything is ultimately equally close to the centre.

This is what phenomenology intends: the disappearance of argument.

This too is presentation. Everything equally close to the centre. Density.

At the same time this is traditional in a bad sense: against thought understood as inference.

Dialectic: argumentative reflection upon argumentation.

---

3) Concepts must be regarded in terms of their configuration.

The fact that concepts acquire truth only in their interconnection expresses the inadequacy of each on its own. – Concepts are determined through their relation

The challenging thought: that there is no such thing as a single truth.

6

Introduction to Dialectic, continued

Rendering our thoughts fluid 35

Hegel's own characterization of the concept.
Propaedeutic p. 214

Gloss 2 (the Phenomenology)[15]

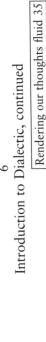

pp. 96f. Dialectic of perception.
Acknowledging the true.
Deception through the activity of consciousness.
'Disparity' = the nugatory aspect in the subject.
Universality in the object of perception (e.g. colour)
The movement arises from the reduction to the pure τόδε τι [tode ti]

97

The purely sensuous is precisely what arises, is product, 'my meaning', is what is mediated.
Return of consciousness into itself: reflection
The true is changed thereby

98

The reduction to consciousness yields the untruth of perception.
Consciousness of reflection: identity
The 'universal' involves us.

99

100 | Determinacy of the various aspects of the object (white in contrast to black)

'Property' = the determination proper to the thing = true properties.

| The thing, the One, is the Also; the universal medium.

The 'Also' and the unity in the thing as mutually opposed

101 The unity of the thing is in consciousness.   The moment One and Also is subject and object.

102 Unity + plurality in itself is in the thing, is not a subjective addition

‖ (NB explicitly develop: we are motivated to such categorization through the mere circumstance of perception itself.)

103 Through determinacy the thing is opposed to all other things, but is thereby preserved for its own part.

Yet the thing is only insofar as it does not stand in this relation to other things.

‖ The thing founders precisely through its own essential property.

7

103–104   Summary
            The principal thought:
            The thing expressed as being-for-itself, as negation of other-being.
            Hence absolute negation.
104 | Hence its self-sublation (i.e., it becomes itself only through its
            relation to something else).

Scepticism and dialectic 163f.
163   Scept[icism] reveals the dialectic in sense certainty, perception, and
       the understanding.
164   Scepticism as consciousness of spiritual freedom (redeemed as a
       moment). 'Self-certainty'.
165   The merely empirical character of sceptical consciousness (read
       out passage).

Re definition.[16]

'Vagueness', other associations not arbitrary or subjective, but something objectively determined.

This is narrowed down by definition, a non-defined concept brings much more along with it.

The art required is this: to preserve what is implicitly harboured in the concept, but specifically to bring it to consciousness.

This is achieved through a constellation.

Example of a word from a foreign language.

Once it has been read 30 times, I understand it better than if it were 'defined'.

The concept is not fixed in the process, but changes through the constellation.

EDITOR'S NOTES

Abbreviations

Adorno's writings are cited from the German editions, *Gesammelte Schriften* (ed. Rolf Tiedemann in collaboration with Gretel Adorno, Susan Buck-Morss and Klaus Schultz, Frankfurt am Main, 1970–) and *Nachgelassene Schriften* (ed. Theodor W. Adorno Archiv, Frankfurt am Main, 1993–); where available, English translations have also been used and corresponding references and publication details provided in the editor's notes to the lectures. The following abbreviations are employed:

GS 1	*Philosophische Frühschriften*, 3rd edn, 1996
GS 3	Max Horkheimer and Theodor W. Adorno, *Dialektik der Aufklärung: Philosophische Fragmente*, 3rd edn, 1996
GS 4	*Minima Moralia: Reflexionen aus dem beschädigten Leben*, 2nd edn, 1996
GS 5	*Metakritik der Erkenntnistheorie / Drei Studien zu Hegel*, 4th edn, 1996
GS 6	*Negative Dialektik / Jargon der Eigentlichkeit*, 5th edn, 1996
GS 8	*Soziologische Schriften* I, 4th edn, 1996
GS 9.1	*Soziologische Schriften* II, Pt 1, 3rd edn, 1997
GS 10.1	*Kulturkritik und Gesellschaft* I: *Prismen / Ohne Leitbild*, 2nd edn, 1996
GS 10.2	*Kulturkritik und Gesellschaft* II: *Eingriffe / Stichworte*, 2nd edn, 1996
GS 11	*Noten zur Literatur*, 4th edn, 1996

GS 14	*Dissonanzen / Einleitung in die Musiksoziologie*, 4th edn, 1996
GS 18	*Musikalische Schriften* V, 1984
GS 20.1	*Vermischte Schriften* I, 1986
GS 20.2	*Vermischte Schriften* II, 1986
NaS I.3	*Currents of Music: Elements of a Radio Theory*, ed. Robert Hullot-Kentor, 2006
NaS IV.3	*Ästhetik (1958/59)*, ed. Eberhard Ortland, 2009
NaS IV.12	*Philosophische Elemente einer Theorie der Gesellschaft (1964)*, ed. Tobias ten Brink and Marc Phillip Nogueira, 2008
NaS IV.14	*Metaphysik: Begriff und Probleme* (1965), ed. Rolf Tiedemann, 1998
NaS IV.15	*Einleitung in die Soziologie* (1968), ed. Christoph Gödde, 1993

Lecture 1

1   No transcription of Adorno's opening lecture of 8 May 1958 is available. The text has been based on a stenographic record of this lecture.

2   In the early dialogue *Gorgias* Plato starts by presenting the Sophist Gorgias (483–375 BCE) as a proponent of the thesis that 'there is no subject on which the rhetorician could not speak more persuasively than a member of any other profession whatsoever, before a multitude' (*Gorgias* 456c4–6; Loeb Classical Library, trans. W. R. M. Lamb, p. 291). His interlocutor Socrates proceeds to distinguish between two kinds of persuasion, a distinction which allows Plato to contrast his dialectic with the approach typically adopted by the Sophists. Thus there is a form of persuasion which can produce only subjective opinion and belief because it understands nothing of the things of which it speaks; and there is a form of persuasion which is supposed to yield knowledge through acquaintance with the nature, concept, and ground of the thing in question. The first part of the dialogue ends with Gorgias conceding that the genuine rhetorician must indeed possess real knowledge of the matter if he is to teach the art of rhetoric (see *Gorgias* 459c8–460b1). In Plato's later dialogue *Phaedrus*, the second main part of the text, which is concerned with the distinction between a good rhetorician and a poor one, begins with the same antithesis between the possession or the lack of genuine knowledge: '*Socrates*: If a speech is to be good, must not the mind of the speaker know the truth about the matters of which he is to speak?' (*Phaedrus* 259e4–6; Loeb Classical Library, trans. H. N. Fowler, p. 513). Adorno underlined this passage in his edition of Plato (Plato, *Sämtliche Dialoge*, ed. Otto Apelt, vol. 2, Leipzig c. 1922), and here wrote 'F' in the margin (for 'Forte': strong). And above the passage Adorno has written: 'core of the theory of rhetoric'. In the *Phaedrus* too the discussion comes to the same conclu-

sion as the *Gorgias*: 'Socrates: One must know the truth about all the
particular things of which one speaks or writes... Until one has attained
to all this, one will not be able to speak by the method of art, as far as
the matter allows, either for purposes of instruction or of persuasion'
(*Phaedrus* 277b5–c6; ibid., p. 571).

3   The *locus classicus* for this ascent from the concrete to the universal,
to the idea, is the concluding section of Diotima's speech in the dialogue
The Symposium, a passage to which Adorno often alludes (and which
is copiously marked and furnished with marginal comments in his
edition of the text. (See *Symposium* 210a–211b; see also p. 15 below
and Lecture 3, note 1.)

4   With regard to this double movement – by which we ascend to the
highest universal concept and descend through the process of logical
division – the passage in Plato which Adorno clearly has in mind is to
be found in the final section of the *Phaedrus*. After the dialectical interpretation of love as a divine form of madness, the text continues:

> Socrates: It seems to me that the discourse was, as a whole, really sport-
> ive jest; but in these chance utterances were involved two
> principles, the essence of which it would be gratifying to learn,
> if art could teach it.
>
> Phaedrus: What principles?
>
> Socrates: That of perceiving and bringing together in one idea the scat-
> tered particulars, that one may make clear by definition the
> particular thing that he wishes to explain; ...
>
> Phaedrus: And what is the other principle?
>
> Socrates: That of dividing things again by classes, where the natural
> joints are [ἢ πέφυκεν / *hē pephuken*], and not trying to break
> any part, after the manner of a bad carver... . Now I myself,
> Phaedrus, am a lover of these processes of division and bring-
> ing together [τῶν διαιρέσεων καὶ συναγωγῶν / *tōn diaireseōn
> kai sunagōgōn*], as aids to speech and thought; and if I think
> any other man is able to see things that can naturally be col-
> lected into one and divided into many, him I follow after and
> 'walk in his footsteps as if he were a god'. And whether the
> name I give to those who can do this is right or wrong, God
> knows, but I have called them hitherto dialecticians. (*Phaedrus*
> 265 c8–266 c1)

Adorno has heavily annotated this passage in his Apelt edition and
translation of the text. Apelt translated the expression *hē pephuken* as
'in accordance with nature' (in the English version: 'where the natural
joints are'), and Adorno has underlined this. And further up, at the side
of the page, Adorno has written, underlined three times: 'διαίρεσις
[*diairesis*] appropriate to nature'. This Platonic demand for an attentive
and non-coercive approach to the nature of the thing in question in the
process of conceptual determination is of central importance for Adorno's conception of dialectic. He develops this thought in detail in *Negative Dialectics*, again with specific reference to the *Phaedrus* (see GS 6,
pp. 53f.; *Negative Dialectics*, trans. E. B. Ashton, London, 1973, p. 43).

As far as Plato's own later conception of dialectic is concerned, what he says in the Phaedrus are merely preliminary adumbrations of his new procedure of definition by conceptual division (*diairesis*), a procedure which is developed and expressly presented as a 'dialectical science' only in the *Sophist* (253d1–e2).

5   Carl von Linné (1707–78), commonly known by the Latin version of his name as Linnaeus. His treatise *The System of Nature* (1735) is regarded as a foundational text for the modern approach to biological classification. But his procedure for dividing and specifying the natural phenomena in terms of genera and species represented, in Adorno's eyes, a perfect example of a merely external method based upon an essentially abstract logical schema.

6   Adorno constructed his opening lecture in such a way as to confront and then gradually undermine three common prejudices with regard to the dialectic: that it is an artificial and purely conceptual method, that it depends on a kind of exaggeration, and that is intellectualistic in character.

7   Eckermann reports a conversation in which Goethe had asked Hegel to explain what he understood by the term 'dialectic'. The philosopher responded by saying that it 'is basically nothing but the regulated and methodically cultivated spirit of contradiction which is innate in every human being' (Johann Peter Eckermann, *Gespräche mit Goethe in den letzten Jahren seines Lebens*, in Johann Wolfgang Goethe, *Sämtliche Werke nach Epochen seines Schaffens*, ed. Karl Richter, vol. 19, ed. Heinz Schlaffer, Munich and Vienna, 1986, p. 603; *Conversations of Goethe with Johann Peter Eckermann*, trans. John Oxenford, New York, 1998, entry for 18 October 1827, p. 244).

8   See Georg Wilhelm Friedrich Hegel, *Werke: Auf der Grundlage der Werke von 1832–45*, ed. Eva Moldenhauer and Karl Marcus Michel, vol. 3: *Phänomenologie des Geistes*; Hegel, *Phenomenology of Spirit*, trans. A. V. Miller, Oxford, 1977.

Lecture 2

1   The tape recordings of the lectures do not include the opening form of address. They have been added here and in the following lectures by the editor in accordance with the transcriptions made from later lectures in the series.

2   G. W. F. Hegel, *Werke*, vol. 3: *Phänomenologie des Geistes*, p. 38; Hegel, *Phenomenology of Spirit*, trans. A. V. Miller, Oxford, 1977, p. 20. [Translator's note: Miller's translation has been adapted in a number of respects: in particular, the common older English translation of Hegel's *Begriff* as 'Notion' has been replaced by 'concept' throughout, and the expression *die Sache selbst*, which recurs constantly in both Hegel and Adorno, has been rendered as 'the matter itself'.] Adorno goes on to interpret this passage in its broader context below; see p. 9.

3 See Hermann Wein, *Realdialektik: Von hegelscher Dialektik zu dialek-tischer Anthropologie*, Munich, 1957; Hermann Wein (1912–1960), professor of philosophy in Göttingen, had personally sent Adorno a copy of his book (Nachlassbibliothek Adorno 619).

4 Adorno is clearly alluding to Karl Marx's observations in the Postface to the second edition of *Capital*, a passage which has prompted a plethora of conflicting interpretations regarding the significance and implications of the concept of the 'dialectic' in Marx's work (see Karl Marx and Friedrich Engels, *Werke*, ed. Institut für Marxismus-Lenin-ismus beim ZK der SED, vol. 23: *Das Kapital: Kritik der politischen Ökonomie*, vol. 1, book 1: *Der Produktionsprozess des Kapitals*, Berlin, 1962, p. 27; K. Marx, *Capital: A Critique of Political Economy*, vol. 1, trans. Ben Fowkes, Harmondsworth, 1976, p. 102). Here Marx defends his 'dialectical method' against his critics by drawing a distinc-tion between the 'form of presentation' [*Darstellungsweise*] and the 'form of inquiry' [*Forschungsweise*], and this raised the question whether Marx's conception of dialectic is *merely* a form which facili-tates the systematic presentation of the subject matter or (also) repre-sents the historical or genetic law of the subject matter itself.

5 'In my view, which can be justified only by the exposition of the system itself, everything turns on grasping and expressing the True, not only as *Substance*, but equally as *Subject*' (Hegel, *Phänomenologie des Geistes*, pp. 22f.; *Phenomenology of Spirit*, pp. 9f.).

6 Hegel, *Werke*, vol. 5: *Wissenschaft der Logik I*, p. 74; Hegel, *Science of Logic*, trans. George di Giovanni, Cambridge, 2012, p. 51 ('the identity of identity and non-identity').

7 'The True is the whole' (Hegel, *Phänomenologie des Geistes*, p. 24; *Phenomenology of Spirit*, p. 11).

8 The quotation is given as it appears in Adorno's copy of the text, and the one from which he probably read out this passage: Hegel, *Phänomenologie des Geistes*, ed. Georg Lasson, Leipzig, 1921, p. 24. (Hegel, *Phänomenologie des Geistes*, pp. 37f; *Phenomenology of Spirit*, p. 20.)

9 Adorno is alluding to the remarks in the Introduction to the *Science of Logic* ('With what must the beginning of science be made?'), where Hegel refers to his *Encyclopaedia of the Philosophical Sciences* and says: 'Here we may quote from it only this, that *there is* nothing in heaven or nature or spirit or anywhere else that does not contain just as much immediacy as mediation, so that both these determinations prove to be *unseparated* and *inseparable* and the opposition between them nothing real' (Hegel, *Wissenschaft der Logik I*, p. 66; *Science of Logic*, p. 46). In his own copy of Hegel's text Adorno had marked this passage (from 'that there is nothing' down to the end) and written 'F' (for 'Forte') in the margin.

10 See Charles de Secondat, Baron de la Brède et de Montesquieu, *De l'esprit des lois* (1748); *The Spirit of the Laws*, trans. Thomas Nugent, ed. F. Neumann, New York, 1979.

11   See Giovanni Battista Vico, *Principi di una scienza nuova d'intorno alla commune natura delle nazioni* (1725); *The New Science of Giambattista Vico*, trans. Thomas Bergin and Max Fisch (from the 1744 edn), Ithaca, NY, 1948, rev. edn, 1968.

12   See Marie-Jean-Antoine-Nicolas Caritat, Marquis de Condorcet, *Esquisse d'un tableau historique des progrès de l'esprit humain* (1794); *Sketch for a Historical Picture of the Progress of the Human Mind*, in Condorcet, *Political Writings*, ed. Steven Lukes and Nadia Urbinati, Cambridge, 2012, pp. 1–147.

13   See Johann Gottlieb Fichte, *Die Grundzüge des gegenwärtigen Zeitalters* (1806); *The Characteristics of the Present Age*, trans. William Smith, London, 1847.

14   A number of Martin Heidegger's former students had engaged more intensively with Hegel partly in the wake of Heidegger's essay 'Hegel's Concept of Experience' of 1942–3 (in M. Heidegger, *Holzwege*, Frankfurt am Main, 1950, pp. 105–92; *Off the Beaten Track*, ed. and trans. Julian Young and Kenneth Hayes, Cambridge, 2002, pp. 86–156). In this connection Adorno may have been thinking of Walter Bröcker (1902–1992), professor of philosophy in Kiel, who had published his book *Dialektik, Positivismus, Mythologie* (Frankfurt am Main, 1958) in the same year that Adorno delivered these lectures on the dialectic. In a later (as yet unpublished) lecture on questions concerned with the dialectic from 1964, Adorno explicitly refers to Bröcker's book, which he thought only rendered the dialectic subservient to ontology (see Theodor W. Adorno Archiv, Sign.: Vo 9098). But it is also possible that Adorno is alluding to the neo-Thomist tendencies which he refers to later in the lectures (see p. 83 and Lecture 9, note 1, below).

15   Adorno is alluding to Hegel's critical analysis, in the opening chapter of his *Science of Logic*, of the first category, namely the category of 'Being' as 'pure indeterminateness and emptiness' (Hegel, *Wissenschaft der Logik* I, p. 82; *Science of Logic*, p. 59). When Adorno speaks of the 'stalest' content here, he may be echoing Hegel's corresponding critique of immediate 'sense-certainty' in the opening chapter of the *Phenomenology*, of 'the Here' and 'the Now' whose truth, as Hegel says, has become 'stale' (*Phänomenologie des Geistes*, p. 84; *Phenomenology of Spirit*, p. 60). Adorno uses this expression on only one other occasion in his published writings (*Zur Metakritik der Erkenntnistheorie*, GS 5, p. 23; *Against Epistemology: A Metacritique*, trans. Willis Domingo, Oxford, 1982, p. 15).

16   Reading *Männchen* [manikins or homunculi] for *Männerchen* in the transcript. [Translator's note: It seems possible that the person who transcribed the tape recording of the lecture misheard the word *Märchen* [fairy tales] here.]

17   Reading *zeitlos* [timeless] for *zeitlich* [temporal] in the transcript. On the basis of the numerous other passages in his work where Adorno talks about 'the temporal core of truth', it seems clear there is a mistake in the transcript of the tape-recorded lecture here (or perhaps that

Adorno himself made a verbal slip in the lecture at this point). Thus, in his essay 'Why Still Philosophy?', we find a comparable opposition between 'the temporal nucleus' of truth and the idea of the 'timeless' and 'eternal'. After discussing the way in which all major philosophers criticize their predecessors, Adorno writes: 'In the progressive unity of such critique even those philosophies whose doctrines insist on the eternal and the timeless acquired their temporal nucleus, their historical status' (*Eingriffe*, in GS 10.2, p. 462; *Critical Models: Interventions and Catchwords*, trans. Henry W. Pickford, New York, 1998, p. 8).

18 In his *Metakritik der Erkenntnistheorie* Adorno makes it clear that he owes this crucial idea of a temporal 'core' or 'nucleus' of truth to the work of Walter Benjamin (GS 5, p. 141; *Against Epistemology*, p. 135). Thus in the materials for the Arcades Project Benjamin writes: 'Resolute refusal of the concept of "timeless truth" is in order. Nevertheless, truth is not – as Marxism would have it – a merely contingent function of knowing, but is bound to a nucleus of time lying hidden within the knower and the known alike. This is so true that the eternal, in any case, is far more the ruffle on a dress than some idea' (Walter Benjamin, *Gesammelte Schriften*, vol. 5.1: *Das Passagen-Werk*, ed. Rolf Tiedemann, Frankfurt am Main, 1982, p. 578; *The Arcades Project*, trans. Howard Eiland and Kevin McLaughlin, Cambridge, MA, 2002, p. 463).

Lecture 3

1 The ascent from the sensuously perceptible individual things to the idea of beauty (see Lecture 1, note 3, above) is concluded when

> suddenly he will have revealed to him, as he draws to the close in his dealings with love, a wondrous vision, beautiful in its nature; and this, Socrates, is the final object of all those previous toils. First of all, it is ever-existent and neither comes to be nor perishes, neither waxes nor wanes; next, it is not beautiful in part and in part ugly, nor is it such at such a time and other at another, nor so affected by position as to seem beautiful to some and ugly to others. Nor again will our initiate find the beautiful presented to him in the guise of a face or of hands, or of any other portion of the body, nor as a particular description or piece of knowledge, nor as existing somewhere in another substance, such as an animal or the earth or sky or any other thing; but existing ever in singularity of form independent by itself, while all the multitude of beautiful things partake of it in such wise that, though all of them are coming to be and perishing, it grows neither greater nor less, and is affected by nothing. (Plato, *Symposium* 210e4–211b5, Loeb Classical Library, trans. W. R. M. Lamb, p. 205).

2 As is well known, Aristotle himself did not describe his principal philosophical text or his philosophy as a whole specifically as 'metaphysics'. What we call 'metaphysics' here is what Aristotle describes as 'first

philosophy' [πρώτη φιλοσοφία / prōtē philosophia], and in the text which subsequently came to bear the title Metaphysics he attempts to define first philosophy in three specific ways: as the science of the first causes and principles of any being whatsoever, as the science of beings as beings, and as the science of the one highest being and the one highest cause (namely God). It remains a matter of debate whether these three approaches in Aristotle can ultimately be brought under the concept of a single unified science or philosophy, or whether they effectively yield two different concepts of first philosophy, namely as physics or as theology.

3 'Diamat' is an abbreviation for 'dialectical materialism'. This and the term 'historical materialism' capture the two sides of the Marxist-Leninist worldview which was officially propagated in the former Soviet Union and the communist countries of the Eastern bloc.

4 Hegel expressed his extremely high regard for Plato in numerous places, but it is not possible to identify any specific passages where he endorses Plato's conception of the first or highest principle in precisely the way which Adorno describes here.

5 Hegel, Phänomenologie des Geistes, Lasson edn, p. 14 (see Lecture 2, note 8 above); Werke, vol. 3, pp. 24f.; Phenomenology of Spirit, p. 11.

6 Hegel, Phänomenologie des Geistes, Werke, vol. 3, p. 25; Phenomenology of Spirit, p. 11.

7 There is a lacuna in the transcription of the tape recording of the lecture here.

8 Reading unterschiebt [insinuates] for unterschied [distinguished] in the transcription.

9 A year earlier, in connection with his lecture 'Zum Verhältnis von Individuum und Gesellschaft heute' [On the relationship between the individual and society today], delivered in Bad Nauheim on 13 February 1957, Adorno had asked his then assistant Jürgen Habermas to select a number of quotations from Arnold Gehlen's book Der Mensch that he could use for his specific critique of Gehlen, who was scheduled to deliver a lecture of his own in Bad Nauheim a week before Adorno. One of the 'particularly striking quotations from Gehlen', as Adorno put it, which Habermas excerpted attempts to define the essence of the human being (see Adorno's letter to Horkheimer of 14 February 1957, in Theodor W. Adorno, Briefe und Briefwechsel, ed. Theodor W. Adorno Archiv, vol. 4: Theodor W. Adorno and Max Horkheimer, Briefwechsel 1927–1969, vol. IV: 1950–1969, ed. Christoph Gödde and Henri Lonitz, Frankfurt am Main, 2006, p. 396). The quotation reads as follows: '...this "unfinishedness" [Unfertigsein] of the human being is a basic part of his physical condition, his very nature. In this sense man must become a being of discipline [ein Wesen der Zucht]: self-discipline [Selbstzucht], education [Erziehung], and training [Züchtigung] in order to achieve a certain state of being and to maintain it are necessary to the survival of an "undetermined" being.' See Arnold Gehlen, Der Mensch, 4th edn, Bonn, 1950, p. 50; Man: His Nature and

Place in the World, trans. Clare McMillan and Karl Pillemer, New York, 1988, pp. 24–5 [translation slightly altered].

10 See Adorno's rather famous aphorism from *Minima Moralia*: 'The whole is the false' (GS 4, p. 55; *Minima Moralia: Reflections from Damaged Life*, trans. E. F. N. Jephcott, New York 1974, p. 50).

11 Thus in §214 of the *Encyclopaedia Logic*, a passage which corresponds to the discussion at the end of *The Science of Logic*, Hegel writes:

> The Idea can be grasped as *reason* (this is the genuine philosophical meaning of reason), further as *subject-object*, as the *unity of the ideal and the real, of the finite and the infinite, of the soul and the body*, as *the possibility that has its actuality in itself*, as that the *nature* of which *can only be conceived as existing*, and so forth, because in it [the Idea] all relationships of the understanding are contained, but in their *infinite* return and identity in themselves. (Hegel, *Enzyklopädie der philosophischen Wissenschaften I*, §214, p. 370; *Encyclopedia of the Philosophical Sciences in Basic Outline*, Part I: *The Science of Logic*, trans. Klaus Brinkmann and Daniel E. Dahlstrom, Cambridge, 2010, §214, pp. 284–5)

The actual expression 'subject-object' does not in fact play such a central role in Hegel as Adorno perhaps suggests. In the *Science of Logic* the expression appears only once, and then specifically with reference to Schelling's philosophy. See Hegel, *Wissenschaft der Logik* II, p. 466; *Science of Logic*, trans. di Giovanni, p. 673.

12 Reading *aufschließt* [yields] for *ausschließt* [excludes] in the transcription.

13 The Greek term ἐποχή [*epochē*] (from the verb *epechein*: 'to hold back') was originally used by the Stoic philosophers to describe a sceptical suspension of belief or judgement. In the context of modern phenomenology, Edmund Husserl adopted the term *epochē* as a fundamental methodological concept to designate the 'bracketing' or 'suspension' of what he called 'the general thesis of the natural attitude', the attitude which spontaneously assumes the presence of the empirical self in an actually existing world. For Husserl, it is the *epochē* which initiates the process of 'transcendental reduction' that is meant to lay bare the hidden but original structure of consciousness. 'Epoche and reduction are the two interconnected sides of the single fundamental methodological operation of phenomenology' (Edmund Husserl, *Die Idee der Phänomenologie*, ed. Paul Janssen, Hamburg, 1968, p. xxx; *The Idea of Phenomenology*, trans. Lee Hardy, Dordrecht, 1999; see pp. 33f. for Husserl's specific discussion of the *epochē* and the 'phenomenological reduction'). For more on the concept of the *epochē*, see Edmund Husserl, *Ideen zu einer reinen Phänomenologie und phänomenologischen Philosophie*, Tübingen, 1980 (reprint of the 2nd ed of 1922), §§27–32, especially §32, pp. 56f.; *Ideas: General Introduction to Pure Phenomenology*, trans. W. R. Boyce Gibson, London and New York, 2002, §§27–32, pp. 51–60, especially pp. 59f.).

For the notion of 'destruction', see §6 of Martin Heidegger's *Being and Time*. He argues that 'the task of a destruction of the history of ontology' is required because the question concerning the meaning of being was already covered over even when it was first posed as such, in ancient Greek philosophy, through a specific concentration upon the temporal mode of the present, and because this approach has only been preserved and intensified throughout the Western tradition. In order to approach an experience of being which is original, in a historical and a structural sense, and to lay bare the meaning of being as temporality in all its implications, the analysis of human existence as *Dasein* must retrace the process through which the tradition has covered over the significance of the question concerning the meaning of being (Martin Heidegger, *Sein und Zeit*, 15th edn, Tübingen, 1979, pp. 19ff.; *Being and Time*, trans. John Macquarrie and Edward Robinson, Oxford, 1967, pp. 41ff.).

14   It appears that Adorno is implicitly alluding to a specific study conducted by the Frankfurt Institute for Social Research into the conditions of the West German coal mining industry. The study was directed by Ludwig von Friedeburg, with the collaboration of Egon Becker, Manfred Teschner, and Klaus Liepelt.

15   It is a linguistic peculiarity of Adorno's that he writes 'Naivetät' rather than the more usual 'Naivität'. This orthography has been retained throughout in the *Gesammelte Schriften* and the *Nachgelassene Schriften*.

Lecture 4

1   The first page of the transcription of Lecture 4 (Sign. Vo 3050) also bears the handwritten observation: 'Tape recording difficult to understand!'

2   G. W. F. Hegel, *Werke*, vol. 3, *Phänomenologie des Geistes*, p. 27; *Phenomenology of Spirit*, trans. Miller, p. 13.

3   Johann Gottlieb Fichte (1762–1814), from 1794 onwards professor of philosophy at Jena, Berlin, Erlangen, Königsberg, and again Berlin.

4   See Johann Gottlieb Fichte, *Grundlage der gesamten Wissenschaftslehre als Handschrift für seine Zuhörer* (1794), introduction by Wilhelm G. Jacobs, Hamburg, 1988. Although Fichte regarded his *Wissenschaftslehre* or 'Doctrine of Science' as completed in its basic form by 1794, he continued to provide several further presentations and elaborations of the fundamental concept.

5   According to Fichte, the task of philosophy is to ground the knowledge of all the sciences in terms of one fundamental principle or proposition (*Grundsatz*) and thereby to present this as a *single* unified system. For this reason, philosophy for Fichte can only be a 'Doctrine of Science', or the Science of Science itself. It is only the proposition 'I am I', according to Fichte, that can fulfil the condition of an absolutely first principle:

firstly, because it is immediately certain and, secondly, because, as an utterly original 'act', it does not depend on anything antecedently given and thus possesses the structure of a productive self-grounding activity: *'That whose being (essence) consists in nothing other than positing itself as existing* is the I as absolute subject' (Fichte, *Grundlage der gesamten Wissenschaftslehre* [see note 4 above], p. 17). Or again: *'The I simply and originally posits its own being'* (ibid., p. 18). Elsewhere Fichte also expresses this in these terms: 'I am *because* I am' (Johann Gottlieb Fichte, *Über den Begriff der Wissenschaftslehre*, ed. Edmund Braun, Stuttgart,1981, p. 61; see Fichte, *Introductions to the Wissenschafts-lehre and Other Writings 1797–1800*, ed. and trans. Daniel Breazeale, Indianapolis, 1994). And, thirdly, this first principle is the absolute principle of all possible knowledge because, in positing itself as existing, it exhibits a subject-object structure in which the I is, on the one hand, absolute subject-object while, on the other hand, it is also in itself the object, and in this object position thus provides the place, as it were, in which objects of experience that are other than the I (the non-I) can also find their place, or be posited as such through the I.

6   See note 2 above.

7   Hegel, *Phänomenologie des Geistes*, p. 27; *Phenomenology of Spirit*, p. 13.

8   Kant defines *phaenomena* as 'appearances so far as they are thought as objects according to the unity of the categories' (Immanuel Kant, *Kritik der reinen Vernunft*, ed. Raymund Schmidt, Hamburg, 1956, p. 298; *Critique of Pure Reason*, trans. Norman Kemp Smith, London, 1933, A248f., p. 265) – in other words, things insofar as they are constituted through the pure forms of intuition (space and time) and the human 'understanding' and its categories; *noumena*, by contrast, are things in themselves, namely things thought or regarded as they would show themselves to a non-sensuous form of intuition – something, however, which is entirely denied to the human faculty of knowing, since this depends on sensuous intuition and the understanding. To that extent the concept of the *noumenon* for Kant remains 'a merely *limiting concept [Grenzbegriff]*, the function of which is to curb the pretensions of sensibility; and it is therefore only of negative employment' (Schmidt, p. 305; Kemp Smith, A255 / B311, p. 272).

9   The formulation 'the Absolute is Subject' is found in this precise form only in the table of contents of the *Phenomenology of Spirit*, although it does designate a section of the Preface where this thought is expressly developed (see Hegel, *Phänomenologie des Geistes*, p. 7 and pp. 20ff.; *Phenomenology of Spirit*, p. xxxiii and pp. 9–11). The claim naturally applies in substantive terms to Hegel's theory of the Absolute in general.

10 In the Introduction to the *Phenomenology of Spirit*, Hegel speaks of the development which 'natural consciousness' must undergo in the course of the experience of its objects. The goal of this development is to reach the point where concept and object correspond with one

another in such a way that knowing is no longer posited as an external means or medium that is separated from its true object, where knowing has thus become identical with the matter itself. In the first instance, this development proves extremely disturbing for the posture of natural consciousness. Instead of rejecting the conception of knowing as an instrument or medium as 'adventitious and arbitrary' (Hegel, *Phänomenologie des Geistes*, pp. 70f.; *Phenomenology of Spirit*, p. 48) and exposing itself to the experience with its object, the natural consciousness seeks refuge in an intellectualistic scepticism where

> its fear of the truth may lead consciousness to hide, from itself and others, behind the pretension that its burning zeal for truth makes it difficult or even impossible to find any other truth but the unique truth of vanity.... This conceit which understands how to belittle every truth, in order to turn back into itself and gloat over its own understanding, which knows how to dissolve every thought and always finds the same barren Ego instead of any content – this is a satisfaction which we must leave to itself, for it flees from the universal, and seeks only to be for itself. (*Phänomenologie des Geistes*, p. 75; *Phenomenology of Spirit*, p. 52)

11 Reading *auftrifft* [encounters] for *auftritt* [appears] in the transcription.
12 Hegel, *Phänomenologie des Geistes*, pp. 27f.; *Phenomenology of Spirit*, p. 13.
13 Ibid.
14 See Lecture 2, pp. 13f. above.
15 Hegel, *Phänomenologie des Geistes*, p. 28; *Phenomenology of Spirit*, pp. 13f.
16 'The form of the sentence [or proposition: *Satz*], or more precisely, of the judgement is in any case unsuitable to express that which is concrete or speculative – and the true is concrete. A judgement is one-sided on account of its form and to that extent false' (Hegel, *Enzyklopädie der philosophischen Wissenschaften I*, §31, p. 98; *Encyclopedia of the Philosophical Sciences in Basic Outline*, Part 1: *Science of Logic*, §31, p. 71). And, with regard to the concept of the concrete, Hegel writes as follows in §164 of the *Encyclopedia Logic*:

> There is nothing said more commonly than that the concept is something *abstract*. This is correct in part insofar as its element is thinking generally and not the empirical concrete sphere of the senses, in part insofar as it is not yet the *Idea*. In this respect the subjective concept is still *formal*, yet not all as if it should respectively have or acquire some other content than itself. – As the absolute form itself, the concept is every *determinacy*, but as it is in its truth. Thus, although the concept is at the same time abstract, it is what is concrete and, indeed, the absolutely concrete, the subject as such. The absolutely concrete is the spirit... – the concept insofar as it *concretely exists* as concept, differentiating itself from its objectivity which, despite the differentiating, remains the concept's *own* objectivity. Everything else concrete, rich as it may be, is not

so inwardly identical with itself, and, for that reason, not as concrete, least of all what one commonly understands by the concrete, a manifold externally held together. (*Enzyklopädie der philosophischen Wissenschaften I*, p. 314; *The Science of Logic*, trans. Brinkmann and Dahlstrom p. 239)

17   In Lecture 11 Adorno returns in some detail to the concept of the 'abstract' in Hegel. See pp. 109ff. below.

Lecture 5

1

Both in the periodization of intellectual history and in terms of his own character, Eichendorff belongs to the declining phase of German Romanticism. He was acquainted with many of those in the first generation of Romantics, Clemens Brentano among them, but the bond seems to have been broken; it is no accident that he confused German Idealism, in Schlegel's words, one of the great currents of the age, with rationalism. Misunderstanding them completely, he accused Kant's successors – he had insightful and respectful things to say about Kant himself – of 'a kind of decorative Chinese painting without the shadows that make the image come alive,' and he criticized them for 'simply negating as disturbing and superfluous the mysterious and inscrutable elements of human existence'. (Adorno, 'Zum Gedächtnis Eichendorffs', in GS 11, pp. 65f.; 'In Memory of Eichendorff', in *Notes to Literature*, vol. 1, trans. Shierry Weber Nicholsen, New York, 1991, p. 72)

2   Friedrich Heinrich Jacobi (1743–1819), writer and philosopher; from 1805 he was a member of the Bavarian Academy of Sciences, and from 1807 he was president of the academy. Jacobi criticized the way in which Kant's critical philosophy insisted upon the self-limitation of human knowledge, arguing instead that an intuitive and immediate rational awareness of both empirical and super-sensible reality is presupposed by the discursive knowledge of the understanding. According to Jacobi, this immediate and intuitive awareness allows us to know things in themselves, human freedom, and God. In this regard, see his work *Von den göttlichen Dingen und ihrer Offenbarung* [On Divine Things and the Revelation of the Same], Leipzig, 1811. For a selection of his philosophical works in English, see Friedrich Heinrich Jacobi, *The Main Philosophical Writings and the Novel 'Allwill'*, trans. George di Giovanni, Montreal, 1994. Jacobi's philosophy of feeling and faith, along with the renewed interest in Spinoza which he helped to produce, furnished an important contribution to post-Kantian idealist thought. In Lecture 11, Adorno returns to Jacobi and discusses him in some detail.

3   The passages where Hegel appears to polemicize against Schelling in an emphatic sense are restricted to that part of the Preface where he speaks of the Absolute as 'the night in which, as the saying goes, all cows are

black' (Hegel, *Phänomenologie des Geistes*, p. 22; *Phenomenology of Spirit*, p. 9). The tone which Schelling later adopted towards Hegel was much more polemical in character. See, for example, Friedrich Wilhelm Schelling, 'Zur Geschichte der neueren Philosophie: Münchener Vorlesungen', in *Schellings Werke*, ed. Manfred Schröter, vol. 5: *Schriften zur geschichtlichen Philosophie 1821–1854*, Munich, 1928, pp. 196–234; Schelling, *On the History of Modern Philosophy*, trans. A. Bowie, Cambridge, 1994.

4   The expression *Rationalismusstreit* or 'dispute over rationalism' was not in fact current in the period of German Idealism or in Adorno's own time with regard to the dispute Adorno is discussing, as the text here seems to imply. It is true that Max Horkheimer had earlier published a substantial essay entitled 'The Dispute over Rationalism in Contemporary Philosophy', in which he specifically addressed these questions. It is possible, therefore, that the expression was quite familiar to members of the Institute for Social Research in Frankfurt at this time (see Max Horkheimer, 'Zum Rationalismusstreit in der gegenwärtigen Philosophie', *Zeitschrift für Sozialforschung* [3], 1934, repr. in Horkheimer, *Gesammelte Schriften*, ed. Alfred Schmidt and Gunzelin Schmid Noerr, vol. 3: *Schriften 1931–36*, ed. Alfred Schmidt, Frankfurt am Main, 1988, pp. 163–220).

5   Hegel also includes Kant's philosophy under the rubric of the 'philosophy of reflection'. For he thinks that the Critical Philosophy employs a mode of thought which he describes as 'external reflection'. He understands this as a movement of thought which 'transcends an immediately given representation and seeks more universal determinations for it or compares it with such determinations' (Hegel, *Wissenschaft der Logik* II, p. 30; *Science of Logic*, p. 350). Hegel's criticism of the philosophy of reflection, which is directed at a specific form of reflection, namely 'external reflection', allowed him to distance himself from the more general critique of 'reflection' which was widespread in this period (a critique to which Hegel himself was closer in his so-called *Early Theological Writings* than he was when he composed the *Science of Logic*). Thus Hegel writes: 'External reflection was also meant whenever reflection, as it was for a while the fashion in recent philosophy, was being accused of all evil, and it and its ways of determining were regarded as the polar opposite, nay the ancestral enemy, of true philosophical method' (*Wissenschaft der Logik* II, p. 31; *Science of Logic*, p. 350). Instead of simply repudiating 'reflection' and trying to replace it with a quite different kind of thinking – such as one which appeals to a sort of immediate intellectual intuition – Hegel modifies the concept of reflection in such a way that it is capable of expressing the true structure of the Absolute. He therefore opposes 'external reflection' with a specific structure of reflection which inheres not only in thought but equally in the objects of thought, which instead of taking pre-given determinations as an immediate point of departure attempts to posit these determinations out of itself. This form of reflection does not compare these

determinations externally in relation to a given universal but undertakes
to present the internally reflected universal as the internal structure of
determination which belongs to every particular determination and
objective actuality as a whole.

6 Henri Bergson (1859–1941), professor of philosophy at the Collège de
France from 1900, was one of the most important representatives of
vitalism or the 'philosophy of life'. Adorno conducted several seminars
on Bergson at the University of Frankfurt between 1949 and 1958.

7 A little further on in this lecture and the next Adorno quotes a passage
from the Preface to the *Phenomenology of Spirit* where Hegel specifically criticizes the attempt to present everything in a kind of 'table'
(p. 47 and p. 50 above). In connection with this criticism Hegel continues as follows:

> What results from this method of labelling all that is in heaven and earth
> with the few determinations of the general schema, and pigeonholing
> everything in this way, is nothing less than a 'report clear as noonday' on
> the universe as an organism, viz. a synoptic table like a skeleton with
> scraps of paper stuck all over it, or like the rows of closed and labelled
> boxes in a grocer's stall. It is as easy to read off as either of these; and
> just as all the flesh and blood has been stripped from this skeleton, and
> the no longer living 'essence' [*Sache*] has been packed away in the boxes,
> so in the report the living essence of the matter [*Wesen der Sache*] has
> been stripped away or boxed up dead. (Hegel, *Phänomenologie des
> Geistes*, pp. 50f.; *Phenomenology of Spirit*, p. 31)

8 'Shot from a pistol' – Adorno is alluding here to an expression which
Hegel was particularly fond of using. Thus in the *Science of Logic*, in the
section 'With what must the beginning of Science be made?' Hegel writes:

> But the modern perplexity about a beginning proceeds from a further
> need which escapes those who are either busy demonstrating their prin-
> ciple dogmatically or skeptically looking for a subjective criterion against
> dogmatic philosophizing, and is outright denied by those who begin, like
> a shot from a pistol, from their inner revelation, from faith, intellectual
> intuition, etc. and who would be exempt from *method* and *logic*. (Hegel,
> *Die Wissenschaft der Logik* I, pp. 65f.; *Science of Logic*, pp. 45–6)

9 There is a lacuna here in the transcription of the tape recording of
Adorno's lecture.

10 Reading 'dispute over rationalism' for 'dispute over irrationalism' in
the transcription here.

11 György Lukács (1885–1971), Hungarian philosopher, literary critic,
and politically engaged intellectual.

12 Lukács, *Die Zerstörung der Vernunft: Der Weg des Irrationalismus von
Schelling zu Hitler*, Berlin, 1964; *The Destruction of Reason*, trans.
Peter Palmer, London, 1980.

13   Hegel, *Phänomenologie des Geistes*, p. 24; *Phenomenology of Spirit*, pp. 10f.

14

> The wealth of experience on which thought feeds in Hegel is incompa-
> rable; it is put into the ideas themselves, never appearing as mere 'mate-
> rial,' to say nothing of example or evidence external to the ideas. Through
> what is experienced, the abstract idea is transformed back into something
> living, just as mere material is transformed through the path thought
> travels: one could show this in every sentence of the *Phenomenology of
> Spirit*. Hegel was in fact granted something praised, usually without
> justification, in artists: sublimation; he truly possessed life in its coloured
> reflection, in its recapitulation in spirit...Like the subject of his theories,
> the man Hegel had absorbed both subject and object into himself in spirit;
> the life of his spirit is all of life again within itself. (GS 5, p. 293f.; *Hegel:
> Three Studies*, trans. Shierry Weber Nicholsen, Cambridge, MA, 1993,
> pp. 50–1)

The essay to which Adorno is alluding here, entitled 'Aspects of Hegel's
Philosophy', was published the year before this series of lectures; it was
republished along with two other pieces on Hegel in 1963 under the
general title *Drei Studien zu Hegel*.

15   Hegel, *Phänomenologie des Geistes*, p. 24; *Phenomenology of Spirit*, p. 10.

16   Reading 'the psychologists' for 'we psychologists' in the transcription.

17   Hegel, *Phänomenologie des Geistes*, p. 48; *Phenomenology of Spirit*, p. 29.

18   Hegel, *Phänomenologie des Geistes*, p. 50; *Phenomenology of Spirit*, p. 30.

Lecture 6

1   The term 'panlogism' was used by the Hegelian philosopher Johann
Eduard Erdmann in 1853, albeit in an essentially positive sense, to
describe the philosophy of Hegel: 'The most appropriate name for
Hegel's doctrine would be panlogism. This doctrine acknowledges
nothing but reason as truly actual; and it allows a merely transient and
self-negating character to that which is irrational' (Johann Eduard
Erdmann, *Geschichte der neueren Philosophie*, vol. III.2, repr. Leipzig,
1953, p. 853. See also Erdmann, *Grundriss der Geschichte der Philosophie*, Berlin, 1856, vol. 2, §329; *A History of Philosophy*, trans. W. S.
Hough, London, 1890–1, vol. 2, §329). In the work of Eduard von
Hartmann the concept of panlogism was specifically applied to Hegel
in a critical sense (see von Hartmann, *Schellings positive Philosophie
als Einheit von Hegel und Schopenhauer*, repr. Berlin, 1969, and particularly the chapter entitled the 'Die Unzulänglichkeit des Panlogismus'
[The Inadequacy of Panlogism], pp. 7–12). And for Benedetto Croce

the panlogism of Hegelian dialectic was regarded as 'a diseased part' of his thought which was wrongly applied by Hegel himself, but which could be eliminated in order to save the valuable aspects of Hegelian philosophy (see Benedetto Croce, *What is Living and What is Dead in the Philosophy of Hegel*, trans. Douglas Ainslie, London, 1915; repr. New York, 1985, p. 79). For Croce's specific criticism of Hegel, see note 14 below.

2 See Lecture 5, note 17, above.

3 See Lecture 5, note 18, above.

4 See Lecture 5, p. 43 above.

5 Adorno frequently referred to this observation of Kandinsky's. In his essay on Arnold Schoenberg (GS 10.1, *Prismen: Kulturkritik und Gesellschaft*, p. 173), and in connection with an aphorism which was not published during Adorno's lifetime, he quotes the relevant passage verbatim: 'The artist thinks that, having "finally found his form", he can now continue to create works of art in peace. Unfortunately, even he himself does not usually notice that from this moment (of "peace") on, he very rapidly begins to lose this finally found form' (*Prisms*, trans. Samuel Weber and Shierry Weber, London, 1967, p. 166). In fact these words of Kandinsky are to be found not in his book *On the Spiritual in Art* but in a brief piece which he contributed to a *Festschrift* for Schoenberg which was organized by Alban Berg in 1912: Wassily Kandinsky, 'Die Bilder', in Alban Berg (ed.), *Arnold Schönberg*, Munich, 1912, pp. 59–64, at p. 61; the contribution is reprinted in *Arnold Schönberg, Wassily Kandinsky: Briefe, Bilder, und Dokumente einer außergewöhnlicher Begegnung*, ed. Jelena Hahl-Koch, Salzburg and Vienna, 1980, pp. 153–6, at pp. 154f.

6 Actually Adorno had alluded to this 'need for security' only indirectly (at the beginning of Lecture 3, for example; see pp. 15ff. below). In the lectures which follow, however, he returns repeatedly to this point (see below, pp. 106–7, 150, 179, 184, 194ff., 198, and 208).

7 Hegel, *Phänomenologie des Geistes*, p. 51; *Phenomenology of Spirit*, p. 31.

8 Ibid.

9 Hegel, *Phänomenologie des Geistes*, p. 24; *Phenomenology of Spirit*, p. 10.

10 Hegel speaks of the 'simply looking on' in a key passage of the Introduction to the *Phenomenology*. Here Hegel is speaking about the appropriate method of philosophical knowing, and he asks, firstly, about the 'criterion' which allows our knowledge claims to be tested and, secondly, about the role which the observing and observed consciousness plays in this process:

> But not only is a contribution by us superfluous, since concept and object, the criterion and what is to be tested, are present in consciousness itself, but we are also spared the trouble of comparing the two and really *testing* them, so that, since what consciousness examines is its own self, all that is left for us to do is simply to look on. (Hegel, *Phänomenologie des Geistes*, p. 77; *Phenomenology of Spirit*, p. 54)

Thus, to simplify somewhat, Hegel holds that, in examining knowing (the relationship of consciousness to its object), we are dealing with an objective criterion and process, since the epistemological distinctions involved (the distinction of object and concept, on the one hand, and the distinction of the being-in-itself of the object and its being for knowing, on the other) are distinctions in the observed consciousness itself and thus fall within the latter. Thus in every case consciousness possesses the relevant criterion within itself, and the examination of whether object and concept correspond to one another is a task which falls within consciousness itself. Where there is a reflexive awareness that these moments do not correspond to one another, consciousness must open itself to the experience that both its knowledge and its object have changed: '*Inasmuch as the new true object issues from it,* this *dialectical* movement which consciousness exercises on itself and which affects both its knowledge and its object, is precisely what is called *experience*' (*Phänomenologie des Geistes*, p. 78; *Phenomenology of Spirit*, p. 55).

11   'The main thing to be noticed is that the antinomy occurs not only in the four specific objects taken from cosmology but also in *all* objects of all genera, in *all* representations, concepts, and ideas' (Hegel, *Enzyklopädie der philosophischen Wissenschaften* I, §48, pp. 127f.; *Encyclopedia of the Philosophical Sciences in Outline*, Part I: *The Science of Logic*, trans. Brinkmann and Dahlstrom, §48, p. 94 [translation slightly altered]). Again Hegel says that the principle of contradiction can be expressed in the form 'All things are in themselves contradictory' (Hegel, *Wissenschaft der Logik* II, p. 74; *Science of Logic*, trans. di Giovanni, p. 381).

12   Friedrich Adolph Trendelenburg (1802–1872), from 1837 professor of practical philosophy and pedagogy at the University of Berlin.

13   Trendelenburg presented his critical analysis of Hegel's conception of logic and dialectic in the following texts in particular: in the chapter specifically dedicated to Hegelian dialectic in his most important work, *Logische Untersuchungen* [Logical Investigations] (Berlin, 1840, vol. I, chapter 2: 'The Dialectical Method', pp. 23–99), and in two shorter polemical pieces which were published together under the title *Die logische Frage in Hegel's System* [The Logical Question in Hegel's System] (Leipzig, 1843), in which he briefly summarized the essential points of his critique. Trendelenburg argued that Hegel's theory of dialectical contradiction rests upon a confusion of logical negation and real opposition. For Trendelenburg, 'negation' is a purely logical phenomenon entirely without extra-conceptual force. Negation thus exists only in thought and can only be considered absolutely universal because it is itself without any positive content and is therefore completely indeterminate. Real opposition, by contrast, is a phenomenon which can be perceived in reality itself. In this case the opposed terms are real principles with a positive content which also belongs to them independently of the opposition and not merely by virtue of the latter. On the

basis of this distinction between logical negation and real opposition, Trendelenburg argues as follows: the 'Science of Logic' as conceived by Hegel is supposed to generate an identity and being entirely through its own resources; but the logical means at Hegel's disposal are quite incapable of achieving this, for the features of determinacy, transition, and changes which are required, the alleged self-movement of concepts, cannot be explained by recourse to logical negation; and so, in fact, whenever Hegel claims in the *Logic* to accomplish a genuine advance by means of negation and dialectical contradiction, he actually has to appeal to the sensible intuition of reality and the real oppositions encountered there. Thus it is only through this unacknowledged recourse to the intuition of extra-logical reality and its real movement that he reaches the identity of thought and being which is supposedly produced by logical-dialectical means.

14   Benedetto Croce (1866–1952), Italian philosopher, historian, literary critic, and politically engaged intellectual. His book *Ciò che è vivo e ciò che è morto nella filosofia di Hegel* was published in Bari in 1907. Croce formulated the core of his critique of Hegel in chapter 4 of the book, entitled 'The Nexus of the Distincts and the False Application of the Dialectic Form' (*What is Living and What is Dead in the Philosophy of Hegel*, pp. 78–99). According to Croce, the basic error of the Hegelian dialectic, and the one from which all the other 'errors' are said to flow, lies in the 'confusion between the theory of distincts and the theory of opposites' (ibid., pp. 98–9). What Croce calls a 'distinct' is a structural principle of a plural order which can be differentiated and organically unfolded in different degrees without the component parts constituting an antagonistic relationship with one another, and where the initial principle of unity is also preserved as a principle of unity in the differentiated whole. A two-term structure of opposites, on the other hand, constitutes an antagonistic structure in the strict sense which can only be resolved through the principle of the synthesis of opposites on a higher level. 'Distincts' and 'opposites' for Croce clearly form two existing aspects of reality which must be distinguished in every phenomenon:

> The organism is the struggle of life against death; but the members of the organism are not therefore at strife with one another, hand against foot, or eye against hand. Spirit is development, history, and therefore both being and not-being, becoming; but spirit *sub specie aeterni*, which philosophy considers, is *eternal ideal history*, which is not in time. It is the series of the eternal forms of that coming into being and passing away, which, as Hegel said, itself never comes into being and never passes away. (Ibid., p. 93)

Thus Croce's critique of Hegel's dialectic is that, in failing to recognize the difference between the theory of opposites and theory of distincts, he 'conceived the connexion of these degrees dialectically, in the manner of the dialectic of opposites' (ibid., p. 95). Hegel thus illegitimately extends the validity of dialectic to non-dialectical domains of reality and tries to force reality as a whole into the dialectical schema of opposites and their synthesis.

15 See Lecture 4, note 16, above and Lecture 20, note 9, below.

16 In the *Critique of Pure Reason* the 'antinomies' are expressly counterposed as 'thesis' and 'antithesis', followed immediately by the 'proof' for each of the two positions. Kant presents the first antinomy as follows:

> Thesis: The world has a beginning in time, and is also limited as regards space.

> Antithesis: The world has no beginning, and no limits in space; it is infinite as regards both time and space. (Kant, *Kritik der reinen Vernunft*, pp. 454f.; *Critique of Pure Reason*, A426, p. 396)

17 The third antinomy is presented as follows:

> Thesis: Causality in accordance with laws of nature is not the only causality from which the appearances of the world can one and all be derived. To explain these appearances it is necessary to assume that there is also another causality, that of freedom.

> Antithesis: There is no freedom; everything in the world takes place solely in accordance with laws of nature. (Kant, *Kritik der reinen Vernunft*, pp. 462f.; *Critique of Pure Reason*, A444, p. 409)

18

> If in employing the principles of understanding we do not merely apply our reason to objects of experience, but venture to extend these principles beyond the limits of experience, there arise *pseudo-rational* doctrines which can neither hope for confirmation in experience nor fear refutation by it. Each of them is not only in itself free from contradiction, but finds conditions of its necessity in the very nature of reason – only that, unfortunately, the assertion of the opposite has, on its side, grounds that are just as valid and necessary. ...

> A dialectical doctrine of pure reason must therefore be distinguished from all sophistical propositions in two respects. It must not refer to an arbitrary question such as may be raised for some special purpose, but to one which human reason must necessarily encounter in its progress. And secondly, both it and its opposite must involve no mere artificial illusion such as at once vanishes upon detection, but a natural and unavoidable illusion, which even after it has ceased to beguile still continues to delude though not to deceive us, and which though thus capable of being rendered harmless can never be eradicated. (Kant, *Kritik der reinen Vernunft*, pp. 449f.; *Critique of Pure Reason*, A421–422, p. 394.)

Lecture 7

1 Nicolai Hartmann (1882–1950), professor of philosophy in Marburg, Cologne, Berlin and Göttingen. For the concept of 'real dialectic', see Lecture 2, note 3, above. Hartmann claimed that Hegel saw the dialectic

as 'a higher mode of experience'. See 'Hegel und das Problem der Realdialektik', in: N. Hartmann, *Kleinere Schriften III* (Berlin 1957), pp.
323–46, specifically pp. 329–32. For Hartmann's general view of Hegel,
see N. Hartmann, *Die Philosophie des Deutschen Idealismus*, 2 vols,
Berlin, 1921–9 (vol. 2 is entirely devoted to Hegel's philosophy) and his
study 'Aristoteles und Hegel', *Beiträge zur Philosophie des deutschen
Idealismus* 3/1 (1923): 1–36.

2 See Hegel, *Werke*, vol. 12: *Vorlesungen über die Philosophie der
Geschichte*; *The Philosophy of History*, trans. J. Sibree (1857), New
York, 1956; and *Lectures on the Philosophy of World History: Intro-
duction*, trans. H. B. Nisbet, Cambridge, 1975.

3 See Hegel, *Werke*, vol. 7: *Grundlinien der Philosophie des Rechts*;
Outlines of the Philosophy of Right, trans. M. Knox, ed. S. Houlgate,
Oxford, 2008.

4 See Hegel, *Werke*, vols. 13–15: *Vorlesungen über die Ästhetik*; *Lectures
on Aesthetics*, trans. M. Knox, 2 vols, Oxford, 1975.

5 Adorno is referring here to the philosopher and psychologist Wilhelm
Wundt (1832–1920), not to the son Max Wundt (1879–1963).

6 Wilhelm Dilthey (1833–1911) developed a specific epistemology for the
human sciences, in contrast to the methods employed in the natural
sciences, and presented it as a theory of *Verstehen* or 'understanding'
(hermeneutics).

7 Richard Kroner (1884–1974), from 1919 professor of philosophy in
Freiburg, subsequently in Dresden, Kiel and Berlin; he emigrated from
Germany in 1938 and from 1941 taught in New York.

8 See Richard Kroner, *Von Kant bis Hegel* [From Kant to Hegel], 2 vols,
Tübingen, 1921–4. [Translator's note: This work has not been trans-
lated into English but, for Kroner's later view of Hegel, see his 'Intro-
duction' to Hegel, *Early Theological Writings*, trans. M. Knox,
Philadelphia, [1948] 1971, pp. 1–66; see also Kroner, *Speculation and
Revelation in the History of Philosophy*, London, 1957, vol. 3, ch. XII:
'The Speculative Dialectic', pp. 274–301.]

9 There is a lacuna in the transcription here.

10 The sociologist and philosopher Georg Simmel (1858–1918) was one of
the founders of sociology as an independent academic discipline; from
1914 he was a professor in Strasbourg. Simmel furnished a detailed
account of the concept of the 'limit' or 'boundary' [*Grenze*], interpreted
in the context of his own 'philosophy of life', in the opening chapter ('Die
Transzendenz des Lebens') of his book *Lebensanschauung: Vier metaph-
ysische Kapitel*, published in 1912 (in Simmel, *Gesamtausgabe*, ed.
Ottheim Rammstedt, vol. 16: *Der Krieg und die geistigen Entscheidungen*,
ed. Gregor Fitzi and Ottheim Rammstedt, Frankfurt am Main, 1999, pp.
209–425, specifically pp. 212–35; *The View of Life: Four Metaphysical
Essays with Journal Aphorisms*, trans. John A. Y. Andrews and Donald
N. Levine, Chicago, 2010, pp. 1–17). There are numerous passages in
Simmel which exemplify the ideas to which Adorno is alluding here.
Thus Simmel describes the self-transcending character of life as a process
in which spirit constantly advances beyond itself:

Our concrete, immediate life posits an area that lies between an upper and a lower boundary; but consciousness of this account depends on the fact that life has become more abstract and advanced, thus transcending its boundary, and thereby confirming the reality of a boundary. Life holds the boundary fast, stands on this side of it – and in the same act stands on the other side of it and views it simultaneously from within and from without. The two aspects belong equally to its establishment, and just as the boundary itself partakes of both its 'this side' and its 'that side,' so the unified act of life includes both boundedness and the transcendence of the boundary, despite the fact that this, considered as a whole, seems to present a logical contradiction. (*Der Krieg und die geistigen Entscheidungen*, pp. 214f.; *The View of Life*, p. 3)

But it is perhaps no coincidence that Simmel's formulations of the problem of the limit or boundary do not in fact correspond precisely to Adorno's own way of putting it and reveal a rather different nuance. For it appears that Simmel did not defend a strictly dialectical conception of the limit or boundary, one in which the latter would bear the principle of supersession internally *within itself*. What Simmel is principally concerned with is clearly evident from his theory of time (*Der Krieg und die geistigen Entscheidungen*, pp. 218ff.; *View of Life*, pp. 6ff.). Here we are basically presented with a self-surpassing (or self-transcendence) of the ego as an essential structure of life, as an original, continuous and immediately 'lived' process which stretches out of the present into the future. And it is only through an act of conscious logical objectification that a limit or boundary is inscribed as a threshold between the Now and the Later. Thus we always already find ourselves on this side of the boundary and beyond it on account of the original underlying unity of life. Thus the supersession of the boundary is already grounded in an original process of self-supersession: 'But this very reference to such boundaries shows that we can somehow step over them, that we *have* stepped over them' (*Der Krieg und die geistigen Entscheidungen*, p. 214; *View of Life*, p. 3).

11   Kroner, *Von Kant bis Hegel*, vol. 2, p. 331.
12   In a famous passage from his *Athenäum Fragments*, Friedrich Schlegel writes:

> Romantic poetry is a progressive universal poetry…It alone can become, like the epic, a mirror of the whole circumambient world, an image of the age. And it can also – more than any other form – hover at the midpoint between the portrayed and the portrayer, free of all real and ideal self-interest, on the wings of poetic reflection, and can raise that reflection again and again to a higher power, can multiply it in an endless succession of mirrors. (*Philosophical Fragments*, trans. Peter Firchow, Minneapolis, 1991, Fragment 116, pp. 31–2)

The particular description of reason as 'reflection of reflection' could not be traced to any specific text of Schlegel's. The expression 'reflection of reflection' is certainly found in Kierkegaard, who used it, like Adorno, to characterize Schlegel's conception of 'romantic irony', which is 'subjectivity raised to the second power, a subjectivity's subjectivity, which corresponds to reflection's reflection' (see Søren Kierkegaard, *The Concept of Irony with Continual Reference to Socrates*, ed. and trans. H. V. Hong and Edna H. Hong, Princeton, NJ, 1989, p. 242). Kierkegaard also refers in a critical sense to self-reflective subjectivity in modern philosophy with specific reference to Kant and Fichte: 'Because reflection was continually reflecting about reflection, thinking went astray, and every step it advanced led further and further, of course, from any content' (ibid., p. 272).

13   In chapter 9 of Book XII of his *Metaphysics*, Aristotle writes as follows: 'Thus what reason thinks is itself, being that which is most excellent, and thought is a thinking of thinking [νόησις νοήσεως / *noēsis noēseōs*]' (*The Complete Works of Aristotle*, 2 vols, ed. Jonathan Barnes, Princeton, NJ, 1984; vol. 2: *Metaphysics*, 1072b 18–30). This idea of reason as 'the thinking of thinking', as pure and eternal actuality, also defines Aristotle's concept of God. Through the exercise of their own faculty of reason, in *theoria* or contemplation, human beings are able to participate, for a time and in a weaker form, in the divine life. Hegel also gave expression to his well-known admiration for the Aristotelian conception of reason when he concluded his *Encyclopaedia* with a lengthy quotation from chapter 7 from the same book of the *Metaphysics*, a passage where the self-relating character of thought is expressly connected to identity of thought and the thinkable or the intelligible (see Hegel, *Werke*, vol. 19: *Enzyklopädie der philosophischen Wissenschaften* III, §577, p. 395; *Hegel's Philosophy of Mind, being Part III of the Encyclopaedia of the Philosophical Sciences*, trans. William Wallace, Oxford, 1971, §577, p. 315).

14   Kroner, *Von Kant bis Hegel*, vol. 2, p. 331.

15   Ibid., vol. 2, pp. 331f.

16   The specific phrase 'direct attention' here is a translation of the expression *intentio recta* employed in Husserlian phenomenology (and originally in scholastic philosophy).

17   It was not possible to identify passages in Hegel's *Encyclopaedia* that correspond to Adorno's allusions here.

18   See Lecture 20, note 9, below.

Lecture 8

1   Reading *sie* (i.e., the dialectic) for *er* here.

2   The transcription of the tape recording reads *dialectic* for *reality* here.

3

To the extent that these final results of idealism are viewed as results, i.e. to the extent that they are viewed as conclusions of a chain of argument, they are '*a priori*' and contained within the human mind. To the extent, however, that argument and experience actually coincide and one views these same results as something given within experience, then they are '*a posteriori.*' For a full-blown idealism, *a priori* and *a posteriori* are not two different things, but are one and the same thing, simply looked at from two different sides, and they can be distinguished from each other only in terms of the different means one employs in order to arrive at each. Philosophy anticipates experience in its entirety; it thinks of experience only as something necessary, and to this extent the experience of which philosophy thinks is – in comparison with actual experience – *a priori.* Insofar as it is given, a given number is *a posteriori.* The same number is *a priori* insofar as it is treated as the product of its factors. Anyone who is of a different opinion does not know what he is talking about. (Johann Gottlieb Fichte, *Versuch einer neuen Darstellung der Wissenschaftslehre*, in Fichte, *Gesamtausgabe der Bayrischen Akademie der Wissenschaften*, ed. Bernhard Lauth and Hans Gliwitsky, Part 1, vol. 4: *Werke 1797–1798*, Stuttgart-Bad Cannstatt, 1970, p. 206; see Fichte, *Introductions to the Wissenschaftslehre and Other Writings 1797–1800*, trans. Daniel Breazeale, Indianapolis, 1994, p. 32)

4 Reading *Durchführung* [treatment] for *Buchführung* [book-keeping] here.

5 Hegel had originally planned this work as the first part of his projected 'System of Science', and the title he initially gave to his book was 'First Part: Science of the Experience of Consciousness'. But when the work was published in 1807 this was changed to read 'First Part: Science of the Phenomenology of Spirit'. Finally, in 1831, in connection with a new edition of the *Phenomenology* which he had just begun working on before his death, Hegel made it clear that the phrase 'First Part of the System of Science' was to be removed from the title. It seems that he wished the work simply to be entitled 'Phenomenology of Spirit'.

6 See Lecture 7, p. 60 above.

7 See Lecture 2, note 9, above.

8 The expression 'dialectical salt' could not be traced to any text of Hegel's. Perhaps Adorno is also alluding to a well-known observation by Lenin in his *Conspectus to the Science of Logic*. He copied out the passage where Hegel speaks of absolute negativity as 'the turning point of the movement of the concept', and then added the remark: 'salt of the dialectic' (W. I. Lenin, *Werke*, ed. Institut für Marxismus-Leninismus, Berlin, 1968, vol. 38: *Philosophische Hefte*, p. 220).

9 Adorno is alluding to the French proverb: 'A farceur, farceur et demi'.

10

> When civil society is in a state of unimpeded activity, it is engaged in *expanding* internally in *population* and *industry*. The *amassing of wealth* is intensified by *generalizing* (a) the linkage of people by their needs and (b) the methods of preparing and distributing the means to satisfy these needs, because it is from this double process of generalization that the largest profits are derived. That is one side of the picture. The other side is the *subdivision* and *restriction* of particular work. This results in the *dependence* and *distress* [*Not*] of the class [*Klasse*] tied to work of that

sort, and these again entail the inability to feel and enjoy the broader freedoms and especially the spiritual benefits of civil society. (Hegel, *Grundlinien der Philosophie des Rechts*, §243, p. 389; *Outlines of the Philosophy of Right*, pp. 220–1)

Or again:

When the standard of living of a large mass of people falls below a certain subsistence level – a level regulated automatically as the one necessary for a member of the society – and when there is a consequent loss of the sense of right and wrong, of integrity and of honour in maintaining oneself by one's own activity and work, the result is the creation of a *rabble of paupers* [*Pöbel*]. At the same time this brings with it, at the other end of the social scale, conditions which greatly facilitate the concentration of disproportionate wealth in a few hands. (*Grundlinien der Philosophie des Rechts*, §244, p. 389; *Outlines of the Philosophy of Right*, p. 221)

And even if, when 'the masses begin to decline into poverty', they were provided with work 'to maintain them at their ordinary standard of living',

the volume of production would be increased, but the evil consists precisely in an excess of production and in the lack of a proportionate number of consumers who are themselves also producers, and thus it is simply intensified by both of the methods by which it is sought to alleviate it. It hence becomes apparent that despite an *excess of wealth* civil society is *not wealthy enough*, i.e. its own resources are insufficient, to check excessive poverty and the creation of a penurious rabble. (*Grundlinien der Philosophie des Rechts*, §245, p. 399; *Outlines of the Philosophy of Right*, pp. 222–3)

Hegel specifically describes this inner connection between poverty and wealth in civil society as 'its dialectic' which 'drives it to push... beyond its own limits' (*Grundlinien der Philosophie des Rechts*, §246, p. 391; *Outlines of the Philosophy of Right*, p. 222).

11 The specific expression 'freedom with regard to the object', which evokes the important theme of 'freedom towards the object' in Adorno's work, could not be identified either in Hegel's *Propaedeutic* or in any other Hegelian text.

12 Reading *folgen* [trace] for *verbinden* [connect] here.

Lecture 9

1 Adorno is probably thinking here of neo-Thomist or neo-Scholastic currents of thought. In the nineteenth century the scholastic tradition of Catholic thought had maintained an extremely conservative outlook

and had regarded modern philosophy in general as an emphatically false trail of thought. In the first half of the twentieth century, however – in the school founded by Maréchal for example – there were numerous attempts to engage productively with Hegel (see Bernhard Lakebrink, *Hegels dialektische Ontologie und die Thomistische Analektik*, Cologne, 1955; André Marc, *Dialectique de l'agir*, Paris, 1949, and the same author's *Dialectique de l'affirmation: essai de métaphysique reflexive*, Paris, 1952). Max Horkheimer had already discussed Scholastic thought in chapter 2 of his book *Zur Kritik der instrumentellen Vernunft*, specifically in the second chapter, entitled 'Gegensätzliche Allheilmittel' (see Horkheimer, *Gesammelte Schriften*, vol. 6: *Zur Kritik der instrumentellen Vernunft und Notizen 1949–69*, ed. Alfred Schmidt, pp. 75–104; *Critique of Instrumental Reason*, trans. Mathew J. O'Connell et al., London, 2012, pp. 34–50). Adorno refers to these neo-scholastic currents of philosophy again in Lecture 11, pp. 108f. above.

2   See Lecture 5, note 14, above.

3   Max Scheler (1874–1928), philosopher and sociologist; professor in Cologne from 1919, he became professor in Frankfurt in 1928. One of the founders of the movement of 'Philosophical Anthropology', he published *Die Stellung des Menschen im Kosmos* [Man's Place in the Cosmos] in 1926. The remark by Scheler to which Adorno alludes could not be traced or identified more precisely.

4   Martin Buber (1878–1965), Jewish social thinker and philosopher of religion; from 1938 to 1951 he was professor of social philosophy at the Hebrew University in Jerusalem. The central focus of Buber's thought was the dialogical principle embodied in the mutual relationship between human beings and that between human beings and God (see Martin Buber, *Ich und Du* (1923), Heidelberg, 1983; *I and Thou*, trans. Walter Kaufmann, Edinburgh, 1983).

5   There is a lacuna in the transcription at this point.

6   *Rudis indigestaque moles*: a raw and shapeless mass. See Ovid, *Metamorphoses*, Book I, verse 7. At the beginning of his *Metamorphoses* the poet describes the original state of the world as follows: 'Before there was any earth or sea, before the canopy of heaven stretched overhead, Nature presented the same aspect the world over, that to which men have given the name of Chaos. This was a shapeless uncoordinated mass, nothing but a weight of lifeless matter, whose ill-assorted elements were indiscriminately heaped together in one place' (Ovid, *Metamorphoses*, trans. Mary M. Innes, Harmondsworth, 1981, p. 29).

7   The original meaning of the Greek verb *dialegesthai* is 'to converse'. But Adorno is obviously thinking of the significance which the word comes to assume in Plato when he investigates the formation of general concepts and the problem of genuine 'definition'. See Lecture 1, note 4, above.

8   Adorno did not in fact return to these points in this series of lectures.

9   'Gestalt theory' was introduced and developed in Germany by Christian
    Ehrenfels (1859–1932), a professor in Prague from 1896 (see Ehrenfels,
    'Über Gestaltqualitäten', *Vierteljahreszeitschrift für wissenschaftliche
    Philosophie* 14 (1890), pp. 249–92), Max Wertheimer (1880–1943),
    Aldhémar Gelb (1887–1936) and Kurt Goldstein (1878–1965). When
    he was a student in Frankfurt, Adorno had attended lectures by Gelb.
    These ideas were subsequently developed by a number of other thinkers
    and provided the theoretical foundation for 'Gestalt therapy'.
10 Max Wertheimer had employed the term 'bad Gestalt' for the initial con-
    fused condition of a problem with which productive thought must start,
    before it could – by virtue of an immanent tendency to 'relief' or 'configura-
    tion' in the thing itself – restructure the original situation and discover a
    unified Gestalt that facilitates the transition from a bad Gestalt to a satisfac-
    tory one (see Wertheimer, *Drei Abhandlungen zur Gestalttheorie*, Erlan-
    gen, 1923). Max Wertheimer was professor of psychology in Frankfurt
    from 1929 until 1933. Adorno formulated his criticisms of Gestalt theory
    more clearly and specifically in his *Metakritik der Erkenntnistheorie*:
    'Gestalt theory has been correctly reproached with wanting immediately
    to uncover metaphysical sense in the datum of the structure of positivistic
    research. It presents itself as a science without paying the price of demysti-
    fication. Hence it serves to lay an ideological smokescreen for divided
    reality, which it claims to know as undivided and "healthy", instead of
    naming the conditions of the division' (GS 5, p. 164; *Against Epistemol-
    ogy*, trans. Willis Domingo, Oxford, 1982, p. 159).
11 See Lecture 4, p. 17 above.
12 See Kant, *Kritik der reinen Vernunft*, p. 206; *Critique of Pure Reason*,
    A160/B199, p. 195.
13 See Walter Benjamin, *Charles Baudelaire: Ein Lyriker im Zeitalter des
    Hochkapitalismus*, in Benjamin, *Gesammelte Schriften*, vol. I.2, ed. Rolf
    Tiedemann and Hermann Schweppenhäuser (1974), pp. 509–690;
    Charles Baudelaire: A Lyric Poet in the Era of High Capitalism, trans.
    Harry Zohn, London, 1997. The controversy to which Adorno is refer-
    ring is documented in the exchange of letters with Benjamin in 1938–9
    (see Theodor W. Adorno and Walter Benjamin, *Briefe und Briefwechsel
    1928–1940*, ed. Henri Lonitz, Frankfurt am Main, 1994, pp. 364ff.;
    *Theodor W. Adorno and Walter Benjamin: The Complete Correspon-
    dence*, trans. Nicholas Walker, Cambridge, 1999, pp. 280ff.). Benjamin
    had sent the central section of a projected but never completed book on
    Baudelaire to the Institute for Social Research with a view to publication.
    Adorno subjected this original version to extensive criticism in his letter
    to Benjamin of 10 November 1938, and these critical observations are
    basically the same as those formulated in this series of lectures. They
    encouraged Benjamin to a comprehensive revision of aspects of his inter-
    pretation – though only in parts of the second chapter, 'The Flâneur'. The
    original version of Benjamin's text is published in the German edition of
    his collected writings under the title 'Das Paris des Second Empire bei
    Baudelaire' (see Benjamin, *Gesammelte Schriften*, vol. I.2, pp. 511–604;

the revised version is published under the title 'Über einige Motive bei Baudelaire', ibid., pp. 605–53; *Baudelaire: A Lyric Poet in the Era of High Capitalism*, 'The Paris of the Second Empire in Baudelaire', pp. 9–101, and 'Some Motifs in Baudelaire', pp. 107–54).

14 *Gesammelte Schriften*, vol. I.2, pp. 519–23; *Baudelaire: A Lyric Poet in the Era of High Capitalism*, pp. 17–21.

15 Victor Hugo (1802–1885); *Les Misérables* was published in 1862.

16 *Banlieue*: the suburbs; Adorno says 'outside the suburbs', but what was meant is 'outside the town gate' (*barrière*). It is not clear whether this is a mistake in the transcription of the recording of Adorno's lecture or a slip on Adorno's part. However, what Benjamin was talking about here was not the suburbs but the town gate which separated the suburbs from the city proper, and where the wine tax was levied (see Benjamin, *Gesammelte Schriften*, vol. I.2, p. 520; *Baudelaire: A Lyric Poet in the Era of High Capitalism*, p. 18).

17 Adorno is summarizing Benjamin's claims here. In this connection Benjamin referred specifically to Honoré-Antoine Frégier, *Des classes dangereuses de la population dans les grandes villes, et des moyens de les rendre meilleures*, Paris, 1840 (see *Baudelaire: A Lyric Poet in the Era of High Capitalism*, p. 18).

18 Adorno is referring both to Benjamin's texts and to their correspondence which touched on these issues (see note 13 above).

19 In his letter to Benjamin of 10 November 1938, Adorno wrote as follows:

> Unless I am very much mistaken, your dialectic is lacking in one thing: mediation. You show a prevailing tendency to relate the pragmatic contents of Baudelaire's work directly and immediately to adjacent features in the social history, and whenever possible, the economic features, of the time. I am thinking, for example, of the passage about the duty on wine (I, p. 23), of certain remarks about the barricades, or especially of the aforementioned passage on the arcades (II, p. 2), which strikes me as particularly problematic since this is where the transition from a general theoretical discussion of physiologies to the 'concrete' representation of the *flâneur* is especially precarious... I shall attempt to supply the theoretical reason for my aversion to this particular kind of concreteness and its behavouristic overtones. The reason is that I regard it as methodologically inappropriate to give conspicuous individual features from the realm of the superstructure a 'materialist' turn by relating them immediately, and perhaps even causally, to certain corresponding features of the substructure. The materialist determination of cultural traits is only possible if it is mediated through the *total social process*. (Adorno–Benjamin, *Briefwechsel 1928–1940*, pp. 366f.; *Theodor W. Adorno and Walter Benjamin: The Complete Correspondence*, pp. 282f.)

In order to understand Benjamin's approach here, one should add that, in the part of the text which Adorno saw, he began by deliberately isolating the philological emphasis upon concrete and particular relations to social history from the mediation on which Adorno insisted with the intention of pursuing this dimension in the projected (though unwritten) third part of the work.

20 Max Weber explained his conception of the 'ideal-type' in his essay ' "Objectivity" in Social Science and Social Policy' (1924). Here he also adumbrates the objection, to which Adorno alludes, that Marx's approach is implicitly metaphysical:

> Thus far we have been dealing with ideal-types only as abstract concepts of relationships which are conceived by us as stable in the flux of events, as historically individual complexes in which developments are realized. There emerges however a complication, which reintroduces with the aid of the concept of 'type' the naturalistic prejudice that the goal of the social sciences must be the reduction of reality to *'laws'*. *Developmental* sequences too can be constructed into ideal types and these constructs can have quite considerable heuristic value. But this quite particularly gives rise to the danger that the ideal-type and reality will be confused with one another... This procedure gives rise to no methodological doubts so long as we clearly keep in mind that ideal-typical developmental *constructs* and *history* are to be sharply distinguished from each other, and that the construct here is no more than the means for explicitly and validly imputing an historical event to its real causes while eliminating those which on the basis of our present knowledge seem possible... We have intentionally avoided a demonstration with respect to that ideal-typical construct which is the most important one from our point of view; namely, the Marxian theory... We will only point out here that naturally all specifically Marxian 'laws' and developmental constructs – insofar as they are theoretically sound – are ideal-types. The eminent, indeed unique, *heuristic* significance of these ideal-types when they are used for the *assessment* of reality is known to everyone who has ever employed Marxian concepts and hypotheses. Similarly, their perniciousness, as soon as they are thought of as empirically valid or as real (i.e., truly metaphysical) 'effective forces,' 'tendencies,' etc. is likewise known to those who have used them. (Max Weber, 'Die "Objektivität" sozialwissenschaftlicher und sozialpolitischer Erkenntnis', in Weber, *Gesammelte Aufsätze zur Wissenschaftslehre*, Tübingen, 1922, pp. 146–214, specifically pp. 203–5; ' "Objectivity" in Social Sciences and Social Policy', in Weber, *The Methodology of the Social Sciences*, ed. and trans. Edward A. Shils and Henry A. Finch, New York, 1949, pp. 50–112, specifically pp. 101–3)

Lecture 10

1   In the preceding winter semester 1957/8 Adorno had conducted a seminar on Max Weber's book *Economy and Society* (Weber, *Wirtschaft und Gesellschaft: Grundriss der verstehenden Soziologie*, ed. Marianne Weber, Bonn, 1922; *Economy and Society*, ed. Günther Roth and Claus Wittig, 2 vols, Berkeley, CA, 1978).

2   In the second part of Spinoza's *Ethics*, 'Of the Nature and Origin of the Mind', we read: 'Propositio VII. Ordo, et connexio idearum idem est,

ac ordo, et connexio rerum'; Spinoza, *Ethics*: 'P.7: The order and connection of ideas is the same as the order and connection of things', *The Collected Works of Spinoza*, vol. 1, ed. and trans. Edwin Curley, Princeton, NJ, 1985, p. 451.

3 See Lecture 13, pp. 128ff. above.

4 The formulation that 'speculative philosophy makes common cause with faith against reflection' could not be found in Hegel's writings in precisely this form. It seems to the present editor questionable whether Hegel would actually have expressed himself exactly in these terms. For even in Hegel's Jena writings, such as *Faith and Knowledge*, where 'speculation' and 'reflection' are not identified with one another, we cannot simply claim that speculation is opposed to reflection (see Hegel, *Werke*, vol. 2, *Jenaer Schriften 1801–1807*, pp. 287–433; *Faith and Knowledge*, trans. W. Cerf and H. S. Harris, Albany, NY, 1977). See also Lecture 5, note 5.

5

> The true is the whole and the whole is spirit, spirit which divides within itself and posits itself as identical with itself, which only arises, and arises for itself, in this process of self-movement. This is the primordial positing, the self-positing positing of Hegelian metaphysics, or we could say, its self-presupposing character, which does not *get* externally pre-supposed independently of the system, but is the process in which the system presupposes itself. ...The system as a whole cannot be demonstrated, for every positing, every pre-supposition, which could demonstrate it is itself only posited through the system in the first place. The contents of the individual positings are one and all contents of the whole, which articulates and explicates itself in and through them. Thus we can say that the system rests, as a whole and in detail, on *intuition*. But to say this would also be to say too little, would only express half the truth here, for it rests just as much on *reflection* and *abstraction*: it is an intuition which thinks itself, an intuition which reflects itself. Both moments are equally essential and act together. (Richard Kroner, *Von Kant bis Hegel*, vol. 2, pp. 342 and 361)

6 Adorno is alluding specifically to György Lukács's *History and Class Consciousness*, which exercised a considerable influence upon Adorno himself and many other thinkers of his generation (see Lukács, *Geschichte und Klassenbewusstsein: Studien über marxistische Dialektik*, Berlin, 1923, repr. in Lukács, *Werke*, Neuwied and Berlin, 1969, vol. 2, *Frühschriften*, pp. 161–517; *History and Class Consciousness; Studies in Marxian Dialectics*, trans. Rodney Livingstone, London, 1971).

7 In the event, Adorno was not able to return to these specific points regarding Hegel in this course of lectures.

8 '*True* and *False* belong amongst those determinate notions which are held to be inert and wholly separate essences, one here and one there, each standing fixed and isolated from the other, with which it has nothing in common. Against this view it must be maintained that truth

is not a minted coin that can be given and pocketed ready-made' (Hegel, *Phänomenologie des Geistes*, p. 40; *Phenomenology of Spirit*, p. 22).

Lecture 11

1   Talcott Parsons (1902–1979), American sociologist who taught at Harvard University from 1927 (as professor from 1944). Adorno also discusses Parsons in Lecture 17 (pp. 179ff.).

2   Jean-Paul Sartre (1905–1979), philosopher and writer, wrote the book which can be regarded as the founding text of French existentialism, *L'être et le néant* (Paris, 1943; *Being and Nothingness: An Essay on Phenomenological Ontology*, trans. Hazel E. Barnes, London, 1969). In his famous description of the waiter in a cafe, Sartre explores the phenomenon of what he calls 'bad faith' (*'la mauvaise foi'*), where the individual attempts to deceive himself regarding his genuine character – namely as a fundamentally free being, a being 'for itself' – by playing a role which he is expected to play in society, such as that of 'being a waiter', as if he were such 'in himself' – i.e., as if he were immediately identical with that role. Sartre thus interprets the waiter who plays being a waiter as an externalized or dispossessed self which consists 'in being what I am not' (*'d'être ce que je ne suis pas'*). (*L'être et le néant*, p. 96; *Being and Nothingness*, p. 60). But since the assumption of the role is only possible as a simulated presentation (*'représentation'*), this already implies a difference between our existence and the role in question: 'As if from the very fact that I sustain this role in existence I did not transcend it on every side, as if I did not constitute myself as one *beyond* my condition' (*L'être et le néant*, pp. 107f.; *Being and Nothingness*, p. 69). In the overall structure of the book, the function of the analysis of the phenomenon of 'bad faith' – comparable to the despairing flight from authentic selfhood analysed by Kierkegaard – is to expose the fundamental structures of the 'for-itself' and the 'transcendence' which intrinsically belongs to human existence.

3   The thought here can be explicated as follows: in the previous lecture Adorno had employed the concept of 'role' in the context of the heteronomous determination of the individual by society as a whole, that is to say, as this is also developed in a way by Sartre's theory; in modern sociology, under the influence of Talcott Parsons, the concept of 'role' is defined, by contrast, as the forms of behaviour characteristic of the person or the individual within society. Adorno formulated the problems involved in this approach more explicitly in a lecture course of 1964 entitled 'Philosophische Elements einer Theorie der Gesellschaft' ['Philosophical Elements of a Theory of Society'], and with specific reference to the concept of the 'character mask', which he will also touch upon in the next lecture here. In the 1964 lecture Adorno says:

Where we are able to speak of social reality in the specific sense, and where alone one is justified in talking about the constitution of a special domain of social science at all, it always appears – and this precisely on account of the general character of a society in which the interests of individual human beings and the structure of the whole are at variance – that individual human beings are also largely character masks even there where they think they are acting as specific psychological individuals, where they believe they are being themselves, believe they are acting freely, believe they are identical with themselves; that is to say, they are doing nothing but what their function, their objective function within the society in question, prescribes for them. This, we may add in passing, is the ultimate source of the phenomenon which it has become extraordinarily fashionable today to describe in terms of 'roles', although the concept of role is particularly problematic precisely because it hypostasizes something that should itself be derived from the structure of society. For human beings here must do something that they themselves are precisely not – and indeed to play a role literally means, in the first instance, having to do something and having to present ourselves as something that we in ourselves are not – and if we disregard this essential aspect the concept of role becomes meaningless. This concept of role, which thus can only be explained by the way that human beings are brought by the social totality to act in a particular fashion other than the way they might determine themselves to act, this concept of role, I emphasize, thoroughly dependent as it is on concrete social factors, gets hypostasized in such a way that the notion of 'role' comes to appear as if it were a kind of primordial characteristic of the social as such, which is rather like trying to derive the ontology of reality directly from the experience of the theatre. (NaS, vol. 12, pp. 150f.; see also GS 8, p. 13)

  In the next paragraph of the lecture we have just cited, Adorno refers explicitly to Parsons as a defender of the concept of role which he is criticizing. (For the concept of 'character mask', see Lecture 12, p. 123, and Lecture 12, note 12.)

4 Hans Cornelius (1863–1947), lecturer in philosophy at the University of Frankfurt from 1910 and Adorno's principal academic teacher.

5 For the concept of *prōtē philosophia* ('first philosophy'), see Lecture 3, note 2, above.

6 Reading *verschränkt* [bound up with] for *beschränkt* [limited] here.

7 In the *Metakritik der Erkenntnistheorie*, Adorno specifically refers to Nietzsche in this connection (GS 5, p. 16; *Against Epistemology: A Metacritique*, pp. 18–19).

8 Hegel provides a systematic account of the relationship between his own philosophy and other philosophical positions in the *Encyclopaedia* version of the *Logic*, in the section entitled 'Preliminary Conception' (§19–§83), which includes a discussion of the three 'Positions of Thought towards Objectivity' (§26–§78). See Hegel, *Enzyklopädie der philosophischen Wissenschaften* I, pp. 67–180; *Encyclopedia of the Philosophical Sciences in Basic Outline*, Part 1: *The Science of Logic*, trans. Brinkmann and Dahlstrom, pp. 67–125.

9 See Lecture 9, note 1, above.

10   See Martin Heidegger, *Die Kategorien- und Bedeutungslehre des Duns Scotus* [The Doctrine of Categories and Meaning in Duns Scotus] (1915), in Heidegger, *Gesamtausgabe I. Abteilung: Veröffentlichte Schriften 1914–1970*, vol. 1: *Frühe Schriften*, ed. Friedrich-Wilhelm von Herrmann, Frankfurt am Main, 1978, pp. 189–412. [Translator's note: The treatise which Heidegger investigates in this book is now generally ascribed not to Duns Scotus but Dietrich of Freiburg. For the remarks on Hegel to which Adorno is alluding, see p. 411.]

11   The editor has been unable to discover what Adorno is alluding to here.

12   See Martin Heidegger, 'Hegels Begriff der Erfahrung' (1942/3), in Heidegger, *Holzwege* Frankfurt am Main, 1950, pp. 111–204; 'Hegel's Concept of Experience', in Heidegger, *Off the Beaten Track*, trans. Julian Young and Kenneth Haynes, Cambridge, 2002. See Lecture 8, note 5. [Translator's note: In a letter to Thomas Mann of 3 June 1950, Adorno also refers to this essay, in the context of remarks concerning György Lukács's recently published book *The Young Hegel*: 'I am afraid I must regard Lukács's big book on Hegel, which I have worked through from beginning to end, as among my most depressing recent experiences. One can hardly credit such reification of consciousness in the very man who coined this concept in the first place. Heidegger's essay in *Holzwege* on the *Phenomenology of Spirit* is almost dialectical by comparison' (Theodor W. Adorno and Thomas Mann, *Correspondence 1943–1955*, trans. Nicholas Walker, Cambridge, 2006, p. 47).]

13   See Lecture 9, note 1, above.

14   The first (grammatically incomplete) sentence of Book I, chapter 1, of Hegel's *Science of Logic* reads: 'Being, pure being – without further determination' (Hegel, *Wissenschaft der Logik* I, p. 82; *Science of Logic*, trans. di Giovanni, p. 59).

15   Herbert Marcuse (1898–1979), philosopher, sociologist and political theorist, from 1932/3 a member of the Institute for Social Research. Having emigrated to the USA in 1933, he was professor at Brandeis University from 1954 and at the University of California, San Diego, from 1964.

16   See Herbert Marcuse, *Hegels Ontologie und die Grundlegung einer Theorie der Geschichtlichkeit*, Frankfurt am Main, 1932; *Hegel's Ontology and Theory of Historicity*, trans. Seyla Benhabib, Cambridge, MA, 1987. Marcuse had originally intended to present this work under his teacher Martin Heidegger in 1928 as his *Habilitationsschrift* (the academic qualification which allowed the holder to lecture in a German university), but it appears, on some accounts, that Heidegger was unwilling to accept it. [Translator's note: Adorno wrote a brief review of Marcuse's book in the same year it appeared (see GS 20.1, pp. 203–4).]

17   Adorno had already commented on Hegel's conception of the 'abstract' at the end of Lecture 4, p. 36 above.

18   In his treatise on *Categories*, Aristotle uses the expression τόδε τι [*tode ti*] to designate a 'this-such' or 'this something of a kind', such as 'this table' insofar as this thing falls under the concept 'table'. For Aristotle,

what is decisive for determining whether or not something is a *tode ti* are above all the criteria of independence and separability, criteria which are satisfied in the first instance by singular or individual objects. In his *Metaphysics*, Aristotle also describes the *eidos* (the form or concept) as *tode ti*, although there is some controversy about the precise sense in which the *eidos* can be said to satisfy these criteria. Adorno himself uses the expression *tode ti* exclusively to signify the pre-conceptualized singular object (a 'this', a 'something') which we indicate by means of the expression. Thus Adorno writes:

> This concept of τόδε τι is also fundamental for the entire tradition of Western thought – this is because all reference to facticity, to the 'this-there', to that which cannot be dissolved in the concept but for which we nonetheless seek a conceptual name, is harboured in this expression τόδε τι. Indeed τόδε τι is not ultimately a concept at all but more of a gesture – which is extremely interesting for the character of the thought in question here; τόδε τι means something like 'this', and indicates or points towards something. And it was thus still clear to Aristotle that it was not possible to form anything like a concept for this essentially unconceptual something, and that we can only express it through a gesture. Yet this notion of gesture subsequently became a sort of technical term which eventually found expression in the concepts of a 'given' or a *datum*, or already in the *hacceitas* of the Scholastic tradition, or however else such concepts may be framed. (NaS IV.14, p. 57)

19 This sense of 'abstract' is also central to Hegel's little essay 'Who Thinks Abstractly?' (Hegel, *Jenaer Schriften*, pp. 575–81; 'Who Thinks Abstractly?', trans. Walter Kaufmann, in Kaufmann, *Hegel: Reinterpretation, Texts, and Commentary*, Garden City, NY, 1965, ch. 9.

20 Reading *haben* [have] for *benutzen* [use] here.

21 Adorno probably cited the *Science of Logic* from the complete edition of Hegel's works by Hermann Glockner: Hegel, *Sämtliche Werke*, 1927–30, vol. 4: *Die objective Logik*, pp. 87f. Adorno cites the first half of the second sentence from the first chapter of Book I ('The Logic of Being'). See Hegel, *Wissenschaft der Logik* I, pp. 82f.; *Science of Logic*, trans. di Giovanni, p. 59.

22 Hegel, *Die objective Logik*, p. 88; Hegel, *Wissenschaft der Logik* I, pp. 82f.; *Science of Logic*, trans. di Giovanni, p. 59.

23 It has not been possible to identify a corresponding passage in Nietzsche.

24 Hegel, *Sämtliche Werke*, vol. 8: *System der Philosophie, Erster Teil: Die Logik*, p. 204; Hegel, *Enzyklopädie der philosophischen Wissenschaften* I, p. 183; *Encyclopedia of the Philosophical Sciences, Part I: The Science of Logic*, trans. Brinkmann and Dahlstrom, p. 137.

25 For Jacobi, see Lecture 5, note 2, above.

26 Hegel, *Die objective Logik*, p. 107; Hegel, *Wissenschaft der Logik* I, p. 101; *Science of Logic*, trans. di Giovanni, p. 73.

27 In his lectures on Hölderlin in the winter semester of 1934/5, Heidegger uses the older form *Seyn* (beyng) instead of the modern standard form

Sein (being). See Martin Heidegger, *Gesamtausgabe. III. Abteilung: Vorlesungen 1923–44*, vol. 39, ed. Susanne Ziegler, Frankfurt am Main, 1980, p. 6: 'Offenbarung des Seyns' [manifestation of beyng]. In 'Die Kehre', a text from 1935, Heidegger specifically uses this form *Seyn* (beyng) to mark a fundamental difference with regard to his own earlier conception of Sein (being). If in *Being and Time* (1927) Heidegger had attempted to think being and beings in terms of human being (*Dasein*), he now attempts to think the human being and beings from the perspective of being itself. See Heidegger, *Die Technik und die Kehre*, Pfullingen, 1962; *The Question concerning Technology and other Essays*, trans. William Lovitt, New York, 1977.

28   A general election for the Bundestag, the Federal Parliament in West Germany, had taken place just the year before, on 15 September 1957. The Christian Democratic Party (the CDU) ran for the third time under the leadership of Konrad Adenauer, while the Social Democratic Party (the SPD) was led for the second time by Erich Ollenhauer. The CDU had won the election with an absolute majority.

29   It is evident from the transcription of the tape recording of the lecture that, at this point, Adorno referred his listeners to Horkheimer's essay 'Der neueste Angriff auf die Metaphysik' of 1937, which had originally appeared in the *Zeitschrift für Sozialforschung*. See Max Horkheimer, *Gesammelte Schriften*, vol. 4: *Schriften 1936–1941*, ed. Alfred Schmidt, Frankfurt am Main, 1988, pp. 108–61.

30   The concept of 'second nature' has a long and complex history which effectively reaches back – beyond the expression itself, which was apparently first employed by Cicero – to ancient Greek thought (see the article 'Zweite Natur' by N. Rath in *Historisches Wörterbuch der Philosophie*, ed. Joachim Ritter and Karlfried Gründer, vol. 6, Basel, 1984, pp. 484–94). The way in which Adorno uses the concept of 'second nature' involves at least three aspects which were already present or implicit in the earlier history of the expression: firstly, the thesis that the 'first' or original nature of human beings is not something immediately given in itself but is always experienced as a 'nature' that is already mediated or altered by human labour or the work of the human mind, so that first and second nature cannot simply be separated from one another (the perspective of Hegel and Marx: see Lecture 8, pp. 76f. above); secondly, the idea that the concept of 'nature' in the expression 'second nature' actually needs to be critically challenged inasmuch as it also stands for the alien and ossified character of society and history – i.e., for the ideological illusion of something which presents itself as if it were nature in some original, positive and immediate sense (the specific contribution of Marx and Lukács; see *Negative Dialektik*, GS 6, p. 48; *Negative Dialectics*, trans. E. B. Ashton, London, 1973, pp. 37–8); thirdly, Adorno reaches back beyond Lukács, Marx and Hegel to Rousseau's reflections on the relation between first and second nature when he speaks of 'allowing to a damaged and oppressed nature what belongs to it'. In his early essay *The Idea of Natural History* (1932),

Adorno had already attempted to think the significance of the relationship involved here in a dialectical fashion so that, with the dissolution of the seemingly natural immediacy of second nature, the historical character of first nature may emerge, and the latter may thereby be liberated from the purely instrumental and exploitative relationship which human beings have established with regard to it. (See *Die Idee der Naturgeschichte*, GS I, pp. 345–65; 'The Idea of Natural History', *Telos* 60 (1984), pp. 111–24.)

Lecture 12

1   Adorno is alluding to Gottfried Wilhelm Leibniz (1646–1716) and his theory of monads. According to the metaphysics of Leibniz, the world consists essentially of 'monads' – i.e., simple unextended substances which are self-enclosed and are furnished either with unconscious representations (in the case of plants and minerals) or with conscious representations (in the case of living beings). In §7 of his *Monadology*, Leibniz writes: 'The Monads have no windows through which anything may come in or go out. The Attributes are not liable to detach themselves and make an excursion outside the substance, as could sensible species of the Schoolmen. In the same way neither substance nor attribute can enter from without into a Monad' (G. W. Leibniz, *La monadologie*, ed. Eduard Erdmann, 1840, §7, p. 705; see also Leibniz, *Monadologie/Lehrsätze der Philosophie: Letzte Wahrheiten über Gott, die Welt, die Natur der Seele, den Menschen und die Dinge*, ed. and trans. Joachim Horn, Darmstadt, 2009, p. 45; *Monadology*, trans. G. R. Montgomery, in Leibniz, *Basic Writings*, La Salle, IL, 1968, p. 252).

2   Francis Herbert Bradley (1846–1924), English philosopher, professor at the University of Oxford from 1876.

3   F. H. Bradley, *Appearance and Reality*, 1893; trans. into German as *Erscheinung und Wirklichkeit*, Leipzig, 1929; *Principles of Logic*, [1883] 1922. It seems that the latter work has never been translated into German.

4   From the times of ancient Greek philosophy onwards the opposition θέσει/φύσει [*thesei/phusei*] has governed the discussion of the specific relation between that which can be said to exist 'by nature' (*phusei*) and that which can be said to exist merely 'by human convention' (*thesei*).

5   See Lecture 10, p. 97 above.

6   The third chapter of Adorno's *Metakritik der Erkenntnistheorie* is entitled *Zur Dialektik der erkenntnistheoretischen Begriffe* (GS 5, pp. 130–89; *Against Epistemology: A Metacritique*, ch. 3: 'Epistemological Concepts in Dialectic', pp. 124–85).

7   See Lecture 7, pp. 68f. above.

8   The Darmstadt investigation to which Adorno refers here consisted of nine monographic studies which were produced under the auspices of

the Institute for Research in the Social Sciences in collaboration with the Frankfurt Institute for Social Research in 1952–4. Adorno, in partial collaboration with Max Rolfes, wrote the introductions for the studies. The study to which he specifically refers in the following discussion is the eighth monograph, which is entitled 'Behörde und Bürger', and dates from February 1952. Adorno's introduction to this study is reprinted in GS 20.2, pp. 634–9.

9   It has not been possible to identify the specific work to which Adorno alludes here.

10   The transcription of the recording of Adorno's lecture indicates a lacuna at this point.

11   Adorno is referring to an investigation entitled 'Betriebsklima: Eine industriesoziologische Untersuchung aus dem Ruhrgebiet, Frankfurt a. M. 1955' [Business Climate: A Sociological-Industrial Investigation from the Ruhr Region], and for which he composed an 'Afterword' which was not actually published with the investigation itself. The 'Afterword' is available in GS 20.2, pp. 674–84, under the title 'Betriebsklima und Entfremdung' [Business Climate and Alienation].

12   Marx employs the concept of 'character mask' or 'persona' in *Capital*, when he proceeds from the analysis of the commodity to his exposition of the process of exchange. Since commodities 'cannot themselves go to market and perform exchanges in their own right' (Karl Marx, *Das Kapital*, p. 99; *Capital*, trans. Ben Fowkes, Harmondsworth, 1976, vol. 1, p. 178), this exposition must also include the human agents themselves, namely the possessors of commodities. Marx reveals his critical intention when he begins by deriving the concept of 'person' from the possessors of commodities in this context. He is offering a critique of the concept of the person in positive bourgeois law which is defined in terms of property rights, and thereby also a critique of a concept of right which simply reflects the historically given economic relationships of the time. In this way, the distortion which is already produced by the commodity form – where quite specific social and historical conditions come to appear to human beings as if they were natural and given features of things – is effectively extended into the relationships between human beings themselves. Thus the concept of person which Marx presents here stands for an alienated mode of existence where human beings can only be 'persons' precisely as personifications of pre-established economic functions, and where they are consequently assigned a role by material relations which have themselves become independent, as if they were performing a role in a play (in ancient theatre the role of the actor was specified by the relevant 'mask' or 'persona'). As Marx writes:

> Here the persons exist for one another merely as representatives and hence owners of commodities. As we proceed to develop our investigation, we shall find, in general, that the characters who appear on the economic stage [*die ökonomischen Charaktermasken der Personen*] are

merely personifications of economic relations; it is as the bearers of these economic relationships that they come into contact with each other. (*Das Kapital*, pp. 99f.; *Capital*, vol. 1, pp. 178–89)

For the relationship between 'individual', 'role' and 'character mask', see Lecture 11, notes 1–3, above.

13 The theses and results to which Adorno refers in the following discussion had been presented in the draft for an essay entitled 'On Popular Music' (see NaS I.3, pp. 402–10). The 'difficulties' he mentions in the lecture may allude to his arguments with Paul Lazarsfeld (1901–1976) at the time when Adorno was also working on Lazarsfeld's Princeton Radio Research Project. These arguments concerned the aims and methods involved in empirical social research in general. The radio project, with which Adorno collaborated, was originally intended, through research into the expressed preferences and dislikes of the radio listeners, simply to put together specific music programmes which would attract as many listeners as possible for the longest duration possible in order to maximize exposure to the lucrative advertisements the programmes would also carry.

14 See Lecture 10 and Lecture 10, note 1, above.

Lecture 13

1 René Descartes (1596–1650), philosopher, natural scientist and mathematician, is generally regarded as the founder of modern rationalism. His *Discours de la méthode* appeared in 1637.

2 Francis Bacon (1561–1626), statesman and philosopher, is regarded as the founder of the British empiricist tradition. See Lecture 15, notes 2 and 3, below.

3 It is obvious that Adorno read out from his own copy of Descartes's text in German translation at this point: René Descartes, *Philosophische Werke* (2 vols), vol. 1: *Abhandlung über die Methode und andere Schriften*, trans. Artur Buchenau, Leipzig, 1922, pp. 14f. See *Discourse on the Method of Rightly Conducting the Reason*, in *The Philosophical Works of Descartes*, trans. E. S. Haldane and G. R. T. Ross, New York, 1955, vol. 1, p. 92.

4 Descartes, *Abhandlung über die Methode*, p. 15; *Discourse on the Method of Rightly Conducting the Reason*, p. 92.

5 It seems that Adorno was not quoting directly from Gottfried Keller himself here but was probably thinking of the quotation that Walter Benjamin included in the fifth of his *Theses on the Philosophy of History*:

The true picture of the past *flits by*. The past can be seized only as an image which flashes up at the instant when it can be recognized and is never seen again. 'The truth will not run away from us': in the historical outlook of historicism these words of Gottfried Keller mark the exact point where historical materialism cuts through historicism. (Walter Benjamin, *Gesammelte Schriften*, vol. 1.2, ed. Rolf Tiedemann and Hermann Schweppenhäuser, p. 695; *Theses on the Philosophy of History*, in Benjamin, *Illuminations*, ed. Hannah Arendt, trans. Harry Zohn, London, 1970, p. 256)

This quotation, which has now found a firm place in the secondary literature on Benjamin and far beyond, has never actually been traced back to the work of Gottfried Keller himself. It is quite possible that Benjamin was mistakenly citing from memory here, but the phrase can indeed be found – and this surely seems no accident – in Röhl's German translation of Dostoyevsky's *Crime and Punishment*, which appeared in 1913. Benjamin read this translation in 1934 in Skovsbostrand around the same time that he was reading Gottfried Keller's *Sinngedicht* (see Benjamin, 'Verzeichnis der gelesenen Schriften', in *Gesammelte Schriften*, vol. 7.1, p. 468). In the first chapter of the third part of the novel, the inebriated and excited Razumikhin defends the idea of personal individuality and appeals to the human privilege of talking 'rot' or 'nonsense' in the following words:

> By talking rot you eventually get to the truth. I'm a man because I talk rot. Not a single truth has ever been discovered without people first talking utter rot a hundred times or perhaps a hundred thousand times – and it's, in a way, a highly commendable thing even. But so far as we are concerned, you see, the trouble is that we can't even talk rot in our own way. Talk rot by all means, but do it in your own way, and I'll be ready to kiss you for it. For to talk nonsense in your own way is a damn sight better than talking sense in someone else's; in the first case, you're a man; in the second you're nothing but a parrot! The truth won't run away from us, but you can certainly ruin your life with that stupid refusal of individuality. There are plenty examples of that. (Fyodor Dostoyevsky, *Schuld und Sühne*, trans. H. Röhl, Leipzig, [1913], p. 307; *Crime and Punishment*, trans. David Magarshack, Harmondsworth, 1951, p.219; the final sentences have been adapted here to reflect the wording of the German translation)

6   It has not been possible to identify who Adorno is referring to here.
7   See Lecture 10, note 2.
8   It is possible that there is a slight gap in the transcription here where the tape was changed at this point in the lecture.
9   Descartes, *Abhandlung über die Methode*, p. 15; *Discourse on the Method*, p. 92.
10   Reading *aufgelöst* [resolved] for *ausgelöst* [released] here.

Lecture 14

1   See Franz Borkenau, *Der Übergang vom feudalen zum bürgerlichen Weltbild: Studien zur Geschichte der Philosophie der Manufakturperi-*

ode, Paris, 1934 (Schriften des Instituts der Sozialforschung, ed. Max Horkheimer, vol. 5).

2   Adorno is alluding here to Karl Mannheim's *Mensch und Gesellschaft im Zeitalter des Umbruchs* (Leiden, 1935), a text he also mentions in his essay 'Das Bewusstsein der Wissenssoziologie' (see GS 10.1, pp. 31–46; 'The Sociology of Knowledge and its Consciousness', in *Prisms*, trans. Samuel Weber and Shierry Weber, London, 1967, pp. 35–49; the issues Adorno raises in his lecture are specifically discussed on pp. 44–6 of this essay).

3   See Adorno's essay 'Über Statik und Dynamik als soziologische Kategorien' (GS 8, pp. 217–37).

4   See Karl Mannheim, *Ideologie und Utopie*, Bonn, 1929, p. 134.

5   The transcription of the tape recording indicates a lacuna at this point.

6   See Helmut Schelsky, *Wandlungen in der deutschen Familie der Gegenwart: Darstellungen und Deutung einer empirsch-soziologischen Tatbestandaufnahme*, Stuttgart, 1953.

7   See Gerhard Baumert (with the collaboration of Edith Hünninger), *Deutsche Familien nach dem Kriege*, Darmstadt, 1954 (with a summary in English).

8   Descartes, *Abhandlung über die Methode*, p. 15; *Discourse on the Method*, p. 92.

9   Reading 'which he still quite openly describes as a rational principle' instead of 'which he still describes as an entirely open rational principle' in the transcription.

10   The infinitesimal calculus was first formulated in strictly scientific form by Leibniz and Newton.

11   For the Hegelian expression 'The position of thought towards objectivity', see Lecture 11, note 8, above.

12   It has not been possible to identify any use of the expression 'freedom with regard to the object' in Hegel's work. See Lecture 13, note 7, above.

13   In his second speech on the nature of love in the *Phaedrus*, Socrates describes love as a kind of divine madness (*Phaedrus* 243 e10ff.). When we behold beautiful things within the world of sensuous perception, this divine madness releases 'the noblest of all enthusiasms' [αὕτη πασῶν τῶν ἐνθουσιάσεων ἀρίστη / *hautē pasōn tōn enthousiaseōn aristē*] (*Phaedrus* 249 e1) among those who are truly inclined to philosophy, for they can here recall the idea of beauty which the immortal rational soul once beheld directly before the soul was lodged in the human body. Adorno interprets this Platonic passage in its original context in the lectures on aesthetics which he delivered in the following semester (see NaS IV.3, pp. 139–69).

Lecture 15

1   Adorno is referring to Joseph Marie Comte de Maistre (1753–1821).

2   In his work *Instauratio magna* (*The Great Renewal*), Francis Bacon (see Lecture 13, note 2, above) projected a foundation for the modern

natural sciences in which the mere observation of nature would be superseded by experience oriented to experiment and active discovery. Bacon begins one of the parts of this work, the *Novum organon*, with a radical critique (*pars destruens*) of tradition, in which he argues that the human mind has previously been hindered in its attempt to acquire a scientific knowledge of nature by a number of persistent prejudices which Bacon calls 'idols'. He goes on to distinguish four types of prejudice: the *idola tribus* (prejudices of the tribe), which is responsible for the human tendency to take ourselves as the measure of nature; the *idola specus* (prejudices of the cave), which derive from our own environment or education; the *idola fori* (prejudices of the market-place), which human beings take over through language; and the *idola theatri* (prejudices of the theatre), with which Bacon identifies the dogmatic adherence to ideas handed down from the past. See Francis Bacon, *Novum organon*, ed. T. Fowler, Oxford, 1889, vol. 1, pp. 36–68. The older use of the term 'idols', in the Church Fathers, referred essentially to the worship of pagan divinities.

3   The new inductive concept of knowledge which Bacon attempted to establish in the *Instauratio magna* (see note 2 above) involved, among other things, the prescription to advance towards the highest propositions of the sciences through several steps or stages of experience. With his expression '*idole d'échelle*' (idol of the step or ladder), de Maistre turned Bacon's own critical conception of 'idol' against the latter's theory of step-by-step induction. In the *Dialectic of Enlightenment*, Adorno had already alluded to this expression of de Maistre's and provided the reference (GS 3, p. 23; *Dialectic of Enlightenment*, trans. John Cumming, London, 1973, p. 7). See Joseph de Maistre, *Les soirées de Saint-Pétersbourg ou Entretiens sur le gouvernement temporel de la Providence*, 5th entretien, in *Oeuvres Complètes*, Lyon, 1891, vol. 4, p. 256.

4   Zeno argued as follows: a flying arrow must at every point in time possess a definite spatial position the magnitude of which is identical with that of the arrow itself. At this point in time, therefore, the arrow is at rest; for at a place which allows it no leeway, as it were, it cannot possibly move. But if it cannot move at one point in time in its flight, then it cannot move at any other point either. Thus the arrow cannot fly at all and motion is impossible. If therefore thought is only ever supposed to move from level to level without flying, then it doesn't really move but only repeats the same thought that it already has and thus produces tautologies.

5   See Ludwig Thoma, *Die kleinen Verwandten: Lustspiel in einem Aufzug*, in Thoma, *Brautschau, Dichters Ehrentag, Die kleinen Verwandten: 3 Einacter*, Munich, 1916.

6   Adorno is probably thinking here of the 'Deduction of the Pure Concepts of the Understanding', the heart of the first part of Kant's first *Critique*. See Kant, *Kritik der reinen Vernunft*, ed. Raymund Schmidt, Hamburg, 1956, pp. 126–91; *Critique of Pure Reason*, trans. Norman Kemp Smith, London, 1933, pp. 120–75 (A84–A130/B116–B169).

7 Adorno produced a large number of reviews of operas and concert performances between 1928 and 1933, in part in his capacity as the main editor of the journal *Anbruch* (see note 10 below).

8 It has not been possible to determine the identity of the 'Viennese friend' to whom Adorno refers here.

9 Eduard Horak (1838–1893) founded the private music schools named after him in Vienna in 1861; they were elevated to the status of 'conservatories' in 1940.

10 Adorno, 'Motive IV: Musik von außen', *Anbruch* 11(9–10) (1920), pp. 335–8 (GS 18, pp. 18f.).

11 Adorno here returns to the concept of immanent critique which he had already broached in Lecture 4 (see pp. 28f. below).

12 See Johann Wolfgang Goethe, *Faust: Eine Tragödie*, lines 323–9, where the Lord allows Mephistopheles to tempt Faust:

> Enough – I grant that you may try to clasp him,
> Withdraw this spirit from his primal source
> And lead him down, if you can grasp him
> Upon your own abysmal course –
> And stand abashed when you have to attest:
> A good man in his darkling aspiration [*in seinem dunklem Drange*]
> Remembers the right road throughout his quest. (Goethe, *Sämtliche Werke*, vol. 6.1: *Weimarer Klassik 1798–1806*, p. 544; *Goethe's Faust*, trans. Walter Kaufmann, New York, 1953, p. 89)

13 The particular expression 'a form in which truth appears' [*eine Erscheinungsform der Wahrheit*] does not correspond precisely to Hegel's terminology. Hegel's principal question with regard to any work of art is the extent to which it may be regarded as an adequate form for the manifestation of the Idea, of the absolute, of spirit. In this sense (artistic) beauty is the 'sensuous show of the Idea' (Hegel, *Werke*, vol. 13: *Vorlesungen über die Ästhetik* I, p. 151; *Aesthetics: Lectures on Fine Art*, trans. T. M. Knox, Oxford, 1975, vol. 1, p. 111: 'Therefore the beautiful is characterized as the pure appearance of the Idea to sense'), but such beauty is 'true' for Hegel, strictly speaking, only in the works of classical Greek art, because the Idea or 'the concept' is here immediately identical with the sensuous form. But at the same time this immediate identity is also deficient for Hegel precisely because the Idea is present here only in a sensuous and immediate way – i.e., the Idea has not yet been consciously realized as such. But since it is only the self-conscious realization of the Idea that is fully or *actually* true, Hegel can write that 'the manifestation of truth in a sensuous form is not truly adequate to the spirit' (*Vorlesungen über die Ästhetik* I, p. 144; *Aesthetics*, vol. 1, pp. 104–5). And, with an eye to his own present, Hegel says: 'For us art counts no longer as the highest mode in which truth fashions an existence for itself' (*Vorlesungen über die Ästhetik* I, p. 141; *Aesthetics*, vol. 1, p. 103).

14   The Greek can equally be rendered as 'making the weaker case or argu-
      ment appear the stronger', which then came to mean simply 'turning
      wrong into right'. This lies behind Plato's critical analysis of the power
      of sophistic rhetoric, but it was also one of the charges raised against
      Socrates himself:

> And in addition to these things, the young men who have the most leisure,
> the sons of the richest men, accompany me of their own accord, find
> pleasure in hearing people being examined, and often imitate me them-
> selves, and then they undertake to examine others; and then, I fancy, they
> find a great plenty of people who think they know something, but know
> little or nothing. As a result, therefore, those who are examined by them
> are angry with me, instead of being angry with themselves and say that
> 'Socrates is a most abominable person and is corrupting the youth.' And
> when anyone asks them, 'by doing or teaching what?' they have nothing
> to say, but they do not know, and that they may not seem to be at a loss,
> they say these things that are handy to say against all the philosophers,
> 'the things in the air and the things beneath the earth' and 'not to believe
> in the gods' and 'to make the weaker argument the stronger'. (Plato,
> The Apology, 23 c2–d7, Loeb Classical Library, trans. H. N. Fowler,
> p. 89)

15   See Lecture 1, p. 1 above.
16   See Lecture 8, note 11.
17   See Lecture 12, pp. 117f. above.
18   In the Preface to his book The Origin of German Tragic Drama, Walter
      Benjamin criticizes both the deductive and the inductive method, at least
      in its traditional form, as a way of presenting the phenomena of art
      history. He claims that the undiminished particular – and thus a certain
      inductive moment – can be preserved only by recourse to an 'idea' as
      distinct from a 'concept':

> The impossibility of the deductive elaboration of artistic forms and the
> consequent invalidation of the rule as a critical authority – it will always
> preserve its validity in the field of artistic instruction – provide the spur
> to a productive scepticism. This can be likened to a pause for breath, after
> which thought can be totally and unhurriedly concentrated even on the
> very minutest object without the slightest inhibition. For the very minutest
> things will be discussed wherever the work of art and its form are con-
> sidered with a view to judging their content. To snatch hastily, as if steal-
> ing the property of others, is the style of the routinier, and is no better
> than the heartiness of the philistine. In the act of true contemplation, on
> the other hand, the abandoning of deductive methods is combined with
> an ever wider-ranging, an ever more intense reappraisal of phenomena,
> which are, however, never in danger of remaining the objects of vague
> wonder, as long as the representation of them is also a representation of
> ideas, for it is here that their individuality is preserved. (Benjamin, Gesam-
> melte Schriften, vol. I.1, p. 225; Origin of German Tragic Drama, trans.
> John Osborne, London, 2009, pp. 44f.)

19 The expression *metabasis eis allo genos* ('transition to another category') has been used since Aristotle to describe an erroneous form of reasoning where we take concepts which are appropriate in one domain and illegitimately move to apply them in a quite different domain. See Aristotle, *Posterior Analytics Book I. 7. 75a38f.* Thus in the 'Transcendental Dialectic' of the first *Critique*, in his discussion of the fourth antinomy, Kant refers to a *metabasis eis allo genos* as an erroneous 'leap' in the argument which indicates a transcendent 'first cause' for the series of sensuous appearances and then makes an illegitimate 'leap' or 'transition' from the domain where the concept of empirical contingency (implying an infinite causal chain) is valid to a different level which employs an 'intelligible' concept of contingency (involving a finite causal chain). See Kant, *Kritik der reinen Vernunft*, p. 468; *Critique of Pure Reason*, A 459/B 487, p. 419.

20 In his *Notes to Literature*, Adorno gives the following German translation as the source for this remark by Degas: Paul Valéry, *Tanz, Zeichnung und Degas*, trans. Werner Zemp, Berlin, [1951], p. 129. (See GS 11, p. 121; *Notes to Literature*, trans. Shierry Weber Nicholsen, vol. 1, p. 104: 'Another Anchorite who knows the train times.') A different German translation gives the cited remark in the following context: 'On one occasion there was much praise for Moreau, and his secluded way of life, which one person described as a veritable anchorite's life. "Yes, indeed", Degas said, "but the life of an Anchorite who knows when the trains leave"' (Hans Graber, *Degas nach eigenen und fremden Zeugnissen*, Basel, 1942, pp. 102f.).

21 'Here I stand. I can do no other. God help me, Amen.' These are supposed to be words with which Luther concluded his own defence before the Diet of Worms on 18 April 1521, when he refused to retract his teachings. There is actually some doubt about their authenticity, and the official records confirm only the final phrase 'God help me, Amen' (see *Deutsche Reichsakten unter Kaiser Karl V*, ed, A. Wrede, vol. 2, no. 80, Gotha, 1896).

22 Wilhelm Reich (1897–1957), psychiatrist, psychoanalyst, sexologist and sociologist. Reich was already practising as a psychoanalyst in Vienna at the age of twenty-three and is often regarded as the founder of 'Freudo-Marxism' on account of his explicit attempt to combine Marxist and psychoanalytic approaches. In his book *Massenpsychologie des Faschismus* of 1933 (*The Mass Psychology of Fascism*, trans. Vincent R. Carfagno, Harmondsworth, 1975), Reich attempts to explain fascism as a form of collective neurosis which springs from a persistent authoritarian repression of instinctual life within patriarchal society. It was his theses regarding the fascistic character structure that led to his expulsion from the German Communist Party in the same year and to his expulsion from the International Psychoanalytic Association in the following year (1934). During the rest of the decade, when the threat of fascism drove him first to Denmark and Norway, and eventually to the New School for Social

Research in the United States, Reich advanced beyond his earlier analysis
of fascist character formation in the direction of a biologically oriented
theory based upon the notion of a specific form of energy (dubbed
'orgone energy') as the essential core of human life ('orgonomy'). This
theory met with almost universal rejection and condemnation, and in
1955 his researches into orgone energy and the therapy he developed in
this connection were legally prohibited in the United States. Reich was
sentenced to two years' imprisonment for ignoring the injunction against
him, and he died in prison in 1957.

23 The notion of a 'qualitative leap', or sudden transition from quantity
to quality, is one of the central themes of Hegel's dialectical theory. In
the Preface to the *Phenomenology of Spirit* he offers a particularly
famous formulation of the way in which a continuous development is
suddenly broken and interrupted by a qualitative leap:

> Besides, it is not difficult to see that ours is a birth-time and a period of
> transition to a new era. Spirit has broken with the world it has hitherto
> inhabited and imagined, and is of mind to submerge it in the past, and in
> the labour of its own transformation. Spirit is indeed never at rest but always
> engaged in moving forward. But just as the first breath drawn by a child
> after its long, quiet nourishment breaks the gradualness of merely quantita-
> tive growth – there is a qualitative leap, and the child is born – so likewise
> the Spirit in its formation matures slowly and quietly into its new shape,
> dissolving bit by bit the structure of its previous world, whose tottering state
> is only hinted at by isolated symptoms. The frivolity and boredom which
> unsettle the established order, the vague foreboding of something unknown,
> these are the heralds of approaching change. The gradual crumbling that
> left unaltered the face of the whole is cut short by a sunburst which, in one
> flash, illuminates the features of a new world. (Hegel, *Phänomenologie des
> Geistes*, pp. 18f.; *Phenomenology of Spirit*, pp. 6f.)

Lecture 16

1 René Descartes, *Abhandlung über die Methode und andere Schriften*,
trans. Artur Buchenau, Leipzig, 1922, p. 15; *Discourse on the Method
of Rightly Conducting the Reason*, trans. E. S. Haldane and G. R. T.
Ross, New York, 1955, p. 92.

2 Kant criticized the rationalism that he encountered in the form of Christian Wolff's metaphysics as 'dogmatism', namely as

> the presumption that it is possible to make progress with pure knowledge,
> according to principles, from concepts alone (those that are philosophical),
> as reason has long been in the habit of doing; and that it is possible to do
> this without having first investigated in what way and by what right reason
> has come into possession of these concepts. Dogmatism is thus the dog-
> matic procedure of pure reason, *without previous criticism of its own
> powers*. (Kant, *Kritik der reinen Vernunft*, p. 31; *Critique of Pure Reason*,
> trans. Norman Kemp Smith, B xxxv, p. 32.)

3   See Lecture 20, note 9, below.

4   Elsewhere Adorno ascribes such criticism of Weber's concept of *Verstehen* to the typical representatives of empirical social research in general. 'The field of empirical social research in its entirety is united in its extreme polemical resistance not only to all socio-philosophical speculation, but also to the central categories of earlier sociology, which was itself largely empirical in orientation, such as the sociology that deployed the concept of "understanding"' (Adorno, 'Empirische Sozialforschung', in GS 9.2, pp. 327–60, specifically p. 347). According to Adorno, Karl Mannheim (see Lecture 18, note 9, below) also developed his account of basic sociological concepts under the influence of American positivist sociology and in opposition to Weber's theory of 'understanding' (and to the historical–dialectical approach) (see Adorno, 'Neue wertfreie Soziologie', in GS 20.1, p. 16).

5   'The Moor has done his work, the Moor can go' (exits): Friedrich Schiller, *Die Verschwörung des Fiesko*, Act III, scene 4 (Schiller, *Sämtliche Werke*, vol. 1: *Gedichte, Dramen* I, ed. Gerhard Fricke and Herbert Göpfert, Darmstadt, 1984, p. 704). The line is frequently misquoted, with 'duty' in place of the word 'work.'

6   Max Weber writes:

> We have in abstract economic theory an illustration of those synthetic constructs which have been designated as '*ideas*' of historical phenomena. It offers us an ideal picture of events on the commodity-market under conditions of a society organized on the principles of an exchange economy, free competition and rigorously rational conduct. This conceptual pattern brings together certain relationships and events of historical life into a complex, which is conceived as an internally coherent system. Substantively, this construct in itself is like a *utopia* which has been arrived at by the analytical accentuation of certain elements of reality. Its relationship to the empirical data consists solely in the fact that where market-conditioned relationships of the type referred to by the abstract construct are discovered or suspected to exist in reality to some extent, we can make the *characteristic* features of this relationship pragmatically *clear* and *understandable* by reference to an *ideal-type*. This procedure can be indispensable for heuristic as well as expository purposes.

And, with specific reference to the ideal type or idea of capitalistic culture, Weber goes on to say:

> It is possible, or rather, it must be accepted as certain that numerous, indeed a very great many, utopias of this sort can be worked out, of which *none* is like another, and *none* of which can be observed in empirical reality as an actually existing economic system, but *each* of which however claims that it is a representation of the 'idea' of capitalistic culture. *Each* of these can claim to be a representation of the 'idea' of capitalistic culture to the extent that it has really taken certain traits, meaningful in their essential features, from the empirical reality of our culture and brought them together into a unified ideal-construct. (Weber, 'Die "Objektivität"

sozialwissenschaftlicher und sozialpolitischer Erkenntnis', in *Gesammelte Aufsätze zur Wissenschaftslehre*, Tübingen, 1922, pp. 190 and 102; '"Objectivity" in Social Science and Social Policy', in *The Methodology of the Social Sciences*, trans. Edward A. Shils and Henry A. Finch, New York, 1949, pp. 89–90 and 91)

7   Adorno presents his own critique along these lines in the section entitled 'Naturalienkabinett' ('Natural History Museum') in his *Metakritik der Erkenntnistheorie* (GS 5, pp. 219–21; *Against Epistemology*, pp. 217–19).

8   In *Minima Moralia* Adorno writes: 'Properly written texts are like spiders' webs: tight, concentric, transparent, well-spun and firm. They draw into themselves all the creatures of the air. Metaphors flitting hastily through them become their nourishing prey. Subject matter comes winging towards them. The soundness of a conception can be judged by whether it causes one quotation to summon another' (GS 4, p. 97; *Minima Moralia*, trans. E. F. N. Jephcott, New York 1974, p. 87).

9   In *Minima Moralia*, in the section entitled 'Monograms', Adorno says: 'True thoughts are those alone which do not understand themselves' (GS 4, p. 218; *Minima Moralia*, p. 192).

10 Max Brod (1884–1968), writer, translator and composer. Brod was a friend of Kafka, as well as his literary executor, who published a number of works about Kafka (see, among others, *Franz Kafka*, Prague, 1937, and *Franz Kafka: Glauben und Lehre* [Kafka: His Faith and Teaching], Munich, 1948). Hans-Joachim Schoeps (1909–1980) had discussed Kafka in his *Der Gaube an der Zeitwende* [Faith at the Turning Point] of 1936. The different, and sometimes strongly opposed, interpretations of Kafka's work offered by Brod and Schoeps are well documented in Julius Schoeps, *Im Streit um Kafka und das Judentum* [The Controversy around Kafka and Judaism], Königstein im Taunus, 1985.

11 Honoré de Balzac (1799–1850) had hoped with his (unfinished) cycle of novels *La Comédie humaine* to furnish a panoramic view of the French society of his time. The ninety-one novels are interlinked by the frequent reappearance of the same characters in a great variety of different stories.

12 Heimito von Doderer (1896–1966) achieved rather belated recognition as a writer during the 1950s with his novels *Die Strudlhofstiege oder Melzer und die Tiefe der Jahre* (1951) and *Die Dämonen: Nach der Chronik des Sektionsrates Geyrenhoff* (1956). In terms of compositional structure, the first of these novels links a large number of particular events by reference to a single place – the *Strudlhofstiege* of the title – rather than by reference to a single narrative thread. The second is linked to the earlier one by the reappearance of one of the latter's principal figures.

13 See Lecture 10 above, pp. 96ff.

14 Reading *es* instead of *er* here.

15 The phrase from the *Phenomenology* to which Adorno is alluding here actually already appears at the level of 'Self-Consciousness' (chapter IV) rather than that of 'Spirit' as such (chapter VI). Hegel writes: 'With self-consciousness, then, we have therefore entered the native realm of truth [*das einheimische Reich der Wahrheit*]' (Hegel, *Phänomenologie des Geistes*, p. 138; *Phenomenology of Spirit*, p. 104). In Hegel's lectures on aesthetics there is a comparable and almost equally famous formulation where he speaks of how 'spirit makes itself at home', and indeed specifically in connection with the idea of 'productive spirit' to which Adorno alludes here:

> In epic proper the childlike consciousness of a people is experienced for the first time in poetic form. A genuine epic poem therefore falls into that middle period in which a people has awakened out of torpidity, and its spirit has been so far strengthened as to be able to produce its own world and feel itself at home in it, while conversely everything that later becomes firm religious dogma or civil and moral law still remains a living attitude of mind from which no individual separated himself, and as yet there is no separation between feeling and will. (Hegel, *Werke*, vol. 15: *Vorlesungen über die Ästhetik* III, p. 332; *Aesthetics*, trans. M. Knox, Oxford, 1975, vol. 2, p. 1045)

Lecture 17

1 In the metaphysical system of Arthur Schopenhauer (1788–1860) a single eternal will lies at the base of the ego and the world as constituted by the intellect in the realm of representation as causally connected individuated appearances in space and time. This underlying 'will', which in a certain sense assumes the place of Kant's 'thing-in-itself', is fundamentally irrational, and its own objective and factical character, which strives for expression as life, essentially precedes the rational constitution of the world on the part of the intellect.

2 'The structure of immanence as absolutely self-contained is necessarily always already system, irrespective of whether it has been expressly deduced from the unity of consciousness or not. Nietzsche's mistrust of *prima philosophia* was thus also essentially directed against system builders. "I mistrust all systematizers and I avoid them. The will to a system is a lack of integrity"' (*Zur Metakritik der Erkenntnistheorie*, GS 5, p. 35; *Against Epistemology*, p. 28). The quotation from Nietzsche comes from the section 'Maxims and Arrows' (no. 26) in *Twilight of the Idols* (see Friedrich Nietzsche, *Werke*, ed. Karl Schlechta, vol. 3: *Jenseits von Gut und Böse, u. a.*, Munich, 1969, p. 392; *Twilight of the Idols*, trans. Walter Kaufmann, in Kaufmann, *The Portable Nietzsche*, New York, 1968, p. 470).

3 The Marburg School was the form of neo-Kantian philosophy founded by Hermann Cohen (1842–1918) and Paul Natorp (1854–1924).

4   The Southwest School was the form of neo-Kantian philosophy founded by Wilhelm Windelband (1848–1915) and further developed by Heinrich Rickert (1863–1936).

5   Heinrich Rickert, *Die Philosophie des Lebens: Darstellung und Kritik der philosophischen Modeströmungen unserer Zeit* [The Philosophy of Life: An Exposition and Critique of the Philosophical Fashions of our Time], Tübingen, 1920.

6   In his foreword to a posthumously published collection of Rickert's essays, Hermann Glockner writes:

> Perhaps the enduring significance of Heinrich Rickert's thought rests precisely upon the fact that he permitted the system builder, which he himself also was, only as much as was strictly necessary. It is quite true that he often declared that he could not possibly conceive of a philosopher without a system. In this regard he felt a certain affinity for Fichte, Schelling and Hegel. And as a philosopher he too desired to build a house, one that would be durable, but also appropriate to life, open for any later development of fresh questions. A house in which a 'whole' human being – someone like Goethe – would find enough room. He hardly concerned himself with the question whether or to what extent such a house can be grounded for all time. (Rickert, *Unmittelbarkeit und Sinndeutung: Aufsätze zur Ausgestaltung des Systems der Philosophie*, ed. Hermann Glockner, Tübingen, 1939, pp. xiif.)

In one passage of his book *The Philosophy of Life*, Heinrich Rickert himself discusses the sense in which the concept of 'system' can be interpreted as a kind of 'house' or 'home' [*Haus*] (as distinct from a mere 'shelter' or 'enclosure' [*Gehäuse*]) (see Rickert, *Die Philosophie des Lebens*, p. 153.)

7   The transcription of the tape recording indicates 'change of tape' at this point. It is impossible to determine whether this has resulted in a gap in the text here.

8   Adorno is probably alluding here to Bruno Rizzi's book *L'URSS: collectivisme bureaucratique: la bureaucratisation du monde*, Paris, 1939. This book, which originally appeared anonymously, had been reviewed by Josef Soudek in the *Zeitschrift für Sozialforschung* (see *Studies in Philosophy and Social Science*, published by the Institute of Social Research, New York, 1941, Vol. IX [1941], No. 2, pp. 336–40, especially pp. 338f.).

9   Correcting 'structure and functional theory of society' in the text; see Talcott Parsons, *The Social System*, Glencoe, IL, 1951.

10   John Maynard Keynes (1883–1946), British mathematician and economist who also actively engaged in political life. Keynes developed a theory of the economic cycle of society as a whole and fundamentally questioned the neo-classical theory of economic equilibrium, defending a degree of state intervention in the economic cycle in order to secure levels of employment and economic investment.

11 The transcription of the tape recording indicates that Adorno here alluded to his earlier essay *Zum Verhältnis von Soziologie und Psychologie* [On the Relationship between Sociology and Psychology] which had appeared in 1955 in the first volume of the *Frankfurter Beiträge zur Soziologie* (see GS 8, pp. 42–85). In this essay Adorno had specifically subjected the theory of Talcott Parsons to detailed criticism. See Talcott Parsons, 'Psychoanalysis and the Social Structure', in: *The Psychoanalytic Quarterly*, Vol. XIX, 1950, No. 3, p. 371ff.

12 See Max Weber, 'Über einige Kategorien der verstehenden Soziologie' (1913), in Weber, *Gesammelte Aufsätze zur Wissenschaftslehre*, Tübingen, 1922, pp, 403–50, specifically pt II: 'Verhältnis zur Psychologie', pp. 408–14.

13 See Lecture 8, p. 73, and Lecture 15, pp. 161f.

14 On the idea of spirit 'making itself at home' in the world, see Lecture 16, note 15, above.

15 In his essay 'The Artist as Deputy', included in *Notes to Literature*, Adorno quotes the relevant passage from Valéry at some length:

> With full rigour and no admixture of ideology, as ruthlessly as any theoretician of society, Valéry expresses the contradiction between artistic work and the current social conditions of material production. As Carl Gustav Jochmann did in Germany more than a hundred years ago, he accuses art itself of archaism: 'It sometimes seems to me that the labour of the artist is of a very old-fashioned kind; the artist himself a survival, a craftsman or artisan of a disappearing species, working in his own room, following his own home-made empirical methods, living in untidy surroundings; using broken pots, kitchenware, old cast-offs that come to hand...Perhaps conditions are changing, and instead of this spectacle of an eccentric individual using whatever comes his way, there will instead be a picture-making laboratory, with its specialist officially clad in white, rubber-gloved, keeping to a precise schedule, armed with strictly appropriate apparatus and instruments, each with its appointed place and exact function' (GS 11, pp. 121f.; *Notes to Literature*, trans. Shierry Weber Nicholsen, vol. 1, p. 104).

Adorno quotes from the German translation (Lecture 15, note 20, above): Paul Valéry, *Tanz, Zeichnung und Degas*, pp. 33f.

Lecture 18

1 Adorno may be alluding to the song 'Are they for, are they against?' of 1932, performed by Marcellus Schiffer (1892–1932) with music by Mischa Spoliansky. The first stanza runs as follows:

> There's something new in town:
> Plays and papers everywhere
> Ask those that read and hear
> About the latest news and views
> It's really critical we know:

Are they soft, or sharp-political?
Do they love to rail without a clue
About affairs of government?
Are they against? Are they for? – and in this sense:
Could they do it better?
Could they – even they – really do it better?
Are they for? Are they against?
Are they against? Are they for?
And why are they against?
And again why are they for?
And why if they're against
Are they against?
Let them be against on my account,
Let them be for on my account!
But why are they against, why are they for? (Quoted in Martin Trageser,
*Es liegt in der Luft eine Sachlichkeit: Die Zwanziger Jahre im Spiegel des
Werks von Marcellus Schiffer*, Berlin, 2007, pp. 313f.)

2 Matthew 12: 30.
3 Reading *konfrontiert* [confronted] for *präsentiert* [presented] here.
4 'If developments in Europe today appear to mark a return to heter-
onomies old and new, I can only passionately protest against this,
even if I recognize the fateful inevitability of this development' (Paul
Tillich, *Gesammelte Werke*, ed. Renate Albrecht, vol. 12: *Begeg-
nungen: Paul Tillich über sich selbst und andere*, Stuttgart, 1971,
pp. 27f.).
5 Adorno is referring here to a long-running debate with Heinz-Klaus
Metzger which eventually led to a radio discussion between them (under
the title *Jüngste Musik – Fortschritt oder Rückbildung* [Recent Music –
Progress or Regression?]) which had been broadcast on West German
Radio shortly before, on 19 February 1958. The radio discussion had
been preceded by a talk by Adorno under the title *Das Altern der neuen
Musik* [The Ageing of the New Music], which was broadcast by South
German Radio on 28 April 1954 (see GS 15, pp. 143–67), and a response
by Heinz-Klaus Metzger under the title *Das Altern der Philosophie der
neuen Musik* [The Ageing of the Philosophy of the New Music], which
appeared in 1958 in the journal *Die Reihe*, vol. 4: 'Junge Komponisten',
pp. 64–80. The radio discussion between Adorno and Metzger was later
published in Heinz-Klaus Metzger, *Musik wozu: Literatur zu Noten*, ed.
Reiner Riehn, Frankfurt am Main 1980, pp. 90–104.
6 See Lecture 5, note 5, and Lecture 10, note 4, above.
7 For Adono's lecture 'Individuum und Gesellschaft', see Lecture 3, note
9, above. Adorno had already given this lecture in a freer and thus
probably rather different form in Munich on 23 May 1958.
8 The Swiss economist Vilfredo Pareto (1848–1923) developed a mathematically oriented theory, specifically in opposition to historical materialism, in order to analyse the interaction between what he saw as the
ultimately irrational socio-economic forces of society and the ideologies

which belonged to them. For Adorno's critique of Pareto, see his *Beitrag zur Ideologielehre*, GS 8, pp. 457–77.

9   Karl Mannheim (1893–1947), professor in Frankfurt am Main until 1933, founder of the 'sociology of knowledge'.

10   The term 'negative theology' is applied to the tradition of religious thought which argues that the absolutely pre-eminent and transcendent character of God cannot adequately be described in positive or affirmative terms, but can only be approached through the experience of divine ineffability in a process of denying all possible propositions about the divine nature. This conception essentially goes back to Dionysus the Areopagite (the fifth century AD), who attempted to combine Christian doctrine with neo-Platonic philosophy. Thus negative theology reached back to the biblical tradition itself, where it could appeal to the Pauline idea of 'the unknown God' and the ban on images of God in the Jewish scriptures but also drew on Platonic sources. Thus the first position which is presented in Plato's dialogue *Parmenides*, where it is argued that each categorical determination in turn is inapplicable to that which is ultimately and absolutely 'One', was already brought by the neo-Platonists into direct connection with Plato's doctrine of the idea of the Good 'beyond being' (*Republic* 509 b5) and thus speculatively reinterpreted as a 'negative' theological concept of God.

11   'For the true is the touchstone of itself and the false' (*The Collected Works of Spinoza*, ed. and trans. Edwin Curley, vol. II, letter 76, to Albert Burgh).

12   'The false is the index (i.e., touchstone) of itself and the truth.'

13   See the words of Prometheus in Goethe's verse drama *Pandora*:

> But Eos ineluctably is rising now,
> Erratically, girl-like, from her laden hands
> Strews purple flowers. On every cloud's rim, look, they bloom,
> Richly unfold their buds and change their multiple shapes.
> So charmingly she appears, at all times a delight,
> Gently accustoming our weak terrestrial eyes
> That could be blinded else by Helios' sudden dart,
> Made as they are to see illumined things, not light. (Johann Wolfgang Goethe, *Pandora: Ein Festspiel*, v, 950–7, in *Sämtliche Werke*, vol. 9: *Epoche der Wahlverwandtschaften 1807–1814*, ed. Christoph Siegrist et al., Munich, 1987, p. 189; *Pandora*, trans. Michael Hamburger, in *Goethe: Verse Plays and Epic*, ed. Cyrus Hamlin and Frank Ryder, New York, 1987, p. 243)

Eos is dawn or Goddess of dawn, Helios the sun or God of the sun. Adorno had taken the same line from *Pandora* as the motto for 'The Essay as Form' (see GS 11, p. 9; *Notes to Literature*, vol. 1, p. 4).

14   There is a comparable passage in Adorno's *Metakritik der Erkenntnistheorie* (GS 5, pp. 25f; *Against Epistemology*, p. 18) where he quotes from the fourth aphorism in the section 'Reason in Philosophy' from Nietzsche's *Twilight of the Idols*:

The *other* idiosyncrasy of the philosophers is no less dangerous; it consists in confusing the last and the first. They place that which comes at the end – unfortunately! for it ought not to come at all! – namely, the 'highest concepts', which means the most general, the emptiest concepts, the last smoke of evaporating reality, in the beginning, *as* the beginning. This again is nothing but their way of showing reverence: the higher *may* not grow out of the lower, *may* not have grown at all. Moral: whatever is of the first rank must be *causa sui*. Origin out of something else is considered an objection, a questioning of value. (Friedrich Nietzsche, *Jenseits von Gut und Böse, u. a.*, p. 404; *Twilight of the Idols*, pp. 481–2)

15   In a comparable passage in his *Introduction to Sociology*, the last series of lectures which Adorno delivered in its entirety, he refers specifically to Scheler's *Probleme einer Soziologie des Wissens* (see Max Scheler, *Gesammelte Werke*, vol. 8: *Die Wissensformen und die Gesellschaft*, Bern, 1960, pp. 15–190; see Adorno, NaS IV, vol. 15, p. 134 and note 160).
16   See Lecture 6, note 10 above.

Lecture 19

1   Conjectural reconstruction of the beginning of the lecture in the transcription of the tape recording.
2   Hegel justifies his view of the limitations of definition as a form of knowledge in his *Science of Logic*. Whereas definition with regard to the products of 'self-conscious purposiveness' and the objects of geometry is quite capable of presenting the true nature of the matter in question, this does not hold for the concrete objects of nature and spirit. As far as the latter are concerned, the practice of definition in terms of the next highest genus and specific difference remains external to the matter, as in the case where we can certainly distinguish human beings from all other living beings by reference to the possession of earlobes, even though this can hardly be said to grasp the essence of the human being as such (see Hegel, *Wissenschaft der Logik* II, pp. 512–19; *Science of Logic*, trans. di Giovanni, pp. 713–18; see also Lecture 7 above, p. 69). This critical limitation on the relevance and applicability of definition is particularly evident in the case of a complex structure such as the state, so that, in the *Philosophy of Right*, Hegel rejects the idea of defining 'right' as a purely formal method and contrasts such an approach with the philosophical – namely the dialectical – method as the only appropriate one precisely because this method alone is capable of grasping the matter itself as a result of a necessary immanent process of development (see Hegel, *Grundlinien der Philosophie des Rechts*, §2, pp. 30–4; *Outlines of the Philosophy of Right*, pp. 18–19). It is interesting to note that Nietzsche comes to the same conclusion – the indefinability of phenomena which have a history – by appealing to the opposite premises: a concept such as 'punishment' is indefinable for Nietzsche not because a definition would fail to capture the historical

essence of the thing in question but because the 'meaning' of the phenomenon has been generated retrospectively in the course of history and externally imposed upon it, and, since this meaning is essentially arbitrary and inevitably plural in character, the unity of the concept is ultimately opaque:

> The whole history of punishment up to this point, the history of its exploitation to the most diverse ends, finally crystallizes in a sort of unity which is difficult to unravel, difficult to analyse, and – a point which must be emphasized – complexly *beyond definition*. (Nowadays it is impossible to say *why* people are punished: all concepts in which a whole process is summarized in signs escape definition; only that which is without history can be defined.) (Nietzsche, *Zur Genealogie der Moral*, in *Werke*, vol. 2, p. 266; *On the Genealogy of Morals*, trans. Douglas Smith, Oxford, 1998, p. 60)

3   See Adorno's 'The Essay as Form', GS 11, pp. 9–33; *Notes to Literature*, vol. 1, pp. 3–23.

4   Reading *definition* instead of *concept* following the transcription of the tape recording.

5   'Art is magic delivered from the lie of being truth' (GS 4, p. 254; *Minima Moralia*, p. 222).

6   At the beginning of the transcription of Lecture 19 there is a note by someone, who cannot be identified, indicating that from this point onwards the tape is in places almost impossible to follow. This explains the numerous lacunae and conjectural emendations in the transcription of the rest of this lecture. The lacunae have been specifically indicated as such by the editor only where they mark a noticeable interruption in the process of the argument. The conjectural emendations here have been adopted from the transcription or sometimes replaced by others.

7   The lacuna in the text results from the tape being changed at this point.

8   'Fate is the nexus of guilt among the living' (Walter Benjamin, *Goethes Wahlverwandtschaften*, in *Gesammelte Schriften*, vol. 1.1, ed. Rolf Tiedemann and Hermann Schweppenhäuser, Frankfurt am Main, 1974, p. 138; *Goethe's Elective Affinities*, trans. Stanley Corngold, in Benjamin, *Selected Writings*, vol. 1: *1913–1926*, ed. Marcus Bullock and Michael W. Jennings, Cambridge, MA, 1996, pp. 297–356, specifically p. 307).

9   Reading *definition* for *dialectic* following the transcription of the tape recording.

10 The 'Tacitean style' of language is characterized by the abbreviated or concentrated reference to the essential concepts involved (often through the deployment of participial constructions) and the use of rare or archaic words and expressions.

11 τόπος νοητικὸς [*topos noētikos*]: Greek expression for 'intelligible place or site' or 'place of intelligible essences'.

12   There is a lacuna here where the tape recording was impossible to interpret.

13   As they appear in the transcription, the immediately preceding sentences are full of lacunae and added question marks which, with one exception, the editor has not reproduced here, since text seems intelligible as it stands.

14   Conjectural emendation of 'Positivismus Jungscher, Marxscher und Avenariuscher Observanz'. Ernst Mach (1838–1916) and Richard Avernarius (1843–1896) are regarded as the founders of 'empirio-criticism', a philosophical movement which attempted to ground objective science in terms of a description of ultimate and immediately given sense data.

15   See T. W. Adorno, Else Frenkel-Brunswik, Daniel J. Levinson and William Morrow, *The Authoritarian Personality*, in *Studies in Prejudice*, ed. Max Horkheimer and Samuel H. Flowerman, vol. 1, New York, 1950; the sections of the text co-authored by Adorno are available in GS 9.1, pp. 143–509. The specific methodological issues and problems are addressed in Section B, 'Methodology' (GS 9.1, pp. 163–73).

16   There is a lacuna in the text at this point. Conjectural emendation supplied by the editor.

17   There is a lacuna in the text at this point. Conjectural emendation supplied by the editor.

18   The text had to be extensively reconstructed at this point on account of lacunas in the transcription of the tape recording. The reconstruction was produced in the light of a comparable passage in Adorno's *Metakritik der Erkenntnistheorie*:

> The original impulse of categorical intuition as one of escape may be detected behind the bad identity of thinking and being. Behind the doctrine that one can have immediate 'insight' into 'states-of-affairs' like arithmetical propositions, stood the misgivings of a structure of objective lawfulness superposed in principle on every intellectual performance. For that structure should be removed from the arbitrariness of our meaning despite Husserl's assumption of our meaning as the basis of epistemological analysis. Husserl is aware of the fact that the state-of-affairs 'seen-into' is more than a mere subjective product of thought. Arithmetical judgement does not simply consist in the subjective performance of the act of collecting whose synthesis it presents. It says that there must be something subjectively irreducible which demands this and no other collecting. The state-of-affairs is not produced purely, but is rather also 'encountered.' The non-arising of the logical state-of-affairs in its constitution by thought, the non-identity of subjectivity and truth, drives Husserl directly to the construction of categorical intuition. The 'intuited' ideal state-of-affairs is not supposed to be a sheer product of thought. (GS 5, pp. 211f.; *Against Epistemology*, p. 209)

19   There appears to be a lacuna in the transcription of the tape recording here.

Lecture 20

1   The opening of the lecture is missing from the transcription of the tape recording and has been hypothetically reconstructed by the editor in connection with the previous lecture.

2   Reading *nicht nur* [not only] in place of *zugleich* [at the same time].

3   In the *Republic*, Plato raises the question regarding the essence of justice. In this dialogue the participants agree that this question, insofar as it concerns the individual human soul, is more easily answered if we begin from the broader model and perspective of the nature and structure of the state. And the hypothetical construction of an ideal polis is pursued precisely with this purpose in view. The basic structure of such a polis involves the division of all the citizens into three fundamental groups or classes: the rulers (the philosophers), the warriors (or protectors) and the productive workers (artisans and agrarians), with specific virtues coordinated with each group: wisdom to the rulers, courage to the warriors and temperance or self-control to the artisans and agrarians (as the rule of the free over the desires of slaves, women and children). Plato then defines justice as the principle that each should perform his 'own part' or function accordingly, which means that each may only exercise the profession which corresponds to his nature and that any change or mingling of professions must be avoided at all costs as the source of misfortune for the community. The discussion then returns to the question concerning justice in the soul of the individual, and it becomes clear that in Plato's eyes the order of the city and the order of the soul share the same structure. For the soul in turn consists of three parts or faculties with which the most important virtues are coordinated: the wisdom of the rulers with the rational thinking part, the courage of the warriors with the spirited part, and the temperance of the third class with the desiring part which pursues pleasures and sensuous satisfactions. As in the case of the state, the soul may be described as 'just' when each faculty exclusively discharges its own function and acknowledges the hierarchy of the three parts of the soul. Insofar as the question concerning the essence of justice in Plato is also equivalent to the question of the 'idea' of justice, it is clear that the order of the classes and professions, of the virtues, and of the faculties of the soul also exemplifies the hierarchical order of the ideas which correspond to the relevant distinctions. But the division of labour also constitutes the model or material ground of the Platonic doctrine of ideas insofar as the construction of the ideal state takes the private individual producers atomized by the market as its primary starting point, its primary given, and its primary assumption, and their isolated activity and isolated property (which is what the Greek word *ousia* or 'essence' originally signified) betray an evident correspondence with the isolated essence of each and every concept (see *Republic* 369b 5ff).

4   Hermann Graf Keyserling (1880–1946), a philosopher of history and culture who founded what was known as the 'School of Wisdom' and the 'philosophy of meaning'.
5   At this point the transcription of the tape recording is marked 'unclear'.
6   See Lecture 16, note 15, above.
7

> Alas! What are you, after all, my written and painted thoughts! Not long ago you were so variegated, young, and malicious, so full of thorns and secret spices, that you made me sneeze and laugh – and now? You have already doffed your novelty, and some of you, I fear, are ready to become truths, so immortal do they look, so pathetically honest, so tedious! (Friedrich Nietzsche, *Jenseits von Gut und Böse u.a.*, p. 202; *Beyond Good and Evil: Prelude to a Philosophy of the Future*, trans. Helen Zimmern, London, 1967, Aphorism 296, p. 263)

8   Aristotle defined the propositional statement as λόγος ἀποφαντικ ὸς [*logos apophantikos*] ('utterance which makes manifest'), which differs from other forms of utterance (such as those expressing a request or a wish) in that it alone is capable of being true or false (see Aristotle, *De interpretatione*, trans. J. L. Ackrill, in *The Complete Works of Aristotle*, ed. Jonathan Barnes, Princeton, NJ, 1985, vol. 1, pp. 25–7).
9   In his reflections on the logical form of judgement, specifically on the twofold aspect of the judgement as an expression of the identity and the double non-identity of subject and predicate, Adorno could draw on Hegel's discussion of this question:

> In this connection, we must observe right at the beginning that the proposition, in the form of *a judgment*, is not adept to express speculative truths; recognition of this circumstance would go a long way in preventing many misunderstandings of speculative truths. Judgment joins subject and object in a connection of *identity*; abstraction is therefore made from the fact that subject has yet more determinacies than the predicate has, just as that the predicate is wider than the subject. Now, if the content is speculative, the *non-identity* of subject and predicate is also an essential moment; but this is not expressed in the judgment. The paradoxical and even bizarre light in which much of recent philosophy is cast for those not intimate with speculative thought is due in many ways to the form of the simple judgment when used to convey speculative results. (Hegel, *Wissenschaft der Logik* I, p. 93; *Science of Logic*, trans. di Giovanni, p. 67)

10   Reading *Urteil* [judgement] in place of *Sache* [matter].
11   Reading *und* [and] in place of *oder* [or].
12   For Henri Bergson, see Lecture 5, note 6 above.
13   Adorno also formulated and developed this conception elsewhere in terms of the 'logic of disintegration' (see *Negative Dialektik*, GS 6,

pp. 148f.; *Negative Dialectics*, trans. E. B. Ashton, London, 1973, pp. 145f.). In a note appended to the second edition of *Negative Dialectics* in 1967, Adorno describes this as 'the earliest of his philosophical conceptions, reaching all the way back to his student years' (the note is not included in Ashton's translation).

14 See GS 5, pp. 7–245.

15 Reading *bedienen* [serve] in place of *bewegen* [move].

16 'Everything that is proven can be disputed. Only the unprovable is indisputable' (Georg Simmel, *Aus dem nachgelassenen Tagebuch*, in *Fragmente und Aufsätze: Aus dem Nachlaß und Veröffentlichungen der letzten Jahre*, Munich, 1923, p. 4; *The View of Life: Four Metaphysical Essays with Journal Aphorisms*, trans. John A. Y. Andrews and Donald N. Levine, Chicago, 2010, p. 161).

17 This reading has been preferred to the slightly different text of the transcription: 'without the assumption that subject and object are not ultimately entirely unlike one another'. But it seems to me that this reading also brings problems of its own. On the one hand, it appears to be naturally implied by the previous course of the argument, where Adorno speaks of the unavoidable assumption of a whole, which at least in Hegel assumes the form of a self-identical whole and an identity of subject and object (in this regard, compare Adorno's own remarks in Lecture 2, p. 12, and Lecture 9, p. 85, above). Adorno certainly begins by referring to this notion of identity, and the corrective which he proceeds to speak about would only weaken the assumption of an identity in favour of the idea that subject and object are not unlike one another. But what speaks *against* this reading is the further development of the argument, for he would then identify the refusal of the assumption of any likeness between subject and object with the notion of a 'completed enlightenment' which, insofar as it understood in a critical sense, could only represent for Adorno the very triumph of identity thinking over the non-identical. But perhaps it is possible that the concept of 'completed enlightenment' is intended in a different sense here, namely as the epistemological position of a radically sceptical dialectic which, in specific opposition to Hegel, refuses the possibility of an ultimate identity and proceeds instead on the basis of the ineliminable non-identity of concept and thing, of subject and object, and thereby falls back into the 'darkest mythology' – that is, into confessing that the world cannot be known at all. Another possible reading would actually be to replace the word 'unlike' with 'like', but the general problem with the passage would still remain here.

18 The lecture course on aesthetics that Adorno delivered in the following semester has been published: NaS IV.3: *Ästhetik (1958/59)*, ed. Eberhard Ortland, Suhrkamp, 2009; *Aesthetics*, trans. Wieland Hoban, Cambridge, forthcoming 2017.

Adorno's Notes for the Lectures

1   Some general observations on the rough lecture notes which Adorno produced for this series of lectures can be found in the editor's Foreword.

2   This date indicates when Adorno produced his 'General Plan'.

3   The dates in the margin generally refer to the day on which each lecture was delivered.

4   The page numbers provided in the general plan refer to the pagination of Georg Lasson's edition of Hegel's *Phenomenology of Spirit*, from which Adorno read out selected passages in the course of his lectures (see Lecture 2, note 8, above).

5   In 1958 Ascension Day fell on 15 May and Easter on 25 and 26 May. There were clearly no lectures on 27 and 29 May either, so the remark 'More on this after Easter' relates to Lecture 5, delivered on 3 June.

6   What appears in Adorno's typescript here is 'but', although on the basis of his remarks in the relevant lecture one would expect 'or'. See Lecture 5, p. 38 above.

7   The date here marks the point Adorno had reached with Lecture 8 on 19 June and thus the beginning of Lecture 9 on 24 June.

8   The date here marks the point Adorno had reached with Lecture 9 on 24 June and thus the beginning of Lecture 10 on 26 June, for which he also prepared a new and detailed outline.

9   At this point (at the end of Lecture 11) Adorno ceased to follow the first outline of his four-page typescript. For the remaining lectures, beginning with Lecture 12 on 3 July, he furnishes a series of new notes on the following pages. The points numbered 3 (*Dialectic eludes the simple alternative*, etc.) to 5 (*Concepts must be considered in their mutual configuration*, etc.) are taken up in Lectures 18 to 20. The marginal notes (*How are we to think?*) are developed in the outline that furnishes the structure for Lecture 13.

10 This represents a single supplementary page to the notes for Lecture 7 of 12 June.

11 The notes on the lower half of the page, which are dated 3.VII.58, were developed by Adorno in Lecture 12. The notes from *How are we to think?* down to *Refusal to accept the fetters* provide the basis for Lectures 13 to 16. For Lectures 15 and 16 Adorno also wrote new outlines.

12 The following notes on sheets 1 to 5, which Adorno clearly conceived as a whole, provide the basis for the remaining lectures delivered from 17 to 31 July.

13 The lecture to which the following notes on this page refer (down to *insight*) was delivered on 17 July.

14 The plan here probably relates back to notes written around 15 July, since the lecture of 31 July was the last one in the semester.

15   The following page references for Hegel's *Phenomenology* relate not to the Lasson edition but to the edition by Hermann Glockner which Adorno possessed (Hegel, *Sämtliche Werke* (see Lecture 11, note 21), vol. 3: *Phänomenologie des Geistes*). Adorno's notes and references relate specifically to chapters 1, 2 and 4B of Hegel's text – i.e. 'Sense Certainty', 'Perception' and 'Freedom of Self-Consciousness' (*Phenomenology of Spirit*, trans. Miller, pp. 58ff., 67ff., and 119ff. respectively).

16   This is an additional sheet for Lecture 19, which was delivered on 29 July.

INDEX

a posteriori   64, 65, 66, 75
a priori   14, 27, 62, 64, 65, 66,
   75, 76, 96, 175
absolute spirit   80, 84, 107
absolute subject   31
Absolute, the   18, 19, 40, 57, 80,
   108, 110, 111, 112, 113
   infinite Absolute   6
   as result   17, 22–3
   as subject   31, 264n9
   the truth and   17, 21
abstract, the   36, 109–12,
   287n19
Adenauer, Konrad   114, 288n28
administered world   47, 114, 141,
   167, 178, 180, 184
   see also bureaucracy
agriculture   158, 159
alienation   11, 42, 44, 74
   see also diremption
America   123–4, 179, 205
analysis   137, 140–3, 147
analytic depth psychology   179
ancient Greek philosophy   5,
   262n13, 288n30, 289n4
   see also Aristotle; Plato; Socrates
antagonistic society   147–9, 179
anthropology   19, 189

antinomies   59, 63, 67, 161,
   271n11, 273n16, 273n17,
   297n19
   see also antithesis; thesis; triadic
   schema
antithesis   30, 38, 46, 49, 53, 55
   see also triadic schema
appearance   181
   essence and   117–18
apperception
   synthesis   65, 66, 173
   unity of   78
Aristotelian logic   56
Aristotle   2, 16, 65, 297n19
   Categories   286n18
   concept of God   276n13
   metaphysics   260n2
   Metaphysics   261n2, 276n13,
   287n18
   propositional statements
   310n8
   reason as thinking of
   thinking   276n13
   'tode ti'   109, 286n18
art   50, 54, 99, 153–4, 200–1,
   296n13
   archaism   303n15
   defining   200

works of art   154, 170–1, 200, 295n13
artisans   121, 303n15, 309n3
artist, the   303n15
artistic nature   155
attitude
  dialectic as   118
  empirical social research   120–2, 125
  generalized attitudes   121
  natural attitude   118
  negative attitudes   120–2, 126
Authoritarian Personality, The   204
Avernarius, Richard   203, 308n14

Bacon, Francis   128, 152, 291n2, 293n2, 294n3
bad faith   284n2
Balzac, Honoré de   171, 300n11
Baudelaire, Charles   88–91, 280n13, 281n16
Baumert, Gerhard   146
beauty   56, 260n1, 295n13
Becker, Egon   263n14
becoming, process of   8, 18, 134
becoming-other   17, 18
being   85, 109–14
  being for itself   45–6, 284n2
  being in itself   44–6
  being in and for itself   45
  Dasein   263n13, 288n27
  in Hegel   85, 109–14
  identity of thought and being   5, 6, 17, 85, 185, 272n13
  as 'life'   109
belief
  religious belief   95
  superstitious belief   135
Benjamin, Walter   260n18, 281n17, 296n18
  on Baudelaire   88–91, 280n13, 281n16
  fate   201, 307n8
  flâneur   281n19
  induction   156

Berg, Alban   270n5
Bergson, Henri   39, 96–8, 216, 268n6
Borkenau, Franz   141
both–and   186–7
boundary *see* limit
bourgeois culture   85, 99–100
bourgeois society   34, 77, 80, 99–100, 144, 146
Bradley, Francis Herbert   117–18, 289n2, 289n3
Brentano, Clemens   266n1
Bröcker, Walter   259n14
Brod, Max   171, 300n10
Buber, Martin   84, 279n4
Buddhism   158
bureaucracy   42, 120–1, 126, 141, 173, 178, 183
  see also administered world

capitalism   89–91, 100, 167
capitalist society   23–4, 32, 142
capitalistic culture   299n6
Cartesian philosophy   37, 39, 94, 101, 147–8, 152
  clara et distincta perceptio   101–3, 129, 132, 134
  knowledge   128–39, 161–2
  reflection   130, 132, 134–9, 147–8
  scientific method   128–39
  see also Descartes, René
Catholic thought   83
censorship   6
character masks   123, 126, 284n3, 290n12
  see also role
Christianity   54
  Catholic thought   83
Cicero   288n30
civil society   80–1, 277n10
clara et distincta perceptio   98, 101–3, 129, 134
class   99, 121, 142–3, 277n10
  defining   196–7
  Plato's ideal polis   309n3
  proletariat   88, 99

class struggle   142
classification   38, 39, 40, 94,
    167
classificatory logic   169
cognition   66–7, 98, 100–1,
    168–9, 199
    conceptual   205–6
    divine cognition   43
Cohen, Hermann   175, 301n3
commodity form   90, 290n12
common sense   33, 52, 103, 114,
    119
completeness   163–6, 172
compulsive character   79, 153,
    206, 216
concept
    constellation and   198–9, 208,
        210, 218
    double movement   24, 256n4
    formation   2, 180
    idea distinguished from concept
        (in Benjamin)   296n18
    labour and exertion of   43, 46,
        48, 50, 77–8, 83, 101, 115,
        213
    movement of   4, 7–12, 17–22,
        29, 30, 98
    nature and   2, 256n4
    object and   2, 24, 98, 256n4,
        271n10
    order of concepts   2–3
    speculative   68, 85
    subject concept   213, 214
    as *tabula rasa*   198, 203
    universal concepts   68, 93, 94,
        110, 168, 171, 204–6, 208
conceptuality   73, 177
    definition and   197
concrete, the   35, 36
Condorcet, Marie-Jean-Antoine-
    Nicolas Caritat, Marquis
    de   10
consciousness   45–6, 61, 62,
    113–14, 119, 160–1, 165,
    174–5, 178–9
    contemporary consciousness
        179, 185, 189

contradiction and   29, 59
    dichotomous consciousness
        189–90, 192–3
    experience of   81
    facts of   107
    freedom of   98
    infinite consciousness   64
    irrationality and   38, 39
    judicial function   187
    natural consciousness   139,
        264n10
    observed/observing   270n10
    pre-dialectical consciousness   55,
        68
    reified consciousness   113
    sense organs and   133–4
    social schizophrenia   193
    speculative consciousness   64–8
    subjective consciousness   75
    unity of   65, 174
continuity   112, 147–51, 180
contradiction   6, 37, 56–9, 126,
    148, 157, 165
    consciousness and   29, 59
    dialectic as organized spirit of   3
    diremption   73–4
    in the given   126–7
    Hegel and   3, 27–35, 58–9,
        60–70, 71–5
    internal contradiction   56
    Kant and   29–30, 58–9, 62–6
    logical principle of   72–3
    movement of   4–5
    non-contradiction   27, 73, 178
    reason and   29–30, 62–6
    universalizing   52–3
    see also antithesis; negation
control   146, 159–61
Copernican Turn   10
Cornelius, Hans   105, 285n4
craftsman   303n15
Croce, Benedetto   56, 269n1,
    272n14
culture
    bourgeois culture   85, 99–100
    cultural industry   154
    dilettantism   210

Darmstadt investigation 120, 126, 289n8
Dasein 263n13, 288n27
de Maistre, Joseph Marie Comte 152, 162, 293n1, 294n3
deduction 26, 27, 131, 148, 155, 176
deductive method 296n18
deductive structure 81
definition 35, 39, 40, 69, 208, 209, 211, 212
conceptuality and 197
dialectical thought and 7, 8
Hegel and 194, 197, 306n2
as logical form 194–5
nature of 194
operational definitions 69, 202, 203, 204
philosophical definitions 201–2
practice of 194–5, 196–207
in rationalist philosophy 131–2
role in philosophy 139
Tacitean style of language 202, 308n10
verbal definitions 200
Degas, Edgar 159, 297n20
deictic approach 195, 196
delusion 54, 96, 101, 122, 123, 161
Descartes, René 94, 147, 162, 174, 291n1
clara et distincta perceptio 101–3, 129, 132, 134
completeness 163–6, 172
Discours de la méthode 128, 135, 291n1
scientific method 128–39
see also Cartesian philosophy
destruction, Heidegger's concept of 22, 263n13
determinate negation 190
development, concept of 143–4
dialectic
in ancient philosophy 1–2, 5
concepts and 2

defining 2
double character of 4, 5, 9
epistemological dialectic 155, 156–7
exaggeration and 3, 257n6
as a form of presentation 5
idealist dialectic 6, 7, 21, 83–4, 85
interpretation of 72, 82, 83, 85
as a method of thought/thinking 1, 2, 4–5, 50
open/fractured dialectic 21, 95
as philosophical method 1
positivism and 3, 104, 108, 113–15, 116–27
real dialectic 5, 60
as state religion 54, 86
transcendental dialectic 58, 62, 63, 66
dialectical contradiction see contradiction
dialectical materialism 11, 32, 76, 77, 83, 85–6, 89–91
'diamat' 16, 48, 54, 261n3
vulgar materialism distinguished 90
see also Marxian dialectic
dialectical method 4–5, 28–9, 32, 57, 155, 198
Marx 258n4
refutation 28–9, 31
dialectical movement 19, 54, 55, 211
dialectical reflection 54–5, 153
dialegesthai 86, 279n7
'diamat' see dialectical materialism
dilettantism 210
Dilthey, Wilhelm 61, 175, 274n6
Dionysus the Areopagite 305n10
diremption 46, 73–4
discipline 7, 19, 57, 149–50, 157, 194
Divine, the 17, 18, 19
divine cognition 43
divine spirit 178
division of labour 13, 141, 209

Doderer, Heimito von   171,
    300n12
Dostoyevsky, Fyodor, *Crime and
    Punishment*   292n5
doubt   118
Duns Scotus   109, 286n10
dynamic principles   88, 145

Eckermann, Johann Peter   257n7
economic theory   179, 194,
    302n10
Ehrenfels, Christian   280n9
Eichendorff, Joseph von   37,
    266n1
either–or   186
empirical research   179, 182
    social research   120–2, 291n13,
        299n4
empiricism   13, 65–6, 67, 81, 125,
    126, 166, 176
    British empiricists   64
    empirical sciences and   141
    first philosophy and   16
    metaphysics and   116
    methodical control in   160
    positivistic empirical
        research   182
    rationalism and   128–9
empirio-criticism   308n14
enlightenment   188, 220
    European enlightenment   41
    Greek enlightenment   210
    process of   41–2
enthusiasm   150, 199
epic poetry   301n15
epistemological dialectic   155,
    156–7
epistemology   132, 157, 168, 191,
    196, 197, 217
    in literary works   170, 171
    positivist epistemology   119
Erdmann, Johann Eduard   269n1
'Essay as Form, The'   199, 211
essence   4, 9–10, 138
    appearance and   117–18
    Husserl and   167, 168–9
    movement of pure essence   8

Eternal, the   12, 17, 18, 19
eternal values   113, 189, 191
European enlightenment   41
exaggeration   3, 257n6
exchange society   146
existentialism   284n2
experience   9–10, 85, 92–8
    givens of   117–27
    Hegel and   73–8, 81
    naive/immediate experience
        106, 164
    pre-conscious level   97
    spiritual experience   81
external reflection   267n5

family   94, 145–7
fascism   42, 80, 144, 297n22
fate   201, 210, 307n8
feudalism   143, 145–6
Fichte, Johann Gottlieb   10, 27,
    28, 35, 36, 75, 83, 178,
    263n3, 263n4, 263n5, 276n12,
    302n6
first ground/principle   15–17, 22,
    26, 27, 28, 36, 100, 106–7,
    112, 116, 128, 159, 218
first nature   115, 289n30
first philosophy   16–17, 106,
    261n2, 301n2
    philosophy of origins   16, 26,
        107–9, 112, 116–17, 119,
        190
flâneur   281n19
Flaubert, Gustave   99
force fields   201
formal logic   40, 67, 68–9, 215,
    217–18
fractured/open dialectic   21, 95
frame of reference   173, 182–4
Frankfurt Institute for Social
    Research   263n14, 290n8
free wage labour   142
freedom   32, 58, 69, 81, 144, 153,
    273n17
    of consciousness   98
    intellectual freedom   159, 198
    press freedom   6

towards the object 81, 150, 156, 278n11
value-freedom 191
Frégier, Honoré-Antoine 281n17
French Revolution 34
Freud, Sigmund 42
Freudo-Marxism 297n22
Friedeburg, Ludwig von 263n14

Gehlen, Arnold 19, 189, 261n9
generalized attitudes 121
German Idealism 37, 39, 165, 266n1, 267n4
German Romanticism 266n1
Gestalt theory 87, 92–3, 106, 280n9
'bad Gestalt' 87, 280n10
givens/givenness 92, 117–27, 132–4
immediate givens 91, 92, 107, 119, 124, 127, 133, 141, 288n30, 308n14
Glockner, Hermann 302n6
God 33, 43, 44, 61
Aristotle's concept of 276n13
negative theology 190, 305n10
Goethe, Johann Wolfgang von 3, 73, 176, 257n7, 302n6
Faust 295n12
Pandora 190, 305n13
Greek enlightenment 210
Greek philosophy see ancient Greek philosophy
groundlessness 158–9
guilt 53, 71, 95, 197–8
fate and 201, 307n8

Habermas, Jürgen 261n9r
Hartmann, Nicolai 60, 76, 273n1
Hegel, Georg Wilhelm Friedrich 4–12, 14, 16–25, 26–36, 38–47, 49–59, 60–70, 71–81, 83–5, 93, 95, 96–7, 100–1, 103, 130–1, 147, 150, 302n6
abstract, the 109–12
Aesthetics 61
'being' in 85, 109–14

contradiction 3, 27–35, 58–9, 60–70, 71–5
definition and 194, 197, 306n2
Encyclopaedia 22, 68, 111–12, 258n9, 265n16, 276n13, 276n17
examples, refusal to give 68
experience 73–8, 81
external reflection 267n5
Faith and Knowledge 283n4
first philosophy 16–17
Greater Logic 40
identity of thought and being 5, 6, 85
immanent critique 8, 31–2
Kant's transcendental dialectic 58–9, 62, 63, 66
language 51–2
mediation 17–21
movement of the concept 4, 7–12, 17–22, 29, 30, 98
natural consciousness 264n10
as ontological thinker 108–14
panlogism 49, 269n1
Phenomenology of Spirit 3, 4, 5, 7, 16, 22, 24, 27, 30, 34, 40, 43, 45, 47, 50, 61, 75, 101, 109, 120, 152, 154, 264n9, 264n10, 268n7, 270n10, 298n23, 301n15
Philosophy of History 61
Philosophy of Right 61, 80, 307n2
on Plato 17, 261n4
Propaedeutic 81
qualitative leap 161
refutation in 28, 31
Science of Logic 22, 40, 45, 61, 110, 217, 258n9, 259n15, 262n11, 265n16, 268n8, 287n21, 306n2
'simply looking on' 39, 55, 58, 192, 270n10
the state, doctrine of 80–1
subject and object 219
system 10, 21–2, 27
triadic form 46–7, 49–50, 53–5

Hegel, Georg Wilhelm Friedrich
(cont.)
'the whole' and   17, 19–25
works of art   154, 295n13
Heidegger, Martin   22, 108–9,
189, 259n14, 263n13, 286n10,
286n12, 286n16, 287n27
Heraclitus   162
historical materialism   261n3,
292n5, 305n8
historicism   189, 191, 292n5
hit songs   123–4, 125
Hölderlin, Friedrich   52, 287n27
Horak, Eduard   295n9
Horak's Music School   153–4
Horkheimer, Max   267n4, 279n1,
288n29
Hugo, Victor, *Les Misérables*   88,
281n15
Hume, David   203
Husserl, Edmund   22, 207,
262n13
theory of essences   167, 168–9
hypothesis   125

ideal types   167–8, 169, 282n20,
299n6
idealism   28, 60, 76, 107, 108,
192, 276n3
closed dialectic   21
German Idealism   37, 39, 165
post-Kantian idealism   64, 165,
174
speculative idealism   107
idealist dialectic   6, 7, 21, 83–4, 85
ideas/the Idea   2, 15, 28, 32,
295n13
concept distinguished from (in
Benjamin)   296n18
the Idea as reason (in Hegel)
262n11
the Idea and art (in Hegel)
295n13
identity   95, 181
absolute identity   6, 72, 85
antithesis   38–9
identity and non-identity   6, 8,

46, 72, 82, 83, 84–5, 87, 155,
165
identity in non-identity   166
moment of   84
of personal consciousness   65
philosophy of   5, 6
of thought and being   5, 6, 17,
66, 85, 185, 272n13
see also non-identity/
non-identical
ideology   3, 48, 54, 122, 125, 144,
154, 183, 219
immanent critique   8, 31–2,
153–4, 295n11
immediacy   3, 34, 35, 40, 51, 52,
72, 73, 79, 86, 94, 110–11,
155
immediate experience   106,
164
immediate givens   91, 92, 107,
119, 124, 127, 133, 141,
288n30, 308n14
immediate intuition   112, 217
micrological thinking   137
see also mediation
impressionism   99
Indian philosophy   112, 209–10
induction   156
inductive logic   105
inductive method   296n18
industrial production   23, 145
industrial sociology   122
industrial workers   122, 127
inference   39, 212–13, 217–19
infinite Absolute   6
infinite consciousness   64
infinite judgements   58
infinite whole   20–1
infinitesimal calculus   293n10
institutions   94, 146–7
intellectualism   3, 37, 42–4, 49
intuition   17, 58, 91, 96–8, 111,
112, 168, 171–2, 207, 216,
217, 266n2
inwardness   186
irrationalism   37–44, 79, 176
ratio   38, 41–2, 132

Jacobi, Friedrich Heinrich   39,
    112, 266n2
Jochmann, Carl Gustav   303n15
Joyce, James   100
judgement   29, 31–2, 57–8,
    212–16, 265n16, 310n9
    infinite judgements   58
Jung, Carl Gustav   210
justice   32, 309n3

Kafka, Franz   100, 170–1,
    300n10
Kandinsky, Wassily   50, 270n5
Kant, Immanuel   42, 44, 75, 88,
    174, 218
    antinomies   59, 63, 67, 161,
        271n11, 273n16, 297n19
    categories   153
    contradiction   29–30, 58–9,
        62–6
    Critique of Pure Reason   29, 58,
        62–3, 78, 297n19
    critique of reason   62–6
    definition and   194
    dynamic principles   88, 145
    knowledge   62–6
    mathematical principles   88
    noumena   264n8
    phaenomena   264n8
    synthetic a priori judgements   62
    system   172
    thing-in-itself   301n1
    time   9, 273n16
    transcendental dialectic   58–9,
        62, 63, 66
    transcendental logic   29, 62, 63
Keller, Gottfried   130, 291n5
Keynes, John Maynard   302n10
Keynesian economics   179,
    302n10
Keyserling, Hermann Graf   210,
    310n4
Kierkegaard, Søren   85, 276n12,
    284n2
knowledge   27, 39, 40, 67, 82–3,
    91, 92–3, 95, 96–9, 101,
    164–71, 208–10

analytic process of knowing
    141
Cartesian philosophy   128–39,
    161–2
as continuity of steps   147–51
contradictions   58–9
division of labour and   209
enthusiasm and   150
experience and   60
finite knowledge   28–9
gradual acquisition   160
ideology and   54
judgement and   213
Kantian philosophy   62–6
objects of   77, 85, 98, 102–3,
    129, 134, 136, 148–9, 164
prejudice and   130, 131, 294n2
scientific see scientific knowledge
sociology of   41
subjectivist theory of   203–4
task of   13
theory of   120
Kroner, Richard   62, 64, 65, 66,
    96, 274n7

labelling   268n7
labour
    as a commodity   142
    of the concept   43, 46, 48, 50,
        77–8, 83, 101, 115, 213
    control of   146
    division of   13, 141, 209
    exploitation   142
    free wage labour   142
    labour power   142, 145
    subdivision and restriction of
        labour   277n10
language   6, 44, 47, 198–200,
    210–14
    foreign languages   199, 210
    Hegel's language   51–2
    linguistic expression   211
    of philosophers   51–2
    Tacitean style   202, 308n10
Lazarsfeld, Paul   291n13
Leibniz, Gottfried Wilhelm   148,
    289n1, 293n10

Lenin, Vladimir Ilyich 277n8
Liepelt, Klaus 263n14
limit, concept of 62–3, 66, 67,
274n10
Linnaeus (Carl von Linné) 2,
257n5
literary works 170–1
bourgeois culture 99–100
materialist critique of 88–91
see also poetry
logic 109, 111, 216–17
administrative logic 180
Aristotelian logic 56
classificatory logic 169
compulsive character of 216
contradiction 72–3
dialectical logic 40, 133, 138,
196, 204, 217
doctrine of absolute identity 72
extensional logic 135
formal logic 40, 67, 68–9, 215,
217–18
identity principle 72
inductive logic 105
logical principles 88
micrological thinking 27, 102,
117, 134, 137
non-metaphysical logic 65–6
of objectivity 75
positivist conception of 202
refutation 31
rules/laws of 27, 40, 72
of science 77, 100, 105, 106,
124, 184
of scientific investigation 93
traditional logic 27, 31, 40,
132, 168, 195, 196, 217
transcendental logic 62
logical positivism 98, 176
looking on 39, 55, 58, 192,
270n10
love 43, 71, 256n4, 260n1,
293n13
Lukács, György 42, 99–100, 211,
268n11, 286n12, 288n30
Luther, Martin 297n21

Mach, Ernst 203, 308n14
magic 112, 164
Mannheim, Karl 141, 145, 189,
293n2, 305n9
Marburg School 175, 301n3
Marcuse, Herbert 109, 286n15,
286n16
Maréchal, Joseph 279n1
Marx, Karl 35, 83, 85, 86, 87,
120, 141
Capital 258n4
character masks/persona
290n12
class struggle 142
dialectic as form of
presentation 5, 258n4
dialectical method 258n4
immanent critique 32
Marxian dialectic 9, 31, 32, 80,
85
see also dialectical materialism
materialism
historical materialism 261n3,
292n5, 305n8
vulgar materialism 90
see also dialectical materialism
materialist critique of literature
88–91
materialist dialectic see dialectical
materialism
mathematics 88, 102, 137, 164,
172, 194, 203
mediation 17–21, 70, 74, 78, 79,
89, 96, 115, 119, 141, 142,
145
becoming-other 17
both–and 186–7
continuity and 147, 148,
149
as critical self-reflection of
extremes 188–9
the whole and the part 96, 101,
105, 106
see also immediacy
Metacritique of Epistemology
120, 217, 308n18

metaphysics 23, 62, 65–6, 91,
  107, 109, 111, 113–14, 117,
  176, 184, 209
  administrative metaphysics 180
  Aristotle and 260n2
  empiricism and 116
  pre-Socratic 210
  self-evidence 131, 132, 138
  speculative metaphysics 117
  of spirit 84
  traditional metaphysics 27
method
  analytical method 140
  dialectic as method of
    thought/thinking 1, 2, 4–5,
    50
  dialectical method 4–5, 28–9,
    32, 57, 155, 174, 198
  scientific method 8, 94, 128–39
Metzger, Heinz-Klaus 304n5
micrological thinking 27, 102,
  117, 134, 137
Minima Moralia 200, 300n8,
  300n9
mobility of thought 154–6, 158,
  161
  see also movement of thought
monads 289n1
Montesquieu, Baron de la Brède et
  de 10
Moreau, Gustave 297n20
motivational analysis 122–3
movement of the concept 4, 7–12,
  17–22, 29, 30, 98
movement of thought 36, 54,
  161–2, 211, 267n5
  see also mobility of thought
music 153–4, 304n5
  hit songs 123–4, 125
  radio project 291n13
  reviews 295n7
  songs 123–4, 125, 303n1
mythology 113, 210, 220

narcissism 45, 94
National Socialism 123, 144

Natorp, Paul 175, 301n3
natural consciousness 139,
  264n10
natural sciences 100, 119, 137–8,
  148, 175, 194, 202
nature 78, 119, 158, 217
  artistic nature 155
  concept formation 2, 256n4
  first nature 115, 289n30
  Hegelian philosophy of 175
  mastering 129
  power of 107
  rationality and 41
  Schelling's philosophy of 175
  second nature 115, 119, 209,
    288n30
  thought and 3
negation 38, 43, 72
  determinate negation 190
  dialectical negation 32, 37
  principle of 61, 65, 85
  synthesis 55
  see also contradiction
negative theology 190, 305n10
negativity 38, 43, 46, 126
  principle of 65
  reflective negativity 34, 65
neo-Kantian philosophy 176
  Marburg School 175
  Southwest School 176
neo-Platonic philosophy
  305n10
neo-Scholasticism 278n1
neo-Thomism 259n14, 278n1
Newton, Isaac 293n10
Nietzsche, Friedrich 42, 111, 190,
  301n2
  Beyond Good and Evil 213,
    310n7
  definition 194, 197
  first philosophy 301n2
  on system 175, 301n2
  Twilight of the Idols
    306n14
nominalism 44, 205, 206
non-contradiction 27, 73, 178

non-identity/non-identical 8, 46,
72, 82–5, 87, 165
antithesis 38–9
identity and non-identity 6, 8,
46, 72, 82, 83, 84–5, 87, 111,
155, 165
identity in non-identity 166
see also identity

object
concept and 2, 24, 98, 256n4,
271n10
continuity 147–9
determinacy 10, 78, 102, 171,
192, 197, 199
double movement 24, 256n4
essence of 168
of experience 47, 97
freedom towards 81, 150, 156,
278n11
identifying with ourselves 213
of knowledge 77, 85, 98,
102–3, 129–8, 134, 136,
148–9, 164
movement of 24, 98, 102,
126
subject and 6, 9, 20, 21, 45,
65, 72, 75, 92, 165, 212, 214,
215, 219–20, 311n17
unity in 75
objectivity 10, 31, 41, 149, 165,
180, 191, 198, 203, 212
historical character 9, 12
logic of 75
of truth 53
Ollenhauer, Erich 114, 288n28
'Om-philosophies' 112–13
ontological anthropology 189
ontological philosophy/
thought 12, 13, 44, 83,
108–14, 206, 211
open/fractured dialectic 21, 95
opinion 30, 31
opinion research 124
origins, philosophy of *see* first
philosophy
Ovid 279n6

panlogism 49, 269n1
paradox 50, 57, 70, 74, 82–3,
110, 144, 152, 156, 165, 166,
203, 214
Pareto, Vilfredo 305n8
Parsons, Talcott 104, 284n1,
284n3
structural-functional theory of
society 179–81
pedantry 149–50, 153, 166, 219
persuasion 255n2
phenomenology 118, 168, 169,
207, 215, 217–18
pigeonholing 268n7
Plato 14, 206
Apology, The 296n14
dialectic 1–2
dialegesthai 86, 279n7
division of labour 209
'enthusiasm' 150
Gorgias 1, 109, 255n2
Hegel on 17, 261n4
ideal polis 309n3
on justice 32, 309n3
on opinion 31
Parmenides 305n10
Phaedrus 1, 255n2, 256n4,
293n13
psychology 209
Republic 305n10, 309n3
on rhetoric 255n2, 296n14
Sophism/Sophists and 1, 109,
255n2, 296n14
Symposium 15, 256n3, 260n1
poetry 52
Baudelaire 88–91, 280n13,
281n16
capitalism and 89–90
epic poetry 301n15
Romantic poetry 275n12
see also literary works
popular songs *see* songs
positivism 44, 56, 60, 156, 168,
175, 177, 203–4, 206
concept of system 182
dialectic and 3, 104, 108,
113–15, 116–27, 134

epistemology 119
hypothesis formation 125
logic 202
logical positivism 98, 176
neutral form of thought 181
science 191
scientific knowledge 23, 24
social science 124, 182, 205
sociology 124
post-Kantian philosophy 37, 64,
165, 172, 174, 266n2
poverty 80, 158, 278n10
praxis 35, 54, 85, 86, 217
unity of theory and praxis 35,
44
prejudice
investigating 202–4
scientific knowledge and 130,
131, 294n2
social prejudice 202–4
presentation 210, 218
epistemological function of 212
form/mode of 5, 53, 210–11,
219
pre-presentation 211–12
process of 211–12
press freedom 6
prima philosophia see first
philosophy
Princeton Radio Research
Project 291n13
productive spirit 173, 301n15
proletariat 88, 99
propositions 27–30, 35–6, 46, 49,
55, 62, 67, 73, 74, 219
hierarchy of 218
inference and 213
judgement and 213, 214, 215
prejudice and 130, 131
propositional statements 310n8
scientific propositions 93–4
speculative proposition 74
Protestantism 186
psychodynamic perspective 123
psychology 94, 97, 98, 105, 146,
153, 158, 190
analytic depth psychology 179

Gestalt theory 87, 92–3, 106
of perception 195
Plato's psychology 209
psychological relativism 218
social psychology 204

qualitative leap 161, 298n23

racism 123, 144
radio project 291n13
ratio 38, 41–2, 132
ratiocinatio 39
rationalism 102, 136, 147, 148,
163, 174
control 160
definitions 131–2
dispute over 39, 42, 267n4
empiricism and 128–9
irrationalism and 37–44, 79,
176
rationality 38–9, 41–2, 179–80,
188
real dialectic 5, 60
realism 205
reason 40–3, 113, 119, 160, 188
contradiction and 29–30, 62–6
as infinite 64
Kant's critique of 62–6
as reflection of reflection 64
as the thinking of
thinking 276n13
reasoning
inferential 219
subjective 38–9, 180
reflection 22, 45, 85–6, 95, 97,
98, 117–19, 156
Cartesian philosophy 130, 132,
134–9, 147–8
concept of 64–7
dialectical reflection 54–5, 153
external reflection 267n5
music 154
philosophy of 39, 56, 267n5
reason as reflection of
reflection 64, 275n12
reflection-into-itself 110, 115
reflective negativity 34, 65

reflection (cont.)
  self-reflection   76, 124, 157,
    187, 211
  self-reflective subjectivity
    276n12
refutation   28–9, 31
Reich, Wilhelm   161, 297n22
reification of the world   11,
  41–2
relativism   20, 30, 157, 158, 187,
  193
  psychological relativism   218
  relativistic historicism   189
  relativistic sociology   189
  sceptical relativism   117
  sociology   189
  universal relativism   18
religion   95
  Catholic thought   83
  Christianity   54
  dialectic as state religion   54,
    86
  religious belief   95
result
  the Absolute as   17, 22–3
  the truth as   27
rhetoric   255n2, 296n14
Rickert, Heinrich   176, 302n4,
  302n6
ritualistic behaviour   153
Rizzi, Bruno   302n8
role
  concept of   104–5, 284n3
  social role   45, 46, 94
  see also character masks
Rolfes, Max   290n8
romantic age   73
romantic irony   276n12
Romantic poetry   275n12
Romanticism   266n1
Rousseau, Jean-Jacques   288n30

Sartre, Jean-Paul   104, 284n2,
  284n3
sceptical relativism   117
Scheler, Max   84, 189, 191, 211,
  279n3, 306n15

Schelling, Friedrich Wilhelm
  Joseph   39, 40, 83, 89, 97,
    175, 266n3, 302n6
Schelsky, Helmut   146
Schiffer, Marcellus   303n1
Schiller, Friedrich   167–8,
  299n5
Schlegel, Friedrich   64, 266n1,
  275n12
Schoenberg, Arnold   270n5
Schoeps, Hans-Joachim   171,
  300n10
Schoeps, Julius   300n10
Scholasticism   109, 287n18
  neo-Scholasticism   278n1
Schopenhauer, Arthur   51, 175,
  211, 301n1
science   91, 93, 95, 102, 173
  applied science   148
  definitions   200
  empirical sciences   141
  Hegel on   27, 268n8
  hypothesis   125, 147
  inductive logic   105
  intuition and   97
  logic of science   77, 100, 105,
    106, 124, 184
  natural sciences   100, 119,
    137–8, 148, 175, 194, 202
  philosophy and   13
  positive sciences   12, 102, 110,
    113
  positivist conception   191
  scientific method   8, 94, 128–39
  self-consciousness   127
  special sciences   114, 118, 202,
    210
  spirit of   128–9
  system   176, 178–9
  tabulation   40, 47
  triadic form and   47, 50
  see also social science
scientific knowledge   23, 39, 106,
  124, 209, 210
  prejudice and   130, 131,
    294n2
scientific method   8, 94, 128–39

Scott, Walter 100
second nature 115, 119, 209, 288n30
security 198
  need for 51, 107, 179, 183–4, 208–9
  sense of 179, 183, 194–5
self-conscious purposiveness 306n2
self-consciousness 127, 295n13, 301n15
self-evidence 131, 132, 138
self-reflection 124, 157–8, 161, 187, 209, 211
self-reflective subjectivity 276n12
sense organs 133–4
sense of security 179, 183, 194–5
sense perception 129
sense-certainty 259n15
seriousness 33, 38, 43, 44, 45, 46
Simmel, Georg 63, 218, 274n10
social role 45, 46, 94
  see also role
social schizophrenia 161, 193
social science 23, 104, 120, 141, 179, 188–9, 204
  empirical social research 120–2, 291n13, 299n4
  positivist 124, 182, 205
  see also sociology
socialism 79
socialist society 32
society 46, 87, 89–90, 91, 99, 144–8
  antagonistic society 147–9, 179
  bourgeois society 34, 77, 80, 99–100, 144, 146
  capitalist society 23–4, 32, 142
  civil society 80–1, 277n10
  compulsive character of 216
  concept of 126, 167, 205
  dialectical theory of 145
  exchange society 146
  frame of reference 183
  immanent critique 32
  relationships in 94
  socialist society 32
structural-functional theory of 179–81
  structure of 23, 90, 127, 171, 180, 181
  as system 147, 148
  totality of 79, 89, 90, 91, 99, 100, 180
  as a whole 77, 90, 100, 122, 125–7, 147, 180
sociology 121, 145, 158, 167, 179, 183, 188–9, 202, 205, 274n10
  industrial sociology 122
  of knowledge 41
  motivational analysis 122–3
  positivist 124
  relativistic sociology 189
  roles 284n3
  see also social science
Socrates 156, 255n2, 256n4, 260n1, 293n13, 296n14
songs 303n1
  hit songs 123–4, 125
Sophism/Sophists 7–8, 19, 30, 113, 156, 273n18
  Plato and 1, 109, 255n2, 296n14
Soudek, Josef 302n8
Southwest School 176, 302n4
space 112
  time and 58, 120, 264n8, 301n1
specialization see division of labour
speculation/speculative philosophy 64–8, 73, 74, 76, 89, 95, 184, 283n4
  consciousness 64–8
  idealism 107
  metaphysics 117
  propositions 74
  speculative concept 68, 85
Spinoza, Baruch 94, 131, 147, 190, 266n2, 282n2
spirit 84, 177
  absolute spirit 80, 84, 107
  divine spirit 178
  metaphysics of 84
  productive spirit 173, 301n15

spiritual bond   61, 177
spiritual experience   81
spiritual intuition   97
Spoliansky, Mischa   303n1
state
    Descartes on   129
    dialectic as state religion   54, 86
    Hegel's doctrine of   80–1
    totalitarian state   80, 185
state employees   122
Stoic philosophers   262n13
structural-functional theory of
        society   179–81
subject
    absolute subject   31
    definition of   131–2
    experimental subject   81, 202
    labour of   43, 101
    movement of   24
    object and   6, 9, 20, 21, 45, 65,
        72, 75, 92, 165, 212, 214,
        215, 219–20, 311n17
    subject concept   213, 214
    transcendental subject   77, 81
    truth as   5
subjective consciousness   75
subjective positing   129
subjective reason/reasoning   38–9,
        180
subjective reflection   90
subjectivist theory of knowledge
        203–4
subjectivity/subjectivism   41, 45,
        75, 136, 165, 192, 212
    self-reflective   276n12
sublation   7, 22–3, 30, 84
substance   118, 131–2
subsumption   48, 88, 167, 182,
        214
suffering   43–4, 46, 74, 123
superstition   135
synthesis   46, 49–50, 65–6, 149,
        154, 214–15
    apperception   65, 66, 173
    as negation of the negation   55
    transcendental synthesis   66, 116
    see also triadic schema

system   35, 74–5, 76, 78–80, 100,
        163–83
    closed world   177–8
    completeness   163–6, 172
    concept of   26–7
    consciousness as unifying
        principle   174
    contemporary appeal of concept
        177–8
    Hegel and   10, 21–2, 27,
        78–80
    as house/home   302n6
    Kant and   172
    natural system   2
    Nietzsche and   175, 301n2
    positivist concept   182
    science   176, 178–9
    society as   147, 148
    structural-functional theory of
        society   179–81

tabulation   40, 47
Tacitean style of language   202,
        308n10
tautology   83, 138, 152, 165, 203,
        213
Teschner, Manfred   263n14
thesis   30, 38, 46, 49, 55, 90, 91,
        185, 219
    reified   159
    see also triadic schema
thing-in-itself   301n1
Thoma, Ludwig   153
Thomistic ontology   109
Tillich, Paul   186, 205
time
    Kant and   9, 273n16
    space and   58, 120, 264n8,
        301n1
    temporal core of truth   14, 34,
        35, 259n17, 260n18
totalitarian mentality   71
totalitarian state   80, 185
totality   23–4, 28, 70, 74, 79, 93,
        95, 148
    abstract totality   140
    concept of   27

dynamic totality 110
internally contradictory 110
of society/social totality 79, 89,
  90, 91, 99, 100, 180
system 175
see also whole, the
transcendent critique 31–2, 154
transcendental dialectic 58, 62,
  63, 66
transcendental logic 62
transcendental synthesis 66, 116
Trendelenburg, Friedrich
  Adolph 56, 271n12, 271n13
triadic schema 46–7, 49–50, 53–5
see also antinomies; antithesis;
  synthesis; thesis
truth 14, 15–25, 101–2
  the Absolute and 17, 21
  as concrete 36
  'emphatic concept' of 69, 70
  finite character 57–8
  Marxist view 18
  objectivity 53
  reality and 30
  reification 11
  as result 27
  as subject 5
  temporal core 14, 34, 35,
    259n17, 260n18
  timeless truth 260n18
  the true as the whole 17,
    19–25, 26, 29, 87, 108,
    238n5
  works of art 154

understanding, the 39, 59, 67,
  119
universal, the 12, 17, 28, 36,
  167–8
universal concepts 68, 93, 94,
  110, 168, 171, 204–6, 208
universal relativism 18
universality 39, 44–5, 52–3, 109,
  169
utopia 32, 35, 71, 299n6

Valéry, Paul 184, 303n15
value-freedom 191
Vico, Giovanni Battista 10

wealth 80, 277n10
Weber, Max 91, 124, 179, 191,
  282n1
  on capitalistic culture 299n6
  on economic theory 299n6
  ideal types 167–8, 169,
    282n20, 299n6
  'understanding' 167, 179,
    299n4
Wein, Hermann 5
Wertheimer, Max 280n10
whole, the 33, 53–4, 70, 89, 171,
  183, 211, 219
  contradictions 6–7
  Gestalt theory 87, 92–3, 106,
    280n9
  Hegel and 17, 19–25
  infinite whole 20–1
  irrationality of 176–7
  part and 87–8, 91, 92–103,
    104–6, 110, 137, 138
  powers of 117, 118, 148–9,
    163
  self-production of 172–3
  society as a whole 77, 90, 100,
    122, 125–7, 147, 180
  the true as the whole 17,
    19–25, 26, 29, 87, 108,
    238n5
  see also totality
wholeness 19–20, 22, 137, 147
Windelband, Wilhelm 176, 302n4
Wolff, Christian 298n2
works of art 154, 200, 295n13
  literature 170–1
worldview 3, 12, 42, 72, 86, 158,
  161, 169, 171, 183
Wundt, Wilhelm 61, 274n5

Zeno 294n4
zoology 17, 35–6